LETTERS TO MY GRANDCHILDREN

Memoirs of a Dragon Lady

by

Carol Williams-Wong

Ngui, Lan Fuhn

LETTERS TO MY GRANDCHILDREN

Memoirs of a Dragon Lady

by

Carol Williams-Wong

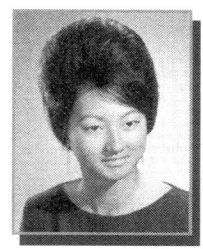

© 2014 Carol Williams-Wong

All rights reserved. No part of this publication may be reproduced, stored in a retrieval system, or transmitted, in any form or by any means, electronic, mechanical, photocopying, recording or otherwise, without the prior written permission of the author.

Book design by Margaret Williams

Cover design by DTP (Designers Typesetters Printers) Inc.

"Letters to My Grandchildren - Memoirs of a Dragon Lady Volume I"

A *Canada 150* series publication.

ISBN 978-1-55307-079-5

Under the auspices of Toronto Hakka Seniors Association

Email: thsa01@yahoo.ca

Dedication

To my beloved Grandchildren:

Mitchell Alexander Wong
Amelie Madeleine Wong
Annika Noelle Wong
Cameron Isla Evans Wong
Annalise Linnea Wong
Hallie Margaret Evans Wong

Back row L-R: Cari holding Cameron, Gordon, Brian, Stephanie, Jason, Ivy holding Annika
Front row L-R: Mitchell, Eddie, Carol, Amelie, December 2012

Inset L: Hallie   2012   Inset R: Annalise

Contents

Prologue & Gratitude   11

The Chinese Zodiac Cycle
   Introduction: Unionville, Ontario, Canada   17

First Chinese Zodiac Cycle: Year of the Snake, 1941-1953
   Life in Jamaica: Williamsfield District, Westmoreland   21
                        Savanna-La-Mar, Westmoreland   31
                        Petersfield District, Westmoreland   39

Second Chinese Zodiac Cycle, 1953-1965
   Life in Jamaica: Kingston, St. Andrew   79
                        Petersfield District, Westmoreland   121

Third Chinese Zodiac Cycle, 1965-1977
   Life in Canada: Montréal, Québec   155
                       Toronto, Ontario   197
   Life in Jamaica: Kingston, St. Andrew   205
                        Montego Bay, St. James   241

More Favourite Photos   305

Appendices:

1. Map of Hakka Chinese Migration — 324
2. Jamaican Hakka Family Relations Chart — 325
3. Map of China (including Hong Kong) — 326
4. Map of Niu-Foo Village, Bao On, Guangdong — 327
5. 20th Century Timeline — 328
6. The Wei Jin Xiu Furong (Chun Yin) Family Chart — 329
7. Foreword from *Our Family Tree* — 332
8. Descendants of Wei Gen Choi — 334
9. The Nathan Williams Family Chart — 336
10. The Gladys Young Williams Family Chart — 337
11. The Wong Family Chart — 338
12. The Williams Families in Jamaica — 339
13. Map of Jamaica — 346
14. Coat of Arms of Jamaica / National Anthem of Jamaica — 347
15. Map of Canada — 348
16. Coat of Arms of Canada / National Anthem of Canada — 349

About the Author — 350

Prologue & Gratitude

In the first year of the new millennium Y2000, my husband and I, then empty-nesters, downsized to a modest sized home in the Angus Glen Development, Unionville, Ontario, Canada. Even though we were still living in the City of Markham, after having lived for almost twenty years at 49 Spanhouse Crescent, moving to the newly-built house on 17 Woodgrove Trail gave me a sense of embarking on yet another stage in my life. With this sense of new beginnings, and in anticipation of the arrival of grandchildren, I felt that it was time for me to begin to write letters to my grandchildren which would serve as my memoirs for them and future generations in our family.

I began to write these memoirs earlier, but put them on hold while I continued to pursue my various interests, including my love of racquet sports and my interest in my Hakka Chinese culture. Just as I had ended yet another Chinese Zodiac cycle of my life – a period which for me has always signalled a significant change in my life – I met the President of the Toronto Hakka Seniors Association, Mrs. Terry O. Bautista. Terry invited me to join their Memoirs Class which met at the Milliken Mills Community Centre in Scarborough.

I accepted the invitation and was introduced to the facilitator of the class, Mr. Harry Van Bommel, who encouraged me to be a part of the "Canada 150: Our Canada – Our Stories" project. The mission of this project is to engage Canadians in a celebration and commemoration of their past by recording stories of their lives, their families, and their communities for the benefit of future generations. Canada will be celebrating its 150th anniversary in 2017 and the stories that are collected in this project are to be stored in the historical archives of the nation's capital in Ottawa. This project prompted me to resume writing my letters to my grandchildren. It was as if I had just been waiting for the opportune moment to revive my plan to record, for posterity, stories about our family's ancestors' lives and the lives of our family in the twenty-first century, as well as about our Hakka Chinese community experience. So it is with much gratitude that I say thanks to Mrs. Terry O. Bautista for the opportunity that she gave me to leave this legacy to my grandchildren. Canada has been good to me and I also thank Terry for the honour of being a part of the 150th celebrations in Canada's history.

As well, I wish to thank my patient editor, Dr. Anne-Marie Lee-Loy, who seemed to have enjoyed my ramblings and would like me to think that she was learning about her Chinese ancestors' lives in Jamaica as well. I thought I would invite my Irish sister-in-law, Margaret Taylor-Williams, to participate in this project by sharing her own stories. In the end, she has proven to be a great help to me and others involved in this project by formatting the many contributions to the Canada 150 Memoir Project.

Tremendous help with proof-reading came from Loraine Lee, co-publisher with her husband and my long-time friend, Patrick Lee, of *Canadian Jamaican Chinese 2000* and *Jamaican Chinese Worldwide 2004*. Patrick kindly gave me permission to use the chart they created to explain the various Hakka family relations in these memoirs. Many thanks to Denise Yap Sam for her assistance, and Maverick Law for his creativity, in producing a very attractive front and back cover for this book.

I am indebted to special family members - my husband, Edward Gordon Wong, my youngest brother and Buddhist monk, Donald Williams (Bhante Kovida), my daughter-in-law, Ivy Lim and sister-in-law, Margaret Taylor-Williams, for their key-boarding skills and computer literacy which were of invaluable help to me in producing the manuscript and including the numerous photographs for this Volume 1 of *Letters to my Grandchildren - Memoirs of a Dragon Lady*.

Thanks also to Polly "Sister P" Lee for keeping some of our cherished childhood photos safely and to my friend, JoAn Chin-Fong Yee in Florida for sending them to me digitally. "Wan luv" and "nuff IRIE" to my *peng-yu*, Ray Chen, for the courtesy of his lovely photographs taken in Jamaica. Much appreciation to Dr. Judith Robinson for facilitating the permission to reprint photographs on pages 80, 82, 83, 86, 93, 94 and 108 which were kindly granted courtesy of Wolmer's Girls' Alumnae (2009) - *In the Light of the Sun: The Story of the Wolmer's Girls' School*. I am very grateful to each and every one who helped in the production of this volume and share with them the Chinese proverb:

> "A bit of fragrance clings to the hand that gives roses."

In closing, I must acknowledge my father, Nathan Williams for having the courage to brave the arduous journey over into the New World, overcoming the hardships and making a successful life in a developing Third World country. Together with my mother, Gladys Young-Williams, they provided a comfortable home and secure life for me and my six siblings, Ricardo, Keith, Patrick, Richard, Elaine and Donald. Our parents also demonstrated community mindedness, getting along with everyone, treating everybody equally and fairly; perpetuating their admirable Hakka work ethics and their Hakka Chinese values based on Confucius teachings of **Respecting elders, Helping each other, Loving and Educating the young.**

Lastly, thanks to my Heavenly Father for giving me three wonderful sons, Brian Martin Wong, Gordon Harrison Wong and Jason Stuart Wong. They in turn gave me three lovely daughters-in-law, Stephanie Wallat, Carolyn Evans and Ivy Lim. In time, they all blessed me with six grandchildren - one handsome grandson, Mitchell and five beautiful granddaughters, Amelie, Annika, Cameron, Annalise and Hallie at this time of writing.

Thanks be to God for all His many Blessings!

Spanhouse Crescent,
Unionville, Ontario

Woodgrove Trail,
Unionville, Ontario

Above: Front Entrance

Below: Backyard with separate garage

The Chinese Zodiac Cycle

Introduction

Unionville, Ontario, Canada 2000

My dear Grandchildren,

The year 2000 was a time of yet another change for our family. We had recently moved to another location in Unionville, Ontario, Canada. Moving was not something unfamiliar to me. Indeed, in some ways, moving is a family legacy. We are, after all, Hakka Chinese people of the Han nationality – sometimes known as "guest people" because of our migratory history. Our family, the Ngui ("Wei" in the Mandarin dialect) can trace its lineage back to the year 661 BC during the Tang Dynasty. At that time, our Hakka ancestors lived in the central plains of China and our Wei ancestors lived in the Wei State, Shanxi Province. Due to the social unrest and hostile invasions that characterized that period, the Hakka people moved away from this area. Over centuries of migration, our Ngui ancestors traveled to Henan Province, then continued southwards and eventually settled in Niu Foo Village, Bao On County, Guangzhou Province, located across the border from Hong Kong.

As a young man, my father, your great-grandfather, left his village in China to move to Jamaica. Decades later as an old man, he left this Caribbean island and joined my family then living in Hong Kong and then, finally, he migrated again, this time to Canada, where he would pass away in 1990 at the ripe old age of 86 years. I have also lived in Jamaica, Hong Kong and Canada. Such changes, as I have said, are not unusual in our family history, so it was not the fact that we had recently moved that made me want to write to you and for you. Maybe, instead, it was the fact that it was the millennium, a time when people examine their past and consider their future, that made me think about how your existence would be very much the product of the twists and turns of fate that have led our family here to Canada and beyond. I wanted you to understand that when you finally arrived, your place in the world would be much more than the physical location of your birth; your place is also deeply embedded in a family legacy of courage, adventurous spirit, hard work and perseverance seeking a better life for future generations. But you would never know that unless I took the time to tell you and so I decided to write these memoirs for you.

This is not my first attempt to document our family history. In 1993, a synopsis of my paternal Williams family migration from China to Jamaica to Canada was published in the booklet, *My Family Tree*. Ten years later, I produced *The E.G. Wong Family Chronicles* and in 2010, I led a committee to publish the *Wei Family History in the Americas and the Caribbean*.

But this writing is different. It is specially for each and every one of you.

Your loving paternal grandmother,
"Ah-Poh" Carol Williams-Wong

First Chinese Zodiac Cycle: The Year of the Snake 1941 – 1953

Life in Jamaica:
Williamsfield District, Westmoreland
1941

My dear Grandchildren,

First, I must introduce myself to you.

My English name is Carol Mearle Williams-Wong and my Hakka Chinese name is Ngui Lan Fuhn (meaning "the fragrance of the Orchid flower"). I was born in the Chinese Zodiac Year of the Snake in 1941 in Williamsfield District, Westmoreland, Jamaica, West Indies and was christened in the Anglican Church of England. I am the second child and elder daughter of Papa, Nathan (Ngui, Bak Tseung) Williams and Mama, Gladys (née Young) Williams.

Papa was the only child of Ngui Siu Len and was born in Niu Foo Village, Bao On County, Guangdong Province, China in 1909 (see Appendix 3). Mama, Gladys Louise Young, was born ten years later in 1919, and lived in Trout Hall District, Clarendon Parish, Jamaica, West Indies. Papa's and Mama's marriage was arranged by well-meaning relatives when it became apparent that his business was doing well enough for him to settle down and start a family. They eventually had four sons and two daughters: Keith, Carol, Patrick, Richard (Dick) Elaine and Donald (Donny). Later, he raised another son, Ricardo, from Hong Kong. (see Appendix).

Papa would reminisce about his Niu Foo Village which was named after the lake that was situated nearby. A long time ago, the village was originally named, "Nao Foo". "Nao" is the name for a huge sea turtle and "Foo" means "lake". Over time, the word "Nao" was changed to "Niu", meaning "cow", and the village became known as "Niu Foo". The lake was beautiful, the surrounding fruit trees were abundant and a large well supplied fresh water for the entire village, which included the Chin, Tenn, Lee and Lo families. These families all lived together peacefully and many would ultimately inter-marry. The Ngui families lived in the old section called "Lao Wee" and the Chins, like Papa's mother's family, lived in the new section, "Sin Wee". Papa told me that, when our ancestors arrived in Dongguan County, Guangzhou Province during the mid-1700s, our 17th Wei generation ancestor, Ngui Gen Choi (see Appendices 5 and 6) worked very hard for merchants in Canton (Guangdong). He saved diligently and became quite wealthy in the mid-1800s. He built the ancestral village with nine adjoining houses, similar to North American townhouses, surrounding an Ancestral Hall ("Tiang") where weddings and other festive occasions were celebrated with relatives and neighbouring villagers.

Ngui Gen Choi had two sons and eight grandsons. Over the years, after buying surrounding rice fields for the family's own cultivation and for renting out to other people, Gen Choi became a respected landlord. He was an astute businessman and

Life in Jamaica: Williamsfield District, Westmoreland 1941

Niu Foo Village and Lake, 1990

Essie and Phoebe at Wei family well, 1994

Wei family ossuaries on hillside, 1980

Road from Lo Wu train station to village, 1980

Relatives and Carol at family ossuary with bones of grandmother, Chin Yu Moi

Life in Jamaica: Williamsfield District, Westmoreland 1941

Village school where Nathan attended and later taught

Carol and Elaine visiting Wei Ancestral Hall after war, 1980

Renovated Wei Ancestral Hall, 2009

Carol visiting grand-aunt, Wong Su Yin, Uncle Wei Hong Sheung and family, 1980

New Wei temple rebuilt in 2003 by donations from Wei families overseas

also bought several shops in nearby towns. The rent collected from all his tenants bought viable trading commodities such as rice and "wet-sugar" (a mixture of cane sugar and molasses). When Gen Choi died, his sons and grandsons mismanaged his business. The lands were sold, shops closed and the remains of the business were divided up among the family. The women-folk toiled in the fields as well as in the homes while some of the men-folk lazed around and even took to smoking opium.

Papa's father, our 18th Wei generation ancestor, Siu Len, died while he was a youngster, leaving him to be raised by his mother (Siu Len's widow), Chin Yu Moi. She was assisted in the home and fields by her young relatives living nearby. One of her nieces, Doris Chung, would help take care of Papa when he was sick and needed babysitting. Papa also tended the fields during his childhood. He had his own favourite buffalo which was so tame, Papa could sprawl across its back and fall asleep while returning home. Papa attended the only school in Niu Foo Village. When he completed his studies, he stayed on as a young teacher. He was very athletic and used to tell us about how many miles he and his cousin, Henderson (Ngui Den Seung) had to walk to play football (soccer) and basketball matches against other villagers after which, they would have to walk all those miles back home again – and would do so without feeling exhausted!

In 1838, slavery was abolished in the British Empire. As a result, the British began contracting indentured labourers to work in the sugar-cane-fields in the West Indies. The Chinese were seen as viable indentured labourers. Many Hakka people went to Hong Kong to sign up as contract labourers. Those who went to Panama became exhausted from overwork and suffered from the prevalent tropical diseases. This resulted in a high death rate amongst the labourers, but this did not deter 475 Chinese workers from seeking work in the sugar factories and canefields in Jamaica.

By 1870, British and American companies started large-scale planting of coconuts and bananas in Jamaican so a second batch of Chinese labourers arrived. After their contracts expired, some Chinese labourers started small grocery shops of their own. The years that followed saw Jamaica entering a period of rapid development. There were no laws restricting the entry of Chinese immigrants to Jamaica, hence, it was a simple matter for Chinese to come on their own or invited by relatives and friends.

Carol's paternal grandmother, Chin Yu Moi

In the early 1900s the first Ngui arrived in Jamaica. His name was Ngui Fwee Len, however, since he was unable to communicate in English, he readily agreed to an anglicized name, created by combining all three of his names. It was thought that "Ngui Fwee Len" sounded like "Williams" and thus, a new family line of Chinese with the surname Williams began in Jamaica. It was said that he was also given the English first name, "John" by the local postmistress who later taught him to speak English.

When our 19th Wei generation ancestor, Jackson (Ngui Hok Len) set up business in Jamaica, he invited his young nephews to join him in this tropical island in the Caribbean.

Life in Jamaica: Williamsfield District, Westmoreland 1941

Youngster tending the fields with favourite water buffalo

With his encouragement, in the late 1920s while still a teenager, Papa and his cousins migrated from China to Jamaica. Once they arrived, they worked with their Uncle Jackson who had already established a business in Petersfield District, in the Parish of Westmoreland. Papa worked extremely hard and for very long hours, sometimes for seven days a week. He and his cousins had never seen Negro people or heard their language before, but pretty soon they learnt their Jamaican patois dialect, which is a language of "broken English" mixed with Spanish and Creole. They also learnt to do business with them and tricks of the trade as well.

They learnt to get along with their customers although Papa related that he and his Chinese cousins were constantly teased and made fun of by the locals This made him so angry that on many occasions, he wanted to jump over the shop-counter, chase them with the "salt-fish machete" and chop them up! As Papa matured, however, he was able to better control his temper with the young hoodlums, especially as he grew to realize that the majority of the local people were warm-hearted, friendly, accepting of the Chinese and would, over time, become valued customers. After gaining business experience and being more fluent in the local Jamaican patois dialect, the nephews scattered to open their own businesses in neighbouring districts in Westmoreland.

Papa moved to Williamsfield District and opened up a shop there. With the assistance of a young man named Ronald, the business flourished. Ronald was a quiet, polite young man, Papa's age, who used to come to Jackson's store as a customer and Papa liked him because he was not as boisterous as the other local boys. Papa also told me that he had to exercise great control when the local boys would constantly tease and taunt him. Ronald, Papa noticed, never joined these hooligans in this behaviour. As a result, when Papa was going to open his own business, Papa encouraged Ronald to leave home and come and work for him in Williamsfield only a few miles away.

Once the business in Williamsfield became established, Papa wanted to settle down and have a family. Papa realized that he could no longer return to his village in China

Life in Jamaica: Williamsfield District, Westmoreland 1941

Nathan & Gladys Williams wedding party with Wei and Young relatives, Kingston, Jamaica 1938

to marry the girl to whom he had been betrothed since birth. Apparently, while his mother was pregnant with him, Papa's father, Ngui Siu Len, made a pact with another friend whose wife was also pregnant, that they would marry their as yet unborn children if one wife had a girl and the other, a boy. So said, so done; Papa and "Ah-Neung" Lam Keow were betrothed. As teenagers growing up, they did not like each other, but in their culture, their fathers' word was law and they understood that their fate was to marry each other, regardless of their feelings towards each other. In fact, Papa had originally planned to come to Jamaica to make some money and then return to Niu Foo Village to marry and start a family with Ah-Neung. In the meantime, she moved into Papa's family home and helped his aging mother like a dutiful daughter-in-law. While Papa was away, however, China became involved with internal and external wars and the possibility of a return to China became, for Papa, increasingly far-fetched. He would have to find a wife in Jamaica.

As usual, when facing an important decision, Papa turned to Uncle Jackson and his family for their advice on how to go about selecting a bride. They decided that the best thing to do would be to go to the capital city of Kingston, where there was a Chinatown, to arrange for Papa to meet an appropriate wife. Chinatown, in the Barry Street and Princess Street area, was the central meeting place for the Chinese across the island. It was where they went to purchase food items for themselves and sometimes for their shops. But more importantly, visiting in Chinatown allowed members of the Chinese community in Jamaica to meet up with each other and keep up with the news from their homeland, China.

Uncle Jackson's family made an arrangement for Papa to meet a young Chinese girl named Enid, but en route to Kingston, Jackson's grandson, Arthur got ill, so they all had to turn back home to Westmoreland. Perhaps it was destiny that Papa should not marry Enid. Not only did this sickness prevent their initial meeting, before arrangements could be made for them to meet again, Enid was introduced to and married someone else. Instead of Enid, Papa was introduced to and ended up marrying a tall and very good-looking young lady named Gladys Young. They were married at the Kingston Parish Church in June 1938 with many relatives on both sides of the Williams (Ngui) and Young families in attendance.

Mama was ten years younger than Papa and the youngest child of Young Bow and Naomi Lue. Her parents had been early immigrants to Jamaica, arriving long before Uncle Jackson settled in Petersfield, Westmoreland. Her parents had settled in Trout Hall, Clarendon and had two sons, Alfred and Clarence, and five daughters, Amy, Florence, Nora, Cisilyn and Gladys. After her parents passed away, Mama lived with her elder brother Clarence and his wife Ella Chin. By the time Mama was introduced to Papa, Alfred, the eldest brother had already died – he died at a young age – and her sisters were already married and had left home: Amy married Papa's older cousin, Isaac Williams; Florence married a Jamaican, Reginald Payne; Nora married Henry Chung; and Cisilyn married Alfred Hoo (see Appendix 9).

Sometimes Mama would take us children to visit Uncle Clarence's family when they were still living in Trout Hall. I remember that their shop was much older than ours and seemed very dark because of its low ceiling. It was illuminated with kerosene oil lamps, which we had to bring to the living area adjoining the back of the wooden, single-story building, at night time when the shop was closed. I enjoyed those visits as I greatly admired my older cousins, especially the older boy, Jackie, who was courting his girlfriend, Dorothy, a nice young lady who would later become his wife. When the shop was closed for business on Sundays, we would all have a picnic by the River Minho and I was fascinated by the huge river boulders and stones we used to climb and sit on.

After their wedding in Kingston, Mama returned with Papa to what would be their first home and business together – the small wooden shop in Williamsfield. They were delighted that Ronald would continue working with them because he had proven to be helpful and was so trustworthy. As were all the buildings in the district, the shop was a wooden single-floor structure. Our dwelling adjoined the shop. It was in this house that their first three children, Keith Alexander, Patrick Wilson and I, would be born. The conditions at Williamsfield were quite primitive. There was no electricity or running water. We had a wooden outhouse latrine (pit toilet) which was actually only used by the adults. Even after we were toilet trained, we children used enamel chamber pots of different sizes as well as a white enamel slop-pail with a carrying handle and a cover. Our maids, local women, did the frequent emptying and washing of those pots and slop pails.

At that time, the roads in Williamsfield were unpaved and there were no motor vehicles. On most Sundays, we would use a horse and buggy cart to travel to Petersfield to get together with other members of the Williams family. Our horse was named Neddy. Because the roads were unpaved, we would have to stop many times on these trips to remove stones from Neddy's hooves. These visits were very important to Papa. He was always happy to meet up with his cousins again and under Uncle Jackson's guidance, they would all discuss business and exchange experiences about their new life in this strange country – including how to deal with the equally unfamiliar African and East Indian people who surrounded them! This was also a good opportunity for Papa to eat familiar Hakka Chinese food and speak freely using his Hakka dialect – Mama, as a second generation Chinese who had been born and raised in Jamaica, was not fluent in Hakka. Ronald also looked forward to these weekend trips as we would take him with us so that he could visit his friends and family in Petersfield as well.

Despite his success, Papa found shop business difficult. As a shopkeeper, Papa had to deal with the local people speaking in a local patois dialect that was still unfamiliar to him, to learn the proper English words for items in the store and to calculate in foreign British currency. Additionally, Papa had been a school teacher in Niu Foo Village so he had been trained to be a scholar and not a businessman. Regardless, with the help of his young wife and the long hours that they both put into running the shop, Papa was able to overcome these and many other hardships to make a good living and raise their three children – that is, with the additional help of hired maids in the home and faithful Ronald in the shop.

Williamsfield was mainly surrounded by farms and cane-fields. The labourers, mostly Negroes, bought breakfast and lunch items at the crack of dawn en route to work, usually with a machete under their arm and a crocus bag over their shoulder. On their way home, they would stop to purchase dinner ingredients, and after supper, some would return to the shop where they would loiter and socialize in the village square which, over time, was created around our small wooden shop. The local people of East Indian descent had similar shopping patterns, but they worked in rice paddies rather than the cane-fields. One of my favourite memories of that shop was of playing in the rice room where loose unhusked rice grains were piled high in one corner. We children would try to climb to the top of the rice pile, but the adults would usually find us and chase us out of the room before we got very far! Then they would have to patiently scrape the rice grains back into a pile in the corner of the room so that the rice would be ready for sale. It was a lot of work for them.

I also enjoyed watching moths flying around the glass globe shades of the kerosene oil lamps. Some of the moths got caught inside the globe causing the cotton wick to start sputtering. The bases of these lamps were either made of glass where one could see the level of the kerosene oil or metal which had been beautifully crafted. The globes were always made of glass and were either rounded with a fluted top or fashioned with a smaller rounded globe with a tall, slim chimney. These were some of the many household items imported from England.

Life in Jamaica: Williamsfield District, Westmoreland 1941

The local postmistress was a spinster named Miss Dawes who was also my Christian Godmother. Miss Dawes taught Papa basic English conversation and vocabulary including names for every item sold in the shop – what we called "shop English". Despite all her teaching, he would always have difficulty pronouncing the "R" sound. Many years later, after he had retired from business and was living in Canada, he still marvelled at his difficulty in differentiating between the words "soap" and "rope"! He was also astounded by the exceptions of the English language, especially how two words could sound the same but have different spellings and meanings.

Our family was also friendly with local farmers and landowners of British ancestry. As a result of these friendships, another important person in our life in Williamsfield was Granny Becky. I am guessing that her proper name was Rebecca. She was an English woman who was once married to an English landowner – I assumed that her husband had passed away. She lived in a large wooden house built on concrete stilts on a huge property. The house was surrounded by many large fruit trees, cane-fields and cow pastures. A river ran through the property and I remember that it always seemed to be moving so fast and furious. There were, however, beautiful white river lilies growing along the banks of the river.

Granny Becky became grandmother to everyone in the district, but our family became especially close to her, her friends and family, people like Lester, Tiny and Carmen, who as a young lady later came to live with our family many years after we moved away from Williamsfield. Some Sundays when we did not travel to Petersfield, our family and other locals from the district would get together to have a picnic under the trees at Granny Becky's home. Granny Becky owned a RCA "His Master's Voice" gramophone with a cute logo of a dog listening to the brass speaker shaped like a horn and she would let me have fun winding it up. I loved to listen to all of Granny's 78 r.p.m. vinyl records. I especially enjoyed playing under the house and hiding behind the concrete stilts, listening to the music blaring away at the highest volume while the adults sat outside on the verandah talking loudly over the music. Occasionally, someone would go inside to either change or flip over the shiny black, vinyl records.

L: Papa, Keith and me   *Middle: Mama and Keith*   *R: Mama and Patrick*

Life in Jamaica: Williamsfield District, Westmoreland 1941

From the verandah, we children would also watch some of the adults play cricket, an English bat and ball game. When we got bored, we ran all over the fields, making sure to stay far away from the cricket pitch for safety's sake. The cricket ball was a composition of dense rubber covered in leather. It was very tough. It would cause you great pain if you were unfortunate enough to get hit by one! In the fields, we would also skillfully avoid the "cow-pies" and make sure to stamp on "shamo'lady" or "dead and wake", a lacey-leaf plant which grew wild all over the field and when touched, would bashfully close up its leaves in shame. There were also many animals to visit or sticks to throw over the fence. I remember the lovely sense of community during these times as people of all different races and classes came together to enjoy each other's company and have fun. These were wonderful times for all of us.

Some time later, Papa decided to move the family to Savanna-La-Mar which was the capital of Westmoreland. Savanna-la-Mar was a shipping port some eight miles away and the town was becoming a thriving place for business, so after conferring with his elders, Papa and Mama decided to move and expand their business there. Even after we left Williamsfield, however, happy times were still spent at Granny Becky's home. Sometimes my older brother, Keith, and I would be sent to spend summer holidays with Granny Becky. Everything seemed luxurious at Granny Becky's. The maid would bathe us in one of the many bedrooms after warming water in the wooden kitchen built outside and bringing it inside to pour into a white bathtub. We ate on chinaware plates, using heavy silverware and even peed in a beautiful decorated chinaware chamber pot that matched the chinaware jug and basin on the wooden mahogany washstand in the corner of the room. As when we had lived in Williamsfield, it was deemed that we were not yet old enough to use the outhouse latrine since it seemed so far away – plus, it housed many lizards and cockroaches! During those summers, we were also taught not to wear underwear to bed and to say our prayers before clambering into a very high four-poster mahogany bed.

I have wonderful memories of the time we spent in Williamsfield. I had such a carefree childhood and felt safe and loved, not only by my parents, but by the whole community around us.

Your loving Ah-Poh

Life in Jamaica:
Savanna-la-Mar District, Westmoreland
1945

My dear Grandchildren,

In the mid-1940s, Papa moved our family from Williamsfield to Savanna-la-Mar. There, we lived in a bigger home, called Trafalgar House, on Great George Street, the main street of Savanna-la-Mar. Trafalgar House was a massive two-storey concrete building with huge round columns in front of the store supporting a verandah with Italian decorative balustrade and the living quarters upstairs.

The family also expanded during this time with the birth of a third son, Richard (Dick) Jeffery and second daughter, Elaine Marie. Mama believed in fresh air and sunshine so she instructed our loving and faithful nurse whom we called "Mother May" to put Dick's cradle out on the verandah while he took his naps. Many times Mother May would forget to take Dick's cradle in, and since he slept so soundly, he was left out in the sunshine for long periods of time. We always said this was why Dick is so much more dark-skinned than the rest of us children!

We spent a lot of time outside. The older children, Keith, Patrick and I, would even take sun baths in a huge zinc metal bath pan in the yard, but we preferred "bathing" when the concrete back patio was being hosed down. Keith and I would soap up our bodies, lathering ourselves real well to slide around on our tummies and bottoms all over the wet concrete. It was so much fun!

The maids cooked in the outside kitchen and would also heat the clothes iron in an open wood-fire made up and blazing in the yard on laundry days. One day, while

Elaine and Dick on the woodpile in the back yard

Life in Jamaica: Savanna-La-Mar District, Westmoreland 1945

learning to ride an adult bicycle in the yard, I lost control and fell into the fire. This resulted in a huge round burn on the inside of my right knee. Dr. Harvey, the family doctor, calmed my crying by applying a cool salve and covered the wound with a huge dressing. I was afraid that I would have a huge scar, but Dr. Harvey reassured me by telling me that eventually, the sore would shrink from the size of a two shilling and six pence coin to a two shilling, then to a shilling, to a sixpence coin size, and then completely disappear. But he lied to me – I am over 70-years of age now and my scar is still the size of a two shilling and sixpence coin, shiny with radial marks like the spokes of a bicycle wheel!

I was not the only one to have accidents while we lived in Trafalgar House. One day, Patrick was playing in the store and while climbing up on the stepladder, he slipped and fell on the edge of the showcase below. Patrick's head was cut in the fall, and since it was a head wound, the cut bled profusely. Papa quickly grabbed one of the towels that were for sale, pressed it to Patrick's wound, jumped into a car parked outside the store piazza and rushed to Dr. Harvey's office. Patrick had a two to three inch curved cut on his scalp that required stitching. He healed well, but as a result of this accident, the dynamics changed in our family. Throughout his entire childhood – even up to adulthood – our parents catered to and sympathized with Patrick. They were even willing to overlook some of his naughtiness!

It was while we lived in Savanna-la-Mar that my formal education began. Keith and I attended Mrs. Chapman's Primary School but most of my memories of that period are just of the fun we had during the walk to and from school with our classmates. We enjoyed stopping by people's houses on these walks to pick up and drop off classmates along the way. We also discovered that we could tie a string to an empty condensed milk can, sink it in the river and tie the end of the cord on the bridge or on a big stone while on our way to school. On our way back, we would pull up the can to find a cache of tiny fishes that we called "tikki-tikki." We would put a little moss in the can, take them home, and watched them until they died.

We always wore brown lace-up shoes for school. We hated wearing those shoes, especially since they were so tightly laced up. We used to remove them as soon as we were out of sight from home, tying the laces together before hanging the shoes safely around our necks, and duly put them back on when nearing school or home. Going barefoot was fun. I liked walking on the rough stony unpaved road and in the gutters during and after the rain, especially when the moss growing in them made the gutters real slippery.

Beside us lived the Guyadene family, an East Indian family. When we weren't in school, Keith and I loved to play hide and seek with their children. We would play in our backyard and sometimes upstairs inside the house. Sometimes, the houseboy, Seaford, would join us in these games. I also enjoyed sharing their spicy Indian food – which I found more appealing than our bland meals. The Guyadenes had a smaller wooden shop than ours, but it also had an adjoining rum bar in front. They lived in a separate wooden house and had a vegetable garden at the back of the house. I remember helping to pick off nice fat green caterpillars crawling on their callaloo plants and wanted to think that my doing so was the reason why the callaloo plants were so healthy looking. You see, the local Jamaicans would tease our East Indian neighbours by saying: "Wha' mek Coolie callaloo so fat? Dem s--t pon it!" Since I loved their food, I did not want to believe that could possibly be true!

Granny Becky's relative, Carmen, came to live with us while we were in Savanna-la-Mar. Carmen was in her late teens and came mainly to learn secretarial skills like typing and taking Pitman's shorthand writing and some bookkeeping skills at our business bookkeeper, Mr. Tucker's Commercial School. She was good company for my mother and she helped with raising us children and working in the store. Mama was particularly happy to be able to have someone around who was fluent in English and had grown up within the same westernized Jamaican culture in which Mama had grown up. Papa was very close to his family in Jamaica, but his relatives were all migrants from China. Since Mama had been born and raised in Jamaica, she was not fluent in the Hakka dialect and did not always understand the cultural nuances and expectations of Papa's relatives. There was something of a cultural divide between them. With Carmen, however, Mama developed a wonderful mother-daughter relationship. Although Carmen was not Chinese, she called my mother, "Auntie", and we children were taught to call Carmen, "Sister Carmen". We loved her as much as she loved Mama.

Carmen was very outgoing and friendly so she and Mama formed friendships with other young middle-class families like the Lee's, Chong's, Ridley's and Pringle's who lived in Savanna-la-Mar. Carmen had a beautiful voice and loved to sing. I remember her practising to sing solos in the Savanna-La-Mar Parish Church for weddings. On the weekends, we would take Carmen home to Williamsfield, which gave us the opportunity to visit Granny Becky, run around the open fields, see the farm animals and go down to the roaring river. It was all so familiar for us – it felt very much like we were also going home, even though we did not live there any longer. Carmen was a vibrant young woman so it was no surprise that eventually, young men started coming by to call on her. Mama was always very hospitable to these young men, but Papa would look on disapprovingly. In his Chinese village experience, parents or other adults would be making courtship and marriage arrangements between young people and young people would never be allowed to sit together so closely when they visited!

Mama and Sister Carmen Fenton

Eventually, with Mama's approval, Carmen began dating Eric, the son of an East Indian family who owned a bakery on Great George Street. Carmen and Eric eventually married and had three children, Richard, Robert and Denise. Many, many years later when we all migrated to Toronto, Ontario, Canada, our two families remained close friends and we continued to share and make wonderful memories together.

Savanna-La-Mar was becoming a thriving town. It was full of life. Great George Street was then the widest street in Jamaica which led straight through the town ending up at the Caribbean seashore where the wharf was situated. A narrow, unpaved road led to an old English fort with a lighthouse where we loved to walk around and explore. At the end of Great George Street, a sea wall had been built along the seaside to protect a busy local market where produce was brought in by local and neighbouring farmers. I remember walking all along the length of the seawall, carefully balancing at the same time as I watched the waves lash against the double walls. I would watch the fishermen bringing in their catch in their dug-out canoes. A crowd of people would gather around as the canoes came ashore, ready to purchase their fish for the day. I also found it interesting to watch the sugar transport trucks traveling to and from the wharf, as well as the constant activity of the strong, able-bodied men loading coarse crocus bags of sugar onto the ships. These ships would collect brown unrefined sugar that had been brought down to the wharf from the Frome Sugar Factory located some miles inland. This supply of sugar would then be taken to England to be refined into white sugar and made into other products, including the world-famous Tate & Lyle Golden Syrup.

Our store and home (called "Trafalgar House"), was constructed out of stone and concrete. It was located close to the imposing colonial style Town Hall. The Town Hall had a beautiful domed wrought iron water fountain on the grassy lawn in front. Adjoining the Town Hall was the Court House, Police Station and City Jail. Across the street was the Anglican Parish Church and cemetery surrounded by a wrought iron fence as well. Beside the church were business offices, the Imperial movie theatre and a drug store. Further up the road were the community library and another movie theatre, Doric Theatre. While we lived there, bakeries and icecream parlours started opening up alongside the smaller business places. The Bank of Nova Scotia and Barclays Bank added to the commercial activities on either side of Great George Street.

Whether for business or pleasure, our house became a popular meeting place for the other Chinese people in Savanna-La-Mar and from around the nearby districts. In fact, our house was much like a Chinese community centre for the Chinese in this area. All during the nights, our relatives and other Chinese folk constantly played the tile game of Mahjong. They and the Mahjong tiles were very noisy which disturbed our sleep, much to my mother's dismay; but we enjoyed walking around the players in our nighties and pajamas before bedtime. Although we hated the face pinching and getting *gah-chucks* (being hit on the head with someone's knuckles), it was worth suffering through them if we received money from the players which was most likely. The winners called this custom of giving money to celebrate their luck "giving sore foot". I believe this expression is only used by Chinese gamblers in Jamaica and it was coined so many years ago that no one seem to know the origin or the meaning.

Life in Jamaica: Savanna-La-Mar District, Westmoreland 1945

Fashion Show at Savanna-La-Mar Town Hall

Similar to the racial harmony that we experienced in Williamsfield, we found that Savanna-La-Mar was a place where people of all races and class status came together at occasions such as church functions, garden parties at Mannings High School grounds, a variety of events on the library premises and major dance events at the

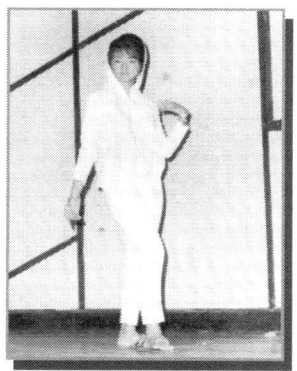

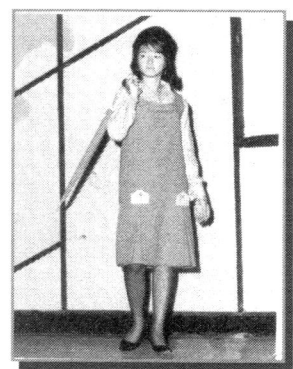

Models on stage:

Left and right - Carol

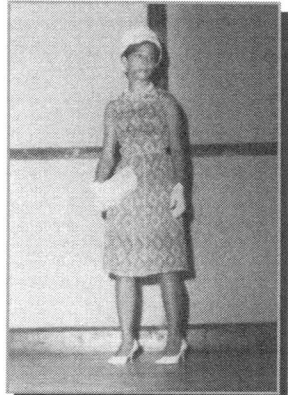

Left - Marianne

Right - Marianne, Jeanie and Carol

Life in Jamaica: Savanna-La-Mar District, Westmoreland 1945

Bandleader Kes Chin

Town Hall. The latter was the first venue where famous and popular dance bands, like "Kes Chin and the Souvenirs" and "Byron Lee and the Dragonaires" made their debuts in the west end of the island. In later years, it was at the Town Hall that my girlfriends and I made our debuts as amateur fashion models for community tea parties.

Our social circle included some of the prominent members of the community such as Drs. Harvey and Carnegie, lawyers Hamaty and McPherson, land surveyor Forrest, Anglican minister Rev. McMillan, Catholic priest Father Knight, Baptist minister Rev. Whylie, the managers of Barclays Bank and the Bank of Nova Scotia, and others. My father's favourite drinking buddies were the wharfinger, Mr. Nash, and the Honourable Judge Gayle. These individuals came from different racial and cultural backgrounds including British, Jewish, Syrian, American, Negro and Indian. We all got along with their families and we children attended the same schools.

As well, there were our fellow Chinese business families like the Chongs, Lyns, Chin-Fooks, Lees, Chins, Lowes, Lims, Moo-Young and others. Many Chinese married local folks as, in those days, it was difficult to send for mates overseas. My uncle married an Indian woman and had many children. "Auntie" proved to be an excellent businesswoman and managed the entire household. She always welcomed us warmly and as kids, we relished the change of food at her house. As teenagers, we looked forward to the dance parties held at their house when we would rock 'n roll and smooch with our cousins from all over Westmoreland as well as with many other friends.

Eventually Grand-uncle, Jackson Williams, (Shuck Goong) and Grand-aunt, May (Shuck Poh) started planning to move from Petersfield to Savanna-la-Mar as well. They built a bigger concrete building adjoining ours. In addition to Grand-uncle and Grand-aunt, the home housed his son, Lincoln and his wife Nancy as well as their seven children: Marie, Arthur, Winifred, Washington, Shirley, Winston (Keung) and Frank (Bim). It was fun crossing between the two houses to play with our cousins. Some of the older children had, however, been sent to Niu Foo Village to learn Hakka Chinese culture or to live with Lincoln's sister, Chin Gim Fung, in Hong Kong. Sending Jamaican-born Chinese children back to their parents' village in China was a common practice amongst the Hakka families in Jamaica at this time. Papa actually planned that Keith and I should also go to China and stay with his mother in the village. I vaguely remember going to Kingston to apply for a passport, where I had my fingers rolled on a black ink-pad in order to take my finger prints. I also remember having my passport photographs taken by the local photographer, Mr. Leakey, at Leakey's Photo Studio further down Great George Street. Even at that young age, I was fighting with my mother about the way I should fix my hair. Now looking at the photograph fading in my old photo album, I wish that I had listened to my mother as my hairstyle made me look like a wild and mad girl, while Keith looked so nice with his hair neatly combed and parted to one side.

I also remember that Mama spent many nights at the Singer sewing machine pedaling away as she cut and sewed many pairs of flannel pajamas for us. As she pedaled, I used to put one foot also on the pedal to feel the movement from the other side of the machine. Despite these signs that changes were being planned, I was not aware of our pending journey because neither Keith nor I were told what was being planned for us. It was not until years later, when we met the "uncle" who was going to take us to China along with another boy, Fredel, from the Moo Young family in Little London District, Westmoreland, that we fully realized what had been going on.

As luck would have it, before we could be sent to China, the Japanese war broke out and it was no longer safe to travel to China. Keith, Fredel and I were not sent to Niu Foo village for our Hakka cultural education. I now reflect how traumatic it would have been to be snatched away from my parents and siblings, to be plunged into the care of strangers in a foreign land and not be able to speak the same language. It would also have been just as horrible to return to Jamaica afterwards and not be able to communicate in English or recognize my own parents and siblings.

There have been many horror stories about these children who were sent back to China. Some families illtreated these overseas born children and the money sent back to the village for their support was spent on the host family and their own children. The Williams men in Jamaica did not discriminate when it came to sending their half-Chinese children back to Niu Foo Village. Unbeknownst to them, however, these children were not readily welcomed in the village and these poor souls found themselves having to overcome racial prejudice at a young age. Perhaps this harsh experience strengthened their characters because, upon returning to Jamaica, they were able to become resettled and made successful and respectable lives for themselves, their children and grandchildren. There was a sad story in the Williams family that a beautiful girl sent by her family in Jamaica to China was always being propositioned by her cousin, son of the uncle with whom she lived. One day after she rejected him yet again, she went to take a bath. While she was taking her bath, the rejected cousin threw acid in her face, which left her scarred for life and ruined her future.

When the war broke out, there was a rush to send these Jamaican-born children back to their families in Jamaica, but some were left behind or could not get across the border to Hong Kong in time to get on the ship leaving for the Caribbean. Those left behind suffered the ravages of war and starvation. They also had to survive the Chinese Communist regime and somehow make a life for themselves despite all the turmoil and hardships of life in rural China in the early 20th century. Their families could not contact them during this upheaval and some guilt-ridden family members have tried to make up for this period by inviting these now grown-up children back to the West after China opened its doors again to migration in the early 1980s. Those who have made such journeys have usually found the transition difficult. Their parents have long since passed away and their siblings are now strangers to them.

Life in Jamaica: Savanna-La-Mar District, Westmoreland 1945

Living in a foreign culture is very hard for them and the difficulty is made even harder if they have left their own children and grandchildren behind. Needless to say, many of them eventually return to China. Their lives there might lack some of the physical comforts of life in the West, but at least it is very familiar to them.

Thank God, I was spared this horrible experience and could grow up with my own parents and siblings, plus be educated in the western hemisphere.

Your loving Ah-Poh

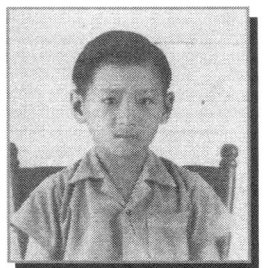 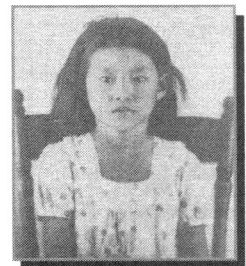 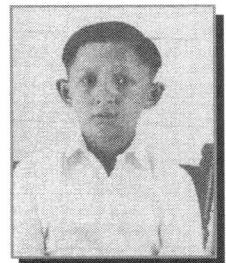

Passport Photos L-R Keith, Carol and Fredel

Sister Carmen Fenton and Sister Polly Lee

Polly Lee and siblings
L-R: Pat, Moi, Sylbert, Polly, Gena, Myrtle

Life in Jamaica: Petersfield, Westmoreland 1947

My dear Grandchildren,

In the late 1940s, the construction of the building adjoining ours in Savanna-La-Mar was completed. When the entire family of Papa's Uncle Jackson had moved from Petersfield into the new building in Savanna-La-Mar, Uncle Jackson's wife, May, insisted on transferring their original family store and premises in Petersfield to Papa. This meant that our family would be leaving Savanna-la-Mar and moving to Petersfield because, in return for being given Uncle Jackson's old business, Papa was expected to turn his business in Savanna-la-Mar over to Uncle Jackson and his family. Later in life, Papa explained this arrangement to me in this way: Aunt May had always favoured Papa over all the other nephews who had arrived with him in Jamaica from China and that was why Aunt May wanted him to have their store in Petersfield. Papa was always obedient to her and proved to be a hard worker. Papa was a strapping young man who had no qualms about lifting 100-pound jute bags of brown sugar and throwing it on the shop counter to be parceled out into smaller amounts for the customers. The same could be said for cotton sacks of flour and cornmeal stored in a far corner of the shop floor.

For as long as I could remember, Papa always felt so grateful to Uncle Jackson and Aunt May for giving him and his cousins the opportunity to seek their fortunes in Jamaica. Even long after both Uncle Jackson and Aunt May had passed away, Papa would continue to demonstrate his gratefulness to them by showing the same respect to their children. Papa always respected and trusted the advice of his elders and considered being the "chosen nephew" to take over their old and already established business in Petersfield an honour. My father had such a kind and trusting heart, he never doubted the intentions of Uncle Jackson and Aunt May or dared to imagine that perhaps, his being asked to take over the Petersfield shop was not done out of pure kindness – that perhaps, Uncle Jackson and Aunt May would rather take over his growing business so that they could pass on this thriving business to their more closer family members, some of whom would arrive from China and Surinam shortly after our family had moved to Petersfield. Whether the exchange of businesses was fair or not, Papa would never have disrespected Uncle Jackson and Aunt May by refusing the arrangement. We moved to Petersfield. This would be our last move as a family in Jamaica. It was a new village for us children and Mama, but for Papa, he was making a full circle: returning back to where he first started his life in Jamaica upon arrival from his homeland in China.

Life in Jamaica: Petersfield, Westmoreland 1947

*Williams Men standing L-R: Papa, Henry, Lincoln, Alfred
sitting L-R: Thomas, Jackson and wife May*

Petersfield was a rural town. It was a beautiful, lush, fertile and bountiful area surrounded by acres and acres of sugar-canefields planted by the West Indian Sugar Company. A variety of trees native to the island dotted the landscape. Fruit trees were found in virtually every yard. There were rivers and streams winding their way all over the various properties. Water tubers, like baddoe plants and lily plants, lined the sides of the banks. We would float on inflated car tubes along these small streams winding among the canefields and drink the river water using the baddoe leaves as vessels. The water was clean and the sparkling drops of water seemed to dance on the broad green leaves. Watercress grew wild along the banks as the fish and crayfish swam freely – although they tried to avoid intruders like us children. Tropical flora and fauna thrived unattended.

The locals, like us, all planted fruit trees and cultivated the land on their properties. The East Indians, whom the local Blacks called "Coolies", farmed rice paddy fields and some did tailoring as a trade. The Blacks who did not work in the sugar cane industry, cultivated other food produce for sale. Some worked at the nearby Dean's Valley Ice factory or worked in various trades like carpentry, furniture and coffin making, creating tinsmith products, dressmaking, baking, barbering and hairdressing.

Many were teachers, nurses, caregivers and maids. A travelling dentist would sometimes pass through town, although the only service he seemed to be interested in or capable of performing was pulling out a patient's teeth to stop dental pain. The only dentist in Savanna-la-Mar was just a step more qualified – he had a permanent office and a dentist chair! More professional and advanced dental treatment would have to be done in Montego Bay, twenty-six miles away.

Our business in Petersfield grew to be very successful. One reason for this was that the district of Petersfield was surrounded by sugar-canefields and the nearby West Indian Sugar Company (WISCo) weigh station was located in the neighbouring district of Shrewsbury. A lot of our business came from people affiliated with the sugar industry. Another reason for the success of this business was that Petersfield was situated on the main thoroughfare from Savanna-La-Mar, located on the southern coast, to Montego Bay, another seaport on the north coast of the island. All modes of transportation came through the town and past our store on this road. In fact, for a very long time, our store was the only business place in the town square. Surrounding the square were the post office, St. Peter's Anglican Church and cemetery, the Public Works Department of the Ministry of Transport and Communications, the open-sided market, the Public Health Office and our store, Nathan Williams & Sons Ltd.

Like in Savanna-la-Mar, our store was a two-storey concrete building with zinc roofing. The sound of the rain falling on the metal sheets of zinc created such a soothing sound – it was wonderful for restful sleeping. As children, unconcerned about safety issues or damage to the roof, we found it fun to count the June plums falling off the tree on the roof, each plum making a satisfyingly loud thud as it fell. But during the hurricane season, the zinc roofs were quite treacherous. Heavy winds could blow off the zinc sheets causing damage to other buildings.

Nathan Williams & Sons Ltd. store, circa 1968

Life in Jamaica: Petersfield, Westmoreland 1947

Left: Ministry of Communications & Works, Petersfield Station, and Shrewsbury Road, opposite our store

Below: St. Peter's Anglican Church, opposite the Post Office and our store

There were four massive concrete columns supporting our residence upstairs and the full width of the wooden verandah overlooking the centre of the square below and the surrounding landscape. A concrete piazza was below the verandah and under our residence was the dry goods, haberdashery, hardware and variety store. Adjoining the store was a one-storey concrete building that housed the grocery shop and rum bar. Next to this building was a petrol station. When Papa first started the petrol station, it had just one pump from which gasoline would be manually served. Years later when electricity came to the district, the petrol station would be expanded with two electrically operated gasoline pumps as well as a pump for diesel oil fuel for trucks and farm equipment machines.

Mama and Papa's last son, Donald (Donny) Anthony was born in Petersfield. Ironically, he was born in the same room where Papa had first slept on arrival in Jamaica from his distant homeland in China. For this birth, Mama was attended to by the local midwife, Nurse Campbell. Actually, Nurse Campbell lived in Savanna-la-Mar and had also delivered Dick and Elaine while we were living there. To deliver Donny, she had to ride her bicycle (the only ladies' wheel bicycle I had ever seen during that era) exactly six miles from her home in Savanna-la-Mar. The trip took her over two hills in Hertford, one at the cross-road and the other at the Tomlinson's property which I will write about later. I am not sure, but it is possible that Nurse Campbell delivered all of us children. After all, she and her bicycle could be seen riding all over the neighboring districts. She was short and stubby and, because of fair complexion and her part British ancestry, was what we called "White Jamaican". She wore rimless spectacles that I thought suited her nice and motherly face well. She had delivered so many babies that her left arm was in permanent cradling position. Long distance cycling did not deter her from visiting us socially as well. I remember that when she would arrive, she would take her white lace handkerchief out of her heaving bosom to wipe the perspiration off her chubby face and arms.

Mama, Papa and Donny

My parents always employed two or three Black maids to take care of the house, laundry, cooking and us children. These women worked tirelessly for minimum wages. They loved us children and we loved them too. Sometimes, they would even return after having dinner with their own families to do extra chores of their own free will or to just to socialize. We especially loved when they would just hang out with us – that was when we learned a lot of local Jamaican culture, customs, music, dance and duppy (ghost) stories based on African folklore. We would also listen to and repeat their colourful local patois.

There were many maids who worked for us over the years, but I always particularly remember the devotion of Louise. Louise used to take the time to massage Mama's legs after a long day of standing up in the store, which Mama Gladys found very painful because of her bulging varicose veins. I recall Miss B running the household and taking care of Papa Nathan, as well as Patrick, Dick and his wife, Margaret, during the 1970s after Mama passed away. I also remember Cissy, who nursed my Chinese step-mother, Ah-Neung, during her final days when she was dying of lymphatic cancer. Ah-Neung was the woman to whom my father had been betrothed as a child but had never been able to return to China and marry. Years after my mother passed away and China had opened its door to the Western Hemisphere, Ah-Neung was finally able to join Papa in Jamaica. Unfortunately, in addition to her old age, she was also suffering from cancer and became terminally ill only three years after she arrived.

Life in Jamaica: Petersfield, Westmoreland 1947

Mama's grave in the Chinese cemetery, Kingston

Ah-Neung's grave in the Anglican Church cemetery, Petersfield

When she passed away, Ah-Neung was given an Anglican burial in the St. Peter's Anglican Church cemetery in Petersfield. Mama was buried in the Chinese Cemetery in Kingston after a Roman Catholic funeral service.

We also had what was then called a "yard boy" to take care of the premises, help with the gardening, and do other odd jobs around the property. The yard behind the store was planted with different citrus trees, June plums, dwarf water coconut, almond, mango, banana and papaya trees. I enjoyed climbing the mango trees; it was fun swaying on the branches in the breeze. It was easy to climb the bigger June plum tree because of it growing so close to the roof of our outdoor kitchen and the spreading almond tree which shaded the chicken coops, providing easier access. As girls, younger sister Elaine and I were fearless climbers and many times the yard boy would have to rescue our brothers by helping them to get back down after they followed us to the top branches.

Years later, Papa received a young Chinese lychee fruit tree which was not as fruitful as Papa wished and prayed for year after year. The climate was not ideal for this oriental tree and there were no other trees of this rare species to cross-pollinate. Although not indigenous to Jamaica, our breadfruit tree bore well because there were many other breadfruit trees in the neighbourhood. Initially in the early 1800's, British

Life in Jamaica: Petersfield, Westmoreland 1947

Captain Blythe brought hundreds of breadfruit saplings from Tahiti on his ship "The Bounty" to Jamaica. The breadfruit was brought to help feed the African slaves on the sugar-cane plantations and today, it is one of Jamaica's favourite foods enjoyed by all classes, especially in the Jamaican diaspora.

There were also yam hills and vegetable gardens. I was fascinated by the curly leaf lettuce, pumpkin vines and Chinese bitter melon *(foo-gah)* trellises. The Jamaicans value the vines of the bitter melon in their home remedies and named it "cerasee'. The dried vines were made into a hot tea for drinking to cleanse the blood and put into a warm bath to soothe the itching associated with tropical skin diseases and the childhood diseases, measles and chicken pox. As a toddler, Donny used to wander into the vegetable garden to pick and eat the tiny tomatoes that he called "up-tup-tup." Mama also loved flowers, especially African violets and gladioli, so these flowers were planted all around the house, along with hibiscus, Joseph's coat (coleus), and canna lily shrubs. In the evenings, we could smell the fragrance of orange blossoms and the jasmine flowers.

Our servants worked very well together. Sometimes, they shared jobs, like cleaning all our shoes en masse, usually on Sundays, and you could hear them all happily chattering in colourful Jamaican patois dialect and laughing together as they went about their tasks. They also would share their food, which was typical Jamaican fare, like boiled yam, potatoes and humongous flour and cornmeal dumplings. I also remember how they liked to eat these with the tinned corned beef, which they called "bully beef," because of the picture of the cow on the red label of the can which came all the way from Argentina. Sometimes, they would also eat tinned herring and sardines from the Maritimes of Canada or roasted breadfruit and cooked salted codfish with fresh ackees or pickled mackerel with callaloo (spinach) and boiled green bananas. We children loved to share their food with them. We would eat from their simple enamel plates, and drink their "wash" – water sweetened with brown unrefined sugar and lime juice – out of the empty condensed milk cans that served as their cups and glasses.

I loved these meals. I think the food tasted so nice because they used unrefined coconut oil that they made from scratch for their cooking. I specially enjoyed the camaraderie they shared and it felt good to be with local folks speaking patois. We children found it to be so much fun just sitting around their outdoor fire with them, being amazed at how they could fashion cooking utensils out of large empty coconut oil tins and cheese pans from the store. They were so innovative, making do with what they had at the moment. They were very relaxed, fun-loving and leisurely, seeming to take everything in stride. We always felt very safe

Donny and the three musketeers: Patrick, Dick and Elaine in the back yard

with them. We knew that they would never harm us. Indeed, they were quite protective of us and ensured our safety as we sat stoking the fire and walked around the yard barefooted. They cared about us all and eventually became part of our family too.

The hired Chinese men, *Foo-Ghees*, who came to work in the store were less loyal. It seemed that as quickly as they arrived to work for us, they left, and Papa would have to find a replacement when he went to Chinatown in Kingston to purchase goods and Chinese food supplies. But the *Foo-Ghees* had one advantage over our other help: they could cook authentic Chinese cuisine -- even better than Papa. Some of my fondest memories are those of the nights after the store was closed, when they would cook white rice steamed with *fah cheong* (pork sausages) and *lap-ap* (salt-preserved duck). I remember being awakened by the smell and would jump out of bed to join them having their late night snack (*seow-yah*). For dessert, we might have Excelsior crackers soaked in sugar water or gelatin made from agar-agar or slices of white hard-dough bread spread with condensed milk and sprinkled with white granulated sugar.

Papa may not have been as able a cook as the *Foo-Ghees*, but he did have two specialties. One was *nu-neuk-gun* (dried beef strips). He made the tastiest *nu-neuk-gun* I have ever had – it was much better than Canadian beef jerky! We would normally steam the *nu-neuk-gun* and eat it as a condiment at meal times, but Papa loved to serve it as a snack to his drinking buddies. When he was ready to make a batch, Papa would order freshly butchered beef, carefully cut it into thin slices, season the slices, mainly with salt and soya sauce, and then place the meat on metal zinc sheets to be dried. When the meat was partially dried, he would fill an empty rum bottle with water to create a rolling pin that he used to flatten each piece of meat. Then, he would use a large packing needle to form a loop of string for each individual slice of meat. The loops of string, with the meat now attached to them, would then be threaded onto broomstick handles and left out to be dried in the winter northerly breezes. This breeze was, according to Papa, the secret ingredient in his *nu-neuk-gun*. He believed that the type of wind that the meat was dried in was important to developing the taste of the meat, so he only made our supplies during the winter months. I am not so sure if the wind really made a difference – I believe it was the type of beef we got in Jamaica that made it so good. The beef was all free range, grass-fed cows that were freshly butchered in our own market next door.

Papa's other specialty was *yuk-choy* soup. He made it using fresh meat which was cooked slowly – for at least four hours -- with a special assortment of dried Chinese medicinal herbs, seeds, berries and stalks (together called *yuk-choy*), a mixture which was obtainable only from Chinese specialty herb stores in Chinatown. Papa would begin the soup by adding his meat – his first choice was to use beef bones, chicken feet, neck and the organs of the freshly killed chicken -- to the *yuk-choy*. Then, after this mixture was brought to a boil, a whole plucked chicken would be added to the pot. When the soup came to a boil again, the stove was turned off to allow for the whole chicken to be truly slow cooked. When the chicken was done, it would be chopped up and eaten with a dipping sauce made from escallion (spring onions), soya sauce and hot oil mixture. The soup that it had been cooked in, containing all the goodness of the medicinal herbs of the *yuk-choy* mixture, would also be consumed with relish.

When it was available, Papa loved to cook and slurp sea turtle soup. The local fishermen knew that they had a sure sale if they were fortunate enough to catch a sea turtle in their nets! Sea turtle soup had top layers of fat which made it delicious and, it was said, also gave the soup aphrodisiac value. Papa was even more delighted if the turtle had eggs which would be cooked in the soup and relished with vim and vigour. These eggs had extra bright orange yolks. I was more fascinated by the beautiful shell of the turtle and by how tiny the claws were on their relatively big feet.

Papa would occasionally purchase a young goat to be cooked with ginger and lime leaves. He would ask his friends to help with the butchering in our backyard. We were more curious than daunted when the goat was killed, then the carcass was hung up and left to become bloated in order for it to be easily skinned and hairs scraped off. After being cut up, the mutton was simmered with Chinese spices, ginger and lime leaves in the traditional Hakka Chinese style. We children were not too fond of this dish but the adults enjoyed eating this meal because it was reminiscent of how the specially raised dogs were cooked back in their village in China, as a winter dish to help keep them warm. Even though outlawed under British rule in Hong Kong, the Chinese always found a way to continue enjoying that delicacy.

Although we did not like the goat dish so much, we children were always happy to have the Hakka-style golden brown roast chicken cooked by the *Foo-Ghees* during their time of employment. The smell of five-spice powder as the chicken or duck was being fried in the huge iron wok was so mouthwatering. After the bird had been cooked to perfection, we watched, fascinated, as the *Foo-Ghees* deftly chopped up the bird on a huge wooden chopping block. We would each vie for one of the drumsticks. Somehow, my sister, Elaine always seemed to be the one most favoured by the cook to receive one!

We children were certainly not faint-hearted. We had grown up witnessing the killing of the chicken and ducks which became our meals. Their heads were bent backwards so that it was easy to remove their neck feathers before their throats were cut. Then their blood was drained into a container to be later cooked into a blood pudding. Finally, the decapitated poultry were thrown down and left to flutter to their death either in the concrete cistern or in an area which would be covered by a straw basket or a metal pan. These were frequent occurrences and we realized that this was a necessary part of life. How else were we going to enjoy the delicious chicken soups with fish bladders (*emn-peow*) and succulent pieces of roasted chicken or duck served on beds of lily roots, mushrooms and red dates brought steaming hot to our dinner tables? We also needed the feathers for our pillows to sleep on.

Papa was not really a good all-round cook like Mama. His repertoire was limited to Hakka dishes – he liked to cook what he enjoyed eating! But Mama had a real interest in non-Chinese cooking and loved baking. She liked the challenge of perfecting the right tartness of local specialty dishes, like sweet and sour pig trotters, or English recipes, like pot-roast beef and shepherd's pie, that she found in the English magazines she bought weekly. She would also cook some Chinese dishes but she made them with her own seasoning and style. She did, however, stick to the traditional Hakka Chinese style of making *shao-bow* (steamed buns) with various fillings and always tried to better my aunts' (the wives of Papa's cousins) recipes.

We were accustomed to having ducks and chickens walking all over the yard during the daytime, but at nights they would go into their respective coops situated at one corner of the backyard. Papa used to say that we should take note that although ducks and chickens played together during the days, at nights they would sleep with their own kind. And in his "Chinglish" he would say, "luck-a-luck an' fowl-a-fowl"; that is, "ducks are ducks and chickens are chickens", meaning that even though we might play and go to school with other Jamaicans, he wanted us to marry our own kind of people (*chee-gah ngin*). We were really too naïve at that age to realize what he was hinting at. It wasn't until much later in life that we understood what he was trying to tell us.

At one time, Papa's aunt, Mary Chin, came from Kingston to live with us. We called her *Tai Goo Poh* because she was the older sister of Papa's father. *Tai Goo Poh* loved taking care of the ducks and chickens. She lovingly tended the baby ducklings and chicks which were soft and covered in yellow down. We would watch her feed them. She would call out "hey-di-di-di" and, recognizing her voice, they would come running over to her. She would cut up and moisten cubes of stale bread to feed them. She was so devoted to them, that she often got sick because she would go out to round up her poultry in the rain! I used to help her collect the eggs but I didn't care to help her wash and clean the feathers of the killed chickens. After picking out the softest feathers, she would stuff the pillow cases she had already sewn out of the empty chicken feed bags made of cloth. She knew how to reuse and recycle long before it was trendy in North America!

After a few years of living with us and being so useful in the home and store, she returned to live with her son, Edwin and daughter Daisy in Kingston. Without the tasks that she had helped us with in Petersfield, she seemed to get older and more feeble. I would visit her when I went into Kingston and I could tell how she missed living in the country with us and being useful by taking care of the poultry and animals. I felt so sad for her.

At least when she was staying with us, she got to see her eldest brother, Ngui, Wei Len whom we called "Bak Goong" (grand-uncle) when he visited Jamaica from Trinidad. She had not seen him for many, many years since leaving her Niu Foo Village in China and all his nephews, including Papa, got together to have a huge reunion dinner at the home of B.J Williams. I noticed she had tears in her eyes when he arrived but Bak Goong was too dignified to be sentimental. We were all happy to meet him and decades later on in life, we would meet his son, Robert "Gan Tong Shuck" and wife, Eileen (née Chin) and their children, Annette and Charles who had all migrated to Toronto, Canada from years of living in Trinidad. I would also have the good fortune to meet Bak Goong's wife, Wong, Su Yin and their other son Wei, Hon Sheung and sons, Wei Ying Xiang and Ngai, Fook Cheung when I visited Niu Foo Village myself in the 1980s.

Life in Jamaica: Petersfield, Westmoreland 1947

*Williams families: Back L-R: Sarah, Violet, Nancy, Daisy, Walton, Lincoln,
B. Joseph, Patrick, Nathan, Arthur;
Middle: Donald
Front L-R: Henry, Thomas, Mary Chin, Wei Len, May, Isaac*

We also had cats and dogs in Petersfield. They were domesticated, but were not really pets. The dogs were kept as guard dogs and were common mongrels yet we grew attached to them. The cats were numerous and were useful to catch the mice and rats that roamed the grocery shop. Of course, there was no fancy dog or cat food for these animals. They were fed our food scraps and coped very well with the bones. They were not toilet trained so they crapped all over the premises like the ducks and chickens. We somehow learned to avoid the mess and tolerate the smell. This was a trade-off for growing up in the country and being close to nature.

Overall, I believe that we children were fortunate to have moved from Savanna-La-Mar which, as the capital of the Parish of Westmoreland, was quickly becoming very developed. Life there was turning into city living rather than the rural life that we were fortunate to be experiencing in Petersfield. In Petersfield, we were exposed to country living and could grow close to the various country folk, the Blacks and East Indians, as well as with the upper and middle-class British in the area. We were also able to maintain the Hakka customs of our parents and create strong family ties with our Chinese relatives. We were lucky in that, without competition, business was good, and we could see that our parents were well-liked and respected in the community.

Truly, God had blessed us with the best of all worlds in this peaceful country setting.

Your loving Ah-Poh

Life in Jamaica: Petersfield, Westmoreland 1947

Canefield of young sugar cane plants

A river roars through the canefields

Photos courtesy of Ray Chen

Life in Jamaica:
Petersfield, Westmoreland
1948

My dear Grandchildren,

By 1948, Papa and Mama and their now six children were quite settled in Petersfield. We were happy living in the solidly-built Jackson Williams family home from which so many of the Williams family who migrated to Jamaica started out. The building had two floors with tall, round concrete columns in front of the store supporting a wooden verandah. This provided a "piazza" for the local vendors and shelter for the people below. The upper living quarters were built of wood while the lower level was built with concrete block walls and concrete flooring.

While our parents toiled away in the store, we children were busy entertaining ourselves. For us mischievous children, the wooden floor upstairs was ideal for peeping down below at the customers in the store. Although we had a small private trapdoor in the floor that allowed someone upstairs to look down into the store if, after the store was closed, we heard suspicious sounds like those of a break-in robbery, we children used the missing wood knot-holes to spy on the customers. My brothers were not naughty like other children who, we had heard, peed through these knot-holes onto the people below. Instead, our mischief consisted of throwing chewed-up marshmallows over the verandah of the living quarters at the pedestrians below. After the deed was done, we would quickly hide from sight. If the people complained to our parents, we would get a spanking with the long cane handle of the Chinese feather duster – the *gai-mao sow* -- used for dusting the goods and shelves in the store. This was a painful punishment and the cane marks left welts on our bodies.

Another way in which we entertained ourselves was by climbing up to the sturdy wooden beams in the ceiling upstairs so that we could get a good perch from which to jump down on the beds below. The wooden stairs leading downstairs into the dining area, kept polished and shined by the maids, served as another play area. We used to slide down the lower portion of the banister to be stopped abruptly by the wooden post and gate at the bottom of the stairs. We would sometimes sit on the stairs and take turns pretending to be

L-R: Patrick, Carol, Donny, Dick and Elaine

driving a bus and letting passengers on and off by opening the gate. We would imagine receiving coins in our palms and giving back the change for this game.

Our dining room had a large rectangular wooden table with wooden benches on the two long sides of the table. In one corner was a wooden cabinet with fine mesh-wired windows to keep the insects out. The upper section stored eating utensils and the bottom section locked away food stuff. Beside the cabinet were empty wooden crates covered and padded with old, used newspapers. We used them as a sideboard for the rice pot and perhaps a soup pot.

We enjoyed many hearty and naturally wholesome breakfasts here as well. Fresh milk was supplied daily, straight from hand-milked, grass-fed cows from a local dairy farmer. Because the milk was fresh, it had to be scalded before the thick rich cream could be skimmed off and enjoyed. The hot milk was used for our morning cocoa and porridge. The porridge was either made with oats, freshly grated cornmeal or green bananas and was sweetened with unrefined brown sugar. Our eggs came directly from our chicken coops and our hard-dough bread was made without additives from our cousin's bakery in the nearby village. Our guava jams were home-made while butter and cheese arrived from New Zealand in their most natural state. They contained no added colours or flavours.

The rest of the surrounding wall space in our dining area was packed close to the ceiling with stock of goods for the store, such as 100 lbs. patterned cloth bags of chicken feed, cartons of canned food, and in later years, automotive supplies for the petrol station that my father built. There was also a heavy duty balance scale stored under the stairs for weighing heavy loads.

The back door leading to the backyard opened to concrete steps and a zinc covered walkway that led to the adjoining roofed building. This building housed a kitchen and a storage room. Next to this building was the maid's quarters and an adjoining bathroom. On one side of this walkway was a concrete cistern that was used for washing pots and pans, plus a huge wooden chopping block. On the opposite side along this covered walkway was an open mesh wire table that served as a draining board and working area for Mama's potted plants. Later on, she added a home-made metal-lined oven and ice-box side by side along the walkway.

The kitchen had a wooden counter table built along one wall and a wooden cabinet against another. The third wall had a solidly built concrete counter top platform with an open iron frame for wood fires to be lit underneath. These fires were used for cooking and for heating bath water. There was always a pile of chopped wood under the wooden counter table to provide fuel for these fires.

We had two bathrooms, one upstairs in our living quarters and the other outside beside the outdoor kitchen. The upstairs bathroom was a wooden enclosure that contained a huge and wide metal bath pan made of tin. When we first moved to Petersfield, there was no "running water," so if you wanted to take a bath, water had to be fetched from reused metal oil drums, which were filled either with rain water or from water collected from the nearby river. For a warm bath, this water had to be taken to the outdoor kitchen where it would be heated over the wood fire and then taken up the stairs to fill the metal bath pan. This was a laborious and dangerous task for the maids. Years later, the government installed huge water main pipes and intermittent standpipes along the road. Watching the labourers manually digging the trenches to lay the water main pipes was quite interesting for us. We would stand on the fresh mounds of dirt by the trenches and patiently watch as the shirtless men continued to dig into the ground to widen the trenches until they were big enough to fit and bury the huge water pipes waiting by the side of the road. After all pipes were connected, we finally had the luxury of running water after doing without for many years.

In the downstairs bathroom beside the outdoor kitchen, was a large rectangular concrete bathtub smoothly rendered inside and outside. Inside the bathtub was kept a low wooden stool and in front of the stool were metal buckets to hold hot, warm and cold bath water. Bathers could sit comfortably on the stool to wash and rinse themselves from the buckets. At the end of the bath, the bather would empty all the remaining water in the buckets over their bodies as a grand finale. Towards the other end of the room, near the doorway, were an ironing board and various sizes of galvanized tin wash tubs and wooden washboards for doing the laundry.

I remember that the maid's room had wooden walls that were wallpapered by sticking old newspapers and colourful magazine pages to the walls with a flour and water paste. A passe-partout glass frame with a picture of Jesus hung over a wooden bed frame on which lay a straw-filled mattress. The clothes closet was a cloth enclosure around a wooden shelf built high up towards the ceiling. These were the bare necessities, but they were very much appreciated by the maids.

A huge June plum tree grew behind the maid's room and a mango tree was near the wooden outhouse. The outhouse had a concrete base, zinc sheet roofing and a window with horizontal wood slats. The door could be closed with a tower bolt inside. Inside there were two oval-shaped holes cut in a wooden platform against one wall. One hole was smaller for the children and that section of the platform was lower to the floor for shorter legs. The other bigger hole higher up served the adults. The wood used was unfinished, but the wooden platform and hinged covers over the holes were straw-dyed in a maroon-red oak colour and buffed to a shine using coconut husk brushes after a coating of Poliflor wax polish was applied. The walls were papered with old newspaper and there were cut-up sheets of newspaper set aside to be used as toilet paper. These needed to be crushed vigorously to be softened before use.

There was no electricity in the outhouse, so the person accompanying you had to bring a "kitchen bitch" lamp to light the way if it was dark so that before you sat down you could check for the lizards and cockroaches who lived in the outhouse. Nevertheless, sitting over the holes, one often could not avoid the occasional tickle on one's buttocks from the feelers of the cockroaches living in the pit toilet! This kitchen bitch lamp was a metal cup with a tin handle that held kerosene oil, and a centre spout on the top part to accommodate a cotton wick or discarded cloth used as a wick. Because of its small size, lightness, and cup handle for easy carrying and the fact that it was made from an unbreakable material, kitchen bitches, which were made by the local tin-smith, were used mostly in the outdoor and open areas like the kitchen, hence its name, and as mentioned before, for going to the outhouse. Because they did not have chimneys, however, the soot from the burning wick went up into the atmosphere or up one's nostrils if held too closely. The latter situation seemed to be unavoidable since, as there were no globes on the lamp, one tended to hold the lamp closely to shield it from the wind. The putrid stench from the pit latrines was tolerated by all of us as natural, normal, and necessary in those days.

We entered our imposing store through the dining area at the bottom of the stairs leading from the living area and bedrooms upstairs. The double-entry doors to the store were made of wood covered with metal sheeting and secured with extra-large tower bolts and heavy-duty padlocks. In addition, the door had to be opened by a huge black iron key. There were six double-doors at the front of the store from the street which were wider and were also made of heavy wood and metal covered with bigger tower bolts. Massive wooden bars were placed across the doors when closed, for added security. The floor of the store was made of concrete and extended towards the road under the upper verandah which covered the piazza and steps leading out onto the asphalt paved street. The walls were sturdy and made from thick concrete blocks. The large windows were covered with mesh wire to allow for ventilation and visibility when open. Straight iron poles were installed in the window frame for security. At nights, metal-covered doors were closed over each meshed window and additional iron crossbars placed horizontally on the outside of these wooden doors which were further bolted from the inside with metal pins.

It was the same security for the adjoining one-storey building housing the grocery shop and the rum bar. Both buildings were separate but we had a connecting door between the two buildings since we all worked at both places at different times to relieve each other, especially during meal times. When we closed up the store at night, the doors and windows were as secure as Fort Knox. As a result, although there were some attempts made at breaking into the shops, they were never successful. I actually only vaguely remember one such attempt made by an outsider from another district in Jamaica. When some of the locals witnessed the robber in the act of trying to break into the shop, they chased and stoned the man. The man tried to run away, but they eventually caught him and gave him a good beating – all the while admonishing him for trying to break into "*their* Chiney Shop". After the beating, they told him to leave Petersfield and never come back. When Papa and Mama heard of this incident, they felt surprised, but so very pleased. The incident seemed to publicly mark the community's acceptance of our family as part the village. After all, the locals had declared that they had been defending *their* village grocer. It had taken some time but "the Chiney Shop" had become a type of community centre in Petersfield and the Chinese family of Nathan Williams living at the shop was considered to be part of the community. We were one of them.

The store that was under our living quarters served dry goods, ready-made wear, hardware, and haberdashery items along with a variety of cosmetics, food and over-the-counter pharmaceutical items. Other than the front wall, where the front doors opened to the street, sturdy self-enclosed wooden counters were built along all the other walls of the store. We would serve our customers from behind these shop counters. The counters formed an enclosure that welcomed the customers off the street, but they also served as a barrier for our safety. One could only get behind the counter at one section where there was a hinged top to the counter and a door beneath that allowed for passage from behind the counter to the front of the store. The door to get behind the counter was kept bolted for security.

Keith and Elaine in front of fabrics shelves

Some sections of the counters had thick glass installed on the top surface and in front so that they could be used as showcases for customers to view and point to articles that they wanted to purchase. There were also separate free-standing and locked showcases to display samples of hats and shoes for sale. Ready-made garments were hung from the ceiling on metal rods suspended above the counter in the clothing department. The wooden shelves behind the counters were stocked with a wide variety of hardware, dry goods and assorted merchandise, including bolts of cloth, sewing notions and accessories.

On one section of the counter were large jars with sweets and biscuits. Further along, at the corner of the counter was a glass showcase filled with baked goods of all shapes and sizes: rectangular loaves of hard dough bread, sweet buns, round flat "bulla" cakes, square "gratto" bread, triangular "coco" bread, all of which were supplied by a nearby bakery in Whithorn District. The Whithorn Bakery was owned and operated by one of my father's cousins on his maternal side, Stanley Chin along with his wife, Madge and family members, including her brother, Eric Hugh.

In the smaller grocery shop and rum bar in the next adjoining building, there were also sturdy wooden counters but only on two sides of the store and each had weigh scales suspended from the wooden beams above. One scale was used for weighing dry food items and the other for wet, salted or pickled items. Beneath the counter below the scales for dry food items were wooden bins of unbleached flour, coarsely ground cornmeal, unrefined brown sugar and unpolished brown rice. Moving along the counter in the direction of the other scale were wooden containers of coarse and fine salt, barrels of salted codfish from Newfoundland, and smaller barrels of pickled mackerel from another fishing port in the Maritimes as well as tinned sardines from New Brunswick on the shelves. It seemed that all our fish was from Canada! Next to the salted food items were square gallon tins of unrefined coconut oil with different sizes of measuring cans hooked along the edges of the open tin, for serving. Kerosene oil was also sold separately and kept carefully away from the edible food items. The measuring cans utilized the British imperial measure of quarts, pints, ½ pint, ¼ pint,

Patrick serving in the rum bar

and were made by the local tinsmith, nicknamed "Man Hawk" because of his facial features and hunched shoulders.

In those days without electricity, the store was illuminated by Tilley gas lamps with mesh mantles, which were lit with cotton fibre lighters soaked in methylated spirits. We did not use the gas lamps in our living quarters. In those areas, we used tall pedestal glass kerosene oil lamps with rounded glass globes with a "Home Sweet Home" design etched in for decoration. Smaller kerosene glass lamps with rounded handles, without a pedestal, were available for smaller areas to be illuminated. These were quite portable for us to move from one area to another. One of the maids' chores was to frequently clean the black soot collected on the inside of the glass globes (shades) from the burning cotton-fibre wicks.

These lamps were also placed on the tables used at the African Pocomania religious meetings. The leaders would set up a table beside the road along our store piazza and below our verandah. From the safety of our verandah we children watched the meetings below. These meetings were entertaining but also somewhat frightening when "Brothers" and "Sisters" got into the spirit and started having convulsive spasms. The Pocomanians had a distinctive dress: white gowns with blue bands. They also wore head turbans into which they stuck lead pencils. The Pocomanians were not the only religious group to use the area in front of the shop for their meetings. Other fundamentalist religious groups met there as well and we enjoyed their harmonious singing of the revival songs. Since we had already learned many of these songs from our maids, we would sometimes sing along.

In this time period, we children were too young to help in the dry goods store or grocery shop, so while Mama, Papa and the *Foo-Ghees* worked, we played underneath the counters or outside in the yard with the children of the maids and neighbours. We frequently pretended to have our own shop, emulating the adults and even chopping up the fallen leaves of the breadfruit tree to be used as salted codfish and wrapping up the purchases with old newspaper after receiving pretend payment and giving back the change. Needless to say, we were the sellers and our Black playmates were the customers! We did not consciously choose these roles based on the colours of our skins; instead, we were simply imitating the reality of our daily lives.

Forgive me, dear grandchildren for writing in such detailed description of our store and home environs in Petersfield, but the fond memories are so vivid to me; and who knows, in years to come you might one day, perchance, visit Petersfield and come across this very sturdy concrete and stone building. It could very well be still standing in the next century! I would just really like you to know of the simple way of life your ancestors used to lead and the innovative Chinese methods they used to cope with the situation at hand. They tried to make the most of what God blessed them with, as they tried to do business in an under-developed tropical island in the Caribbean: Jamaica, West Indies.

Your loving Ah-Poh

Life in Jamaica:
Petersfield, Westmoreland
1950 -1951

My dear Grandchildren,

Life was good and carefree growing up in Petersfield during the 1950s.

My eldest brother, Keith, and I were not yet allowed to serve the customers who patronized our store and we were free to roam safely and without fear all around the district. My parents and the maids were not worried about us because we were warmly greeted by everyone on the street and welcomed into the homes of the local people. On our jaunts, we often walked through many of the homes of our schoolmates and their relatives would greet us, feed us, and would not hesitate to take care of our sores and boils. I clearly remember someone's mother making a poultice of castor oil and chopped up hibiscus (locally called "shu-black") to cover my infected boil. These people would also not hesitate to give us a scolding if need be! Everyone cared for each other and acted as if we were their children. It does take a village to raise a child!

We liked to visit the post office next door and speak with the staff. There was Miss Icy, the head Post Mistress who lived upstairs with her husband, Mass Bertie; Miss Joyce who lived nearby; and Miss Gascoigne, who rode her bicycle from Hertford, a district about two miles away. They used to let us play around and help them get the mail bags ready for when Her Majesty's Royal Mail van would arrive to collect them. They showed us how to write up a telegram and we listened to them sending off the telegrams using the military code, A for "Abel", B for "Baker", C for "Charlie" and so on. Eventually we got the hang of how the post office was run and how to sort out and deliver the local mail as it arrived. Years later, these same ladies taught me how to crochet, do tatting and embroidery. They also made items for my hope chest as soon as I was engaged to be married in the 1960s.

Our usual jaunt would take us across the street to the Anglican Church, where we could help to put up numbers for hymns to be sung by the choir at the upcoming church service on Sunday. We thought it was so much fun when we were also allowed to assist with the lengthy ringing of the church bell before service started, since that meant swinging on the rope used to ring the bell!

We were not afraid to play in the cemetery surrounding the church during the day. We tried not to point our fingers at the graves, however, because we believed that we would be cursed if we did. If, by some chance, we happened to accidentally point at a grave, we would make sure to bite each finger to break the curse of the dead!

Life in Jamaica: Petersfield, Westmoreland 1950-51

Mrs. Icy Smith, Head Postmistress

The spreading Poinciana tree provided us with long, hard pods with tough elongated seeds to play with as shakers. When its red and orange flowers were in bloom, we would pick the unopened blooms to get at the curved stamens. Then, we would challenge each other in a game to unhook the head of the stamen. The flat top of the tombs were ideal to play the game of "Jacks". In this game, each player would take a turn catching star-shaped metal game pieces with the back of their hand. The pieces not caught would be picked up afterwards by tossing a small rubber ball and catching it also with the errant metal game pieces.

After we passed through the cemetery, we entered the Petersfield Elementary School grounds. There, we would climb the star-apple tree, then raid the guava tree overhanging the river at the bottom of the school property. It was fun to jump from the limb of the tree into the river where sometimes local women were washing clothes. They would sometimes lather the clothes and then spread them out on the grass or rocks to be bleached by the sun. We never heard of liquid bleach and powdered laundry detergent in those days. The soap used was natural unscented brown bar soap which was cut up into smaller bars and sold in our shop. I recall that there were soap berries on the trees across the river and we only picked them to play with the suds they created. The headmaster of the school was Mr. Dunn who lived with his family in the house adjoining the school premises. His wife, Mavis was nice and hospitable, not as stern as her husband. They had three sons, Errol, Dennis and Peter who were good playmates and very smart in school.

Further along the main road lived an East Indian family named Burgess. Mrs. Burgess kept a small shop beside the road and "Tailor" Burgess, who might have been a tailor by trade before, farmed and cultivated the property behind their house. They lived in a modest wooden house and owned a gramophone to play 78 r.p.m. vinyl records like Granny Becky had in Williamsfield. The children's favourite record, which we played over and over, was "Who put the wind in the donut under the yum-yum tree". We did not understand the lyrics, but loved the tune. The Burgesses had two daughters. The older one, Gloria, defied her parents and ran off to marry her first cousin, Eric. The younger one was named Constance. She was our age, so we played a lot together. She spent a lot of time at our house too and my brothers thought that she was pretty and shapely. One day we took "Conse" to the beach with our family and she wowed the boys in her green and white floral bikini! She was also a party girl and when she became a teenager, she got pregnant at a wild party at her friend Cissy's house, which was located further down the road. Conse had a baby boy named Trevor out of wedlock. The baby was cute and extremely good-looking like his mother and his suspected father, Sinclair. Because of Conse being around with us so much, however, Papa asked me to go and check out the baby as soon as he was born. I was to report back to him if the baby's eyelashes were curved or straight down. Trevor's eyelashes were indeed curled so Papa was relieved because he had feared that the baby's father might have been Chinese!

Conse's friend, Cissy, was raised by her grandmother in a nice concrete house on a lovely property with flower gardens in front of the house and a long driveway along from Petersfield's main road. It was obvious that there was British ancestry in the family background because of their light skin colour and long brown wavy hair. Their house furnishings were also like those in the Dunn family house adjoining the school. There were upholstered sofa sets and British Victorian style furniture which were not yet available to the ordinary local folks like ourselves. Other such families were the Jones family still further along the Petersfield main road towards Savanna-la-Mar. The maternal parents in that family were Caucasian and the family had apparently inherited the vast surrounding property as well as a concrete and tiled roof house on top of a hill. They raised cattle and hired farm hands. Their darker-skinned son, Bertie, worked at the Singer Sewing Company and he was quite friendly and outgoing.

Across the street on top of another hill overlooking another huge property, lived the wealthy Tomlinson family who had older light-skinned children. Lawyer Tomlinson had his law office in Savanna-la-Mar, about five miles away. Mrs. Tomlinson, (Miss Maggie), was head of the Savanna-la-Mar branch of the Women's Federation of Jamaica which was originally formed by expatriate wives to assist local women over the island. Miss Maggie was very benevolent and helped our local women and girls in Westmoreland, which was quite inspiring to Mama. Mama did not hesitate to join the Federation and help out the local women in the environs of Petersfield. The Tomlinsons had two children. The older daughter, Elinor was (and still is) a free spirit. Her father bought her a beach property in Negril when she got married to a German fellow named Hans, and they started and operated the Negril Beach Club. The younger son, Alfred, was irresponsible. The family owned many properties all over Westmoreland and the neighbouring parish of Hanover which included canefields that Alfred was supposed to oversee. Instead, he seemed to spend all his time driving his sports car all around the island. When Alfred got married to a beautiful and lovely girl, Cherry, who was the daughter of another "Jamaican White" family, his parents built them a modern home on top of another hill on their Petersfield property. They hoped that that the marriage and home would make him settle down, but very soon after the lavish wedding, the young couple separated and got divorced. Their house was later rented by the Bank of Nova Scotia, for the new branch manager, Mr. Sanguinetti, also another "Jamaican White", who had a wife and young children.

I was now an expert cyclist and because there was hardly any traffic on the roads, it was safe for me to ride on the main road. I would sometimes ride my bicycle and stop at the house of one of my teachers at the Petersfield Elementary school. Miss Gunning was a spinster and was feared by all her students, but she was a different person at home. She was more easy-going and looked less cross and spoke kindly while entertaining me with lemonade and biscuits. When she retired, she opened a

Life in Jamaica: Petersfield, Westmoreland 1950-51

Carol honouring her math teacher, Miss Gunning

basic school in her home. On Sundays, she would play the organ at church and conduct the choir. It was always amusing to watch her short legs pumping away at the pedals of the upright air organ, her neck stretching up to read the sheet music while her spectacles kept sliding down her nose.

My memories of attending the Petersfield Anglican Church, located across from our store and home, are very pleasant ones. This is where I received much of my early religious training. The Reverend Haughton, and the church wardens made sure to come to the store to inform Mama about weekly programmes at the church and to ask for donations as well. The experience must have had a good influence on me because throughout my life, I continue to worship at and belong to the Anglican Church wherever I visit or reside. I recall the happy times I had making Easter baskets fringed with tissue paper of all colours and filling them with fruit to take up to the altar as offering during Easter church service. Everyone was dressed in their finest and wearing Easter bonnets to celebrate the resurrection of Jesus.

Unlike the church service on Easter Sunday, the long three-hour Good Friday service was not something to look forward to, although Mama would make bun and cheese sandwiches for us to take with us to help sustain us through the service. When she was not needed in the store, Mama would attend church with us. I do remember her singing voice and the bright red lipstick she used to wear on those occasions. During this era it was mandatory for women to wear hats to cover their heads in church and I used to envy her half-hat with its delicate half veil. My hat was a Panama straw hat with a broad rim. I liked my hat, so I did not mind taking a photograph wearing it.

Mama liked to take photographs of us after attending church because we were already dressed up. She owned a Kodak Brownie box camera, which was a rarity at that time.

Life in Jamaica: Petersfield, Westmoreland 1950-51

Before you could take a picture, a roll of film had to be first wound on a spool within the camera. To take a shot, you had to hold the box shaped camera close to the body for steadiness, look at the image reflected on the lens on the top surface, then press the lever to close and open the shutter to capture the image. When the film had been completely filled with captured images, the roll had to be sent to the photo studio to be developed in chemical solutions and later printed on special photo paper which was then cut up into the individual shots.

It was more common for people to engage the services of a professional photographer when they wanted to take family photographs. Sometimes, we would contact Mr. Leakey who would arrive from Savanna-la-Mar with his professional camera equipment. He would set up his tripod and cover himself with a long black cloth once we were posed and ready to smile. Thanks to our parents, we have photographs of ourselves as children at different stages of our childhood.

We were very fortunate to be born in these times in Jamaica. Our innocent childhood was spent at a time when we were free to roam around safely in our neighbourhood among caring and loving Jamaicans of all classes of society, creating beautiful memories.

Your loving Ah-Poh

Back: Carol, Patrick
Front: Elaine, Donny, Dick

Life in Jamaica: Petersfield, Westmoreland 1950-51

Men cutting mature sugar cane

Harvested sugar cane ready for transportation to the sugar factory

Photos courtesy of Ray Chen

Life in Jamaica:
Petersfield, Westmoreland
1952

My dear Grandchildren,

I must mention some other people and influences which shaped our lives growing up in Jamaica, West Indies.

I previously mentioned our jaunts along the asphalt-paved main road towards Savanna-la-Mar, but sometimes my siblings and I would turn off the main road to Bastard Cedar Walk where the Ridguard family lived. They were fair-skinned people but they had distinct Negroid features despite their colouring. In our adult years, one of their daughters, Erma, worked at the Bank of Nova Scotia's branch in Savanna-La-Mar and became the trusted person to whom I could send money for my ex-maid Gurzel after I had married and migrated to Toronto, Ontario, Canada.

We always stopped in at the house of the Brownie family as we were sure to receive some homemade coconut sweets like "drops" and "sham-shuku". If we were lucky, we might even witness how they were made with diced and grated mature coconuts. Another treat was shaved ice which was served with different flavoured homemade syrup. A huge block of ice would be delivered by the truck from the ice factory nearby in Waterworks. The purchased block of ice would be stored in a thick crocus bag, (previously used for transporting or storing brown unrefined sugar) and insulated with dried banana leaves. A heavy metal shaver with a hinged cover, made in England, was used to scrape the ice using forward strokes. When the shaver was opened, it revealed a rectangle of shaved ice which was hurriedly formed into a ball with bare hands. Syrup was poured on the ice ball – we rotated the ball as the syrup was poured to ensure maximum coverage – and then the ball was ready to be sucked on with great delight. It was such a refreshing treat in our hot, tropical climate.

Mr. Brownie was not as fair-skinned as Mrs. Brownie. He was also frequently drunk. Mrs. Brownie was industrious, hard-working and had great ambitions for her children who were also high achievers. At night, the children would sit on the pavement under the street light outside their house and study for hours. As adults, their study habits paid off: the eldest girl, Norma, became a nurse, and the son Dana, became an agronomist. We lost track of the younger siblings, but I am sure that they did well in life too -- Mrs. Brownie would never have allowed them to become worthless.

Next door was the wood-working shop belonging to Ronald, the same young man who had initially helped Papa in his first shop in Williamsfield. Ronald's woodworking shop was a wooden four-post structure with a roof. One side of the structure was open. This was the working area and it was usually filled with sawdust. The closed half was the finishing area and sometimes we would see coffins being made, although Ronald usually worked on making cabinets for homes. Across from Ronald's was a tailor's shop perched high off the ground on long round wooden logs. The door to this small wooden shop was usually closed, but it had a huge open window in the front where you could see Tailor Barnes sitting at his Singer sewing machine, pedaling away so that the spindles and shuttles would work. His wife, Mrs. Barnes, was a fat, quiet, but friendly woman who was usually tending the garden in front of the house which was located behind the shop.

Beside and set way back from the road lived a slim, tall, good-looking and dashing man, Jackie, and his nice wife, Mrs. Muschette. Jackie owned the first motor car in the district, so our family depended on him for transportation. Their next door neighbours were Dudley, who owned a big truck to haul goods from Kingston, and his business-minded wife, Miss Iris. Every Saturday, early in the morning, Miss Iris would have a cow butchered to provide the district with fresh beef at the open market next to our grocery shop. As a result, it became traditional in our family to have fresh beef soup for lunch every Saturday. Even after I had left home for Canada and became a mother to my own three children, Saturday lunch was beef soup! The hearty soup was prepared by the Jamaican cook with locally grown ground provisions, dumplings, seasoning and, of course, long macaroni pasta to slurp when our soup cooled. Dudley and Iris Vassell had two daughters, Delores and Blossom, who were in Keith's and my class at school.

Another family's home which was a refuge for all of us children over the years was that of the Gilfillians who owned a huge property of canefields and fruit trees. A river ran through the property. The family matriarch, "Miss Gill," was a warm, friendly and extremely outgoing lady who ran the house, home and cane-field plantation as a liberated woman in these conservative times. She would not hesitate to work in the fields alongside the hired hands "like a man", as my sister once described her to me. Through her hard work, she educated her daughters, Inez, Cynthia, Helene, Daphne, Jeanette and Claudette who have remained friends with us throughout their grown-up lives. Later in life, Miss Gill herself would migrate to Toronto, Canada and at this time of writing, she is feisty as ever and living in a nursing home at the ripe old age of 101. Perhaps Miss Gill is proof of what my mother used to tell us when reprimanding us for laziness: "Hard work never killed anyone; only laziness did!" I recall that sometimes Mama would follow that statement with a further warning: "And if you can't hear, you will feel!" which we understood to mean: "And if you do not obey my orders, you will get a painful spanking!"

Petersfield Elementary School was the next stage of my formal education, after I had attended Mrs. Chapman's Basic School in Savanna-la-Mar. Because Jamaica was a British colony at that time, we had a very traditional British education – and I believe that the British education system, offering subjects like English grammar, comprehension and penmanship, is simply the best. The teachers were strict and disciplined and demonstrated respect for authority. Headmaster Dunn and Mrs. Dunn taught the higher classes (grades). Mrs. Dunn taught Home Economics and ran the soup kitchen which was the name given to the place for serving hot lunches, including a variety of healthy soups, for all students. Mrs. Brown, a quiet and dignified lady, taught English. Mrs. Pennycooke, a friendly and likeable person, taught Geography. The previously mentioned Miss Gunning was the dreaded Arithmetic teacher. There were other junior teachers who taught the lower classes. These teachers had earned the respect of the community and no parent questioned their method of discipline. If a student was punished, she or he would not dare complain to or inform their parents for fear of additional spanking. Sometime, we would mischievously hide the teacher's leather straps to prevent us from being punished -- although that did not stop Miss Gunning from wringing our ears.

Our classrooms were furnished with rows of long wooden desks and matching benches. We used exercise books to complete our lessons. The older classes used those with single lines while the younger used those with double lines to develop good penmanship. The very youngest students used a slate bordered by a wooden frame and slate pencils to use for writing. The middle classes used wooden lead pencils that needed sharpening frequently to keep their points, while students in the higher classes used ink and pens. The pens had slim pointed wooden shafts with a metal fitting for the pen-nibs. There were ink wells counter-sunk intermittently along the top of the long desks, and I recall that I had to be constantly on guard to fend off the boys from dipping my long braids or ponytail in the ink well in the desk behind me! The teachers taught us our lessons by using a blackboard and sticks of white chalk. All these school supplies and curricular materials were imported from England.

A large brass bell was rung at the start of classes and at the end of the recess period. Once you had moved up to the higher classes, you had a chance of being assigned the great privilege of ringing the bell. At recess, the girls often played "rounders" which is a ball game similar to North American softball. Like softball, the ball is pitched underhand, but we used our hands or made fists to hit the hollow rubber ball instead of using a bat. The boys loved to play cricket or games with marbles. The favourite marble game involved first marking a circle in the dirt with a stick and drawing a line a few feet away from the circle. All players would wait for their turn to play behind this line. Each player would start by throwing his marble towards the circle and hope that his marble would roll in the safe area within the circle or hit someone else's marble out of the circle. If a player's marble fell outside of the circle, he would wait his turn and then, when his turn came, he would try to flick his marble at another one of the marbles that was outside of the safe circle. If he successfully hit another marble, he would capture that marble. Needless to say, my brothers did not have to worry too much when their marbles were captured – they had an unlimited supply of marbles from our father's store.

At this time, my closest friend was Ethel, a local girl. My mother was not fond of Ethel. She believed that Ethel had infected me with lice because she was told that someone saw Ethel take a lice from her hair and put it in mine. I did not believe that rumour and was still friendly with Ethel because I liked her quiet disposition. Needless to say, Mama had the task of purchasing a special treatment from the chemist in Savanna-La-Mar, to disinfect my entire scalp. Then the maids spent many hours picking out the lice from my hair with fine tooth combs and killing the white nits (eggs of the lice), which clung to my long black hair strands.

The school grounds were vast, so they were used as a venue for community events like garden parties and country fairs. We enjoyed the festivities at these events, such as the English Maypole Dancing – certainly one of the legacies left behind by the British. I also remember that at one fair, there was an enclosed booth that advertised that you would get to see the mysterious-sounding "Boney on the Rhine" if you entered it. When you paid your money and entered the booth, you found a display of chicken bones placed on the rind of an orange! Talk about Jamaican trickery! This was not something left behind by the British – it was pure Jamaican inventiveness. Another money grabbing game at these fairs was called "Grab Bag". You would pay a fee to grab a gift out of a bag full of prizes. Of course, the majority of the prizes in the bag was never worth the fee charged to play, but the enjoyment was in the mystery of what was in the wrapped gift you grabbed – as well as the hope that you had grabbed a jackpot prize! Live Mento music, performed by self-taught local musicians, was always part of these events. These were most enjoyable times in which the entire community had a chance to come together, dressed in their finest wear, for some fun and an opportunity to dance the night away. My younger brothers, Patrick and Dick would have the opportunity to wear their cowboy outfits which were gifts brought back from the USA by our family friend, Mrs. Gayle, wife of the Supreme Judge in Savanna-La-Mar.

Mento music must have originated amongst the slaves on the sugar plantations because the lively music has always sounded to me like a mixture of African rhythms and English quadrille music with a catchy beat. The basic musical instruments used were hand-made from items available. The saxophone was fashioned out of a stalk of bamboo and the banjo out of wood sheeting. For the bass, there was the "rhumba box" made out of a wooden box with varying lengths of tin strips placed along the base of a cut-out hole in the front of the box. The unusual but vibrant mellow sounds of this instrument came from plucking the tin strips to create the beat of the tunes. The lyrics for mento songs are usually funny and tell a tale in Jamaican patois. Mento music is so soul-stirring and uplifting that one cannot resist moving to the rhythms – to "wine up yu waist" and gyrate – when the music is playing. Up to this day, I agree with those Jamaicans who would say when mento was playing, "Di music sweet, cyaan done"!

*Dick, left, (Hopalong Cassidy)
and
Patrick, right, (Roy Rogers)
in their cowboy outfits*

Life in Jamaica: Petersfield, Westmoreland 1952

For a long while, we were the only Chinese children amongst the mostly Black children attending Petersfield Elementary School, until Willie (William) and Madge started attending. Their parents, Edwin and Blanche Forchin (Li) had started doing business in the neighbouring Whithorn District so they enrolled their children after arranging with Papa and Mama that Willie and Madge would go home with us after school and stay with us until they could be picked up later in the evening. My eldest brother, Keith and I had so much fun playing with Willie and Madge and they were added support when we were all constantly teased with the expression "Chiney nyam dawg", (Chinese eat dogs). We never denied this claim because it was an unspoken fact that the Chinese in China and those in Chinatown did eat dogs as a delicacy, especially during the cold winter months. It was believed that eating dog meat would keep you warm and certain dogs were specifically raised for the table. So, instead of denying this claim, we would retort by saying Negroes "nyam di shit" (Negroes eat the feces of the dog the Chinese eat) or Negroes "nyam jancro" (Negroes eat vultures).

We schoolchildren would freely verbally abuse each other, then forget our differences. Other than those times, we students got along fairly well, although I found that we gravitated to the East Indian children because they were less aggressive and less boisterous than most of the other local children, and to the teachers' children, who were typically more well-mannered than the other village children. I recall only one instance of getting into a fight. I was told that a mulatto boy, nicknamed "Bakkra", had bothered my younger brother Patrick, so I quickly walked over and confronted him. He would not stop picking on Patrick so I used a sparring technique that I had learned from my older brother, Keith, and gave him a fake jab to the upper part of his body, before quickly landing a punch to his stomach. When he doubled over in agony, I gathered up Patrick and left the scene before a crowd gathered.

I was a real tomboy, but very early in life, I had adopted a motherly and protective role towards my siblings. Both aspects of my character were clearly revealed in that incident!

Your loving Ah-Poh

Mama and Elaine

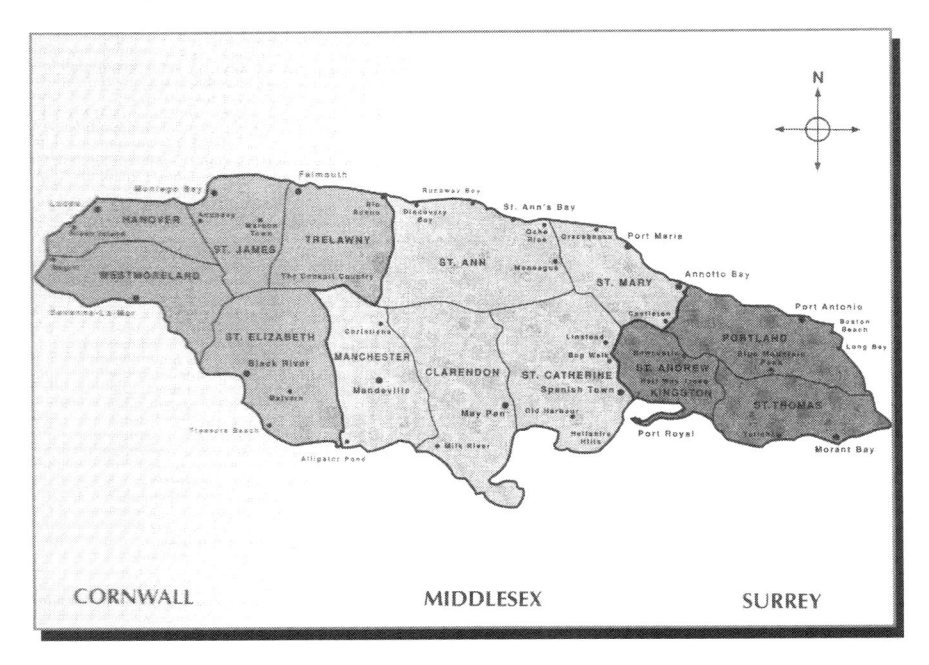

Life in Jamaica: Petersfield, Westmoreland 1952

Above: Map of Jamaica showing the three counties and fourteen parishes

Below: part of the county of Cornwall, showing Westmoreland and St. James

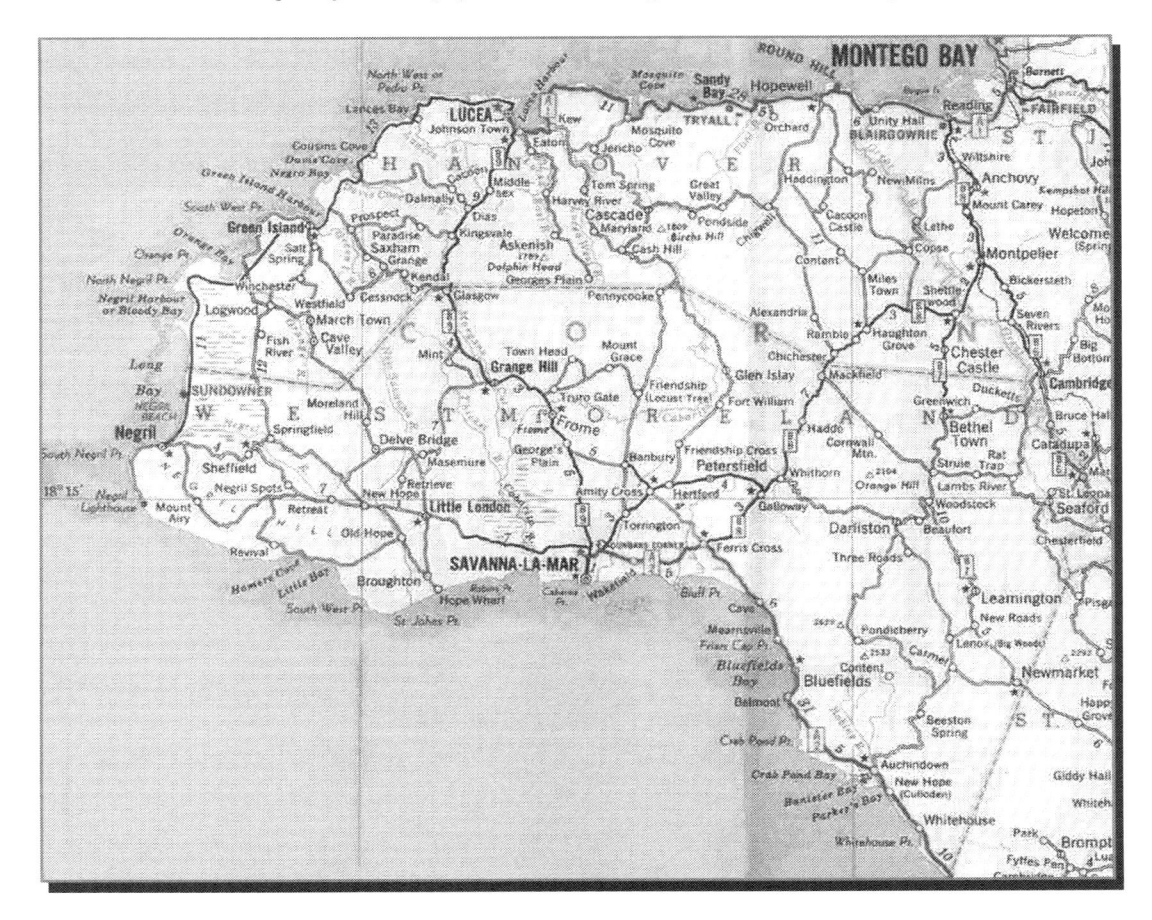

Life in Jamaica:
Petersfield, Westmoreland
1953

My dear Grandchildren,

Being the eldest daughter in the family, I developed a sense of responsibility for taking care of the younger siblings early on. I had to keep an eye on the other children when our parents were busy in the store or when the maids were having difficulty with them and especially during the long summer holidays.

Since I had become adept at riding an adult bicycle built for males, I used to take my younger sister, Elaine, on the cross-bar, to her piano lessons with "Parson" Whylie, a Baptist minister, in Savanna-La-Mar, which was six miles away. Elaine would sit side-saddle style on the cross-bar of the bicycle while I pedalled away. When going uphill, she would alight and walk, while I pedalled the bicycle and waited for her at the top. One day on our way back home, she felt tired and dozed off to sleep, so her foot got caught in the spokes of the front wheel, which caused the bicycle to stop abruptly. We toppled over on the street. Elaine woke up in time to see me, the rider, fly over her head and the handle bars, to land in the street ahead of the fallen bicycle. Although her foot was twisted and she was in great pain, she and I laughed and laughed while we limped home. She never forgot the incident and as adults, we always remember this hilarious accident when reminiscing about our childhood days. However, all this labour I exerted to transport Elaine to and from piano lessons was lost. Elaine was a poor student and her piano lessons came to naught. Mama had wanted to introduce us girls to the finer arts and music appreciation so she signed us both up for piano lessons. Too bad she did not pick up on Patrick's mellow voice, his love of music and talent for singing instead of focusing on Elaine!

When the Morning Star bus, which travelled daily from Montego Bay to Savanna-La-Mar, passed through Petersfield, that was the signal for the maids that it was bath time for the younger children. I would help to round up Patrick, Dick and Elaine, who, when they saw the bus, knew that it was time to avoid their bath by running away to hide in the Anglican Church graveyard across the street. Sometimes they would go

Carol and Elaine in their respective school uniforms

even farther away and hide under the school building, which was built on concrete footings to avoid flooding from the river running through the school property. This run and hide, seek and catch game became a ritual they enjoyed, but it was wearing down the patience of the maids so it was good that they grew out of that habit when they were old enough to bathe themselves.

I would also watch the three younger children when they came into the store, as they had a tendency to steal candy or to take money from the till, which was a deep wooden drawer built under the shop counter for storing cash sales. The children wanted money to share with their school friends or to buy homemade coconut sweets from vendors on our store piazza. The latter was absolutely forbidden by Mama who did not trust the sanitary conditions of locally-made food products. One day Elaine was hovering around the candy counter and acting suspicious, so Papa chased her away. As she ran, a huge bar of Cadbury milk chocolate fell out of her panties! Elaine was the ringleader of their little trio, and Dick was her able partner in crime. Poor Patrick would end up following along with them. Whenever they were caught in any mischievous deed and a spanking was coming, Dick and Elaine would quickly scamper out of sight leaving Patrick to bravely and stoically take whatever punishment was meted out.

As I got older, I started helping in the store and became too busy to keep track of the other children. My first responsibility in the shop was *kun poo* (watch shop). Basically, this meant that I was to carefully watch the local people coming into the store to prevent them from stealing the goods and raise the alarm if they did. I guess I did a great job moving around conspicuously in a watchful way because I never witnessed anyone stealing anything and I never had the opportunity to shout out an alarm! Our customers did not usually steal anyway. More typically, they would try to cheat us by saying that they had already paid for something when they had not done so or by claiming that they had not received the correct change for their purchase. They did not try those ploys with my parents, but they would sometimes try them with the *Foh-gees* or my elderly aunt, *Tai Goo Poh*. They must have figured that they would not understand the calculations of the British currency. But when the *Foh-gees* or my aunt held their ground confidently, the cheating customer would back down and simply slink away.

Gradually, as my mental arithmetic skills developed, I was trusted to serve and sell smaller priced items, eventually progressing to the sale of multiple articles, until finally I was confident enough to collect large money bills and give change. I learned to calculate quickly and mentally without writing down the items separately and adding them up on paper. I also learned not to put the customers' payments away in the till until the customers had counted their change. That way, I had proof of what they had paid, just in case they tried to claim that they had paid for their purchase with a larger amount of money than they actually had. Our customers tried many different ways of cheating us. We had to always be on our toes to outsmart them!

Long before the advent of plastic credit cards, Chinese shopkeepers in Jamaica would extend credit to their customers. Shopkeepers would allow customers to come to the shop and have certain items without paying for them at that time, with the understanding that these goods would be paid for at a later date. All of these items were, or course, scrupulously recorded. Despite extending this kindness, some customers still tried to cheat us. My mother once caught a respectable woman, the wife of an employee at the Public Works Department of the Ministry of Transportation and Communications, trying to scam us. This woman had been given a weekly credit of groceries. Because she was literate, she kept a copy of what she was purchasing on credit in her own notebook. At the end of the week, however, instead of paying for the groceries, she would go into our larger store for a few moments, then return to the grocery store. She would show us the notebook where she had noted that she had paid her bill in the bigger store, and then order more groceries for the next week. The problem was, however, that she was not paying anything in the other store! Because she was literate and the wife of a respectable man with a good job, at first no one suspected anything. But then Mama had a hunch that she should double-check whether or not this woman had actually made the payment that she had claimed to have made. When it was discovered that she had not made a payment – and in fact had not been making any payments – the woman began to cry, and Papa, who was always so sympathetic, decided to overlook the incident. He knew that the family could never repay the amount of debt they had accumulated under this scam and still feed their family of six.

Little did I know that many years later, the youngest little girl in that family would greet me as an adult in Merrickville, Ontario, Canada. She had made a decent life for herself in Ottawa and had sponsored one of her brothers to Canada. We met at a Jamaica Independence celebration which was organized by another Jamaican lady, Elinor, also originally from my home district of Petersfield and I was happy she greeted me as I would not have recognized her all grown-up. By this time, my parents had already passed away, but I could not help reflecting on how my father's benevolence had allowed her and her family to survive the poverty in Jamaica so that she was able to eventually migrate to Canada like myself.

I suppose these attempts to cheat us were just part of the mentality of always trying to get something for nothing and to feel good about getting away with something! Our customers seemed to feel no shame in trying to pull something over on us. Their attitude seemed to be more along the lines of: Nothing ventured, nothing gained. And we also got something out of these attempts to cheat us. We had the joy of out-witting them and cursing them roundly as they left the store! We all knew that soon enough, they, without showing any signs of shame or remorse, would return to the store; and we, in turn, would welcome them back!

Sister Polly Lee

Life in Jamaica: Petersfield, Westmoreland 1953

Helping in the store and living with us at this time was Phyllis Lee the daughter of the Lee family whom Mama had met when we lived in Savanna-la-Mar. Mama had grown close to them, probably because they could relate to each other. The Lees were Chinese but, like Mama, did not speak Hakka fluently. Phyllis was affectionately known as Polly or "Sister P" in our family. Polly's sisters were Myrtle, Gena, Moi and Patricia and she also had an only brother, Sylbert, whom they doted on. Like, Carmen, Sister P was a lovely companion for Mama and Papa appreciated her quiet disposition. I also liked being around Sister P. She was so kind and loving to all of us. I especially admired her cursive hand-writing and just to watch her write I would hover as she learned bookkeeping from our business bookkeeper, Mr. Tucker whenever he came to do Papa's books! Like Carmen, Sister P would attend Mr. Tucker's Commercial School when she moved with us from Savanna-La-Mar to Petersfield. She would now cycle home to her family in Savanna-La-Mar on Sunday mornings when the business was closed and cycle back six miles on Monday mornings to start working when the store reopened. On her way home, she would attend bookkeeping classes which Mr. Tucker kindly gave on Sundays specially for her so that she could attend before visiting her family.

Sister P used to give Mama home hair permanents, making Mama the envy of the other Chinese women in the community who were not as glamorous as Mama! She also introduced Mama to her younger friends in the Parish, like the Moo Young family in Little London, outgoing Daphne Pringle and the Ridley brothers in Savanna-La-Mar. With Sister P around, Mama was able to have a rich social life and was not limited to having to socialize with Papa's village relatives. Because Mama was a Jamaican-born and raised Chinese and not a migrant from China, she often found herself in the position of trying to gain the approval of Papa's immigrant relatives, especially their criticizing wives. A good play to avoid their gaze was to head for the beach on Sundays. Mama would organize the picnics at Negril and invite Miss Icy and Mass Bertie Smith while Sister P invited her friend, Mavis Moo Young. It seemed like a long journey but it was well worth these days of fun at this natural beach stretching six miles of white sand, swimming in absolutely clear blue sea and under sunny skies.

L-R: Mavis, Icy, Bertie, Mama
Kneeling: Carol

L-R: Icy, Carol, Polly, Mavis

Icy & Bertie Smith

Life in Jamaica: Petersfield, Westmoreland 1953

While Keith, Mama, Papa, Sister P and I worked in the store, Patrick, Dick and Elaine would entertain themselves in much the same ways that Keith and I had done when we were too young to help in either the store or grocery shop and definitely not in the rum bar! The rum bar was set up next to the grocery shop and was heavily patronized by the locals. Jamaicans loved their liquor and as soon as they got paid for cutting the cane, sending loads off to the sugar estate to make sugar and the rum factory to distill into rum, they would head for the rum bar to drink themselves crazy and behave outrageously. They would also curse bad words in Jamaican patois. We became accustomed to their bad language and oblivious to their bad behaviour. Indeed, there was big profit for us in the rum shop. We would receive large wooden casks of over-proof rum which we would decant into glass bottles and dilute with water. Shopkeepers could be charged for watering down rum and the strength of the rum and water mixture was randomly tested by the Government inspectors. Somehow, not many Chinese rum-shop operators were found guilty or charged.

When the delivery truck arrived at night after the shop was closed, Papa and the local men he hired would lift the large heavy wooden casks of rum across two long wooden benches from our dining table in order to remove the natural cork and pour out the rum from the middle of the cask into an empty waiting metal tub on the floor underneath. Using a metal funnel, the rum was bottled into a variety of glass bottles for easier handling. I clearly remember the heady smell of the vapour of the alcohol and to this day, I find it comforting to rub this Jamaican over-proof rum as the scent alone brings back memories of my childhood. Later on, instead of wooden casks, rum would be delivered in beautiful, thick round twenty-five gallon glass bottles with a small neck and cork for pouring. These lovely bottles were beautifully covered with woven rattan which, when empty, were kept for other uses like being converted into a fish tank. To make a fish tank from these bottles, the rattan covering was first removed and the neck of the bottles ground away to leave a nice glass dome for us to enjoy watching little fishes swimming around among moss collected from the river. And still years later on, rum of all different blends with whiskey, brandy, coloured rum and good old favourite over-proof rum were delivered in quart bottles, nicely labeled and screw-corked.

Other than serving customers in the store, Mama helped the local people in many other ways. Mama took care of the initial applications for birth certificates and passports during the mass exodus of Jamaican immigrants to England and to the USA as farm workers. When people received those documents, Mama would help them complete the remaining documents that they needed to travel and help make flight arrangements for their departures. Later, she would help the families left behind to write letters to the immigrants, read the letters they sent in response, and exchange the money drafts that were often sent in these letters. As we got more literate, we children would also help out in this manner, at least until the children of the families left behind were old enough to assist their illiterate parents. As mentioned before, Mama was also involved with the Federation of Women rendering assistance to women and girls of the parish of Westmoreland. One of her projects was the local orphanage which was located nearby in Water Works District, above the Dean's Valley Ice Factory.

Life in Jamaica: Petersfield, Westmoreland 1953

Papa was also quite benevolent to everyone, but especially to the children who hung around the store looking hungry. Papa was always most hospitable to the travelling salesmen, many of whom were quite happy to interrupt their island-wide business trips with a home-cooked meal and some company. When our fruit trees, especially our famous June plum tree, was laden, almost all of these salesmen returned to Kingston with bags full of plums or whatever fruit was in season. All this community service, kindness and compassion that we saw in our parents influenced the choices we children made in the future, especially the way we treated those around us; and hopefully, we will be able to pass on these values to our future descendants.

Our business opened six days per week from Monday to Saturday so we looked forward to Sundays when our parents would take us to the beach in Bluefields, not too far from Petersfield. Papa had learned to swim in the rivers of China and taught us to swim in the manner that he had been taught. I can still remember his first instruction. In Hakka Chinese he would tell us: "*Dah pin bong*" meaning for us to kick our legs hard to make huge splashes in the sea while he held us buoyant in the water. After many, many Sundays of practice – and with the help of the natural buoyancy of the salt water – all of us children eventually became good swimmers and divers.

Papa with Donny in the sea at Bluefields

Donny, the baby of the family, was still too young for the jaunts around the district neighbourhoods that the other three siblings went on, so he was cared for by a special "Nursie" who was not the same maid hired to work in the house or kitchen. Elaine, Dick and Patrick especially liked to go to "bird bush", a wooded area where they could catch birds. They would either make and set spring-traps or use a sling-shot to capture or kill the small birds. The sling-shots were fashioned out of a tree crook branch which was scraped to a smooth surface for a Y-shaped handle and the sling was made out of strips of rubber from old inner tubes of bicycle tires. When the birds were captured and killed, they would light a small fire in the woods and singe the fine down feathers off the plucked birds, then gut and clean them. The birds would then be ready to be cooked, and would either be strung together to be brought home to be cooked or they would be roasted on the open fire and devoured right there in the bush.

Looking back, this was a strange practice for Dick to engage in because he later became a bird lover and began raising birds instead of killing and eating them! Dick had a huge cage of mesh wire within which were tree branches used as perches for his birds, mostly ground doves or warble doves. He spent a lot of time caring for his birds. He would feed them often and watch over their unhatched eggs laid in small boxes made of plywood and nested with straw. Dick came by his love of bird-raising

Life in Jamaica: Petersfield, Westmoreland 1953

honestly. When he was younger, Mama had raised budgerigars and we had all enjoyed looking at these beautiful and colourful little birds in their small cages. They needed special care, especially during the nesting period. Apparently, Mama had passed on her love of birds to Dick.

Mama loved animals in general, not just birds, so we grew up with many dogs and cats. The dogs were mongrels and the cats were common breed so they were fed scraps from our table. Larger dogs received an additional food of cooked cornmeal and salted cod-fish tails. The cats additionally caught rats and mice which was their main function in the household. The dogs guarded the premises and us children. Patrick's favourite dog was Frisky, but the dogs and cats were not really our pets, although we sometimes played with them.

Patrick, Elaine & favourite dog Frisky

I recall that at one time, our parents tried raising one or two dairy cows but they found the work too tedious as our backyard was too small for cattle grazing and Mama had to hire someone to daily tether the cows at another property. We also had ducks and chickens and hutches for raising rabbits as pets. One of our chores was to go collecting certain bushes for feeding the rabbits. They ate a lot and pooed a lot so we had to clean the hutches quite often. They had many baby rabbits and it was fun petting and playing with them.

Growing up in the country really exposed us to all kinds of domestic and farm animals – as well as insects -- indigenous to the tropics. As a result, we were not scared of them and actually, Elaine liked to catch lizards for the fun of it. We learned firsthand about each of them, their care, survival and – to our childish amusement – their mating habits. We all took it in stride as part of the cycle of life. In some ways, we received a better education about life outside with the animals than inside our classrooms!

Villagers were not hesitant to let us ride their larger animals like horses and donkeys or to take us for a ride in the horse-drawn cart or sit in the straw hampers across the backs of the donkeys – their frequent unbridled ablutions and braying amused us too! We were indeed fortunate to learn about life in a natural setting and in a friendly and safe environment.

With the hope that you might someday enjoy this natural type of education and fun, I remain,

Your loving Ah-Poh

Life in Jamaica: Petersfield, Westmoreland 1953

Jamaican country yard

Boys playing cricket

Cow pasture

Photos courtesy of Ray Chen

The Second Chinese Zodiac Cycle 1953 – 1965

Life in Jamaica: Marescaux Road, Kingston 1954

My dear Grandchildren,

I was born in the Chinese Year of the Snake in 1941, so in January 1954, I had completed one 12-year cycle of the Chinese Lunar Calendar and was embarking on the second Chinese Zodiac Cycle of my life. I was ready to be sent off to the Wolmer's High School for Girls in the big city of Kingston, the capital of Jamaica.

Mama made the decision to send me to Kingston for high school – and it was the best decision! Education is the key to one's future life and my life was greatly influenced by the British education system under which I was instructed. I was taught by British teachers, but found my strongest influence was under the guidance of the English Headmistress at Wolmer's, Mrs. Evelyn Skempton, who was also the founder of the Wolmer's boarding hostel. She was born in England and her family was sent to Russia because her father was appointed Manager of the British Iron and Steel Works in southern Russia. There, she received her early education and Teacher's Training Diploma. She came first at Final Matriculation and received the God Medal, awarded annually by the Tzar Nicholas II. Returning to England she furthered her education in Modern Languages and supposedly got married before being appointed as headmistress of Wolmer's Girls School in 1941.

At that time, students who wanted to enter high school had to sit entrance exams to test the level of their former elementary education. Since my religious training was by the Anglican Church of England, my parents did not think that it would be right for me sit the entrance exams of Roman Catholic high schools, the high school system in which most Chinese children in Jamaica were educated. The plan was for me to write the exams at two other prestigious high schools in the capital: St. Andrew's High School for Girls and Wolmer's High School for Girls. I travelled to Kingston to write the exams with my cousin Shirley, who, only a few months older than I, was also writing the exams.

We first went to St. Andrew's which was located off Half Way Tree Road. As soon as we drove in to the school gates, I took an immediate dislike to the atmosphere of the school. The towering and mature trees along the driveway were eerie and I found a tall wooden statue of a horse near the entrance to the school just plain creepy. The main hall that we entered was gloomy, with dark wood-panelling, and strangely bare. The members of staff whom I met were just as stone-faced and unfriendly as the

Life in Jamaica: Marescaux Road, Kingston, 1954

Wolmer's Girls School Staff Room and administrative offices, 1940s

Entrance to Wolmer's Girls School and Domestic Science Building, 1968

buildings. I felt no warmth in that environment. I truly did not want to spend five years of my life in that dreary place – or to attend school with my bossy cousin! As a result, I chose to deliberately do poorly on their entrance examination.

My reaction to Wolmer's was entirely different. As soon as I reached the entrance, off of Marescaux Road, and saw the unimposing cast iron arch that bore the name of the school and the face of a smiling sun, I felt at ease. The buildings were widely spaced and the beautiful blooming lignum vitae trees planted intermittently along the asphalt driveway felt welcoming. (The national flower of Jamaica is actually that of the lignum vitae tree and the wood is a beautiful wood suitable for carving as well.) I found the staff to be just as friendly and helpful as my first impressions of the grounds had suggested they might be. While waiting to take the exams, I took a closer look around the grounds to make sure that this was really where I wanted to spend my next few years. The tennis courts on the right side of the grounds had open wire fencing which created an illusion of open space. To the left was the Domestic Science building and the Headmistress's office. The school office and staff room had an open-sided porch with white lattice trellis of climbing flowering vine that was lined with chairs for us exam takers.

There was a Biology laboratory building further along the walkway that led towards an interesting looking building. Covered walkways surrounding rows of classrooms with many glass-pane windows and shuttered doors led to the Assembly Hall, which had a high ceiling and doors opened to the Hall from all directions, making the space feel inviting and airy. There was gym equipment neatly packed to the back of the Hall and huge ropes were hanging from the high ceiling. At the front of the hall was a wide stage with a podium and an upright piano.

More covered walkways led to the washrooms that were next to the Arts building. A long open asphalt walkway led to the library, decorated with imposing concrete columns on either side of the entrance. On either side of the library were more classrooms for the upper form students. Together the buildings formed a quadrangle. An open grass square with a high open-air stage at one end was at the centre of the quadrangle. Behind that section of building alongside the quadrangle were the netball fields which fronted onto Mico Training College and were adjacent to the Wolmer's High School for Boys.

I learned that Wolmer's School was one of the oldest schools in the Caribbean and was bequeathed in 1729 by an English goldsmith, John Wolmer in his Last Will and Testament. The history of Wolmer's Girls' School really began in the 1770's, however, with the establishment of a female adjunct to the Boy's division. The schools were formally separated in the 1860s. In 1941, Mrs. Skempton was appointed the fourth Headmistress of the Girl's school. The previous Headmistresses were Miss Maud Barrows, Miss Kate Howson and Miss Mary Cowper after whom the school houses were named. The school house system was instituted during Mrs. Skempton's era. In addition to the Barrows, Howson and Cowper houses, there was also Forbes house, named after the longest serving teacher at that time. The house colours were red, blue, green and yellow. This house system proved to be an excellent system to foster camaraderie and encourage a competitive spirit among the students.

With such a rich history, needless to say, I wanted to attend this secondary school, so I tried very hard on that entrance exam. I did very well and I was mightily overjoyed to be accepted into the school, as well as into the Boarding hostel, which was located across Marescaux Road. To my delight, I discovered that the music room building and additional tennis courts were located at the Boarding hostel site. If I had not gotten into the hostel, I might have had to stay with my relatives living in Kingston and I would have to commute to school daily. I really wanted to live at the Hostel. By that time, I had read the adventures of Nancy Drew and was anticipating new English experiences that I would not be able to have if I was to stay in a Chinese home that would be very similar to my own home. I was looking forward to an all-round education away from home and I received the right vibes that this was the place for me.

Life in Jamaica: Marescaux Road, Kingston, 1954

I was totally happy during the five years (1954 – 1959) that I spent at Wolmer's. I never felt homesick like some of the other girls. In fact, I always looked forward to returning to school after holiday breaks. I would usually take the diesel engine train, which journeyed across the island, from Montpelier Railway Station, about 18 miles from Petersfield. The train's route ran from Montego Bay to Kingston and would be filled with students returning to their respective schools. At each stop along the way to Kingston, vendors would hurry towards the train compartments, plying their products or wares held high under the windows, trying to make a quick sale before the train pulled out of their station after picking up more passengers. There were peppered and dried shrimps, roasted cashew and peanuts packaged in cellophane wrap, strings of oranges and tangerines tied together plus sweets and biscuits. All of the treats were so appealing to us students. We would buy them and share them with other students and make friends with each other on the way back to Kingston. The boys would naughtily throw the tangerine and orange peelings at each other while the girls would giggle and admire the boys from afar. When the train arrived at the end of the line in the city of Kingston, I would walk to my Uncle James's place of business called Lee Fah & Co., which was near to the station. I would wait there until closing time when my cousin Joe would drive me uptown to the boarding hostel. The hostel was close to the Race Course which later became Jamaica Heroes Circle, housing the statues of many important figures in Jamaica's history.

The boarding hostel was the refurbished Cavaliers Great House, a huge wooden Victoria-style house with a stone basement situated on a fairly big property. It most likely had been the great house of a wealthy family in its past. Tall palm trees lined the paved driveway leading up to the hostel. These palm trees provided a boundary for us boarder girls. The Headmistress, Mrs. Skempton, whom we girls affectionately called "Skempie", had declared that after supper time none of the boarders were allowed to go beyond 12 feet from where the line created by the palm trees ended. (Likewise, there was another unwritten rule: all of the Wolmer's girl students were forbidden to go closer than three feet to the barbed wire fence that separated the Wolmer's Boys

Wolmer's Boarding Hostel - former Cavaliers Great House

Life in Jamaica: Marescaux Road, Kingston, 1954

and Wolmer's Girls Schools.) The "sweetie man", a male vendor who plied his wares on foot by carrying a wooden tray balanced on one shoulder, was allowed to come in past the palm trees after suppertime. At that time we were allowed to purchase treats like Cheese-trix biscuits, Cadbury milk chocolates, pepper shrimps, popcorn, guava cheese, candies and cookies with our pocket money. Also allowed on weekends was "Fudgie", who sold ice treats out of his box with dry-ice that was tied onto his bicycle. Our pocket money was kept by the matron of the hostel, Mrs. Myers, who doled out daily allowances every morning as needed, but it was never enough! So we kept an eye on the cherry tree near the dining room and the huge Bombay mango tree near the kitchen and, when our money ran out and those fruits were in season, we would eat those as treats.

Towards one corner of the hostel property were additional asphalt surfaced tennis courts surrounded by a high chain link fence and shaded by lignum vitae trees. These courts were very much used by me and my friend, Sonia Thompson, especially on weekends. Looking back, I can hardly believe that on some occasions, when my canvas and crepe soled shoes got too hot, I would play barefoot! My first tennis racquet was a wood-framed Dunlop Maxply, which came with a wooden racquet press and turning screws at the four corners. With the year-round heat and humidity of Jamaica, it was easy for wooden racquets to get warped out of shape so it was imperative that after playing, one had to place the racquet in the wooden press and tighten the flanged screws.

Behind the main house was an annex for older girls. I assume these buildings had probably been the servants' quarters in days gone by. Across the grass lawn was a cottage, probably the caretaker's residence in days of yore, where Headmistress Mrs. Skempton resided. The grounds had lots of shade trees to sit under and were nicely landscaped and kept beautifully by the gardener. The Water Commission grounds were on one side of the rear of the property, and on the other side was an unused open field which was part of the Cavaliers Great House once stood among the tall grass. I used to steal away from the boarding hostel. I would crouch low to the ground and sneak across the open field and head directly to Arnold Road where I would go to a grocery shop to make purchases, hoping to catch a glimpse of Fernando Chung, a good-looking boy who might be helping in his father's grocery store. On one of the rare occasions that Skempie allowed the girls to have a dance party with boys present in the Assembly Hall, I managed to invite Fernando to escort me, under the watchful eyes of the teachers of course. He was not a great dancer but he was quite polite and after the party ended without mishap, he escorted me across the street to the boarding hostel as far as he was allowed. I was in Seventh Heaven!

On the tennis court side of the property was a road named Connolly Avenue. This is where my piano teacher, Mrs. Hickling lived. Further down the road was the Wolmer's Preparatory School for the youngest students preparing to enter the high school system. When I reached Grade 3, in the British Royal School of Music, I was

Life in Jamaica: Marescaux Road, Kingston, 1954

12-year-old Carol at the hostel

allowed to practise on the piano at the Prep school to prepare for music examinations. In my adult life, I have regretted not progressing past Grade 3 in piano, but in my youth, playing netball and tennis always took priority over piano lessons!

At the corner of Connolly Avenue and Marescaux Road was a Chinese grocery shop that sold home-baked "coffee strips" pastry, tinned sardines, "bully beef" and Excelsior crackers. When my tuck supplies ran out, I used to sneak out through the fence at dusk, between supper-time and homework prep-time, to purchase these items for midnight feasts in the dormitory. If Skempie was patrolling the perimeter of the premises with her beautiful Alsatian dog, Judy, I would wait until dark. I was not worried to walk to the shop in the dark -- at that time in Jamaica, it was quite safe to walk the streets at night and no one would have dreamed of hurting a child.

The Cavaliers Great House had solid stone steps leading up to the front door. Once one entered the house, one would find the sick bay, or "isolation room" on the left of the foyer. To the right was the bedroom and living area for Mrs. Myers, our very serious and stern matron. I believe that the stone steps leading up to the house were the only remnant of the original house left intact, probably as a reminder and legacy of Mrs. Skempton's boarding hostel, when years later, following Mrs. Skempton's retirement in 1962, the hostel was closed. The building was demolished in 1967 to make way for additional classrooms and a swimming pool. Although it is not a huge pool, I would have appreciated having a swimming pool during my days of boarding! Instead, while I was at school, Wolmer's girls would take the public bus, "Jolly Joseph", to Immaculate Conception High School for swimming lessons. During one of the bus strikes, we had to walk from the hostel up to Constant Spring, which was approximately four miles away. Walking there via Cross Roads and Halfway Tree was fine – everyone was eager with anticipation of swimming – but walking after the swim class, there were numerous complaints. I was just as tired as the other girls but did not complain. I was simply happy for the freedom of being allowed out of boarding school to walk the streets of Kingston.

Once one passed the foyer of the hostel, one would find two open areas which might have been the grand sitting room and the banquet room at one point, which we referred to as the Common Room, and were used as the homework prep rooms. My years living at Wolmer's hostel instilled good study habits. There was assigned homework prep-time two hours before dinner and two hours after. The senior girls studied in the former sitting room area while the junior girls did their school homework in the Common Room under the watchful eagle eyes of Mrs. Myers. We nicknamed Mrs. Myers "Froggie" because of her facial features and body shape. She used to favour my tennis friend, Sonia, so I appropriately nicknamed Sonia "Taddy", short for tadpole!

Life in Jamaica: Marescaux Road, Kingston, 1954

Upstairs was the attic which served as one large dormitory of single beds for the younger new girls. Mrs. Skempton's initial living quarters adjoined this area at one end. Despite Mrs. Skempton's strict surveillance, my Chinese friend, Sonja Lue, sometimes managed to perform her night dance to the strains of Nerine Barrett's rendition of "All Through the Night" on her violin. While she performed, I kept my ears close to the connecting door to listen for the muffled footsteps of "Skempie". If detected, I would raise the alarm for the show to cease and everyone would quickly get under the bedcovers – in Nerine's case, with violin and all. I was relieved of my watchman duties if Mrs. Skempton was entertaining her guests or had a gentleman caller.

What had previously been the bedrooms in the lower level of this grand house had been converted into dormitories of single beds and double bunk beds. The beds were separated by white wooden cupboards for each boarder. I used to love sleeping in the upper bunk beds, but when matron Froggie did her nightly rounds to check on us after lights-out, I would most likely not be in my bed. Over time, I perfected a running leap from the floor up into my upper bunk bed, sometimes barely touching the steps of the ladder!

On som,e nights while others were asleep, I would quietly awaken my compatriots in crime to meet in the corridor to the washrooms to share whatever food I had sneaked out to purchase. The other alternative was to eat surrounding someone's bed or stash our supply under our pillows for a later midnight snack. I was not really hungry but it was exciting to break the rules and run the risk of being caught. I also remember making a make-shift tent out of my blanket or counterpane on my bed and with my flashlight would read more Nancy Drew mystery and adventure books and in later years, romance and movie magazines underneath my tent when it was "lights out" and Froggie had returned to her bedroom.

At this point, goodnight Grandchildren!

Your loving Ah-Poh

15-year-old Carol at the hostel

Life in Jamaica: Marescaux Road, Kingston, 1954

Refurbished Library, 1993, with Wolmer's Crest and Motto "Age Quod Agis"

Refurbished Wolmer's Girls School Assembly Hall Block, 1993

Life in Jamaica:
Marescaux Road, Kingston
1955

My dear Grandchildren,

At Wolmer's hostel, meals were taken in the lower level of the stone basement, a space that was quite similar to present day walk-out basements.

Our dining room had rows of long wooden tables and benches under a low ceiling. Fellow boarders often complained about the food we received but I ate heartily and enjoyed everything at every meal. I even ate what the other girls did not care for and were trying to get rid of! The meals were different from the Chinese and local food served at home, which was a nice change for me. I also appreciated learning British table etiquette, which was not practised at my home. I quickly learnt not to speak with food in my mouth and to daintily place the white damask napkins in my lap after unfolding it carefully from its serviette ring neatly placed in front of my place setting. I also learned to use the fork in the left hand with tines convex side down, knife in the right hand and to use the flatware setting from outside in towards the plate.

The kitchen staff serving the tables were always neatly dressed in English style dark-coloured uniforms complete with white aprons and lace trimmed caps. They were fully trained local Black ladies. These women always had their favourites among the girls. Beatrice favoured me, and when my pocket money ran out and I could not buy lunch at school, she would make jam sandwiches out of the bread "backs' (end) slices for me, without the other girls knowing! I will not forget the special Sunday dinners of either fricassee chicken or roast beef with rice and peas plus mouth-watering cinnamon sugar buns that "Cookie" used to bake. The smell of them baking would drive us girls wild with anticipation. When they were ready, dripping with a sugary glaze, no one ever was willing to give up her share! All through my life, I have never had a sugar, raisin or cinnamon bun as delicious as those baked by Cookie then enjoyed and craved for at the boarding hostel. She was the main cook and boss of the kitchen staff. Cookie slept on the premises next to the dining room and it never dawned on me to ask her for the recipe which must have been handed down by her former English employer. Cookie also had a Rediffusion set in her room so some of us used to sit outside her window to listen to Radio Jamaica, when we were forbidden to turn on the set in the Common Room.

The rest of the kitchen staff also lived on this level and in the next section on the opposite side of the dining room were the bathrooms and laundry room. Washer-women were hired to do the laundry by hand. Each item of our clothing had to be

Life in Jamaica: Marescaux Road, Kingston, 1955

permanently marked with our names so that the laundry women could put the clean clothing into the open cubicles assigned to each border when the washing was completed. Our school uniforms were starched stiff and perfectly ironed before being hung in rows waiting to be identified and collected. Another thing I preferred at Wolmer's over St. Andrews School was the uniform. Wolmer's was an aqua coloured tunic with white collared blouse and aqua wool beret. White socks and brown shoes completed this nice looking uniform I was proud to wear. I was told that this school uniform that I so enjoyed wearing was actually a uniform that Skempie chose. Apparently the previous Wolmer's uniform was a navy skirt, white blouse, maroon tie and a jippi-jappa straw hat.

In a completely separate area on the ground level was the tuck room, the place where each girl was assigned a cubicle to keep her personal edible items under lock and key. From my parents' grocery shop, I would bring non- perishable items including crackers, cookies and tins of Milo, Ovaltine and Horlicks drink mix and condensed milk which did not need refrigeration. My mother would not have approved of my mixing the drink mix and condensed milk without adding water but that was the trend among the boarders. We would lick this thick sweet chocolate or malted mixture off the spoon stuck in the mixture we made in our mixing mugs. It looked like muck but it was so delicious to eat it that way!

We had a disciplined regimen at Wolmer's hostel: announced by the ringing of a bell, there was a set time to arise, to get ready for the day, to arrive for breakfast, lunch (on weekends), afternoon naps, tea-time as well as a specific time at which we were allowed to enter the otherwise locked tuck-room to access our padlocked cubicles of goodies. There was also shower time, homework prep time, dinner time followed by another homework prep time before bed time and lights out. On weekends we could get permission to visit the dentist or doctor and perhaps, attend religious confirmation classes. We usually had to sign out and in, and, when we were younger, to be accompanied by a "big girl" from a higher form or an appointed prefect on these outings.

Every Sunday, we boarders would all attend church service at the St. Luke Anglican Church in Cross Roads. Occasionally on Saturday afternoons, the boarders would be allowed to attend a carefully chosen movie as a collective outing at either Carib Theatre or Tropical Theatre. Both theatres were within walking distance from the hostel. We would walk in a double file on these outings, excitedly chattering amongst ourselves all the way. I totally enjoyed these outings and carefully took note of the routes taken, in case I ever wanted to try and visit some of the places we passed on my own. Because of this habit, I knew how to get to the Carib Theatre when "Bill Haley and the Comets", an American rock and roll band, arrived in Jamaica on tour to perform there.

At the time of the concert, I had graduated from sleeping in an open dormitory and had been moved to a single room that contained one double bunk bed, called "The Cubicle". My roommate was my previous dancing roommate from when I was in the attic dormitory, Sonja, and both of us were crazy about Bill Haley and the Comets. We had to see them! And I knew how we could do so. We decided that we could

Life in Jamaica: Marescaux Road, Kingston, 1955

make it for the early matinée show. We would tell the matron at the hostel that we would be late from school and would not be at our first homework prep-time. Then, we would slip out of school and head over to the Carib Theatre to watch Bill Haley's afternoon show. And that is just what we did.

The first part of our plan – sneaking away to the concert – went perfectly. Unfortunately, the second part of our plan – sneaking back to the hostel – did not go off as well. We had planned to return to the hostel during the pre-dinner period. This was a free-time period when girls often strolled around the ground. We figured we could slip in and mingle unnoticed with those who were out strolling. But, the show ran later than we expected, and to our dismay, we returned to the hostel during the quiet homework prep time. At this time, everyone was seated and accounted for, so our absence would be obvious. And that was exactly the case. By the time that we returned, the matron and Headmistress had both been advised of our absence. It turned out that even if we had managed to sneak back at our planned time, we still would have been in trouble. Unbeknownst to us, one of the teachers had also attended the Bill Haley show and had seen Sonja and me there. That teacher had already reported to Mrs. Skempton that not only had we gone to the concert, but that we were also dressed up "like puss back foot" (dressed to the nines)!

Being absent from the grounds without permission was an offense worthy of expulsion. It was quite the disgrace! Poor Mama had to leave the busy store in Petersfield, spend time and money to journey down to Kingston and find her way to the boarding hostel to plead with Mrs. Skempton not to expel me. To my great relief, Mama's pleas were successful. Sonja and I were not repentant, however. We were really crazy about Bill Haley's music and thought that the drummer in the Comets was so handsome and groovy (sigh). We thought that our little adventure was well worth the trouble! We also did not realize how serious the consequences might have been if we had been expelled, not the least of which was that there was a very real chance that we might not be accepted at another school with the prestige of Wolmer's.

Looking back, I wonder if, despite the inconvenience of having to come and plead on my behalf, Mama may have enjoyed meeting with Mrs. Skempton. After all, this episode gave her the opportunity to take a break from life in the country. She got to visit with her brother's children and other relatives who now lived in Kingston. Additionally, since Mama had been born and raised in Jamaica and was fluent in the English language and customs, unlike some of the parents of the Chinese students at the hostel, Mama would not have been too intimidated by the thought of having to meet with Mrs. Skempton. Sonja's parents did not come to plead her case so I guessed that she shared the same reprieve -- thanks to Mama who could be as articulately charming and apologetic as any other middle-class Jamaican parent who might be called in to speak with Mrs. Skempton about his or her daughter's behaviour!

Needless to say, there were other incidents of my being caught leaving the hostel without permission during my time at Wolmer's hostel, although Mama never knew of these occurrences! I was quite outgoing and became popular with the older Chinese boarders like Wilhel Kong, Mildred Cheung, Sonia McPherson, Wilhel Chen and

Life in Jamaica: Marescaux Road, Kingston, 1955

Schoolfriends: Left - Minnie Chin, Right - Mabel Hoo Sang

Connie Chung. When these girls decided to sneak out to a party or to an event like a Chinese New Year function -- events that they felt we Chinese girls had the right to attend – I was allowed to tag along with them. If Skempie happened to find out about these surreptitious outings, the older girls would find themselves facing serious scolding and punishment. Since I was so young, Skempie seemed to believe that I had been inveigled by the older ones into the misadventure and would let me off!

There were not as many Chinese students at Wolmer's as there were attending Roman Catholic Schools like Alpha Academy and Immaculate Conception High School. There were even fewer Chinese students in the boarding hostel. Nevertheless, I had a wonderful circle of Chinese friends outside of the hostel who were day students at Wolmer's. I recall Minnie Chin, Mabel Ho Sang, Isabel Chang Fong, Daisy Tenn, Jeanette Chung, Joyce Lyn and Dorothy Ho. I became so close to Elsie and Annie Yap Sam that, with permission, I would spend half-term holidays at the Yap Sam's house on Lady Musgrave Road. I got to know numerous members of their extended family, including Cecil, Joyce, Ferdinand, Bernard and the youngest brother, Clive. He would eavesdrop when we were conferring in our bedroom about serious matters like "secret crushes" on boyfriends!

I also had older cousins, Norma and Hilma, boarding at the hostel and I would go with them to visit the Allerdyce residence of our cousin Joe and Mavis Williams and their young children, Janet, Annette and Joan. I felt closer to the younger sister, Hilma who is affectionately called "Pearlie" by her family, because she was so caring of me, her young cousin. She would notice that the white socks I was wearing and had washed myself, were not washed clean enough and promptly proceeded to wash them for me. It was good to have help with such dreary chores but most of all, to have someone watching over me. We have kept close ties over decades as we grew up and, later in life, became grandmothers. Tagging along with Wilhel Chen, I visited her classmate, Deanna Chin Loy's home and toured the family's Royal Cremo ice cream factory. With Sonja, I attended parties at our schoolmate, Jeanette's family home on Milford Road which was a nice place for teenagers to hang out. I recall seeing Errol, Raymond, Colville, Tassy, Spoakie, Jeanie, Monica, Kitty, and others who attended

Life in Jamaica: Marescaux Road, Kingston, 1955

Alpha Academy High School, St. George's College or some other Roman Catholic High School. Sometimes, Sonja's friend, Tyrone Chen would borrow his father's old car to take us for a drive towards the Palisadoes Airport. The drive was a scenic route all along the picturesque Kingston harbour. The car was in such bad shape, however, that the engine would keep overheating. When it wasn't overheating, I could still feel the heat coming up through the floor of the car, but I did not complain. After all, at least I was having an opportunity to leave the hostel and get to know other places in Kingston!

Earlier I mentioned some of my friends within the Chinese circle but I was also friendly with other Chinese and non-Chinese classmates and boarders that attended Wolmer's. Some of those whose names come to mind were Sonia and Lorna Roach, Norma and Faye Jones, Emily and Marie Kong, Joy and Flora Coleman, Claudette and Shirley Lee Shue, Eileen and Barbara Swaby, Paulette Davis, Effie Dunbar, Sonja Vassell, Alzie Dyce, Doreen Chong, June Rhynie, Judith Robinson, Dahlia Morris. I would meet up with many of these friends later in life. One of the things that I enjoyed about being a boarder was that it gave me the opportunity to meet a wide range of students of all ages and from different forms at school. Living together forced us to get along with each other and care for each other.

When I first arrived at the hostel, I found that the older girls made a real effort to get to know the newcomers. In fact, upon my arrival, one of the older girls called out to me a friendly greeting but I was not aware that she was speaking to me, so she called me again: "Hey you with the porcupine hair, come here!" From then on, I was nicknamed 'Porky", a name which stuck long after school days were over and I was an adult living in Canada! I was not at all insulted by being called "porcupine hair"; instead, I felt welcomed and special because an older girl had taken the time to notice me! In fact, the only real thought that I had when the girl called me was that my hair must need a good brushing! My mother thought that I would look prettier with curly hair and had given me a fresh home perm before sending me off to school. Unfortunately, she had over-permed my naturally straight hair and the ends did stick out like porcupine quills! Many people at Wolmer's were puzzled when they heard my nickname for the first time because they did not know that "Porky" referred to a porcupine and not a pig. They could not figure out why this skinny girl was being called a fat pig!

While in school, I was friendly with my form-mates like my best friend, Grace Clarke, Beulah Stone, Loris Beckford, Mary Gordon-Martin, Paula Davis, Marjorie Black, Shirley Stephens, Anita Matalon, Angela Desnoes, Dorothy Walters, Merle Campbell, Paulette Case, Yolanda Bogues and others, most of whom moved up with me as we progressed to higher forms. While at the hostel, I fondly remember Sharon and Hilary Creary, Olive and Norma Williams, Pat Broderick, Annabelle Creary, Elaine, Jean and Nerine Barrett, Audrey Jean Lamb, Valerie Anderson, Dawne Abrahams. There were so many friendships, too numerous to recount all the names here, but I have never forgotten all the fun interactions with the friends I made at Wolmer's, especially the boarder girls.

Life in Jamaica: Marescaux Road, Kingston, 1955

We boarder girls would sometimes spend Friday and Saturday evenings jiving and rock and rolling in the Music Room. We quickly learned to dance together or dance solo using the wall or post as our spinning partner. On Sunday mornings, it must have been a beautiful sight to see about thirty of us girls wearing white dresses walking double file along Marescaux Road to attend church service at St. Luke's Anglican Church in Cross Road, much to the delight of Rev. Maxwell. Whether walking together to church or going to Carib Theatre or Tropical Theatre to see a movie, we would chatter away excitedly, strengthening our bonds of friendships over topics like our favourite movie stars, like Elizabeth Taylor, Lana Turner, Rock Hudson, John Derek, or perhaps Mario Lanza in the classic *Student Prince*. Some of us attended weekly confirmation classes together at St. Luke's Church and further established closer camaraderie over a banana split or chocolate sundae at the Dairy Farmers after class. We learned to support each other. For example, when, for the big Confirmation Day, I did not like the dress my mother had made and mailed to me, Hilary Crearey did not hesitate to lend me one of her more fashionable ready-made dresses from the USA for this important step in my religious up-bringing.

Some of these friendships would become life-long, continuing well into our lives in Canada, especially since, as strong supporters of the Toronto Chapter of the Wolmer's Alumni Association, destiny would allow us to meet up again. One of our annual obligations is to get together for Wolmer's Founders Day Church Service, and strange as it may seem, I find that fond memories of the many school assemblies we attended in the Wolmer's Assembly Hall during the 1950s flood into my mind as we solemnly sing "I vow to thee my country". I find myself proudly holding my chest high, and most times I cannot prevent myself from becoming misty-eyed. The same is true whenever I go to worship at Anglican churches in different parts of the world and I get the chance to sing the familiar church hymns I had sung at Wolmer's. I always sing lustily, all the while envisioning Mrs. Skempton at the podium and Mrs. Hazel Lawson Street at the piano.

These lasting memories reflect how much I enjoyed and appreciated school assemblies held every morning at Wolmer's during my formative years. I did like having the entire student body and staff coming together each morning. The lowest form students would file into the Assembly Hall to be in the front rows while students from the higher forms would follow so that the oldest girls would end up at the back of the hall. It should be noted that Mrs. Skempton respected other religions so the room next to the Assembly Hall was reserved for girls of other religious persuasions and they were excused from attending assemblies. During assembly, we would sing a chosen hymn from the *Songs of Praise* hymnal followed by a reading of a scripture passage from the Bible by one of our School Prefects or a student with good diction, like Patricia Priestly. Then Mrs. Skempton would impart her words of wisdom, inspiration or, on occasion, reprimand. On the latter note, I remember how one morning, after Mrs. Skempton had been speaking on a serious matter, she suddenly screeched out loudly, "It's not funny Carol Williams – wipe that silly grin off your face!" I was greatly astonished since I was on my best behavior, but then I noticed that she was staring at another Chinese girl, Isabel Chang Fong across the row

Life in Jamaica: Marescaux Road, Kingston, 1955

from me. I did not complain or protest, however; I knew that my dear third form teacher, Mrs. Roper, who was standing nearby, would later apologize for Mrs. Skempton's mistake. So with due respect, there was absolute silence as Mrs. Skempton proceeded to leave the stage. After assembly, we would march out of the Hall briskly to a marching tune played by either Mrs. Lawson Street or another advanced music student like Elaine Barrett or Sonia Roach.

My dear Grandchildren, this episode where Mrs. Skempton mistakenly reprimanded me was not detrimental to me; and if we accept that anyone can make a mistake – including ourselves – then we should be quick to overlook peoples' mistakes. I would not even dream of being upset with or, for a moment losing respect for our esteemed Headmistress and a great lady, Mrs. Evelyn C. Skempton. She started her tenure at Wolmer's in the year I was born, 1941, and all Wolmerians who went to school during the "Skempton era" should be thankful and feel fortunate to have learned under her direction of the school. Mrs. Skempton was highly qualified and experienced, having worked at another girls' school in England before coming to Jamaica. She had high goals for all "her girls"; and, with her visionary, modern approach to education, she was able to steer Wolmer's High School for Girls through the World War II years and well prepare "her girls" for life abroad or to face life in an independent and self-governed nation once Jamaica gained its independence from Britain in 1962.

We should always have great respect for our principal and teachers who will educate and prepare us to face our adult lives ahead of us.

Your loving Ah-Poh

Front stone steps left standing as a memento after the demolition of Wolmer's Boarding Hostel for the new addition of the Cavaliers Campus

Life in Jamaica: Marescaux Road, Kingston, 1955

Aerial view of Wolmer's Girls School Campus, 1990s

*Carib Theatre where Wolmer's boarders watched movies
(and some of us sneaked out to the Bill Haley and the Comets show!)*

Life in Jamaica:
Marescaux Road, Kingston
1956 – 1957

My dear Grandchildren,

Although I was enjoying my high school years at Wolmer's and the camaraderie at the boarding hostel, I still looked forward to going back home to Petersfield, to country living and being with family and friends at the western end of the island for summer holidays.

As a teenager, I was not allowed to go and spend the long summer holidays at another student's home. I always felt so disappointed at not being able to accept the invitations, especially from my best friends, Grace Clarke and Valerie Anderson who filled my head with stories about her parents' "ranch and farm". Like in most Chinese families' homes, I was expected to return home to help in the family business and earn next term's school fees and pocket money. I was also expected to return home by myself via the railway from Kingston. I would disembark at Montpelier Train Station where someone would transport me directly to Petersfield. When my eldest brother, Keith, got his driver's license, I managed to arrange with him to pick me up a few days later in Montego Bay. Montego Bay was two stops away from Montpelier. It was where my roommate Sonja lived, and I would get the opportunity to spend a few days at her home without my parents realizing it.

Sonja's mother, Mrs. Viola Lue, was most hospitable and I enjoyed a few days of holiday before returning to work in my parents' store. Sonja's family owned "Commercial Restaurant" and I had fun reading the comics meant for sale and returning them to the shelves in an impeccable condition. I loved their food. It was while I was staying with them that I was initiated into such treats as eating ice-cream with jello, as well as other desserts sold in the restaurant. I enjoyed meeting Sonja's many younger brothers, Warren, Trevor and Horace; sisters Yvonne "Honey", Arlene, Karen and Wendy; and her young aunt, Darrieux "Sugar". I marveled at Mrs. Lue's patience and I was envious of the pretty dresses that she would painstakingly make for Sonja

Roommate Sonja Lue

and her sisters. Keith did not mind cooperating with my plan for a few days holiday by picking me up in Montego Bay as he got the chance to meet with Sonja, Sugar and his male school-friends from Cornwall College who used to come around to see Sonja and me, her roommate, returning from boarding school in Kingston.

Life in Jamaica: Marescaux Road, Kingston, 1956-57

Sister Polly Lee

Back in Petersfield, there were a number of changes happening in our household. Sister Carmen had gotten married and left Mama's care to start her own family. Sister Polly's bookkeeping studies paid off and she got a job in the City of Kingston where two of her sisters, Myrtle and Moi, were already living, so she left as well. She did not leave our family in spirit, however, as she constantly wrote to Mama and we visited her whenever we visited Kingston. Decades later, after she had migrated to Florida, USA and we had moved to Toronto Canada with our own grown-up children, she still continued to maintain a lasting relationship with us, "Auntie's children". And we continued to refer to her fondly as "Sister P".

With Carmen and Sister P gone, Mama opened up the door of our home again to a young lady named Novlet, who was closer to our age. Novlet's family lived in the neighbouring district of Darliston. Novlet came to us so that she could learn bookkeeping and secretarial skills from our bookkeeper, Mr. Tucker. Later on, her brother, Wilson joined her and the rest of us in Petersfield. Mama was always helpful to the young people in our community and Papa was also quite generous in his help to the bachelor Chinese men seeking work in Jamaica. I have been told that during the war days, Papa made a point of helping out less fortunate Chinese families when there were food shortages. I watched everything they did. Without knowing it, both my parents were teaching me to be compassionate and give help to my fellow man.

Like our other "big sisters", we all liked Novlet, whom we endearingly called "Novie" instead of "sister" since she was closer to my age. She was a sweet girl and fitted in

L-R: Carol, Novlet, Dulcie Williams, Bobette Chin, Dick, Patrick and Mama at Negril Beach

A more mature Novlet Chen

Life in Jamaica: Marescaux Road, Kingston, 1956-57

nicely with our family. About a year after coming to us, Novie went to stay with her godmother in Kingston and we frequently visited her. She eventually migrated to New York, USA and then to Montréal where we would meet up again. At this reunion, she served as the chief bridesmaid at my wedding. Later, she got married to Dr. Russel Chen and moved to Cambridge, Ontario where her husband opened a successful Optometry practice. They have a daughter, Andrina and a son, Alexis. Novie and Russel attended at our wedding in 1965 and over forty years later, we attended Andrina's wedding. We still continue to remain family friends.

Lorraine Tong and Carol

Actually, as time went on, Keith and I started going to parties further and further afield, so driving as far to Kingston to visit Novie and back was no problem for Keith to accomplish after we closed the store in the evenings. In addition, there were many events at the Chinese Athletic Club on Derrymore Road, the Chinese Freemason "Chee Gung Tung" Hall and at the Chinese Benevolent Association for us to meet up with our cousin from Whithorn, Edmund "Eddie" Chin who was now working at a commercial bank in Kingston. Through him, we met other young Kingstonians like Eva Yee and her friend, Lorraine Tong, whom we liked a lot. In fact, we even invited them to visit us at our home in Petersfield.

In later years, Lorraine would move to Montego Bay with her husband, Walton "Wally" Chin and much later, she would move to Toronto, Canada where we have now shared experiences as grandmothers together.

Going mid-island to Mandeville was a shorter trip and there were many parties held at Little Rock Club and private homes that Keith and I attended. We met other young Chinese boys and girls from Mandeville like the Lyns, Chungs, Fungs, Hughs, as well as from the surrounding districts like Borough Bridge, Christiana, Chapelton, Porus, Maggotty, and Troy.

Our cousins, Maurice from Little London district and Antonio "Tony" Williams from Savanna-La-Mar were the regulars who drove with Keith and me to our various parties. Looking back, I seem to have been the only girl on these trips, but I felt safe with my brother and cousins – and I did not mind being the useful emissary and go-between for this car-load of guys scouting for girlfriends, especially when visiting their homes under the watchful eyes of their protective fathers. As a matter of interest, there were a few romances from that period which actually blossomed into marriages.

Life in Jamaica: Marescaux Road, Kingston, 1956-57

Dances at the Savanna-la-Mar Town Hall and parties at our cousin, C.J Williams' place attracted young folks from Green Island, Lucea, Montego Bay, Grange Hill, Black River, Strathbogie and other remote districts like Blackness and Locust Tree. Most of us enjoying these shindigs were cousins and ultimately a few romances developed, but they were quickly quelled by our well-meaning parents and elders. Within the Chinese tradition, cousins were forbidden to marry but later on, these rules were applied less strictly and marriages between distantly related cousins were approved. This prohibition of marriage between cousins was quite a different practice from the African-Jamaican society. There was actually a patois expression which meant that it was okay for cousins to marry each other: "Cousin and cousin mek good soup."

When Keith finished attending high school at Cornwall College and with Novlet and Wilson helping out in the store and grocery shop, Mama was finally able to take more time off work and visit her own family during the summer holidays. Since our family had always been more closely involved with Papa's side of the Williams family, this was also an opportunity for me to meet some of my mother's side of the Young family. I recall one occasion where Mama and I stayed with her cousin Sylvia and her husband, Choy Hing in Kingston. Mama had served as one of her bridesmaids at their wedding before Mama herself got married to Papa.

Mama as Sylvia's bridesmaid

I liked playing with Agnes and Maureen, their daughters, who were close to my age, but thought that their older brother Richard, was stuck up since he completely ignored us. Later in life, I would meet up with Richard and his wife, Pat in Toronto, Canada and their daughter Kathy would be the classmate of my son, Gordon in Optometry School at the University of Waterloo, Ontario.

Uncle's Inn Chinese Restaurant in Cross Roads was a most popular restaurant that everyone spoke of and when we went there, I was delighted to discover that the owner, F.K Young, was the real uncle of my mother. I also got to know my first cousins when my mother visited her siblings: Nora on Spanish Town Road; Cisilyn "Cissy" on Windward Road; and Florence "Florrie". Since Mama was the youngest sibling in her family, most of my cousins were older than I, but it was nice for them to meet me and for me to know about them. At Aunt Nora's, there was a pretty older daughter, Joyce who would later marry a Chinese diplomat; a studious looking son, Ronald who was smart to be studying at a university in the USA; Dorothy, the outgoing cousin who would later marry the son of the owner of a lively "Club Havana". I especially liked the pet-name "Coolo" for the youngest daughter, Carmen. The youngest child, Keith, was too young to pay attention to me.

Aunt Cissy's sons, Charlie, Albert and Bebe were quite entrepreneurial and opened the Ding Ho Chinese Restaurant downtown far from their modest family grocery

Life in Jamaica: Marescaux Road, Kingston, 1956-57

Clockwise from top left: Jean Chin, Aunt Cisilyn Hoo, Joyce Chin, Dorothy Chung

store on Windward Road. They and their sister, Barbara, were quite friendly and cheerful like Aunt Cissy. The youngest son, Winston would become more friendly with my youngest brother, Donny in years to come during their summer holidays. Aunt Florrie and Uncle Reggie were equally welcoming when we visited. Their only son, Ricardo got married and moved to Venezuela and their grandson, Robert "Bobby" Payne would spend summers with us in Petersfield.

Uncle Clarence's daughters, Cherry, Pat, Carole, Madge "Bobbi" and Geraldine, had moved from Trout Hall and lived in Kingston. While I was at school, they would invite me to spend the weekends with them on Victoria Avenue, in front of the J.B. Machado cigarette factory where Four Aces, Royal Blend & Buccaneer cigarettes were manufactured and sold. They used to take me to Hope Gardens when the Royal Constabulary Band was performing in the open-air bandstand. These were enjoyable outings – the gardens were so beautiful. The band conductor and members were almost as impressive as the gardens in their full dress uniform and regalia!

Life in Jamaica: Marescaux Road, Kingston, 1956-57

The Williams side of the family maintained close, cohesive ties, similar to how they had lived in Niu Foo Village in China. I would come to appreciate these ties later in life. In those days, we were living closer to those on the same branch of the family tree. As a result, we children would spend a lot of time with the children of Uncle B.J Williams, "Kee Shuk" and Aunt Sarah (née Chin) "Shuk May". Their children went to the Roman Catholic Schools, Alpha Academy and St. George's College. Their eldest daughter, Rosa got married to "Dockie" Chin from Montego Bay. We would meet again years later when I also got married and was living in Montego Bay. Decades later in Toronto, we would become closer friends as we age into the twilight years of our lives.

Enjoying breakfast at Farm Pen L-R: Novlet, Carol, Elaine, Rosa, Colleen, Elsa

Their younger daughter, Audrey "Nicey", was my age and while attending Alpha Academy, used to correspond with me using my childhood pet-name, Pat. She used to ward off unwanted boyfriends by saying she already had a boyfriend – Pat! Elder son, Edwin would take care of the family sugar-cane business after finishing high school, while younger son, Leonard attended St. George's College like Edwin. The youngest child, Elizabeth "Betty", who was the same age as my younger sister, Elaine, attended Alpha Academy. We have kept in touch with all the family members all through our adult life. We also keep in contact with Kee Shuk's youngest sister, Jasmine. She used to live with their family. Later she went to study hairdressing in England and married a fellow Chinese Jamaican, James Tenn Lyn.

Another Williams family to whom we were close was the Uncle Walton Williams family. His eldest son, Antonio "Tony" was the fellow party-goer that I mentioned in one of my earlier letters. He was a frequent visitor to our house. He was followed by his younger brother, Donald who attended the local Mannings High School. The eldest daughter, Evelyn studied nursing in England and later migrated to Canada. I was particularly close to the younger daughter, Dulcie who worked at Barclays Bank in Savanna-La-Mar and later in Kingston for years before she retired to help her aging parents and youngest brother, Winston in

Walton Williams family:
Back L-R Antonio (Tony), Winston, Dulcie, Donald
Inset: Evelyn
Front L-R Walton, Daisy

Life in Jamaica: Marescaux Road, Kingston, 1956-57

Cecilia & Abraham Williams, 1950s

Abraham Williams family:
Back L-R Fred, Hyacinth, Louis, Enid
Front L-R Shirley, Winston

the family business located in front of the Savanna-la-Mar market at the end of Great George Street. While in Kingston, Dulcie became the god-mother of my second son, Gordon and proved to be a reliable house-sitter and baby-sitter for all my sons.

We loved Uncle Abraham who also lived in Little London, Westmoreland. He would come around at Christmas time dressed in a funny imitation of Santa Claus and give us special candy. We would actually call him Santa Claus and made sure to put gobs of white cotton wool to replicate snow on the fir tree outside before he arrived. Uncle Abraham was such an interesting man who seemed to be always on the go. This left us to wonder why he was different from from the other uncles. Earlier in his life, during the early 1900's, he left China and traveled to London, Paris, New York, Vancouver and Panama before arriving in Guyana and then moving on to settle in Jamaica. While in Paris, he spent three years as a cook so he was much more exposed to the western way of life and traditions than his relatives. Mama got along with Aunt Cecelia (née Chung) who could not speak Hakka dialect like herself and also with her children who were much older than us children. Louis, Hyacinth and Enid went off to England and would frequently correspond with Mama who proudly showed off the photograph of Louis in his Royal Air Force uniform. Their younger siblings, Fred, Winston and Shirley were closer to our age so Keith and I would interact with them.

Another fellow party-goer, Maurice and his sister, Gloria lived with their grandfather, Henry and mother, Violet Williams in Little London district. Maurice's father, Thompson, died early on and they were left to manage the business. During the weekdays, after the store was closed in the evenings, Maurice and Antonio "Tony" would drive to Petersfield to visit with my older brother, Keith to discuss the next party being held on the following Saturday night.

Life in Jamaica: Marescaux Road, Kingston, 1956-57

While chatting, Maurice and Tony would also help us prepare for the next day's business by helping us replenish our stock of wrapped goods in the grocery section. To suit the pockets of our low income customers, we would pre-wrap affordable small amounts of food items like flour, sugar, rice, salted cod-fish, salt into quarter-pound (4 ounces), half-pound (8 ounces), and one pound packages. Because we did not yet have paper bags to package these items, the first step in preparing them for sale was to cut up squares of brown paper. These squares of paper would be used to deftly wrap up these small portions. We would use cut up greaseproof paper sheets to wrap the small slices of butter and margarine. It was more challenging to make newspaper funnels to hold black peppercorns and mini-packets for straw dye crystals. To compensate for our wrapping materials and handling, we learned to produce five quarters to a one pound weight and improved our knowledge of profit and loss. When Maurice and Tony visited, these chores were made lighter by the numerous and heated arguments we had on a wide variety of subjects, as well as the sharing of grouses within the Williams clan. Tony was the most vocal while Maurice was more subdued. At the end of the evening, plans were in place for our next Saturday evening trip to go rockin' and rollin'.

Maurice's older sister, Gloria married Henry Moo Young from Frome district, had two daughters and lived in Negril where they built and managed the successful White Sands Villas and Apartments complex. Gloria had a huge wedding and I was excited to be one of her many bridesmaids. I had to journey to Kingston to be fitted by Flossie Thomas, one of Jamaica's top fashion designers, who created beautiful gowns

Gloria (née Williams) Moo Young's wedding
L-R: Shirley, Shirley, Carol, Gloria, Novlet, Rosa, Dulcie

Life in Jamaica: Marescaux Road, Kingston, 1956-57

Henderson Williams family
Standing L-R: Hopeton, Shirley, Eldith (Joyce), Jenneth (Cutie), Leonie (Sweetie), Norma
Sitting L-R: Henderson Paul, Hilma (Pearlie), Milword Rose, Warrington

for the entire bridal party. The wedding reception was held at the Frome sports ground and I remember that outgoing Mrs. Mary Lowe was the life of the party.

Although they lived out of the parish, Papa and Mama would occasionally take us to visit Papa's cousin, Henderson "Den Seung Back" and Auntie Milword Rose (née Wong) in Green Island, Hanover. Henderson had a special place in Papa's heart because he and Papa had played sports together as children. They had six daughters, five of whom had cute pet-names: Norma "Dodo", Leonie "Sweetie", Hilma "Pearlie", Eldith "Joycie", Jenneth "Cutie". The sixth was Shirley. They also had three sons, Hopeton, Warrington and Paul. Norma and Hilma would attend Wolmer's High School for Girls and we three cousins shared memorable years at the boarding hostel during our teen years before migrating overseas.

Papa was also close to Uncle Henry "Choy Sang Goh" who arrived in Jamaica via Guyana where his father was registered as Ngui, Chun Tait. Because the colonial officials were ignorant of how Chinese names were organized, there was a mix-up at the Immigration Department and the family ended up with "Chun Tait" as their surname instead of "Ngui". Choy Sang Goh and Aunt Elinor (née Chin) lived in Grange Hill, Darliston, Frome, Kingson before settling on Great George Street, Savanna-la-Mar.

They went into the millinery business so most Williams businesses, including Papa's, started selling ladies hats. They added sugar-cane farming as the sons grew old enough to manage the canefields. They had one daughter, Shirley, who migrated to England and three sons, Nelson, Edward and Peter. Nelson used to drive his Volkswagen "Bug" car very fast so he was nicknamed "Speedy", Edward's nickname was "Bubbles", and Peter got saddled with his nickname, "Big Load", during their teen years. These nicknames

Henry (Choy Sang) & Eleanor (Fui Lan) Williams

Life in Jamaica: Marescaux Road, Kingston, 1956-57

would follow them into their adult lives. After attending St. George's College, Edward went off to the Seminary in the USA. Many years later, after I had moved to Toronto, Canada, Choy Sang Goh invited me to attend his performance as part of a Chinese Band at the Tsung Tsin (Hakka) Association of Ontario. This would be my first introduction to this Hakka Chinese association located in Scarborough, Ontario, Canada.

Needless to say, our ties with the family of grand-uncle, Jackson Williams were never severed even when his son, Uncle Lincoln "Min Shuk" and Aunt Nancy (née Chin) "Shuk May" and their grown children migrated to the USA and Canada. Eldest daughter, Marie, went to study in the USA and got married to an American Chinese, Larry; first son, Arthur and his wife, Olive (née Chin-Fook) worked in the family business; second daughter, Winifred "Winnie" went to learn hair-dressing in England and married a Trinidadian Chinese, Tony Lee Lum; second son, Washington also worked in the business; youngest daughter, Shirley was my age and after attending St. Andrew's High School, she went to study and stay with her big sister, Marie in California. Third son, Winston "Keung" completed high school at St. George's College and studied Civil Engineering at McGill University, Montreal, Canada; the last child, Frank "Bim" was an excellent soccer player on the school team when he was attending St. George's College and later went to Montréal for further studies at Loyola College.

Later in life, Lincoln and Nancy would retire in Miami, Florida. Nevertheless, their business in Jamaica would continue, first under the leadership of their two sons, Winston "Keung" and Frank "Bim" after they returned from overseas, and even later, when Keung's grown sons, Andrew and Cary joined the business. The business finally folded in 2012. The closing of the business marked the end of an era; for it was our first ancestor, Jackson Williams of the lineage of Wei, Gen Choi, who had encouraged his nephews, including Papa, to brave the high seas across the Pacific Ocean, travel by

Wedding of Andrew & Tracy Williams, 1998

Paul Wong, Warren, Brian Wong, Susie Phillips holding Justin, Cary, Winston, Damian, Joshua Phillips, Arthur, Rhea Howell, Larry Chung, Nancy, Washington, Tracy, Andrew, Shirley Wong, Frank 'Bim', Nick Wong, Winnie Lee Lum, Olive, Marie Chung, Kylie Wong, Melanie Wong, Janet, Tricia

rail across Canada and take a banana boat sailing on the Atlantic Ocean to join this business in Jamaica, one of the most beautiful tropical islands in the Caribbean Sea. And now Jackson and his nephews are all deceased and their once flourishing store, Jackson Williams & Sons Ltd., has ceased to exist as well. Indeed, it was the end of a historical era in the Wei family!

As mentioned before, in the 1940s Papa eventually moved back to where he had started in Jamaica, the original Jackson Williams business in Petersfield, Westmoreland. Along with Mama, he worked hard to provide for us six children while instilling the Hakka Chinese values system which was itself based on Confucius teachings: respect elders, help each other, love and educate the young. Papa was adjusting to the Jamaican way of life as well. At first, if Papa needed to go to Kingston on business, he would hire a chauffeur named Wolsey to drive us into the city and take me shopping. It took quite a few years, but eventually, Papa was confident enough with his driving to feel that he could handle both the long distances between Petersfield and Kingston, plus the drive up Spur Tree Hill when passing through Mandeville. Spur Tree Hill was so steep that after getting to the top of the hill, we usually had to stop for a while in order for the engine to cool down and the radiator to be refilled with cool tap water. We children never minded these stops as it gave us the great joy of getting out of the car to run around in the nearby farmer's field.

On some of these occasions when I was returning to the boarding hostel from holidays, Papa and I would be driven directly to Chinatown on Barry Street upon arriving in Kingston. Here, he was welcomed at all the various business places and associations. It was educational for me to accompany him while he was purchasing food products imported from China. I would look around in bewilderment at strange and unknown food items. We went to shops like Hen Fah, Nam Keung, Tack Sing, and I felt proud and happy when my father introduced me to the owners like the Changs, Chungs and Chins. Many years later, I would meet some of them in Toronto, Canada as a grown-up woman. On Barry Street, I would listen to my father speaking with the owners loudly and rapidly in Hakka Chinese dialect. They always seemed like reunited long lost friends. I remember on one trip, I saw a young Chinese lady, Gladys, wearing a beautiful Chinese cheongsam dress in Tack Sing. Papa proudly told me that she had been sent to her family village and had just returned from living in China. He thought that she had become so cultured from her time in China.

Papa and I would have lunch at an upstairs Chinese restaurant on Princess Street. We would sit together slurping a soup made with lots of meat and noodles. Years later, I learned that this was a traditional Hakka Chinese dish called *Shui Mein*. Despite the fact that the dish was not native to Jamaica, I remember many locals also enjoying the hot steaming soup – albeit under the cooling breeze of the electric fans in the restaurant! After lunch, Papa and I would finally walk to King Street to see the Syrian merchants whose salesmen usually traveled around the island taking orders from shop owners. Papa was a valued customer and the merchants greeted him warmly as well.

On one of these trips, Papa had promised to buy me a swimsuit for swimming lessons. I had been longing to buy my swimsuit from one of the fashionable stores in

Life in Jamaica: Marescaux Road, Kingston, 1956-57

downtown Kingston. I waited patiently for Papa to finish conducting his business. When he was finally free, I showed him the one that I liked -- a bright royal blue one-piece with bamboo buttons for decoration which stretched and hugged my figure tightly, just like the starlets in the movie magazines. My father thought that it was expensive at £10, but I pleaded and he relented. And I got to strut around the swimming pool at Immaculate Conception High School in my new skin-tight swimsuit way before swim classes started! This swimsuit was definitely going to help me swim like movie star Esther Williams!

Thank you Papa for this gift – not only of the extravagant bathing suit – but for the greater gift of taking me around Chinatown to expose me to the Oriental side of Jamaica.

Your loving Ah-Poh

Breadfruit with Ackee (Jamaica's national fruit)

Jamaican fruits in season

Lignum Vitae flowers (Jamaica's national flower)

Photos courtesy of Ray Chen

Life in Jamaica:
Marescaux Road, Kingston
1958 – 1959

My dear Grandchildren,

I was coming to the end of my time at Wolmer's and preparing to sit the Senior Cambridge Examinations. These exams, set and marked in England, were written for schools in the British colonies at the end of one's high school study in order to receive a high school certificate. Students could graduate with a Cambridge School Certificate or stay on for another two years to sit and receive the Higher School Certificate. Unfortunately, because of poverty, many brilliant students were not able to further their studies unless they were lucky enough to be sponsored by a benefactor.

Success on these exams would play a large part in determining whether or not one would be able to attend university. Your success or failure would indicate to your parents whether it was worthwhile spending their hard-earned money to provide further education for you or whether you ought to stay at home to find a job or help in the business. As well, these exam results would be a good indication to the universities abroad whether you should be accepted into their programs or not. School certificates from the British Senior Cambridge Examination Board were highly regarded by the American and Canadian universities. Obtaining one was a sure way to be accepted at these universities.

I had enjoyed the social life at Wolmer's, particularly at the boarding hostel, but I was also a good scholar and enjoyed the academic side to life at Wolmer's as well. Throughout my time in high school, I had excelled in each form and easily progressed up to the next form each term. I learned to appreciate the excellent teachers like Mrs. Scott, (Mathematics), Mrs. Roper (History), Miss Cusak (Geography), Mrs. Evans (English Literature), Mrs. Vidal Smith (English Grammar & Penmanship), Miss Maughan (Domestic Science & Sewing), Mrs. Lyons (Drama & Elocution), Miss Dutt (Biology), Miss Baxter (Chemistry), Mrs. Hamilton (Art/Drawing), Miss DaCosta (Art/Painting), and Miss Stokes (Sports & Gymnastics). Senorita Ruby Feres (Spanish), Rev. Ram (Religious Knowledge), Mrs. Hazel Lawson Street (Music). Miss Walker, Mrs. Segree Girvan and Mrs. Burrows Carberry also come to mind.

I buckled down to studying all my subjects, but of course, I had my favourites. I really enjoyed participating in drama festivals and elocution contests, as well as sports. I played tennis and netball, and participated in gymnastic demonstration. I especially

Life in Jamaica: Marescaux Road, Kingston, 1956-59

Wolmer's Headmistress, Mrs. Evelyn Skempton (centre) and teaching staff

enjoyed gymnastics and giving gymnastic demonstrations, although I would frequently get black and blue marks on my thighs from not clearing the pummel horse cleanly. Unlike most of the girls, I quite liked my white gym tunic and even the baggy bloomers which, in those days, were thought necessary for us girls to wear to maintain modesty.

My report cards revealed, however, that my strength lay in the Fine Arts. In fact, I excelled in Geography mainly because of the artistic component of geographical mapping! Triumphantly, I won the island-wide poster art competition. When Papa found out, he said: "Hrumph! All artist poor till dem dead". At that time, I felt so crushed by his remark. I was deeply saddened that he did not seem to share my joy and everyone's jubilation over my win. Ironically, later in life, I found myself saying something similar to my artistic sons when they began making post-secondary school plans: "Focus on engineering or science so that you can make money to buy your art supplies"; or "Go into a higher paying profession so that you can afford to feed your family and still have time and money to do what you truly enjoy."

In addition to my studies and art, I was also a Girl Guide. I loved the Friday afternoon meetings where we learned outdoor survival skills, as well as the campfire sing-along at sunset. The Girl Guides served as Honour Guards whenever any dignitary or a member of the royal family visited Jamaica. I remember standing for long hours in my Girl Guide uniform in the hot sun outside the Wolmer's main gate along Marescaux Road on the occasion of the visits of King George VI and Queen Elizabeth (known as the Queen Mother), of Queen Elizabeth II and Prince Phillip, and finally of Princess Margaret and Lord Snowdon. When they drove by and gave us the royal wave; it was so exciting! We thought it was well worth the wait in sweltering heat!

Life in Jamaica: Marescaux Road, Kingston, 1958-59

Another highlight of attending Wolmer's High School was the exposure to theatre in all its forms. Drama festivals were held at the British Army Up-Park Camp while larger productions were put on at Ward's Theatre. We were able to be exposed to so many plays – from Gilbert and Sullivan's *The Mikado* to George Bernard Shaw's *Arms and the Man*, to William Shakespeare's *Midsummer Night's Dream* to Jamaican Pantomimes. These festivals, along with the dramas that we performed at school, helped develop a life-long love of the theatre in me. I appreciated every moment of the theatre, whether I was on stage or in the audience. Because of my height and deep voice, I was mostly cast in male roles. I did not mind this at all because going to various rehearsals allowed me to leave the school grounds, and learn about stage make-up from Miss DaCosta, acting from Mrs. Doyen Fitchette, diction from Mrs. Lyons and even stage construction and creating back-drops.

I graduated from Wolmer's in 1959. I was almost 18-years old and believed I was ready to take on the world. Throughout my time in high school, Mrs. Skempton had repeatedly told all her students that her girls could be anything they wanted to be. We were told: *"Never give up! It is wiser and better always to hope than once to despair"*. She expected us to aim high in our goals for ourselves and to exemplify the school motto, *Age Quod Agis* – whatever you do, do it well! Mrs. Skempton ran Wolmer's High School for Girls with tight precision. She turned out girls who not only excelled academically; they behaved like proper young ladies. Posture and Elocution formed part of the curriculum. I remember how Beulah Stone won the posture prize and Pat Priestly excelled at elocution – she had great diction. Gymnastics, lawn tennis and netball were deemed acceptable sports for young ladies, but not track and field events. These were considered "unladylike" activities. After all, ladies should walk briskly -- they do not run! Year after year, Mrs. Skempton surely turned out well-behaved and high-achieving young ladies into the world.

I planned to travel and study Fashion Arts abroad, perhaps in New York City where my best friend, Grace Clarke was moving to, but this dream was put on hold. Mama had been diagnosed with a serious throat ailment after having an operation to remove a goiter some years before in Savanna-La-Mar Hospital. Although she had seen medical specialists at the University of the West Indies Hospital, Papa did not have faith in Western medicine, particularly the new "radium" treatment for cancer that was still in its experimental stage in the United States. He sent Mama to Hong Kong so that she could undergo Chinese medical treatment; and, as I was the eldest girl in the family, it was my duty to take her place while she was away. So, as I was completing the next Chinese Zodiac cycle, I found myself being thrust into the roles of mother to my siblings, partner to my father, household manager of the servants, overseer of the store staff, and a hard working business woman managing our expanding family business.

In hindsight, these family obligations complemented my academic achievements with valuable lessons learned outside the classroom. I was plunged into the real world acquiring much common sense and initiative while learning how to get along with a variety of personalities and deal with different types of situations. I also imitated my

Life in Jamaica: Marescaux Road, Kingston, 1956-59

parents by taking on a benevolent role in the community. I found myself giving credit to the customers even when they were deemed bad debtors. I had actually threatened many of them with lawsuits and daunting letters of credit collection; but, like my father, when they came begging for credit to feed their families, I could not say no. I also found myself continuing the roles that Mama had played in the community: providing generous contributions for the orphanage in Water Works; assisting anyone needing help writing, reading or replying to letters; and endorsing parcel post and registered articles. It just seemed natural to help the illiterate customers, especially when I knew that the correspondence was with family members who were working abroad so that they could send money back, usually for the children who had been left in the care of grandparents.

The two years that I would spend working closely with Papa drew us closer together. It was also an opportunity for my father to reinforce my knowledge and appreciation of my Hakka heritage. I learnt from Papa the Chinese way of making and saving money; namely, being thrifty, and not wasting anything. He drilled into me the importance of my ties to the Williams (Ngui) family, our Hakka Chinese culture, traditions and the Confucius-based value system on which our culture was based: respect elders, help each other, take care of and educate the young. He taught me to be proud of being Chinese and to be patriotic to the motherland of China. Papa subscribed to Chinese periodicals to keep abreast of the political scene in China and supported what was best for the Chinese people. Today, he would have been so proud to witness China's rise in power and world recognition from the foreign leaders. It became a ritual that on Sunday mornings after coming home from attending the early morning Anglican Church service, Papa and I would have our one-on-one conversations and discussions on the veranda while he sat in his rocking chair reading the magazines coming out of China, especially one called *China Communes*.

Years later when I would start having babies, Papa would send this very rocking chair to my home; and much later in life, I would rock my own grandchildren in this very same heirloom rocking chair.

During this period, Papa also passed on parenting advice. Like Mama, I was prone to spank my younger siblings when they misbehaved. Papa would chide me gently by saying in his Jamaican patois, "Di more you lick di donkey, di more him kick up. Koaks him, koaks him" (The more you beat the donkey, the more stubborn he will become. It is better to coax him to do what you want). Sometimes he would switch

Carol with Papa in the rocking chair

to Hakka and say, "Mao dah, gao ghee" meaning "Do not hit, teach them instead!" These wise sayings would be carried with me throughout my life. I have often relied on them in my various dealings with people of all ages.

Papa felt strongly against me marrying outside the Chinese race and even threatened to shoot me if I did! But he needn't have worried about that. Papa had always had a strong influence on me. I respected him, especially because I saw the kindness with which he treated others, and the more time that I spent with him, the more I loved him. I would not have done anything to hurt him, especially in terms of something as important as marriage. He did not have to "lick me" to get me to follow the path he wanted me to take; he had already "koaks'd" me with his love.

Perhaps because of the closeness we developed in those years, people have said that I was Papa's favourite daughter. But Keith, as the eldest son, destined to take over the family business and carry on the family name as per centuries of Hakka history, was clearly the favourite child. At that time, Keith was already out of high school and highly involved in the business. Once I returned home, Papa gave Keith and me free rein to expand the business.

Keith expanded the hardware section and started selling panes of clear glass for window construction. He had an extension built on to the outer wall of the building to create a storeroom for the wooden crates of sheet glass delivered carefully by the transport trucks. I added fashionable ready-to-wear garments, shoes and hats made by the wife of Papa's cousin, Aunt Eleanor from Savanna-La-Mar, to our stock. We also expanded the storeroom at the back of the shop to accommodate more grocery items and to create an eating area for customers. We bought a Wurlitzer Juke Box for the Rum Bar to encourage patrons to stay and have an extra drink. The juke box created much enjoyment for everyone. Later on, we built a separate building just to house the juke-box and accommodate our customers' desire to dance and eat the foodstuff, things like tinned herring, corned beef with bread, or bun and cheese, that they had bought in the grocery store. Our customers were not fancy. They did not demand hot meals; they were content with just a space within which they could eat their purchases. We also found that our customers spent money freely – they spent the money as soon as they worked for it! It did not seem to us as if they saved anything for a rainy day, which was a strict Chinese philosophy with regard to managing money.

At about this time, Papa's friend Vincent Lee, from Little London, had the idea that we could also make money showing movies. There was no cinema in the area and anyone who wanted to see a movie had to travel Savanna-la-Mar six miles away. Papa and Vincent figured that they could share the cost of renting the films from the Palace Amusement Company in Kingston. They only needed a place to show the films. Papa had previously established a petrol station that offered fuel to both gas and diesel powered vehicles on our property. It was believed that the ideal place to build the movie cinema was on the land behind the service station, although this meant that Mama's coconut and banana trees would have to be chopped down. Lucky for us, the fruitful paw-paw (papaya) tree which produced the largest and sweetest papayas (since it had been planted over the site of our no-longer-in-use pit latrine), the orange, grapefruit, lime and huge June plum trees were safely away from the area.

Since the entire family was made up of "movie buffs", we were all very excited and enthusiastic at the thought of building a movie cinema. From the time that we were young, every Sunday evening, our parents would take us to either the Doric or Imperial movie theatres to see a show and no one ever wanted to miss out on that – even if some of us actually fell asleep before the movie was over! My mother was a big fan of Hollywood. She bought movie magazines weekly and had named me after the 1940s movie stars Carol Lombard and Merle Oberon. When we were younger, my brother Patrick would do a great imitation of the cry of the ape man Tarzan as he swung from tree to tree. We would mimic the gambling cowboys we saw in the movies when we were playing cards, complete with an un-lit cigarette dangling from our lips! We would also imitate the movie stars when we posed for photographs.

Papa was the self-appointed architect and building supervisor of the new cinema. He designed a two-storey, open air structure made from cement blocks and mortar with zinc sheet roofing. The building went up in no time. The main ground level had a ticket office with meshed wire frontage and an entry door in front of the building. The concrete floor sloped down towards the inner back wall which was painted white to serve as the cinemascope screen and bordered in black. From the main entry door, there were wooden stairs leading up to the upper balcony. The projection room was located in the centre of this balcony. There was a side entrance closer to the screen which opened to the area assigned for the cheapest priced ticket holders. The mid-section and the back were the next price up and the balcony tickets were the most expensive because the balcony had the most elevated and, thus, prestigious seating. In addition, unlike the areas on the ground, the balcony seats were fully covered by the zinc sheet roofing.

At that time, Dick and Donny were away from home. Donny was attending Cornwall College in Montego Bay and Dick had won a scholarship to attend Kingston College. Dick boarded in the city with the Chong family. They owned a business called Classic Restaurant and accepted boarders attending either St. George's College or Kingston College as they lived near to both schools. Boarders were also accepted next door at Garden City Restaurant, nicknamed "Donkey City" because they sold a popular biscuit, jackass corn. Even though he was not home, Donny did find a way to contribute to the new cinema – it was his idea to call it the Venus Theatre! Patrick and Elaine were commuting to high schools in Savanna-la-Mar, Manning's High School and St. Mary's Academy, respectively, so they were home to help us with this new endeavour. Elaine sold tickets to the cinema patrons and I would collect tickets at the front door while Patrick collected at the lower side door. Keith would play recorded music as the patrons entered the theatre while he was setting up the large metal rolls of celluloid film in the 16 mm Bell & Howell projector. When he was ready, he would play the screening song we unanimously selected, which was the theme song from "A Summer Place" by Billy Vaughan and his orchestra. This was the cue for everyone to promptly sit down and be quiet for the start of the screening of a short trailer film, known as "shorts", before the main full-length feature film.

Keith and I were also in charge of promotions. We used to drive out to remote districts with a P.A. system in the car and a speaker on the roof. As Keith drove, I would announce the name of the upcoming film and its stars, as well as provide a brief synopsis of the plot. The cinema soon became a popular source of entertainment for the local people, especially since so many of them lived without electricity or could not read. Sometimes during the screening of a western film, if there was a bar-room brawl, many members of the audience would start hitting the person next to them, imitating the action on film. On occasion they would get so emotionally wound-up that they would get up, lift up their seat and throw it down to the ground in either victory or sorrow for the cowboys. This enthusiasm caused more work for us as we had to repair the wooden seats that were damaged by these emotional outbursts. Eventually, we started building benches with metal handy-angle fittings for added reinforcement. It was also common for audience members to shout at the actor in the film as if he could hear them or as if they were actually having a conversation with him, much to the amusement of all – that is, until they were shushed by the other more intelligent patrons.

Our lives were not, however, all about work. Papa gave Keith and me free access to money and the use of the family car. Unlike some of our peers, Keith and I did not have many restrictions in terms of what we did with our money and recreation time. We worked hard in the family business and Papa treated us as full partners. We considered ourselves to be self-employed and were free to do what we wanted to do with the money we made. Papa never balked, for example, at the money I spent on clothes. My mother had taught me to sew my own dresses, and pajamas for the boys. When the fashions got more intricate and my mother was away in Hong Kong, the lady who worked in the store, Mrs. Wallace, used to help keep me in the latest fashion as soon as the new fabrics were delivered to the store. She would cut the pattern and I would do the sewing under her supervision.

Papa also did not interfere when Keith and I learned to drive and gave us the choice when purchasing cars. Keith and I chose the jazziest cars: a Chevrolet Bel-Air (turquoise & white) and later, a red Chevrolet Impala sedan. We had actually started out with

Mrs. Wallace, flanked by daughter Karen and son Winston (Carrol), with adopted toddler Annette, leaving for England

Life in Jamaica: Marescaux Road, Kingston, 1956-59

a blue Zephyr Six which Keith crashed in Big Bridge District when he went to pick up schoolmate, Eric, from Grange Hill to return to Cornwall College High School in Montego Bay. Keith was a fast driver and was driving too fast to negotiate a curve. He hit a low concrete bridge and almost sent himself and the car down into the Cabarita River where crocodiles lived.

Although the Williams families were close-knit, Papa and Mama had socialized and become friends with other non-related Chinese families in the parish. There was the Lue Lim family from Strathbogie; the James and Myrtle Hue-Sang's and Wilson Lue family from Locust Tree; the George Lai family from Grange Hill; the Edwin and Blanche Forchin family from Whithorn; the Lym Family from Darliston; the

Carol beside the Chevrolet Bel Air family car

Austin and Lizette Chong family; the David "Ah-Yeung" and Mabel Chin, "Cool Ken" Lee and Vincent "Young Boy" Lee families in Little London; the Moo Young and Watson and Mary Lowe families in Frome; the extended Reggie and Louise, George and Ina, Bobby and Terry Lyn families originally from Black River, among many, many others. I recall that Papa was particularly close with his Mahjong buddies, David Chin and Vincent Lee who would come quite frequently to take him with them to play in Montego Bay. On one occasion, after an unexpectedly large win, all three grown men took a trip to Disney World, in Orlando, Florida. Mama shared a special bond with Lizette Chong who was as community-minded as herself and also had a modern and westernized outlook on life.

As a result of these friendships amongst our parents, we children got along well with their children in our age group, like Marjorie and Aston Lue Lim; William "Willie" and Madge Forchin; Ickia and Alex from Locust Tree; Violet and Eric Lai from Grange Hill; Crosby, Jean and Valerie Lym; Al, Peter, Jennifer, Herbie, Bobsie and Gene Chong; Lloyd, Nadine and Lorraine Lyn are a few names which come to mind. Actually, in hindsight, Mama and Papa taught us to have a wide circle of friends outside of our family circle without any discrimination of class, status,

Mahjong buddies L-R: David Chin, Papa, Vincent Lee

race, colour or wealth. Everyone was equal, their company valued and their friendship treasured.

Papa also did not restrict his children's social lives in the way that some Chinese parents tried to do with their children. Some people thought I was lucky that I was permitted to go out to parties because I had an older brother to chaperone me, his "helpless sister", who might be swarmed by boys on these outings. In reality, I was Keith's passport to get into the homes of girls with strict fathers! I suppose Papa also realized that we were reaching the marrying age. He encouraged us to socialize with other young Chinese people and was always happy when our Chinese friends came to visit – even when they ended up staying over at our house. Initially because of owning our car and our seeming affluence, Keith and I were very popular and well-liked by our peers. Keith had an unbridled outgoing personality. He was nicknamed "Ding Dong" and he, his cousin, Eddie Chin and his friends often wore signature pink and black custom-made shirts sewn by Mrs. Wallace when they went out. We were invited to attend many parties and weddings in places as far away as Montego Bay, Mandeville and even Kingston. In Montego Bay, we usually stayed over at the Tai household if the party ended late, but we might also drive around for hours after a Saturday night party like crazy teenagers and, much later, fall asleep under the almond trees at either Cornwall Beach or Doctor's Cave Beach before driving the 26 miles home to Petersfield the next day.

This was the rock and roll era of the 1950s and 60s. I would wear the widest crinoline skirt possible and a low cut blouse to these parties. I followed the fashion of the day with my hairstyle as well – a pony-tail with stylish bangs. Keith and I used to practise the dance moves and steps we saw in the American bandstand movies and were able to put on quite a show at the various parties we attended. We were an unusual brother and sister dancing pair at parties wherever we went! At these parties, boys outnumbered girls, so there were usually a few fights over girls. I found that when such fights occurred over me, it was very effective to simply walk away and into the arms of the other boys who were dying to dance. During my time away at Wolmer's, I knew that at many of these parties in Montego Bay, there was a certain level of mystique about me. After all, I was that girl who only appeared during school holidays!

It was at one of the frequent parties at the Chinese Club on Creek Street that I first noticed certain young men, Edward (Eddie), his young uncle, Washington (Washy) and their friends, Edmund, Freddie (Frisbie) and Henry (Junior). At weddings, I would notice others from out-of-town like Leo and Oscar from Falmouth and Percival driving over from Duncans.

In my next letters, I will tell you how it was my destiny to marry one of them.

Your loving Ah-Poh

Life in Jamaica: Marescaux Road, Kingston, 1956-59

Party fun in Montego Bay
L-R: Doris Chin, Janet Tai, Rosie Lym

Back: Charles Chin, Peggy Woon-Sue
Front: Patrick Williams

Eddie and Carol dancing cheek-to-cheek

Cornwall College Sixth Form party at Montego Bay Chinese Club

Life in Jamaica:
Petersfield, Westmoreland
1960 – 1961

My dear Grandchildren

Our beloved mother was now settled in Hong Kong. She had met, for the first time, the woman Papa had been betrothed to and was considered number one Chinese wife, Chan Lam Keow, and his many relatives who had escaped to this British Colony during the Cultural Revolution in China. Mama had sought medical treatment at St Mary's Hospital. The doctors diagnosed her condition as thyroid cancer. Mama had always been a positive person and went willingly to the hospital for whatever treatment they had to offer. In the meantime, she was thankful that she was able to reside in Hong Kong and worshipped at the St Teresa Roman Catholic Church, Kowloon where she made a good friend, Una and enjoyed the fellowship of the other church members. She would write about sightseeing and about all the wonderful times she was having, never mentioning her illness. She got along with Papa's relatives, especially the younger ones like Cynthia, her brother Rex, Steve, Shiu-Ki, Ricardo (Ricky) and his sister's family. Mama also developed a special bond with a young boy, Ralph Lue whom I got to meet much later in life.

Mama with St Theresa Roman Catholic church members in Kowloon, Hong Kong

Life in Jamaica: Petersfield, Westmoreland 1960-61

Mama and Una

L-R: Ralph Lue, Rex Williams, Ngai Shiu-Ki

Mama and friends

L-R: Ricky, Cynthis, Shiu-Ki

Before she left, Mama had arranged for a Chinese lady to come and live with us to take care of our youngest brother, Donny and help in the store as well. We called her "Auntie Girlie". She was from the Chin Shue family who had a restaurant and ice-cream parlour in Savanna-la-Mar. Auntie Girlie was a great help with Donny – especially as I had my hands filled with Patrick, Dick and Elaine. Older brother, Keith was more concerned with the business, soccer, and partying than in helping to raise his younger siblings.

Without Mama, our family settled into the routine that she had printed out on a huge sheet of cardboard and posted on the wall. She would have been pleased with the bond which was created among us siblings while we followed the routine she left behind – even though I was required to dole out the dreaded spoonful of raw cod-liver oil in the mornings! Mama always insisted that we sit together as a family wherever we went. I recall that while we were living in Savanna-la-Mar, we would, at a very young age, all go to the movies at the Imperial or Doric Theatres. Mama would command us all to sit together in a row although Keith and I would object since we would rather sit with our older cousins than have to sit with our younger siblings and her. Papa would sometimes accompany us, although he was not fond of English speaking movies. He was needed in attendance at these shows, however, to help lift up the younger ones who would invariably fall asleep during the screening.

Mama also insisted that we all sit together for lunch when, as school children in Petersfield, we would come home from school. She made this time together more appealing and fun by purchasing a metal cocktail shaker to serve us foamy Milo, Ovaltine or Horlicks milkshakes. Unknowingly, I would practise Mama's method of fostering sibling bonds among my own sons when I became a mother myself.

Because of this early investment in family bonding, as we grew up into our teenage years, we children would still spend time and share experiences together willingly and looked out for and cared for each other. Keith and I drew the line however, about taking Elaine out with us when she was not yet a teen. Elaine would cry to go with Keith and me to parties in the late evenings and Papa would threaten that he was going to make her sleep outside on the verandah if she would not stop crying and kicking up a fuss. Patrick, Dick and Donny did not care about parties or staying out so late and were happy to stay home. Elaine was so young that she would definitely have fallen asleep as soon as she had gotten in the car, but she just wanted to be with people much older than herself and could not wait to grow up.

As soon as we were able, we just knew that it was our duty to help in the family business in any way we could and in whatever capacity – whether it was to chop the salted cod fish, sell one cigarette, cut a yard measurement of linoleum or khaki material, weigh half-pound of two-penny nails, cut a quarter bar of soap, scoop a tablespoon of lard, outfit someone going as a farm worker to the USA, convince someone that the shoes or hat she or he was trying on fitted "perfectly" when it did not, transfer yards of material onto a more manageable bolt, dispense home remedies, sell half-a-loaf of bread, pump gasoline or just clean the shelves with a feather duster.

Life in Jamaica: Petersfield, Westmoreland 1960-61

These feather dusters were famous within the family. They were imported from Hong Kong and were called in our Hakka Chinese dialect, *Gai Mao Sow*. They were made of beautiful rooster feathers glued to a long, narrow and flexible cane about twenty-four inches long. There was at least one of these feather dusters in every Chinese household and business and they had a dual purpose: it was used for dusting, but the bare cane section, the side without any feathers, was ideal and convenient to use for spanking naughty children! Almost all Chinese who grew up in Jamaica during my childhood have knowledge of how painful that cane felt on bare skin! It ultimately left raised red welts for days as evidence of our parents' discipline.

When the business was closed on Sunday, we would hasten to get the store and shop ready for business on Monday before any customer would come banging on the doors for emergency supplies. We were anxious to take advantage of our only day off and head for the beach either at Bluefields or Negril or to Roaring River. Although it was a nuisance when customers showed up on a Sunday, if they did come, we would never turn away our customers, especially when it was a true emergency like if there had been a death in the family and burial supplies were needed for making the coffin. We were, after all, the only business in the district to help them in their time of need. Additionally, we were business-minded people!

After helping out our customers, we would hurry to enjoy a lovely day at, more than often, Bluefields. Most of the time, it would be sunny all year round and even when it rained, it was fun being in the warm, salty sea while the fresh rain drops splattered around our bodies. Bluefields beach hugged the coastline on the south coast of our parish of Westmoreland and was naturally perfect for swimming and relaxing under the sea grape trees growing randomly along the roadside. By now, after Papa's initiation to *Dah ping-bong*, we had taught ourselves to swim, and we, of course, watched out for each other in the water. Bluefields was not yet developed and only offered a stand-pipe by the roadside to rinse the salty sea water off our bodies as we shampooed our hair, but this was enough to make us feel fully refreshed after a day of swimming and enjoying the company of our relatives and friends.

In later years, our C.J. Williams cousins would own a motor boat and Elaine was sometimes offered a ride on the older boys' shoulders as they were water-skiing.

At Bluefields Beach
L-R: Patrick shampooing and Earle (Ah Pin)

L-R: Ricky and Carol at Doctor's Cave Beach

Other Williams cousins and friends would join us on many of these Sunday outings. Before she got ill, Mama would also join us, and once our stepbrother, Ricky, arrived from Hong Kong, so would he. We shared such wonderful memories at this Godgiven beautiful beach in Bluefields.

Other Sundays, we would be invited to Dean's Valley by the Dale family to spend the day at their residence. Mr. Dale was the manager of the Dean's Valley Ice Factory. Mrs. Dale was a nice motherly lady. They had four children: Kenny, Peter, Ditty and James (Jimpy). They had a swimming pool which was naturally fed from the river which ran through their property and down the hill to the ice factory so the water was cool and refreshing. This was a lovely setting for looking out over the lush vegetation of the district of Water Works and ideal for taking photographs. Peter's hobby was photography so he would take many photos of our family and we were not bashful to pose for him either.

Other Sundays were spent going to Roaring River, not very far from Petersfield. We drove along the unpaved roads through the cane-fields of Shrewsbury District to find this natural underground spring coming from the mountain which created a tranquil oasis and provided a source of clear and clean running water. This peaceful place overlooked the surrounding cane-fields of green blades of leaves waving in the breeze and coconut trees dotting the countryside.

Further down the hillside, the river roared downstream to the Filtration Plant before going under the road. We would park our car there and then tie a long rope, letting it hang into the water. From here, we would walk up the road as far as we could and then we would fearlessly jump into where the water was raging after leaving the Filtration Plant.

We would grab onto the dangling rope and hold on as the river took us under the road. We would eventually reach a wider pool of calmer water further down river.

Carol and Patrick at Roaring River, getting ready to take the plunge

Carol at the Roaring River Filtration Plant

Life in Jamaica: Petersfield, Westmoreland 1960-61

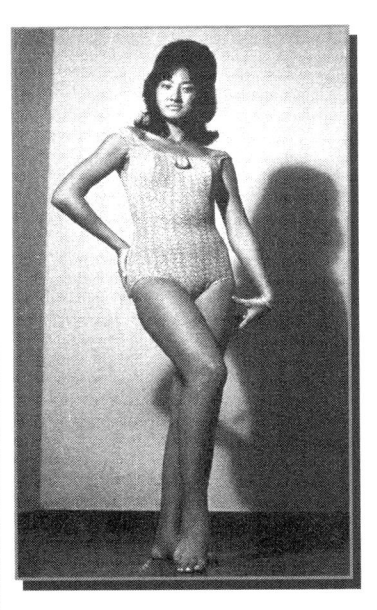

"Calendar Girl" Carol

122

Life in Jamaica: Petersfield, Westmoreland 1960-61

Carol horse-back riding

L-R: Ronald, Guide, Elaine, Carol, Dick, Melvin

Here, the river slowed down enough for us to walk out onto the grassy bank to safety. It was dangerous fun – but, again, we watched out for each other and also for our friends, whom we sometimes took with us to share this experience at one of the hidden beauty spots in our parish of Westmoreland.

My younger siblings Dick and Elaine shared my love of horseback riding at Circle V Ranch. The ranch was owned by our insurance agent, Bobby Charlton in Red Hills, Kingston. Later on, we would travel closer to Montego Bay and towards Rose Hall estates where we could ride our horses along the coastline.

Our visits to Montego Bay also included a day pass to enjoy the facilities at Bay Roc Hotel and hanging out at the Montego Bay International Airport. There from the waving gallery we would watch the planes descending and taking off. Later, we would devour half of a crispy deep fried chicken served with a huge helping of french fries, which was an American entrée we were not exposed to in our Chinese homes. Still later, we would go to the newly opened Montego Pharmacy to gorge on banana splits or hot fudge sundaes which we had read about in the American comics of Archie, Jughead and friends. Then, we would drive twenty-six miles across the western part of the island to get home, feeling quite satisfied with our Sunday outing with our Chin cousins and friends.

Another Chin cousin, on my father's maternal side, was Foster Chin from Maroon Town who came to stay with us after our Hong Kong brother, Ricky left our home to set up his own

Carol at Bay Roc hotel

Life in Jamaica: Petersfield, Westmoreland 1960-61

Ricky and Diana's wedding, Hong Kong

business in the neighbouring district in Locust Tree. This process of taking in family members until they could set themselves up in business seemed to be the Williams family tradition and key to their progress in Jamaica. Later, once Ricky's business was more established, he returned to Hong Kong to marry Diana Chan and then moved to Old Harbour, away from the parish of Westmoreland.

Our young uncle, Foster, was the son of Papa's mother's younger brother who was slightly older than us. Regardless, as usual, we welcomed him as we had everyone else who had come to live with us. Foster was tall and good looking, but he was quite proper in his speech so we promptly imitated him in a teasing way. He would eventually get his driver's license but not before we had a chance to tease him while he was learning to drive from our local driver, Jackie. We would be sitting in the back seat during his practice drives down a small side street to Carawina under Jackie's direction. One of these times, we made fun of him as we watched him losing control of the steering wheel. His arms flayed like a windmill as he tried to correct his over-steering so we nicknamed him "Windy". Regardless of our teasing, he was a good help to Mama and Papa in the shop and rum bar since our business had become quite prosperous and all hands were needed to help out, especially during the busy sugar-cane or rice harvest time.

In due time, Foster would leave our home which would allow us to get to know his family and learn more about our relatives on Papa's maternal Chin side of the family. We had always maintained close ties to the Williams side of Papa's family – the paternal side of his family. Through Foster we were made aware of the Chin connections. We learned that we were related to grand-uncle L.G. Chin who lived not too far from us in the district of Darliston. He had a son, John and two daughters, Babs and Bobette. Young uncle John married Pat Lym who introduced us to her

The Lym family at Negril

L Crosby & Lillian

Eddie and Sworney's wedding
L-R Chester, Madge, Gilbert, Tyrone, Eddie, Andrew, Sworney, Ronald, Penelope, Melvin
(insets left - Earle (Ah Pin); right - Stanley Chin)

lovely Lym family. Babs married Kenneth Forchin who opened a business in Petersfield some years later – which expanded Petersfield from a one "Chiney Shop" district. Bobette married a handsome East Indian man, Wesley Guyadene, who was one of the children who had lived next door to us when we were living in Savanna-la-Mar years before.

Papa's only other relative on his mother's side was Uncle Chue whom we met later when Papa took us to Heywood Street, Kingston to visit. He had a thriving business selling chicken feed so he was dubbed "Uncle Chicken Feed Man". My brother Dick used to board with the Chue family when he attended Kingston College so he got closer to this family. I recall that prior to that time, Dick and Patrick had also boarded at and attended the only Chinese Public School along with other Chinese youngsters. It was situated on North Street in Kingston They had a great time and made wonderful friends but they did not become in any way proficient in the Hakka Chinese dialect – which had been Papa's original intention when he sent them away in the city to be schooled.

We already knew that the Stanley Chin family living closest to us in Whithorn District, which was only a few miles from Petersfield, were relatives on Papa's maternal side. Uncle Stanley "Foo-On" and Aunt Madge (née Hugh) had eight sons and one daughter, Penelope. The boys were Earle, Ronald, Chester, Edmund, Gilbert, Melvin, Tyrone and Andrew. Through our cousins, we got to meet their relatives on their maternal Hugh family side, like Aunt Madge's siblings: Enid, who was married to Batt Chen; Alvin married to Doris; Cecil, Eric and cousins from Borough Bridge. As well, friends would visit from Kingston like Shirley Chang and Denise, who was the daughter of Aunt Madge's friend, "Miss Dolly" Lee.

Papa and Foo-On were close cousins and got along well together. They would go to play mahjong in Montego Bay together. Mama and Aunt Madge were both first generation Jamaican Chinese and related well with each other mainly because they were of different personalities. Mama was more outgoing and Aunt Madge more quiet and conservative. As a result, we children of both families got together very often and shared many happy times visiting each other's homes.

My siblings would agree that this was truly a happy period of our lives when we were able to grow up with family members living so close to us and not spread out all over the world. At this time, we were not too concerned about Mama's illness and absence from home. Although we missed her, we were not worried about her since she was with Papa's family members in Hong Kong but we looked forward to her getting better and returning home.

Your loving Ah-Poh

L-R: Carol, Uncle Joe, Audrey, Washy at Negril

Life in Jamaica: Petersfield, Westmoreland 1962

My dear Grandchildren

My younger siblings and I made a lot of wonderful memories at various beaches. Learning to swim, going snorkelling and crab-hunting were among some of the fun activities which cemented our bond as siblings. During this time, however, I believe that I was really looked up to by my younger siblings as a mother figure because when they went away to high school, I was very much their guardian in Mama's absence. It was quite funny when Dick asked his friend, Ken Lue Phang to write me while he was attending Kingston College to request long pants instead of short pants.

Dick at Hope Gardens in long pants

Ken was actually attending St. George's College located in front of the Classic Restaurant where Dick was one of the boarders along with Johnny and the Chin Lyn brothers, Astor and Colville. Ken was also much older than Dick but he seized the opportunity to correspond with me and befriended my younger siblings in order for him to visit me in Petersfield during his summer holidays. On one occasion, Ken had planned to take my siblings to the movies in Savanna-la-Mar with the hope that I would go along with him. I had already planned to go with someone else and after I left, Ken was so enraged, he drove off dangerously and recklessly with my dear frightened younger siblings in the car. Patrick got quite angry with Ken and was the only one brave enough to quarrel with him – while the rest of the children were just hanging on for dear life! After that incident, Ken was no longer a favourite visitor of my siblings and eventually he gave up trying to date me.

I had to keep track of Elaine's activities at Alpha Academy, which was also located in Kingston, because she would somehow invite herself to other students' homes for the holidays without asking our permission.

Elaine in her graduation gown at St. Mary's Academy

Life in Jamaica: Petersfield, Westmoreland 1962

One time, Keith had to drive mid-island to get her in Christiana from the Chin household where she was, of course, enjoying the company of girls older than herself. After some time boarding at Alpha Academy and making life miserable for the nuns, Elaine got ill and had to return home so she finished her high school days at St. Mary's Academy in Savanna-la-Mar. Keith would take her and pick her up daily from school so she was under stricter supervision.

Patrick would ride his bicycle to and from Mannings High School which was located in Savanna-la-Mar, six miles away from Petersfield. He did not give much trouble once his bicycle was in good working order. Donny was quite happy in Auntie Girlie's care. We found him entertaining, especially when he used to perform exotic dancing shows for us. He was also fond of chasing the girls to kiss them and all the older girls found him very cute. In later years, he became a good scholar at Cornwall College and was like a mad scientist making small chemical explosions while doing experiments at home. Since he was a boarder, I only had to arrange his transportation to and from Montego Bay. When your grandfather, Ah-Goong Eddie would visit me, he would offer to take Donny back to boarding school and took delight in watching Donny devour a quart of Northshore Ice Cream before entering the gates of Cornwall College.

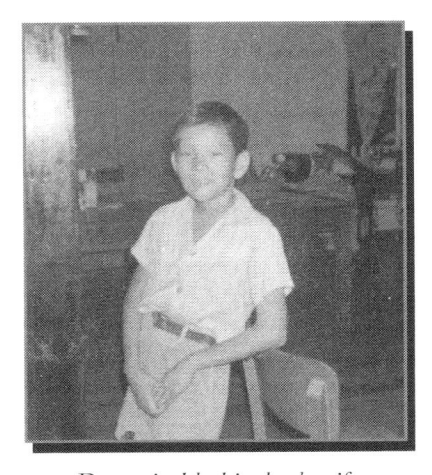

Donny in khaki school uniform

All this time taking care of my younger siblings, Patrick, Dick, Elaine and Donny, must have prepared me for motherhood and wanting to care for others. However, over the years, even as grown-up men and woman, my siblings still looked towards me as more than an elder sister and more like a surrogate mother. This attitude was in accordance with the Hakka Chinese cultural system that my father had instilled in them. I pride myself that I have brought them up right and that they were ready to take over the family business when Keith and I left Petersfield. This would seem like the trend which would follow me over my life – my doing a good job to the best of my ability, then moving on for others to follow a fine example and making me proud of this achievement, especially when further improved upon. I was mighty proud when they followed our example in making the family business prosper and continued serving the community even when other businesses started moving into the district. Patrick, Dick, Elaine and Donny would indeed get as good a grounding for their future life just as I got growing up in our parents' business.

For the community, they continued to help our illiterate customers to write and read letters for them and sign postal notices for their registered mail. My now grown-up siblings also continued to provide electricity for political meetings and local campaigns. Before electricity came to the district, from our verandah, we would witness numerous religious meetings like the Pocomania, the Salvation Army and other fundamentalist meetings. They used kerosene metal "Kitchen bitches" and glass lamps before graduating to Tilley gas lamps. Once we got electricity, my parents freely let them drop an electrical extension cord from our verandah to provide electricity to the sound system of both political parties. As a result, over the years, all of us have listened to the Most Honourable Alexander Bustamante and the most Honourable Norman Manley, his son, Hon. Michael Manley and the Hon. Edward Seaga among other government leaders at the microphone making political speeches and promises. After listening to the political propaganda made by these politicians, we learned that it was best to respond like Papa used to do. When questioned, Papa, without hesitation, declared that he was a "Comrade-Labourite", covering himself without bias as a supporter of both the Jamaica Labour Pary and the People's National Party.

Patrick was based in the grocery shop, Dick's forte was in the hardware section, and Elaine was in the dry goods section of the store – but all were able to relieve each other at all times. They continued to take weekly cash deposits to the Bank of Nova Scotia and Barclays Bank in Savanna-la-Mar. Only Elaine took longer than necessary on these trips to the bank. I learned that she would make personal stops along the six mile journey by car. Later, I found out that on a few occasions, Elaine would stop by the home of our family friends, the Forrests, hide the money bag under one of their beds, and then promptly have a nap – leaving a very nervous Mrs. Forrest to watch over the proceeds of the family business. At this time, Mr. and Mrs. Forrest's elder daughter, Marianne was already married to Harry Norton and lived at the Norton's family farm. The younger daughter, Virginia, who would serve as one of my bridesmaids, had also married Peter Chong. They were then living in Savanna-la-Mar.

To their credit, I believe my younger siblings probably bought fewer records and books during this weekly banking duty than Keith and I used to buy when it was our turn to take the money to the bank. As teenagers, we were more into American popular music – all forms of swing, bee-bop, rhythm & blues and soul music we had heard on the American Bandstand and Motown on WINZ radio station in Florida, USA. Keith and I left behind a huge collection of 33 1/3rpm long playing, 78 rpm, medium size and smaller 45 rpm vinyl records when we left home, which now seems like a waste of money but in those days, we were crazy teenagers without a budget restriction. Patrick, Dick and Elaine were more into the Jamaican music. Radio Jamaica Rediffusion (RJR) was becoming more established and the Jamaican music scene began to change.

Actually, World War II had changed everything. The British Empire was already crumbling before the war and broke up even faster in the post-war period. Under pressure from the colonies, like Jamaica, Britain began to grant independence to countries within its commonwealth. In 1962, Jamaica received its independence and became self-governing while still remaining a member of the British Commonwealth. Jamaican music began to reflect these political changes. A new music and dance called the "Ska" emerged which expressed the aspirations of the newly liberated masses. The next sensational rhythm to emerge was the "Rock Steady" which would be very popular amongst the Jamaican diaspora. My Jamaican circle in Montréal during the late 1960s was introduced to the Rock Steady music and dance moves by a cheerful friend and visitor, Beverly Wong, whom I nicknamed Miss Rock Steady for years to come.

The Seventies saw the birth of "Reggae" music which was performed by a whole slew of musicians, artists as well as record producers including Bunny Lee, Leslie Kong, Lee Perry and Duke Reid and Clancy Eccles, to name a few. It is said that Clancy Eccles claimed to name this new beat as "Reggae" from the Jamaican slang for a female street walker, "Streggae". Numerous singers like Jimmy Cliff and Toots & the Maytals began to emerge in the Jamaican music scene, including a young Robert (Bob) Nesta Marley. He was undisputedly an extraordinarily gifted and conscious artist who was blessed with the talent of translating the anguish of the Jamaican ghetto into universally meaningful music and lyrics. For many people all over the world, Bob Marley has come to represent Jamaican music. Over the following years, numerous dance crazes came out of the ghetto like "Dance Hall" and "Ragga-ragga". Society orchestra bands like Whylie Lopez performed successfully as did Byron Lee and the Dragonaires who were moving more towards performing the Trinidadian calypsos and music with a soca beat.

Mama in the new kitchen

Mama returned to Jamaica to find many changes to more than the music scene in our home. We now had a television station – JBC (Jamaica Broadcasting Station) – which could be viewed in black and white for a few hours each day. She was pleased that the old outside kitchen was demolished and an extension had been built at the back of the house. This elongated addition stretched the whole width of the store and had an open recreation room which opened into a modern kitchen and a washroom. The recreation room had a sitting area with a television set and a table tennis table. The kitchen was furnished with cupboards above and below two walls of counter space. We had purchased modern appliances including a gas stove and oven and a sink with running hot and cold water. Keith and I decided to have a long dining table covered with our choice of a black and gold speckled laminated sheeting. A new refrigerator was installed in one corner of the recreation room. The washroom was completely tiled with a deep bath enclosure and modern toilet facilities – a true upgrade from our pit toilets and outdoor wood fires. The maid's room and outdoor washroom were also demolished to leave an open patio for Patrick's open-air work-out gym that he was using in an attempt to meet his body building goals like Mr. Universe, Steve Reeves. However, the old concrete bath was left intact – it would become a fish tank.

I recall seeing Mama again when she arrived from the airport. She was looking so glamorous and trendy. It was as if she had only been away on holidays. I was confident she would not regret coming back home to our old-fashioned way of living.

Life in Jamaica: Petersfield, Westmoreland 1962

Montego Bay, Jamaica
Standing L-R: Jean, David, Eddie, James. Sitting L-R: Aunt Amy, Vincent, Gloria, April (Pat)

While Mama was away, Papa had started to play mahjong with a Chinese group in Montego Bay on Sundays so now, she seized this opportunity to go with him to visit this tourist town and her eldest sister, Amy. In her absence, Aunt Amy and Uncle Isaac Williams had retired and closed their business in Savanna-la-Mar. They moved to a sprawling house with a nice view on High Level Road in Montego Bay. This was

Ontario, Canada
Front: Anthony holding Estelle, Gloria, James
Back L-R: Vincent, Greg, April (Pat), Jean

131

also the town where their daughter, Gloria, had moved to once she married Vincent Chin. Their son, Noel and wife, Grace (née Wong) moved to Kingston with their children, Clinton, Dorothy and Winston, leaving their eldest son, Eddie with his retired grandparents.

Gloria was our eldest cousin so out of respect, we called her "Aunt G". She and her husband, Vincent owned and operated a bakery, Midway Bakery, on St. James Street. They had a son, Vincent Jr. and two daughters, Jean and April, whom most called "Pat". Uncle Vincent was a very fun-loving and outgoing person who mingled with American movie stars, Cornel Wilde and other tourists visiting Jamaica. We were so saddened when he passed away from a ruptured appendix and Gloria was left to carry on the business with Vincent's brothers, James and David. Gloria later married James and had two more sons, Anthony and Gregory. When the family migrated to Toronto, Canada, all three sons studied medicine and became medical doctors which made their parents and family mighty proud. Mama got along much better with her niece, Aunt G than with her older sister, Amy so we visited Midway Bakery very often, especially when Keith boarded there before he got into the boarding school at Cornwall College.

When I was growing up, it was as if our home had an open door and every bed had to be filled, so it was no wonder that after I left Jamaica, when Elaine met a half-German girl, Barbara at the home of our Williams cousin, Clive and wife, Jasmine, Elaine promptly invited her to come and stay at our home. Of course, Mama and Papa would not disapprove. Barbara would be great company for Elaine and she would write to me about this, plus a news-breaking item which was reported in the local *Gleaner* newspaper.

Years later, I would meet Barbara and she would relate the incident as follows: After Keith and I left home, Patrick, Dick and Elaine followed in the footsteps of their older siblings and would drive to various parties. One Saturday evening, they had driven to Mandeville for one of their usual parties after the store was closed. Barbara decided to stay home with Mama and Papa. She slept in the adjoining bedroom and felt very safe with them. Dick had become the responsible keeper of the family firearm, but since Patrick, Dick and Elaine had decided to go out for such a long period of time, Papa decided to take the revolver from Dick's room and keep it in his room for their safety.

MAN SHOT DEAD

SAVANNA-LA-MAR, Wd., J. 19 (From our correspondent. Ezekiel Davis, 25, truck sideman of Petersfield, was fatally shot by Nathan Williams, businessman, at Petersfield at 2 a.m. today.

According to the police, Williams heard strange sounds in one of his sons' room. He armed himself with a .38 pistol and went to the room to investigate.

A man pounced on him as he entered the room and he fired three shots. Three men then jumped from the room through a window.

At about 5 a.m. the dead body of Davis was found lying at the rear of the premises. He had on three shirts and a pair of gloves.

As a result of police investigations carried out by Detective Sgt. Ira Williamson of Savanna-la-Mar CID, the following persons have been arrested and charged with burglary with intent:

George Wallace, 22, labourer of Savanna-la-Mar; O. C. Baboo, 22, labourer, and Chester Clarke, 18, labourer of River Head. The men are now in custody at Savanna-la-Mar police lock-up and will appear before His Hon. Mr. H. Boyd Carey, acting R.M. for Westmoreland, on Tuesday, June 21.

During the night, he woke up to hear rustling sounds in the boys' room across the hall so he got the loaded revolver and went to investigate. He came upon four local boys searching Dick's room. They were as frightened as Papa was! Apparently, they had overheard in the grocery shop that my siblings were going to a party as far away as Mandeville so they decided to climb up the drain pipe leading to the upstairs of the building to see what they could take from our house. A startled Papa fired his revolver three times and the boys scattered down the inside stairs to let themselves out of the building. Barbara, Mama and Papa thought that the three shots fired had scared the thieves away and promptly went back to sleep. Early the next morning, however, the party-goers returned home to find one of the thieves, known to them as Ezekiel "Whole-a-fowl", dead in the doorway downstairs. A huge crowd quickly gathered and there was much commotion around the body in our backyard until the police arrived on the scene. Upon investigation, Papa was not charged and the autopsy showed that one of the shots Papa fired in fright, shot Ezekiel straight through the heart. He must have run downstairs on sheer adrenalin only to collapse outside the doorway. His two accomplices escaped unhurt but were caught by the police. Papa was a hero and a sharp-shooter making the news. And Barbara would not forget her stay at Petersfield!

With this exciting news of good triumphant over evil coming from Petersfield, I close with love,

Your loving Ah-Poh

Movie idol James Dean's pose at Bluefields Beach by...

...Donny

...Keith

...Patrick

Life in Jamaica: Petersfield, Westmoreland 1962

Front L-R: Dick, Peter
Back L-R: Robert (Gen Sang), Carol, Frank (Bim), Donny

Left: Madge, Ricky, Carol, with Donny stooping

Below: Carol and Tyrone

Life in Jamaica:
Petersfield, Westmoreland
1963 - 1964

My dear Grandchildren,

At this time in our lives, it seemed that all the hard work of making a living and of sacrifices made by our parents in order to educate us, the younger generation, was paying off. Most of our friends had graduated or were graduating from high school and were either thinking of, or actually making, plans to continue their studies abroad in places like the United States, Canada or England.

In 1959, four of my male friends, Eddie, Washy, Oscar and Percival, were preparing to study in Montréal, Québec, Canada. The farewell parties were planned, and they had all promised to correspond with me while they were away, when, suddenly, there was a hitch in the plans. Eddie, who was planning to enter the Civil Engineering program at McGill, discovered that his birth certificate was inaccurate. As was a common practice at that time, when Eddie was born, his father, Kelly Wong, asked the midwife who had delivered him to register his birth at the Registrar of Births and Deaths office. He specified that Eddie was to be named Edward Harrison – Edward after the ruling King of England and Harrison after the Reverend Harrison of the Anglican Church Diocese in Montego Bay. Acting on her own secret agenda, however, Nurse Gordon apparently decided to honour herself and registered Eddie's name as Edward Gordon Wong instead. No one knew what she had done, so Eddie had always referred to himself as Edward Harrison Wong and had used that name throughout all his schooling and ultimately on his applications to McGill. Only when Eddie applied for his birth certificate so that he could complete his passport application was Nurse Gordon's action uncovered. This meant that, while the other boys went off to Montréal, Eddie was stuck in Jamaica sorting out the legal issue pertaining to his inaccurate birth certificate. Basically, he needed to get an affidavit stipulating that the "Edward Harrison Wong" indicated on the McGill University application was the same person as "Edward Gordon Wong", as listed on his birth certificate before his application for a passport could proceed.

While waiting for all the legal work and documents to be completed, Eddie had the time to visit me in Petersfield without the other boys around and I got to know him better – although this also meant that I would have my siblings to tow along on our dates. Papa did not take it kindly when Eddie would hasten the closing of the store so that we could drive the six miles to Savanna-la-Mar in time for a movie or dance date. One Saturday evening, we attended a Kes Chin dance at the Town Hall and ended up at Bluefields beach in the wee hours of the night to chill out after many hours of

Life in Jamaica: Petersfield, Westmoreland 1963-64

Carol and Eddie sitting at beach after Kes Chin and the Souvenirs dance

dancing. Actually, we were privileged to have Kes Chin and his band the Souvenirs travel all the way from the opposite end of the island to entertain us Westmorelites so we made the most of it. Little did we dream that Kes Chin's musical talent would be passed down to his grand-niece, Tessanne Chin who has become a famous world class singer after winning the popular talent televison show, "The Voice", in the USA.

I had liked Eddie in the same way that I liked many of the other boys that I hung around with. I was just having fun and kidding around with these boys and had no intention of finding a special boyfriend at this time in my life. One night after a party in Montego Bay, a group of us was trying to decide what to do. The group of us considered it much too early to go home, and in the case of Keith and me, it was much too far to drive home; so the boys came up with another plan. We would all drive along the deserted road up to the Rose Hall Great House. I suppose the boys thought this would scare us girls. Local folklore has it that during slavery days, there lived a White slave mistress at Rose Hall Estate, a sugar-cane plantation, who, it was claimed, murdered her husbands one after the other. It was said that the ghost of the wicked "White Witch of Rosehall" was still roaming the property. As it turned out, we girls were not scared and did not lunge into the arms of the boys for safety (as they had hoped we would), so we sought other ways to create some excitement.

We decided that we would drive along the coastline towards another town named Falmouth. In Falmouth there were many make-shift stands of wood that were used to display collections of sea shells, star fish and conch shells in the hopes of selling them to passing foreign tourists during the daytime. These stands were located near to the homes of the owners. We decided that we would steal some of these shells from these stands. In those days, of course, there were no streetlights, so it was very dark. As we snuck up to the stand, invariably the dogs belonging to the household would start barking at us trespassers. This would waken the owners of the stand who would come running out of their darkened houses to shout at us as we drove off as quickly as we could. This made us laugh hysterically in the safety of the car. It was just a bit of harmless fun in the safe environment that Jamaica was in those days.

After Eddie started attending McGill University in Montréal, Québec, Canada, he would return home for holidays and would continue to visit without the other boys with whom we used to hang around so my parents got to know him better as well. He was shy and awkward without the other friends. In fact, my father thought he was not

Carol and Eddie walking on the beach at Bluefields

very polite since, as polite Chinese boys were supposed to do, he was often too shy to pay his respect to his Chinese elders by greeting them upon his arrival in the household. At least he had the good sense to keep his distance from me in my parents' presence – but the time he spent kidding around with my brothers made my father mutter, "Him so foolie-foolie" (meaning "He behaves foolishly"). In the summer of 1963, Eddie had a job working at the Kaiser Bauxite Company in Mandeville and would often visit and overnight with our family en route to his work because Petersfield was on the way to Mandeville. Although at that time, I was still unwilling to commit to an exclusive relationship with Eddie – I was still, with Eddie's awareness, corresponding with other boys – our friendship continued to grow.

In the meantime, I was having a spate of local courtiers. One was Simon who used to bring me gifts which I promptly threw away over the back verandah. Sometimes he would bring me boxes of chocolates and Chinese dried plums (*Chan Pei Mui*) which met the same fate. Undaunted, Elaine would scurry over the wooden verandah railings to pick them up from the zinc sheet roofing and thoroughly enjoyed them with her brothers. There were some silly love-struck boys who would send me 45 rpm vinyl records of Neil Sedaka's hit song, *Oh, Carol* through the mail. I did not have to break these to destroy them because in those days, the mail had to be manually stamped with a heavy metal stamping tool and the records arrived already broken.

I noticed that Papa was not fond of non-Chinese or even half-Chinese boys visiting me, which would bring his earlier words of warning back to me: "duck-a-duck and fowl-a-fowl". Some of my young male relatives would come visiting and sometimes get romantic but I could also tell that this relationship would be a no-no from my father. There was no need to see Papa's disapproving looks; I could just visualize his furrowed brow if he knew about their attentions! Anyway, I myself was not quite ready for any serious one-on-one dating and loved to be having fun in a group without any romantic attachments. I would say that I was spreading joy and sharing the wealth of myself; and later in life this would become my grown-up philosophy.

As our families became more affluent after their years of hard labour behind the shop counter, we were able to start really appreciating the beauty of our island. My cousin, Ronald went to work in Kingston and boarded with Mrs. Lim who we knew as the mother of our teenage friend, Rose. Mrs. Lim was a pleasant and hard-working lady who would become my friend for many years to come when we both migrated to

Life in Jamaica: Petersfield, Westmoreland 1963-64

Carol with Yvonne and Ronald at Fort Charles, Port Royal

Canada. She had one son, "Sonny" and four daughters, Linette, Faye, Rose and Violet and we would remain friends as well. While staying with Mrs. Lim, I met their neighbour, Dennis Yapp and family. They were also hospitable and friendly and I became friends with daughter, Yvonne and one of the sons, Gregory without imagining that years later, we would be playing on the same badminton team and still later, playing tennis together in Canada.

During one of Eddie's summer holiday visits from university, we went to Kingston and Yvonne and Ronald went with us to go sightseeing in Port Royal where we learned all about the days of English Admiral Horatio Nelson and Captain Henry Morgan, our most famous swashbuckling buccaneer. Eddie would also go with me to Copacabana Beach with Anthony and his friend. Perhaps one of the reasons why I started liking Eddie more than the other boys was that he did not disrupt my socializing with others and just fitted into my social life until it was time to head back to McGill University, Montréal. It was after this summer, that I started to play the record *Eddie, My Love* sung by the American group, The Cordettes, more frequently than the other records in our vast record collection in Petersfield.

Going to Kingston on one occasion to visit Ronald and his brother, Edmund, we drove to Portland and went rafting on the Rio Grande in Port Antonio. It was such a relaxing ride and the local rafting punters knew every inch of the river winding its way to the sea, so with their guidance, we got the chance to swim alongside the rafts as well. I was always wanting to see Navy Island, the island owned by the movie stars, Errol Flynn and Patrice Wymore, and I had read all about the exclusive Frenchman's Cove for the

Rio Grande rafting with cousin Ronald Chin

rich and famous so this was the time to go sightseeing after our rafting experience. Another tourist site we visited was Folly House which, according to legend, is 'the remains of a huge great house foolishly built using sea water in the cement which caused it to disintegrate'. Another version is more likely: that local people raided the house after it was abandoned and took away anything that was not nailed down, including the second floor columns supporting the roof, so it collapsed!

In 1964, New York City was hosting the World's Fair. Eddie and I were getting much more serious by then but he had decided not to return home that summer. When he heard that I was planning to travel to New York with my friend, Faye Yee, to go to the World's Fair, he figured he would meet me there. Faye was going steady with Eddie's roommate, Winston Chin Fatt, who was returning to McGill University after visiting his family in Alley District, Clarendon, Jamaica. We planned for Eddie to take the Greyhound bus from Montréal to New York and join us there. Afterwards, we would all travel up north together so that Faye and I could see what Montréal was like.

Faye and Winston said that they would be staying with friends in an apartment in Manhattan and invited me to stay with them. I agreed, but little did I know that this was a tiny studio apartment – it only had a double bed and a kitchenette – and was rented by three single boys Patrick Lee, Alfred "Freddo" Kong and Bobby Lue who was studying aeronautics. The apartment building was old and the intercom system was not working, so when Eddie arrived, he kept buzzing and buzzing the apartment number without any response from us. Eventually, he found himself waiting out in the street until another tenant let him in. Understandably, as he had traveled overnight on a Greyhound bus from Montréal to New York, he was quite put out by this delay!

New York World's Fair globe

Life in Jamaica: Petersfield, Westmoreland 1963-64

Bobby, Carol and Freddo strolling around Central Park, New York

Freddo, Carol and Patrick Lee resting in Central Park, New York

That night five adults slept across the double bed and two more of us slept in old armchairs. The next morning, we all headed to the World's Fair. When we arrived at the subway, however, Patrick discovered that he had left his sweater back in the apartment. Eddie offered to go back with him to get it and rejoin the rest of us at the gates to the Fair. For some reason or another, the group decided to attend different events and Eddie and I got separated; however, we planned to meet at a specified time and location. Due to the huge crowds and long line-ups, I arrived at our agreed upon location very late. Once again, Eddie was fuming – he had been stuck all day with Patrick and not with the girlfriend whom he had travelled all that way to be with!

The following day, Winston, Faye, Eddie and I flew to Montréal and stayed in Winston and Eddie's more spacious three-bedroom apartment. After our experience in New York, their apartment seemed perfectly luxurious! Oscar Chin, the third roommate, occupied one bedroom, Eddie was in another, and it was decided that we two girls would take over Winston's larger bedroom. Winston would sleep on the sofa in the living room. Somehow, by the end of the visit, Faye and I found ourselves sleeping in our respective boyfriends' bedrooms! The address of this apartment was 3515 University Avenue, across the street from McGill University campus and many years later, these four digits still served as our secret codes, perhaps as a reminder of our illicit tryst.

Carol on cruise around Manhattan Island, N.Y.

Life in Jamaica: Petersfield, Westmoreland 1963-64

Enjoying the brilliant fall colours in Rawdon, Québec

Montréal was an interesting city to me. With its cosmopolitan mix of French and English and old buildings, the city had a very European atmosphere. No one seemed to make a distinction whether you spoke French or English, but I did notice that French speakers and English speakers lived in different sections of the city. I found the mixture of old Colonial buildings in Vieille Ville and the modern cross-shaped building in Place Ville Marie was part of what gave the city its charm. I also enjoyed hiking up Mount Royal for the view that it allowed of the city, Beaver Hall Hill, and the surrounding park. Another Jamaican engineering student, Winston and his wife, Althea took us for a long drive up north to see the Fall colours in a small French town outside of the city called Rawdon.

I loved the changing colours of the maple leaves and was fascinated by this transformation. I liked this place, Québec, "La Belle Province" very much; and it would become even more special to me when, one night on bended knee, Eddie proposed. I realised that marriage to Eddie would mean leaving Jamaica and I did wonder if I was ready to leave the carefree life I enjoyed in Jamaica – running my father's business and enjoying an easy lifestyle, complete with servants and yard boys at my beck and call, not to mention being surrounded by people who loved, respected and supported our family – all this to get married. But I could also not imagine a future without Eddie, so I accepted. Eddie gave me a beautiful white gold diamond engagement ring that he had purchased at Birks Jewelry Company but I told him that I would not wear the ring until he returned to Jamaica to ask my father for my hand in marriage and to receive his blessing. He agreed and planned to do so in a few months during the Christmas holidays.

By this time, Faye had already returned to her job at Kaiser Bauxite Company in Mandeville, Jamaica. Since I was a self-employed businesswoman with money at my disposal, I decided to spend a few more weeks in New York again before returning home. I was not looking forward to returning to Jamaica and trying to keep my engagement a secret! Eddie had begun studies for his Master's degree that Fall, so he was happy to have me leave so he could buckle down to serious studying!

I decided that I could not stay in the dingy Manhattan apartment again, and went to stay with my friend, Beryl and her roommates, Madge and Sakina. Beryl's apartment was near to Columbia University, which she was attending. However, I had a great time sightseeing with Bobby, the aeronautics student and cruising around Manhattan Island; shopping at Saks Fifth Avenue with Beryl, where we bought daring black fish-net trimmed swimsuits; walking around central park with Patrick and Freddo; skating for the first time at Rockefeller Centre, and attending church services at Episcopalian, United and Presbyterian churches. I also went to Radio City Music Hall, stage shows and movie theatres, all by myself when the others were either at school or at work. The trip was worth having to send Beryl money postal orders to cover my expenses when I returned to Jamaica. I loved the Big Apple as well as La Belle Province!

When I returned to Jamaica, I went back to working diligently for long hours in the store, but once again, life was not all about work. Before my cousin Ronald went to work in Kingston, the two of us decided that we would use materials from my hardware department and the labour of his local boys from Whithorn to build a concrete badminton court on Papa's property in Petersfield. The court would be built under the June plum tree in our backyard between the Venus Theatre and Dick's concrete crab pen. Once the court was created, it attracted all our Chinese friends and

Crab feast in Petersfield

Clockwise L-R: Patrick, Dick, Mama, Elaine, Shirley, Steve, Arthur, Olive, Keith

relatives from the surrounding districts. We organized badminton matches against the Montego Bay Chinese Club – even though most participants were more interested in the food, including local land crabs, that was provided than the actual badminton game! We always had great mounds of fresh seasonal fruit, especially June plums, and a whole variety of mangoes. We would also have huge crab feasts for the family. After the stores and shops were closed – and especially after a heavy rainfall when the crabs were sure to be out of their holes at night -- we would all pile in the Chin's bread van, armed with machetes, crocus bags and kerosene torches to go on crab-catching outings to Negril to replenish Dick's crab pen.

Of course that was not the only time we went to the beach in Negril. We would often go in the daytime on Sundays with other families or friends, bringing our pots of rice and peas, fricassee chicken, and other food. It was so much fun to hack our way through the undergrowth from the unpaved road to reach the pristine white sand and blue sea. Negril beach hugged the coast for miles – it stretched as far as the eye could see. Such natural beauty! At one point, my father was offered land at Negril as an investment, but because the price was £1 per acre, my father turned down the offer. He had six children to take care of and was too timid to take a chance with his hard earned money on what seemed like such a risky investment. No one could have envisioned the massive tourist development about to take place in Negril!

A wealthy American, Mr. Beymiller, proposed building "The Negrillion Hotel" and offering "Underwater Sea Expeditions" to kick start the tourist industry in the area. As part of this project, two scuba diving instructors, Joe Strykowski from Chicago and Ralph Speas from Fort Myers, Florida, arrived to scout out the best location for the hotel.

When we learned they were in the area, without any hesitation, a group of us, Ronald, Dick, Patrick, Elaine, Robert (Gen Sang) Chin and myself, started taking scuba diving lessons from them. We would go for frequent scuba diving expeditions around the Negril area and very soon we were able to dive 65 feet below surface to investigate the ship wrecks below the lighthouse point. Patrick was content to snorkel above and had the lung capacity to dive deeply without using scuba-diving gear. Joe and Ralph also taught us to respect the underwater sea life and the coral reefs. Keith did not accompany us on these outings. He was more interested in snorkeling and spear fishing with other Williams' cousins and his friend, Eugene. Ralph became a particularly good friend who introduced us to so many new things: fondue parties, underwater cameras, trips to Montego Bay beach hotels, water skiing, etc. We even drove all the way out to St. Ann's Bay to watch him being filmed as an extra in the movie *High Wind in Jamaica* starring Anthony Quinn!

Mr. Beymiller's development did not materialize, so Joe and Ralph left Jamaica. Joe went back to the States leaving illegitimate kids in Negril and I never heard from him again, but Ralph and I stayed in touch. Ralph would lead an eventful life over the years. When he left Jamaica, Ralph returned to Fort Myers, began teaching at a Black college, got married and had two daughters and a son, Kevin. Ralph's determination to help Black students by teaching at that particular college attracted the attention of White racists who threatened his family. The stress was too much for Ralph's

Caucasian wife and she eventually left him taking the children with her. Ralph stubbornly refused to give up his post. Eventually he married again, this time to an ambitious and bright Black student named, Betty. Unfortunately, this marriage did not work out either. After Betty obtained her PhD degree and started lecturing all over the United States and even Toronto, where I met her for the first time, she decided to divorce Ralph.

Eventually, Ralph moved to Greensboro, North Carolina where he became a sex therapist and focused on developing the Blues Society in Greensboro. Years later, Eddie and I were driving back to Toronto from Florida and decided to stop in Greensboro to visit Ralph and Betty. It was only then that we learned that not only had Ralph and Betty divorced, but Betty had died in a plane crash en route to one of her speaking engagements. Kevin had come to live with him in the house so that he could help with the household chores, but Kevin had not been well and later passed away also. In this time of great loss, however, a blessing entered Ralph's life. Unknown to Ralph, while he was in high school, he had impregnated a girl who left town and had a baby daughter. Now that daughter, Rebecca, had used the internet to find him. She brought so much joy to him in this difficult period of his life. Not only had he lost so many people important to him, he had, by then become so debilitated by his rheumatoid arthritis and other ailments. Regardless, he still keeps busy doing part-time car-jockeying and being involved with the Blues Society. He remains cheerful and witty. Whenever I ask him how he is, he replies "I am vertical" with the usual smile and glint in his grey-blue eyes.

My dear Grandchildren, it is people like Ralph who have taught me to always look on the positive side of things and be grateful for small mercies and God's blessings as we cope with what life has thrown our way and the path created by our destiny.

Your loving Ah-Poh

Scuba divers L-R: Carol, Robert, Joe, Patrick, Chester, Dick

Life in Jamaica: Petersfield, Westmoreland 1963-64

Ronald and Carol underwater among sea wreck

Patrick snorkeling underwater

Elaine underwater among rocks

Ralph in scuba gear

Life in Jamaica: Petersfield, Westmoreland 1963-64

Ralph (extreme left) on the movie set of the film "High Wind in Jamaica" starring Anthony Quinn

Scuba diving, snorkeling and spear-fishing canoe with coral and conch, manned by local Jamaican fisherman

Life in Jamaica:
Petersfield, Westmoreland
1965

My dear Grandchildren,

True to his word, Eddie came home to Jamaica for the Christmas holidays and asked to speak with my father. I could not help but eavesdrop on the conversation and found it quite amusing. My father was dead serious throughout the conversation and did not exchange any words or pleasantries with Eddie and Eddie was so nervous! Eddie told my father of our intent to marry and live in Montréal while he was completing the requirements for his Masters in Engineering degree. Papa was somewhat ambivalent about our engagement. He was not too thrilled about losing his hard-working business manager, but was pleased that I was stepping into womanhood and making a life for myself. Mama on the other hand, had no such mixed feelings. She was ecstatic! She had always liked Eddie, who took the time to take her to the big Savanna-La-Mar market whenever he visited. Mama had always wanted to travel. She had totally enjoyed living abroad when she had been to Hong Kong despite being there for medical treatment. She had been excited to show us all the photographs of the places and people that she had visited while she was abroad. Now she was delighted that I would be going abroad too and would have the chance to travel as well. Mama must have forgotten that I was just waiting for her to return from her medical treatment in Hong Kong and settle back into her familiar family life so that I could go abroad to study Fashion Designing in New York. Of course, Eddie's proposal and my liking Montréal so much had changed my plans somewhat. I would now have to find a school of Fashion Arts in Québec.

While he was home for the holidays, Eddie and I were invited to spend a week in Kingston with Sakina, one of Beryl's roommates whom I had met while I was in New York. Sakina had returned to Jamaica and was living with her doctor parents, the Parboosinghs in the affluent Jacks Hill area of Kingston. The Parboosinghs were associated with Nuthall Medical Centre and had actually met at medical school in England. Sakina's mother was English and her father East Indian. They were wealthy

Carol and Sakina's friends at Jonkanoo Lounge, Sheraton Hotel, New Kingston

landowners in addition to being doctors. This visit was an introduction to a real upper crust, jet-setting lifestyle! Sakina's family had maid and butler service during meals. Their circle of friends smoked, laughed loudly in public, drove fast cars and hung out in the evenings at Jonkanoo Lounge at the Sheraton Hotel in New Kingston.

Eddie and I did not join this fun-loving group for New Year's Eve, however. Instead we rang in the New Year at the Chinese Athletic Club on Derrymore Road where we had planned to meet up with Faye and Winston, who was also home for the Christmas holidays. We wanted to break the news of our engagement and pending marriage, which we had planned to take place in Montréal. Eddie seemed to be in a rush and wanted to plan our wedding in the Fall, before he resumed his university studies at McGill. Eddie promised my mother to return in the summer so that she could organize our engagement party and we could have a professional photographer to take a complete group family photo before I left the family home. In the meantime, I would start getting my trousseau ready.

When Mama returned from Hong Kong, it took awhile for her to settle back into her family life. She found that, in her absence, her children had grown up and the business had also grown and was doing well, even without her presence. She found it a bit difficult to adjust to return to a rural Jamaican lifestyle and to accept that the household and business could run without her. A huge plus from her time abroad was, however, that she could now speak fluent Hakka and could freely converse with Papa about her experience in Hong Kong, Ah Neung and his village relatives whom she had met, as well as update Papa on all the changes happening in the Orient. Mama had written to Papa while she was away, but, since she could not write Chinese and it was hard for Papa to read the English words crammed together in a folded air-letter, it was easier for them to communicate when she came home.

Mama never spoke about her illness and treatment with us children so when she resumed helping in the store and shop, we assumed that she was well and cured. Later on as adults, we surmised that she was in remission from thyroid cancer, and had not actually been cured. In hindsight, I had noticed that she still had a cough and she would always examine her phlegm hidden in her handkerchief. In any case, neither Papa nor Mama ever said anything that might indicate that she had not been cured. And Mama looked healthy and glamorous as usual, making sure that her hair was permed and her make-up was in place whenever we went out. I was patient, giving Mama some time to readjust to life in Jamaica and I was well aware that, ever since Keith had left home to work, first in Savanna-la-Mar and then in Kingston, Papa was depending on me to keep the business running successfully. My patience eventually paid off. I knew Mama was getting resettled when she went back to trying out new recipes from her weekly English magazines and planting her African violets.

Since I believed that Mama was well and fully readjusted, I felt that I had fulfilled my obligations as an eldest daughter and could now throw my energies into planning my wedding and enjoying my last few months as a single lady. I went into Kingston to look about having my wedding dress custom-made by Mrs. Chung on Milford Road, bought white satin shoes at Nathan's Department Store and ordered a three-tier traditional Jamaican dark rum-soaked wedding cake from Mrs. Chuck at the Deanery Bakery. The cake would be assembled in Montréal, so Mrs. Chuck gave me detailed instructions on how to decorate and assemble the cake. I also designed bridesmaid's dresses to co-ordinate with my wedding gown for my three bridesmaids: Novlet, who used to live with our family, Ouida, my future sister-in-law, and Jeanie, my church-going girlfriend. The girls sent me their dress measurements and I had their dresses made -- bright peach for Novlet as maid-of-honor and jade green for Ouida and Jeanie. I also did not forget to order new linens for my new home.

I had met my bridesmaid Jeanie (her real name is Virginia) when her father, Mr. Gordon Forrest, a tax collector, was transferred from Mandeville to Savanna-La-Mar. Mr. Forrest, his wife Norma and his two daughters, Marianne and Jeanie,

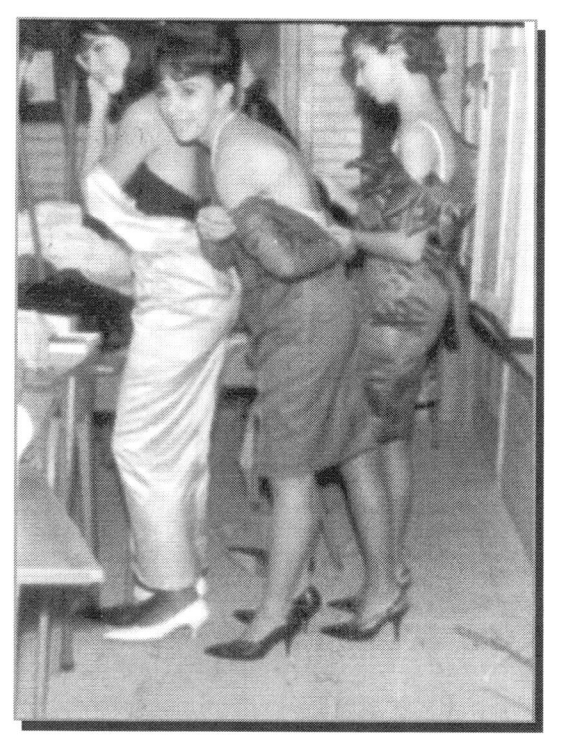

Carol modelling at Mannings with Marianne and Jeanie making a quick change

settled in Petersfield. Their rented house was close to our home and store. This was the beginning of a lifelong friendship between the families. Mr. and Mrs. Forrest became friends and customers of my parents and their two daughters and I also became close. We went to the Savanna-la-Mar Anglican Parish Church together nearly every Sunday morning as well as other church functions and fundraising tea parties. When there were fashion shows at the tea parties, we three girls were usually the models. Our lives have always remained intertwined. Not only was Jeanie a bridesmaid at my wedding, we asked Mr. Forrest to become the Godfather of my second son, I am the Godmother to Marianne's daughter, and Eddie is the Godfather to Jeanie's youngest son!

In addition to preparing for my wedding, I was conscious that this brief period was the opportunity for me to have a last fling of my single, carefree life before I settled down to married life in a foreign country. I took every opportunity to enjoy myself. Papa never verbally objected to my leaving the business on these jaunts, and with Mama back and helping him in the shop, I did not feel guilty about these trips either. On most of my trips into Kingston, I would drive up Spanish Town Road and meet Freddo, one of the single boys I had stayed with in New York, at his dry cleaning establishment. After closing time, he would accompany me into Kingston so that we could see a movie or perhaps go to some type of live performance. I will not forget when he took me to Carib Theatre to attend the performance of the London Philharmonic Orchestra conducted by Sir John Barbirolli. This was a most pleasant evening and I thank Freddo for this overwhelming experience and introducing me to this level of classical music.

On another occasion, I headed to Kingston in the family's red GM Impala sedan for a wedding dress fitting and to have some fun. Instead of driving via Spanish Town Road as I usually did, I decided to drive directly to the Chuck family's establishment, the Deanery Bar and Grill on Deanery Road. God must have been guiding me, because as I drove up to the double zinc gate of Deanery Bar and Grill, I saw that the gates were locked. Suddenly, Mrs. Chuck and the bakery staff rushed out to open the gate while shouting frantically for me to drive inside the premises quickly. As soon as the car and I were safely inside, they hastened to close and lock the gates again. Only then did Mrs. Chuck tell me that a riot against the Chinese had started on Spanish Town Road and all Chinese people had been advised to stay inside until the burning and looting was under control. Apparently there had been a dispute between the Chinese owners of Coronation Bakery and one of their Black employees. The urban masses in Kingston were particularly frustrated by their poverty and lack of opportunities in the 1960s and this disagreement proved to be just the spark needed to allow their frustrations to explode.

In truth, I felt totally safe with Mrs. Chuck. Mrs. Chuck always treated her staff well so they were very loyal to her. We had no fear that they would turn against us during the violence. So, I spent the three days under lockdown with Mrs. Chuck, getting to know her and her family better – her son Freddie, her daughter Faye, her husband Philip and youngest daughter, Eleanor. Eleanor was always known as 'Dimps' because of her prominent dimples and she was my age. She also attended Alpha Academy with some of my cousins. When the anti-Chinese riot was finally quelled, I safely had my wedding gown fitting done and bought a few ready-made dresses before driving back to Westmoreland. I did not feel I had any reason to fear along the journey. The riot appeared to be an isolated incident. It did not spread to the rest of the island – everyone outside of Kingston simply read about it in the *Daily Gleaner* newspaper over the next few weeks. The father of my friend "Freddo", Mr. Alfred Kong Sr., used to travel around the island and would stop in Petersfield frequently on business and I soon realized that he was an educated and cultured man. Mr. Alfred Kong Sr. promptly wrote a letter to the editor of the *Daily Gleaner* about the riots against the Chinese which was published thus:

THE EDITOR, Sir, I am deeply hurt over the recent disturbances with racial feelings. I have been proud as a Jamaican to state that Jamaica is a place with the greatest tolerance and the question of racial difference has never been our trouble.

The recent disturbance is caused through some difference between an employer and an employee. The question of race should not have been involved. Another thing we Jamaicans can be proud of is our law of justice which is one of the best in the world as we follow the British tradition and favour no individual. Whatever differences between the employer and the employee could easily have been settled in full justice in one of our courts. Unfortunately, this incident happened in an area where personal control is not as would have been expected in other areas and thus a small disturbance resulted. However, this disturbance has been well quieted by the police and that should have been all there was to it. It is rumoured that because there has been a disturbance involving two races, some politicians have taken advantage of the situation and incited further disturbances to embarrass our government. If this is true, it is the most dastardly act that can ever be committed against Jamaica as a nation.

Politicians, irrespective of which party they belong to, are supposed to do their best for our country and only for that reason should they seek election and be elected. An act to abuse our national slogan, "OUT OF MANY, ONE PEOPLE" for the sake of promoting a few more votes from irresponsible persons is a sinful crime against our nation and I am sure all well thinking level-headed Jamaicans should agree with me to this effect.

I sincerely hope that the rumour I have heard is not true and that these flare-ups are just spasmodic in which case it should be settled in no time.

I am etc., ALFRED KONG – August 30, 1965

With that incident for the annals of Jamaican history behind us, Eddie came back for the summer holidays and Mama was able to fulfil her wish of hosting a lavish engagement party for us in our extended living and dining area. We were pleased that so many friends and family came from all around the island to celebrate with us. Our friend, Hugh Ken and his girlfriend Winnie, even came all the way from Kingston. Eddie was so overwhelmed by the elaborate party and all of the guests, most of whom he was not familiar with, that he distractedly forgot something important. His mother had sent a lovely slab of roast beef to be served at the party, and he left it outside the

Life in Jamaica: Petersfield, Westmoreland 1965

Engagement Family Photo:
Back L-R: Donny, Shirley, Keith, Dick, Carol, Ricky, Elaine, Patrick
Front: L-R: Papa, Mama

entrance to the house. We did not find it until days later when it was no longer fit to be eaten! Anyway the roast was not missed because there was a lot of food. Even the ice-cream vendor who peddled his treats on our store piazza contributed a whole bucket of home-made and freshly churned ice-cream to be served during the evening as we danced the night away.

The weekend before the party, Papa fulfilled his wish and hosted a separate celebration dinner for his elder relatives, friends and our immediate family. One of the purposes of this party was to also take a group photograph. As Papa must have foreseen, this photo would be the last complete family group photo of our generation with Mama and thanks to Papa, it has become an important record of the Nathan Williams family in Jamaica.

All too soon, Eddie returned to Canada to continue his studies and I began to turn my full attention to packing in preparation for leaving the life that I had grown accustomed to and the land of my birth, for a life of an unknown future in a new foreign country.

Your loving Ah-Poh

The Third Chinese Zodiac Cycle 1965 – 1977

Life in Canada:
Montréal, Québec
1965

My dear Grandchildren

I was entering into my third cycle in the 12-year Chinese Zodiac cycle – those years corresponding with ages 24 - 36 – and it was time to move on to the next stage of my life.

As family members on the waving gallery of Montego Bay airport waved goodbye, I boarded the plane to Montréal, Québec, Canada. My trip would take me through La Guardia Airport, New York, USA before I would finally arrive in Montréal. During the flight, I was my usual friendly self and was quite sociable to the Black Haitian man sitting beside me. I disembarked in New York and began walking through the terminal to make my connecting flight. I arrived at an elevator and waited for the doors to open. The elevator arrived and I stepped inside. Only then did I notice something strange – the Haitian man whom I had been speaking to on the airplane was close behind me. He made a move to follow me into the elevator but two security officers suddenly stepped between us, barring his way onto the elevator before the doors closed. When I got to the Eastern Airlines counter, the manager advised me that airport security personnel had noticed the Haitian man trailing me suspiciously from the moment I had disembarked from the plane and had decided to prevent him from being alone with me in the elevator. I had been totally unaware of any danger! The good Lord was watching over this naive immigrant girl making her way alone to be married in Montréal, Canada! Little did I know that many, many years later, I would return to Jamaica and work for Eastern Airlines at the Montego Bay International Airport. At that time, that same manager who had looked out for me at La Guardia Airport would be transferred to the Montego Bay Branch as supervisor of Eastern Airlines in the entire Caribbean! It was a pleasure to see Mr. Eric Worrell again after that episode.

To continue, after a few hours' wait in the LaGuardia airport terminal, I caught my next flight and arrived safely at Dorval Airport, Montréal. Eddie met me, and I did not mention my escapade en route. We drove downtown and arrived at 3575 University Avenue. Eddie had rented a one-bedroom furnished apartment in a building designated for McGill married students which was across the street from Divinity Hall campus. I unpacked and settled in while Eddie returned to the apartment at 3515 University Avenue which he shared with Oscar and other Jamaican Chinese students. Eddie would stay at 3515 University Avenue until we were married. Then he would join me at 3575 University Avenue to start our married life together.

Life in Canada: Montréal, Québec 1965

Eddie had already taken care of the marriage ceremony details. We were to be married by the Reverend Dr. Knowles at the Divinity Hall Chapel on September 18, 1965; our reception would be held at Bill Wong Chinese Restaurant on Décarie Blvd.; and our honeymoon would be in Niagara Falls, Ontario, the Honeymoon Capital of Canada.

I had brought the three heavy square tins of Jamaican black fruit wedding cake and the bridal and bridesmaids' gowns with me. My chief bridesmaid was Novlet, who had lived with my family for some years before migrating to Montréal as an office worker. The other two bridesmaids were Eddie's sister, Ouida, who was attending McGill as well, and Jeanie Forrest, my girlfriend from my home district, Petersfield, Westmoreland. Eddie's groomsmen were Oscar, the best man, Percival Chen and Clinton Chin. My father was the only member of my family who was able to leave the business for the occasion. He had made the big effort to walk his "favourite daughter" down the aisle. My younger sister has always lamented her inability to attend saying that while I was getting married in Canada, she was chopping salt-fish in Jamaica! Papa planned to visit Hong Kong after the wedding before returning back home to Jamaica. Eddie's parents, Kelly and Catherine, were able to fly up for the wedding as well. His aunts, Lucille and Doris, who were living in Hamilton, Ontario, also attended. Eddie's older brother, Vernon, was a Rhodes Scholar studying at Oxford University, England and was heading for post-doctorate studies at Trieste, Italy so he was not able to stay for the actual wedding day. However, he stayed long enough for us to go to a photo studio and take a group photo, which included Papa and me, of the Wong family.

Pre-wedding Family Photo
Front L-R: Kelly, Ouida, Catherine, Carol, Nathan
Standing L-R: Vernon, Eddie

Life in Canada: Montréal, Québec 1965

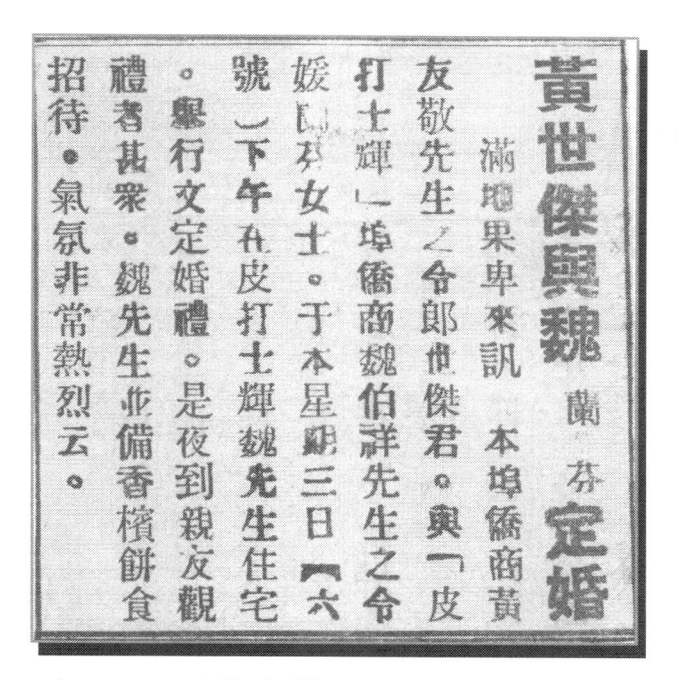

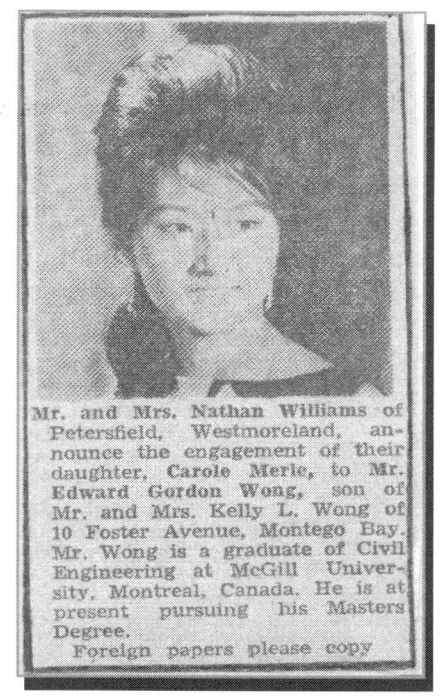

Announcement in Daily Gleaner and Chinese newspaper

Before leaving Jamaica, my cousin, Winifred had hosted a 'ladies only' bridal shower for me at her family home in Smithfield, Westmoreland. Everyone had seen the announcement of my engagement in the *Daily Gleaner* newspaper and knew that I would be getting married in Canada. All the ladies attending the shower were aware of my baggage travel allowance and gave me mostly linen and non-breakable items or gifts that could be easily packed. Monetary gifts were welcome from the patriarch and matriarch of the Williams family, Jackson and Amy Williams, plus all the other uncles and aunts in Westmoreland. The men arrived to join the dinner after the gift opening. In fact, the bridal shower get-together became more like a farewell party than a bridal shower! This was good, however, as I was unsure as to when I would be seeing these Westmorelites again and I felt so happy and appreciative to Winnie for planning this nice gathering.

Now in Montréal, instead of throwing me a bridal shower, Novlet wisely hosted a get-together for me at her apartment which she shared with two Trinidadian girls in the Notre Dame de Grace area. This was an opportunity for me to meet the other Jamaican Chinese in Montréal, some of whom were students while others were already in the work force. Over time, the numbers of this group grew to include people like Wilhel Chen and Arthur Lyew; Yvonne Toyloy, Elorene Chen See, Ina Lowe Ching, Enid and Madge Lyn, Winston Wong and Althea Ho, Roger Chen and Barbara Kong, Rose Chin, Russell and Raynor Chen, Ken Chin, Norman Chin You, Winston Keung Williams and Penny Chung, Frank Bim Williams, Lorna Chung, Mayling Chin, Marcia Hew, Doreen Chong, Connie and Rolston Wong, Daniel and Janet Chin, Audrey Williams and Rennie Chong Kit, James Yap, Calvin and Dorothy Chong, Delores Chin You, Eric Lee, Paulette Chung, and Doreen Chin. I also met other international students who became friends and part of our circle like Myrna,

Life in Canada: Montréal, Québec 1965

Stella and Daphne Young Kong from Guyana; Jim Tong, Koko, Sin Lam and Chee Yee Chong from Malaysia; Wilson Look Kin, Philip and Eddie Young Lai from Trinidad; Francis from Mauritius; Jean Carter and Neville Gibbs from Jamaica; King Li and Dunstan Chen from Hong Kong; and Canadians, Bruce and Malcolm Jue.

Some of the girls felt I should have a bridal shower in Canada as well, so Yvonne and Elorene hosted one in their apartment on 3474 Hutchison Avenue. I was thrilled to get to know them better and they also knew what essential items I needed to set up my very first kitchen. Most of them were invited to the wedding by Eddie so I was meeting them for the first time and they were also curious about me too.

The boys had a stag party for Eddie, but I have never uncovered the details of that evening. Sometimes, I overhear talk of a night club called " Lucky Seven" and French Canadian girls when Eddie is with his friends, but Eddie always insists that they were not talking about the stag party but about something that happened during his freshman year!

My wedding day, Saturday, September 18, 1965 was a sunny and crisp Fall day. Novlet had arranged for me, the bride, and all the bridesmaids to overnight at her apartment so that early in the morning, we could go together to the hairdresser and be dressed in time for fellow-student photographer, Winston, to take our photographs. The corsages and bouquets were delivered on time as arranged. Jim and Papa arrived in a white Cadillac to chauffeur us to Divinity Hall Chapel on University Avenue. The bridesmaids followed in Winston's red Mercedes Benz. By the time we arrived, all the

Carol getting ready in Novlet's apartment with bridesmaids
L-R: Ouida, Novlet, Jeanie

158

Life in Canada: Montréal, Québec 1965

invited guests were already seated inside. In fact, Eddie and Reverend Dr. Knowles were getting anxious because the bridesmaids and I were late and there was another marriage ceremony booked after ours!

After I finally got out of the car and up the stone steps of the chapel, I had to stop for a few minutes so that the bridesmaids could hook up my beautiful long satin train to the lace bodice of my white satin wedding gown. Papa was ready right on cue

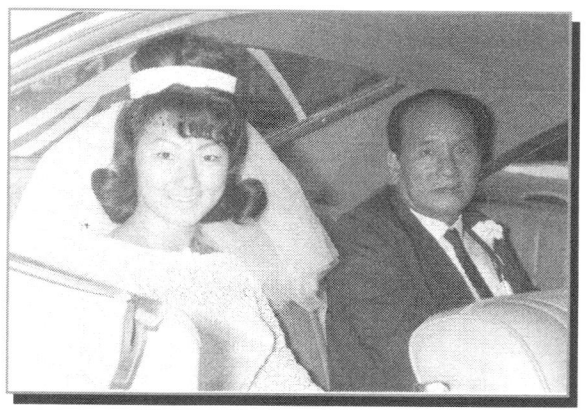

Arriving at the Chapel in the Cadillac with Papa

and I held on to his arm tightly as I nervously entered the chapel. I was so nervous that I actually do not have any recollection of the walk up the aisle or the vows taken. When Eddie and I finally went into the adjoining vestry to sign the marriage certificate, tears filled my eyes, but I was not crying out of fear for the married life that awaited me. Instead, I was crying tears of relief since the tension of the wedding ceremony was over and I could enjoy the rest of our wedding day!

The wedding photos of Eddie and me exiting the church after the ceremony really capture how happy we were to start our new life together in this strange new country. The black and white photos of the wedding party taken inside and outside of Divinity Hall turned out very well despite the drab grey stone walls. We did receive some colour photos from some of our guests but in those days, the technology for colour prints was not yet very advanced so the quality of these pictures was poor. However, we were thankful for all of the prints received and I am so grateful to Winston Wong for putting together a lovely wedding album and also Philip Young Lai for filming the event on his Super 8 movie camera. As students, we could not afford to hire professional photographers and videographers, but these photos and film lasted quite well – so well that we were able to reproduce them and present a slide show at our Silver Wedding Anniversary which we celebrated at the Embassy Suites Hotel in Unionville, Ontario, in September 1990.

After we took photos, Eddie and I greeted our guests in a receiving line before dispersing for the wedding reception at Bill Wong's Chinese Restaurant on Décarie Boulevard. As we got ready to leave, I did

The happy couple exiting the church

Life in Canada: Montréal, Québec 1965

notice that our young ushers, Norman and Raynor, seemed to be quite busy. They were rushing around gathering up the floral arrangements at the chapel to take them over to the reception hall. These arrangements really made the reception hall look beautiful. The wedding cake looked beautiful as well. It was displayed on a separate table from that of the wedding party. It was well worth the trouble of bringing the cake all the way from Kingston, Jamaica. The cake decorators at Woolworth Pastry counter did such a fine job that we knew that we would be able to keep the first tier of the cake for the christening of our first born child.

The Cantonese style banquet that was served at the reception was good and the service was excellent. The proprietor, Mr. Bill Wong, also a past McGill graduate, hovered around making sure that everything was going well. (Incidentally, Bill Wong is the father of author and journalist, Jan Wong. In her young idealist years, Jan, a Canadian-born Chinese left Canada to join Mao Tse Tung's Red Guards during the Cultural Revolution in China. Her bourgeois upbringing clashed with the Red Guard lifestyle and Jan ended up marrying a foreign student and returned to Canada quite disillusioned. Her story is told in the book *China Blues*).

Wedding cake brought up from Jamaica

Seated together were Eddie's engineering classmates Joan and Yin Hum Woo, Jerry Uniat, Valentine Rutkis, Ray and Francine Chen. John Van Oostrom was not able to attend and we were pleased that his parents came in his place. Daisy Hugh was visiting from Mandeville, Jamaica and arrived in time to attend our wedding. Fifty-five guests at our wedding was a lucky number – it made the whole affair very intimate and, at the whopping charge of $10 per head, affordable too.

Eddie's speech seemed to make everyone laugh

Life in Canada: Montréal, Québec 1965

Bridesmaid Jeanie catching the bride's bouquet, to the relief of the other single girls

Our master of ceremonies was Percival Chen, a student of Agronomy at MacDonald College of McGill University. I can only recall one speech from the floor; the speech my cousin Keung made about our childhood days growing up together in Westmoreland, Jamaica. Eddie gave one of the few speeches in his life, and I don't really remember what he said. The reaction of the people listening to Eddie's speech in the photographs indicate, however, that it must have been a very funny speech! After the speeches, the cake was cut and Eddie and I engaged in the cake feeding ceremony. This was followed by the traditional throwing of the bride's bouquet. The bouquet was caught by Jeannie – which turned out to be very appropriate because very soon afterwards, Jeannie was engaged to be married to Peter Chong. She truly was the next young lady in the group of single ladies who had lined up to catch the bouquet to be married! After that, there was dancing and, when the lovely wedding reception finally ended, the party continued at Clinton's apartment on Milton Avenue. Eddie and I returned to our apartment to change into traveling clothes and dropped in on the party on our way to catch the flight that would take us to our honeymoon destination.

To reach Niagara Falls, Eddie and I flew to Toronto and then took a taxi in heavy fog to the Inn on the Park Hotel on Eglinton Avenue near Don Mills Road. I tried to peer through the dense fog as we drove from Pearson International Airport because I wanted to get a sense of Toronto. The only thing I could make out on the trip was, however, the huge Molson Brewery. From that I could only surmise that Torontonians drink a lot of beer! The Inn on the Park was quite luxurious for us students. We were particularly taken aback by the large screen TV in the room. The balcony overlooked the vast green Don Valley and Seaton Park. Compared to Montréal, everything in Toronto seemed more spread-out, lush, green, spacious and very clean.

Life in Canada: Montréal, Québec 1965

Niagara Falls Honeymoon Certificate and souvenir cut-out silhouettes

The next day we took the Greyhound bus from downtown Toronto to Niagara Falls where we stayed the night in a humble Bed & Breakfast. Years later, these Bed & Breakfast establishments would become trendy and hardly affordable with their sky-rocket prices! The next day, we checked into the Brock Motel which was across from the Rainbow Bridge leading to the USA and facing the American Falls. (This simple motel has since been demolished and replaced by the upscale multi-storey Sheraton Brock Hotel).

During the day, Eddie and I would stroll along the walled banks of Niagara River, which were shrouded in mist, and gaze at the amazing amount of water falling over the rocks. This is indeed one of the Seven Wonders of the World! In the evenings as darkness fell, coloured spotlights were shone on the thunderous falls – it was a sight to behold! We joined the rest of the tourists taking the "Maid of the Mist" boat tour to get up closer to the Falls, and got even closer by going through a tunnel leading to a rocky path behind the Falls. The roar of the Falls from this spot was deafening but exhilarating and luckily, rain coats were supplied to all. Further along the river, we took a Whirlpool Aerocar over the Niagara River. Whirlpools swirled below us. Along the street, we had cut-out silhouettes done of us. This was the only souvenir we could afford of our trip, other than picture post-cards that we purchased. We stopped in to see the Ripley's Believe It or Not Museum and Madam Tussaud's Wax Museum. We also visited the Seagram Tower overlooking the falls and the beautiful Sir Adam Beck Floral Clock which kept accurate time. We felt special when we received a Honeymoon Certificate from the mayor of Niagara Falls– at that time, all honeymoon couples received certificates from the mayor of this Honeymoon Capital.

All good things must come to an end and it was soon time to leave. We returned to Toronto by bus and stayed downtown at the Lord Simcoe Hotel on York Street nearby to the famous Royal York Hotel and across from the historic Union Station Building. Many years later, the Lord Simcoe Hotel was refurbished and renamed the Syncona Hotel. We walked around downtown to Nathan Phillips Square and City Hall. Compared to the swinging cosmopolitan city of Montréal, Toronto seemed rather dull and everything seemed to shut down early in the evening. The people were mostly white Anglo-Saxon and one could hear at times Scottish, Irish and English accents. They were quite polite and rather British. I also noticed that everywhere seemed cleaner than Montréal and traffic was more orderly – especially when it came to crossing the streets. There was no jaywalking and the motorists seemed more patient and less hurried than in Montréal. At the end of our honeymoon, we took the train from Union Station back to Montréal. The journey took four hours, but with the dining car and the beautiful scenery to entertain us, the trip was not at all boring for us newlyweds.

The honeymoon was indeed over, Eddie resumed graduate studies in the Soils Lab located in the basement of McGill's famed Engineering Building and I fell into the role of homemaker – which was so foreign to me. I had grown up with maids, yard boys, and shop employees who had handled many of the household tasks that I now had to learn to do. Cooking was one of my biggest challenges. Our McGill married students apartment building was virtually across from the McGill Soils Lab so Eddie would often seize the opportunity to come home for lunch – and lunchtime became yet another chance for me to create some type of cooking disaster. In my case, the way to a man's heart was definitely not through his stomach! I burned the rice for many weeks before I got the hang of cooking steamed rice on the stove top – the electric rice cooker was not yet invented! Novlet taught me how to make a one-pot beef pot roast with potatoes and carrots which, she told me, was the best way to cook a cheap cut of beef. I may not have looked forward to my time in the kitchen, but I was fascinated by the coin-operated washing machines and clothes dryers in the basement of the building and was eager to try them out. When I finally got my opportunity, I promptly shrank Eddie's all-wool pants which were meant to be dry-cleaned only. I was also not a good "dummy" when it came to playing Bridge, but I sure was a gracious hostess, greeting and serving the drinks and simple snacks.

Marriage is certainly an adjustment, but I realized that I had made a solemn commitment when I took my sacred marriage vows. I had decided to give up my carefree life in Jamaica and I was now determined to learn to be an excellent homemaker as well as a faithful wife to your Ah-Goong!

Your loving Ah-Poh

Wedding Party and Family outside Divinity Hall Chapel:
L-R: Oscar, Papa, Ouida, Novlet, Eddie, Carol, Jeanie, Catherine and Kelly Wong, Percy, Clinton

Carol and Eddie signing marriage registry

Life in Canada: Montréal, Québec 1966

My dear Grandchildren

Montréal was indeed an exciting cosmopolitan city to live in. At that time, the English-Canadian and the French-Canadian people lived amicably together, although there seemed to be unmarked geographical boundaries between the two. It seemed that each group had remained settled amongst their respective linguistic groups ever since the British General Montcalm defeated French General Lafayette on the Plains of Abraham. Over time, the French-speaking Québecers had settled on the east side of Montréal while English speakers moved to the west of University Avenue and the McGill University campus.

During the daytime, when Eddie was at the university, I enjoyed walking around checking out my new environs – the old houses along the street had wooden steps leading up to the front doors and circular wrought-iron stairs at the back serving as the fire escape. This was not uniquely French architecture – I had seen this type of housing in the Puerto Rican neighbourhoods in New York and when I watched the musical film *West Side Story*. The corner convenience stores looked more impoverished to me than shops in Jamaica, but Steinburg Supermarket was another matter. I spent hours examining each strange new item on the shelves. At the Bay department store, it was the winter woolen merchandise and Hudson Bay traditional blankets that held my attention. In the kitchenware department at Eaton's, I marveled at tri-ply stainless steel pots and Corning ware that could go from freezer to stove….wow!

The now-famous Ben's Delicatessen was not too far away and I'm still fond of their specialty – Montréal Smoked Meat! The other delis along the street boasted huge jars of colourful pickled peppers which were more like window decorations than food as they never seemed to be eaten! The steak houses served large cuts of beef steak on an oval wooden cutting board, large foil-wrapped baked potatoes, piles of golden hand-cut French fries, and bowls of coleslaw – I recognized this food as the North American fare seen in the American teen movies I had watched in Jamaica! As well, there was the soda fountain inside Kresge's and Woolworth where one could have milk shakes of all flavours and ice cream, too. Can't say I was crazy about ice cream floats, though. Root beer? No way!

If I continued over to the east end of St. Catherine's Street towards the St. Lawrence area, I could take in an afternoon foreign movie in the French section of town – but I stopped doing that the day I noticed men wearing open raincoats inside the theatre. Actually this did not really matter to me at first because the men did not sit close to me; however, once while watching the movie, *Mondo Cane*, I suddenly became aware that someone had sat down quietly beside me in the darkness when I felt a hand on my thigh. Just as quietly, I got up and moved to another row of vacant seats – I was determined to finish seeing the movie and not waste my money! But I never went back to that side of town again!

My first winter approached. I loved my first sight of snow flurries. Actually, they reminded me of the dandruff I would brush out of my hair when I would bend at the waist and hold my head upside down. I loved playing in fresh fallen snow – in fact, I still like playing in fresh fallen snow! Some nights, when Eddie had to return to the Soils Lab after dinner, if he needed to get a reading, for example, I would go with him and we would make snow angels all over the deserted campus and throw snowballs at each other. It was such a wonderful winter scene that I never complained about the cold or the harsh Québec winters to come!

But eventually, playtime was over. I had not forgotten that my original plan upon graduation from Wolmer's High School for Girls was to attend a fashion design school and I decided to register for a Fashion Designing Course in the evenings. I enrolled at the Fashion Arts Academy on Mansfield Avenue which was only two blocks away. I quickly started sketching figures for fashion designing and learned that the head was one-eighth of the height of the body -- contrary to what my art teacher at Wolmer's had taught me. After that, I progressed to mannequin draping which I liked. But most of all, I enjoyed watching what all the chic designers and the trendy sassy instructors were wearing in this place of fashion. I was so elated and felt so at ease to be in the company of these haute couture artists. This place was well worth the long wait that I had endured since leaving high school!

I needed to find a day job to pay the fees for my course. This was going to be my first real experience looking for a job and I figured that since my past working experience had been in the retail business, for a change, I would seek employment in an office like the other girls I had met since coming to Montréal. Having learned speed writing by correspondence course and typing on my own in Jamaica, I made appointments to various office placement services over the phone. When I would go in person, however, I would astonish the office managers when this Chinese girl would answer to the very Anglo name of Carol Williams. When I filled in "Jamaica" as my place of birth on various forms, or opened my mouth and spoke with a Jamaican accent, I seemed to confuse them even more. As a way of avoiding some of the confusion, I started using the name "Williams-Wong", but that did not stop the questions. When people found out I was from Jamaica they always asked, "How come you are not Black?" But I had the statistics to answer that question: 97% of Jamaica's population is Black, I would say, but the remaining 3% consists of Chinese, East Indian, Syrian and British. Further questions about who I was and what Jamaica was like, however, led me to realize how insular, less travelled and uneducated many Canadians were about world geography. Imagine asking if Jamaica was in Africa and if we lived in trees or huts! I guess it was similar to the same type of ignorance that is evident when some Americans think that all Canadians live in igloos!

Life in Canada: Montréal, Québec 1966

I also thought that it might be different for me to work in the hotel environment and went to take a speed typing test at the long established Queen Elizabeth Hotel, part of the Canadian Pacific chain of hotels. I only had to take one look at all the women in the secretarial pool to be totally turned off. They were not neatly or nicely dressed and they were chattering so much that the place sounded like a hen house. I never even bothered to check back with their personnel office to see how my test had gone! By then I realized that it was more appealing for me to head back into retail. I thought that one of the larger department stores might have a more sociable working atmosphere than the smaller stores, so I filled out application forms at the established Canadian institutions like the Hudson Bay Company, Eaton's, Simpson's and the British owned, Ogilvy's Department Store. I found that I responded to the application process for department store work in much the same way that I had responded to deciding which high school to attend: the atmosphere mattered. I did not like the atmosphere at most of the stores; everyone seemed cold and unfriendly.

As soon as I entered the stately building of Ogilvy's Department Store with its tartan logo, however, I felt good vibes and was most comfortable speaking with Mrs. Kirkham, head of the Personnel Office. She advised me that there was an opening in the shipping department office and, without hesitation -- and disregarding other job offers that I had received -- I gladly accepted the job. It paid $1.15 per hour. The head of our office was a kind, cheerful, white-haired lady named Peggy, who was assisted by a dour-faced woman named Margaret. The three young office clerks were a Black girl from Trinidad, Maggie, a white girl from Scotland, Irene and myself, a Chinese girl from Jamaica. All three of us were in our twenties and as new Canadian immigrants, Maggie, Irene and I immediately gravitated to each other. The guys next door from the shipping department never failed to stop by to chat with us despite the steely glares from Margaret. The French-Canadian guys quickly informed us that the best and easiest way to learn to speak French was to sleep with a Québecois, of course!

Maggie used to be a teacher in Trinidad and when her fiancé died in a traffic accident, she just wanted to get away from the island. She learned that the quickest way to immigrate to Montréal was applying to come as a domestic servant. When her contract as a domestic servant was up, she was able to stay in Canada but since she did not have a Canadian teaching diploma, she turned to clerical work. Irene and her husband, Ian, got married in Fife, Scotland, on the very same date as Eddie and I were married: September 18th, 1965. They immediately immigrated to Montréal where they knew folks from Scotland and very soon after they settled in Ville St. Laurent. Ian was a licensed scale mechanic. Both of them had never left the shores of Scotland before and knew little about life anywhere else. In fact, when I started working at Ogilvy's with her, Irene told me that she had excitedly written home to her family that she had met a "real live Chink" and who could speak English fluently! Irene also wrote home about the horror of discovering a tea bag inside a teapot in Canada instead of the loose tea leaves she was accustomed to. She had never seen a tea bag before!

Irene was very outgoing, a girl after my own heart and we behaved crazily together at work, during our coffee breaks in the cafeteria, walking arm-in-arm through the different floors of the department store and spilling out on to the streets of Montréal! We didn't care if we were being looked at – we were happy to be in Canada and free to have fun among those who had never seen us before!

When I got pregnant three months after our honeymoon, Eddie and I planned to move out of the downtown area because children were not allowed in our married student housing. We moved out to the suburbs like all the families and chose to move to Ville St. Laurent where Ian and Irene also lived in a duplex apartment. We got on well as couples and we looked forward to celebrating the Irish annual tradition of St. Patrick's Day Dinner Dances as well as eating haggis on Robbie Burns Day. Our Jamaican and Scottish humour and attitude to life were so similar! Eddie and I enjoyed their circle of British friends although we were referred to as "Sassanachs" in jest which apparently meant "traitors" or "outsiders". We were not offended because for us, the name was the equivalent of how Chinese refer to Caucasians as *Gwai-lo*, meaning "foreign devils" or "white ghosts". But we knew that they did not mean it as an insult; and who cared anyway what they happened to call us? A rose by any other name smells just as sweet!

Ogilvy's Department Store was about ten blocks away but I never took the bus to work as I loved walking along fashionable Sherbrooke Street. I would stop to watch the wealthy guests going in and out of the Ritz Carlton Hotel en route. During the winter, I enjoyed walking in the uncleared snow on the sidewalks in my black, high-heeled, zippered, fur-lined leather boots. When it was time for me to go shopping for my first winter coat in Canada, Novlet advised me to buy a very warm and traditional camel hair coat from an upscale store like Holt Renfrew, but the styles and colours of these coats were too drab for me. One day I strolled by the show window of a low-budget clothing store, Reitman's. I stopped suddenly when I saw this bright blue coat with black oriental frog-like buttons to match the black fur-trim collar and cuffs. The price for this coat was much less than that of all wool or camel coats that I had seen and it was probably not as warm as those coats, but I didn't care – tropical blood ran through my veins and I was not yet fazed by the Canadian winter. I loved this bright oriental-looking coat and I purchased it. In my bright blue winter-lined coat with its black fur trimmed collar and cuffs, I felt like a movie star -- like Audrey Hepburn, playing Holly Golightly in *Breakfast at Tiffany's.*

During the summer months, I took out my high fashion dresses that I had brought up from Jamaica and strutted around like a fashion model into work. Many years later, while reminiscing about our days in Montréal, Irene confessed that she was so envious of the dresses I used to wear and how I completed my ensembles with my pointed toe and stiletto heeled shoes! I also liked walking through the McGill University campus during the summer months. I would enter at the University Avenue iron gates, walk past the Engineering Building, down the impressive central walkway and exit through the majestic entrance on Sherbrooke Street. I never had any desire to pursue an academic degree nor did I wish to attend university, but I did

Life in Canada: Montréal, Québec 1966

enjoy going through the hallowed halls of learning and feeling the long history of these ancient buildings.

I did, however, relish attending university functions, especially the social ones, so that I could meet people from Eddie's Engineering Department, like the Dean and his professors. I liked to joke with them and ask what degrees they were pursuing! Before we married, Eddie used to write me about the McGill Annual Plumbers' Ball, a black tie affair for the entire engineering faculty. I was delighted when I was finally able to attend these Balls – and Eddie appreciated not having to hunt around for a date! One year he had taken Norma Loshusan and another time, Novlet. I guess he was not like the other Jamaican students who fancied dating French-Canadian girls.

McGill Plumbers' Ball 1963
Seated L-R: Norma, Delores, Doris
Standing L-R: Eddie, Percy, Harry

I also enjoyed meeting Eddie's fellow students as they were from other foreign countries and I was interested to hear about their backgrounds. It was good to meet the Canadian boys who had gone to Survey School with Eddie and eventually meet all the wives at the McGill Dames Society. This was a society for all of us wives who were pursuing our PHT degrees -- "Putting Hubby Through" university, that is! Very soon I was voted in as Vice-President at our Annual General Meeting and we Dames met once per month. Actually the McGill Dames Society was formed to help the wives, especially foreign ones, of graduate students get settled in Montréal. We would organize outings, tours and sightseeing to familiarize ourselves with the country our husbands might eventually settle in for good. We provided information about facilities and programmes offered by the city and the school boards, like language classes, recreational sports, exhibitions and festivals. As well, we would

Eddie and Carol at McGill Plumbers' Ball 1966

provide information re group homes for disturbed children, char services and relief personnel. We also created a newsletter including all these activities and added information about used children's furniture and toys, sublet housing and general information about student living and survival. It was fun helping each other and we made great friendships that lasted long after we had spread out all over the world upon the graduation of our husbands.

Picnic at McDonald College

McGill also organized outings to their property on Mont St. Hilaire in the Eastern Townships and Eddie and I would participate in these outings. We would go for picnics in the summer and were introduced to the lake with its freezing water and slippery stones at the murky bottom that moved around suspiciously like frogs. I was never homesick for Jamaica, but after seeing what passed for beaches at Mont St. Hilaire, I began to miss the warm Caribbean sea and the ability to see one's toes under the clear, blue water!

I considered myself to be on a new adventure in a new country and was quite excited to go skiing and skating with the McGill group during the winter at Mont Habitant,

Carol skiing with instructor and (right) skating on outdoor rink at Mont Habitant

Saint-Sauveur. My first time on skis was challenging. I used wooden skis that needed waxing and the leather ski boots took as much time to lace up as ice skates, but it was so much fun!

I went skating more often than skiing since there was recreational skating time at the hockey arena on campus. Winston and Althea used to pick up Daphne and me to go skating. We were glad for the ride because although the arena was close to our homes, it was built on the hillside of Mount Royal. By the time we walked uphill, we were too pooped to skate! On these trips, we were ever so careful not to let the blades of our skates scratch Winston's pride and joy – his red Mercedes Benz 4-door sedan!

I got along well with Eddie's friends and whenever I walked past their apartment or faculty building I usually looked up at the windows to see if I spotted anyone I knew. It always made me happy when Bruce would shout and wave to me from the top floor of the Chemistry Building. He was a nice, friendly Canadian-born Chinese who was the son of one of the Chinese immigrants who had come to Canada to build the railroads in the 1800s. In the 1800s, the Canadian Pacific Railway built a railroad linking all ten provinces across Canada from east to west. The Chinese labourers hired from Hong Kong and the China coastline, mostly Cantonese and Taishanese speaking, were treated terribly and were used for the most dangerous assignments like placing dynamite explosives used to blast through the Rocky Mountain range. It is said that "one China man died for every mile of the railroad" and as the railroad progressed, the dead Chinese were buried along the way and the sick were left to die by the wayside. It was later discovered that native Indians had rescued some of these men and nursed them back to health. Many of these Chinese men stayed on with the good-hearted Indian rescuers and eventually intermarried. Years later, half-Chinese were discovered on Indian reservations in British Columbia and Alberta and there were Indian Chiefs who, it was discovered, were of part Chinese ancestry. As if these hardships were not enough, to add insult to injury, when the railroad was completed and the last spike was driven in the ground, the surviving Chinese workers were not invited to the ceremony and celebrations with the other workers. These abandoned Chinese men were to face yet further loneliness and despair with the imposition of the Chinese Head Tax and the Chinese Exclusion Act. Decades later, although it was considered too late by many, these insulting and unfair practices were acknowledged when the Canadian Government offered an official apology and redress to these Chinese Canadians.

After Bruce graduated and became a professor, he got involved in the association to organize the "Commemoration of the Chinese Railroad Workers of Canada". In later years, I would support his efforts by attending the annual wreath laying ceremonies at the base of a huge monument downtown Toronto on each Canada Day, July 1st and much later, attend the screening of the movie, "Iron Road" depicting the plight of his forefather and other Chinese ancestors during the 1800s.

One day, as I was passing Eddie's old bachelor apartment at 3515 University Avenue and waving to the guys, someone shouted down that a friend, a new arrival from Jamaica, Donald Nam, was going to get his driver's license later that day and asked if I would like to go with them and give the test a shot too. Sure thing, I said. I joined them and was amazed that the written and road tests were so simple compared with the Jamaican/British-type road tests with which I was familiar. So, without any preparation for the multiple choice written test and having never driven on the right side of the road, I received my driver's permit – there is nothing like common sense and living by your wits to get you through life! Getting my driver's permit prompted Eddie to start thinking of buying our first "brand new" car – a second-hand, maroon Corsair two-door coupe!

I was also getting along with everyone at work, from the cafeteria staff to the sales girls, to the interior decorator of the show windows, to the buyers of each department. I liked working at Ogilvy's and felt free to behave with my Jamaican outgoing friendliness in that environment. However, I also maintained my Hakka Chinese work ethic. The senior lady in my office, Margaret, was constantly admonishing me when, if I felt it was necessary, I would stay past 5:00 p.m. in order to finish my paperwork. I guess I was bringing attention to her habit of leaving her desk at 4:45 pm when she would head for the ladies room to get ready for a hasty departure at 5:00 p.m. on the dot! I had run my own business in Jamaica and knew how important it was to be efficient in order to keep the shipping department running smoothly so I did not mind working later to complete my assignments if needed.

I guess this non-Canadian work ethic did not go unnoticed and very soon I was promoted to the top floor of the administrative office in the Payroll Department. Mr. Boire was a nice and polite Office Manager and he introduced me to a lovely French-

Clinton and Suzanne Chin's wedding photo
L-R: Oscar, Daphne, Clinton, Suzanne, Carol, Wilhel, Arthur

Life in Canada: Montréal, Québec 1966

Canadian young lady in charge of payroll. Her name was Suzanne Pichette and she was patient teaching me the ropes and how to operate the old Gestetner machines that we used to make up the payroll for the employees on all floors of the department store. Little did the buyers and staff realize it, but this little Chinese immigrant had already been the boss of a similar operation, albeit on a smaller scale, in Jamaica! Moving up the ranks did not make a difference to me, as I had been quite happy in my old position -- although I did receive a 10 cent per hour raise. I would now get $ 1.25 per hour. I just enjoyed getting along with everyone, especially with the less educated ladies who worked in the cafeteria. In return for my friendliness, I received many favours like extra helpings and free tea and dessert with my meals. The only person I didn't meet at Ogilvy's was Colonel Nesbitt, the President of the company although many times I would peek into the Board Room only to see his stern and dignified portrait on the wall over the head of the Board table.

Suzanne was not a sophisticated Montréal city girl and hailed from a small town outside the city named Rawdon. Eddie and I, along with Althea and Winston, had visited Rawdon on my previous visit to Montréal when I was still a single girl. We had gone on a long drive to look at the beautiful Fall colours and I marveled at how different the vivid colours were from the foliage in the tropics. Suzanne was neat, meticulous and very efficient in her work. We got along and worked well together, so it was only natural to invite her to my First Wedding Anniversary party.

The party was held in the recreation room of our apartment complex – Royal Court Apartments, across from the Cote Vertu train station in Ville St. Laurent. We had invited our Jamaican Chinese circle of friends in the city, as well as the new friends we had made since my arrival in Montréal. One of Eddie's groomsmen, Clinton, had come up from Jamaica to visit us, so of course, he was in attendance as well. Everyone mingled well together, but towards the end of the party, we noticed that Clinton and Suzanne were no longer mingling with everyone else. Instead, they were dancing very intimately in the corner of the room – it was love at first sight and first meeting!

Needless to say, Clinton made a few more visits to Montréal and to Suzanne's hometown, Rawdon, to meet her folks which eventually led to a very nice bilingual wedding in the Westmount area. Suzanne quit her job at Ogilvy's and packed her bags to join Clinton in Montego Bay, Jamaica. He was in the family business, Jamaica Car Rentals, and they lived on the premises there until they bought a lovely house in Ironshore Estates.

Assisting one's friends to find the love of their life is a great feeling but in my case, it also left me feeling a certain sense of responsibility to ensure that their marriage worked out! And I guess, over the years Clinton and Suzanne might have felt some sort of obligation to Eddie and me for introducing them, so we became close friends and confidantes. We celebrate our wedding anniversaries together whenever possible and, over forty-nine years, have developed a lasting friendship – and lasting friendships, my dear Grandchildren, are something that we should always try to cultivate and nourish.

Life in Canada: Montréal, Québec 1966

Friendship is not about whom you have known the longest, it is about who came and never left your side!

Your loving Ah-Poh

McGill Engineering Building

McGill University Gate

McGill University Married Students Apartments at 3575 University Ave.

Eddie's bachelor apartment at 3515 University Ave.

Ogilvy's Department Store, Ste. Catherine St.

Life in Canada:
Ville St. Laurent, Québec
1966

My dear Grandchildren,

1966 was the year I entered yet another stage in my life—motherhood. I was not quite ready to be flung into motherhood. There was still so much I wanted to do -- I was yet to be a graceful ice-skater like Sonja Henie and a downhill skiing champion like Nancy Greene!

I am from a large family of six siblings and before getting married, I remember asking Eddie to agree that if we couldn't have children, we would adopt. I wanted to have lots of children and God chose this time for me to start my family because I was nearing the ripe old age of twenty-five. He also granted me a wonderful pregnancy and gave Eddie the bouts of "morning sickness" for me. I was hale and hearty while Eddie had the retching feeling of nausea which expectant mothers usually experience during their first trimester! I designed and sewed my own maternity dresses to suit my inner glow of happiness. The ready-made maternity dresses were most comfortable and roomy but I found that the fabric of these dresses was quite dowdy and plain. I must remark, however, that the style of maternity wear in the new millennium is too form-fitting – it brings attention to the protruding stomach and is not as elegant as the maternity wear of the 1960s. Even though I was pregnant, I still walked everywhere I went. In fact, I thought that being pregnant gave me the license and permission to boldly raise my arm and point my finger anytime I needed to cross the street whether or not I was at a crosswalk! I did make one change to accommodate my pregnancy: I changed from stilettos to sensible, but still pretty, low-heeled shoes!

I kept healthy and well during my entire pregnancy. That spring, my sister-in-law, Ouida, and I took the train to Ottawa for the annual Tulip Festival. It was a sunny weekend and the tulips were a magnificent sight for me. I found myself wishing that my mother, who had so loved flowers, could have shared this vision of tulips in

Carol at Tulip Festival, Ottawa

Life in Canada: Ville St. Laurent, Québec 1966

Carol with Canadian Mountie in front of the Parliament Building, Ottawa

full bloom with me. In recognition of Canada's help during the war years, the Dutch government presents hundreds of tulip bulbs from Holland to Ottawa, our nation's Capital. When these tulips bloom in the spring it is truly a beautiful sight. Later in my advanced state of pregnancy, my father-in-law, Kelly and mother-in-law, Catherine, came up from Jamaica with their friends, Mr. and Mrs. Miller and Herman Chen: and I was able to take them sightseeing and cruising among our Thousand Islands on Lake Ontario.

I would eventually quit working at Ogilvy's that summer in order to get the nursery and baby's layette ready for baby's arrival in the Fall. Before leaving, the staff had a nice little baby shower for me with members of staff from the different departments, like Annie Lewis (Dept. 82) Marjorie Ravioli (Dept. 47) Elizabeth Toburn (Returns) May Gore (Adjustment) Louis Razavet, Hieke Ehassake (Receiving), Bill Russell (Imports), Agnes Ferguson (Freight), Irma Vasareins (Accounts), Peggie Cairns, Magdalene Antoine, Joan Marks, Susan Marsh (Traffic), Susanne Pichette (Payroll) and the boss himself, Mr. Albert Boire. This baby shower was also a fond farewell and retirement party as I was planning not to work outside of the home once my baby arrived. I was a firm believer of Dr. Ginnot that this mother, if she could manage to do so, should endeavour to stay at home for at least seven years since these are the formative years of a child's life.

My cousin Keung's wife and my friend, Penny also had a baby shower for me and invited personal friends like Dorothy, Stella, Veronica, Magdalene, Cherry, Daphne, Elorene, Rosie, Yvonne, Francine, Marcia, Doreen and Ouida. This was a lovely get-together, especially since I was thinking that as we had moved out to the suburbs of

Ville St. Laurent and since I would soon have a baby in tow, I would not be able to see these kind folks for a while. In my mind, I would soon be tied down as a suburban housewife and mother.

On October 6, 1966, some time after Eddie left for university, I began to have strange sensations in my abdomen. I calculated that it was about two weeks before my due date so I was not sure if I was in labour. Besides, in the movies, the pregnant actresses were always so dramatic when they were in labour. They seemed to be going through pain that was nothing like the mild contractions that I was having. Nevertheless, I decided that I had better be safe than sorry, especially since we now lived in the suburbs and the Royal Victoria Hospital, where I planned to deliver my baby, was downtown at the top of University Avenue. I phoned Penny, who was already a mother, to ask her if my symptoms were similar to her labour contractions. She figured everyone's labour was different and suggested that I should drive down to her place on Pine Avenue, which was closer to the hospital and city, where we would wait for a while to see if I was really in labour or if this was a false alarm. I would bring my hospital bags, just in case. When I got to Penny's place, I rested on the sofa while Penny continued preparing dinner and taking care of her toddler Andrew, who was playing on the floor in the living room. After a while, I realized that although my contractions still felt mild, they seemed to be coming more regularly and closer together. I phoned Eddie, who was at the McGill Soils Lab, and told him to walk up to Penny's place so that he could drive me up the hill to the hospital.

Indeed I was in labour, but I was not too uncomfortable. As Eddie and I drove up to the hospital, I was still comfortable enough to notice how the hospital buildings and the buildings surrounding the hospital were so drab and gloomy. The place looked ancient and depressing. Many years later when our family was visiting Montréal, we drove up to the hospital to show Brian where he was born. His response was to remark that the hospital looked like a haunted castle. Indeed it did!

We calmly checked in and while Eddie was taken to the Waiting Room for expectant fathers, I was ushered alone into a bare and sparse "labour room". A nurse occasionally came in to check the progress of my dilation which seemed to be happening smoothly. I still was not perturbed by the contractions. After one of these examinations, however, I was led to the Delivery Room, and I could hear wailing and screams coming from the rooms on either side of me. I felt as if I was in one of a series of rooms on a baby production line. As I made my way onto the delivery table, I asked the nurse what all the screaming was about and she told me that some Greek women were giving birth. Apparently, Greek women believed that the louder they screamed while giving birth, the stronger their babies' lungs would be. I figured my baby would just have regular healthy lungs as I would not be screaming and embarrassing myself like some kind of a Greek banshee to improve my baby's lung strength!

The nurses were getting prepared around me when my quiet and fatherly looking Obstetrician/Gynecologist, Dr. Tweedie, came in all masked and looking very sterile. He encouraged me to have an epidural injection but I knew that the Royal Victoria

Life in Canada: Ville St. Laurent, Québec 1966

was a teaching hospital and figured that the anesthesiologist was probably just looking for an opportunity to try out what was, at this time, a new medical procedure. I had been reading about the risks of epidurals and was not willing to have a long needle stuck into my spinal column and risk becoming a cripple if it was done incorrectly! Nevertheless, the contractions were now getting much stronger and more uncomfortable, so between contractions, I told Dr. Tweedie that I was okay with the injection. Before I had a chance to change my mind or realize what was happening, I was sat up at the edge of the table and someone behind me said the epidural had been administered.

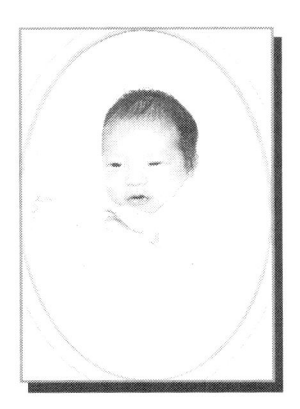

Baby Brian at birth

The shot might have been a placebo for all the good it did me. I did not feel any pain relief and the baby was ready to be delivered. Dr. Tweedie also felt that, since I was a first time mother, I needed an episiotomy, so away he went incising and next thing I knew, I heard a baby wailing. Dr. Tweedie announced that the baby was a boy and disappeared out of sight. The nurses gave me a glimpse of the baby boy and they too disappeared out the door into some other room in the baby production line of rooms. I wanted to go out too, and share this joyous news with Eddie, whom I had not seen since registration and checking in, but it seemed as though the nurses forgot about me. I just lay there on this table in a cold room by myself. They had not even left me with any covers! Although I was shivering, I tried to remain still and patient, and come to grips with the realization that I was now a mother and had a son born in the Chinese New Year of the Horse, 1966.

After what seemed like a long time, I was wheeled to my room in a ward and Eddie came in excitedly telling me that they had taken the baby out to him and he swore that the baby had looked knowingly at him, as if he had recognized that Eddie was his father. I eagerly chatted back, but at some point, my eyes rolled back in my head and I suddenly got quiet. This frightened Eddie who immediately buzzed for the nurse. She assured him that I was just exhausted and had fallen asleep and that he should leave so that I could continue sleeping. Eddie told me the following day what had happened. He also told me that after leaving me, he had returned to Penny with the good news, stayed for dinner and played mahjong games afterwards. During the game, he was extremely lucky, pulling seven flower tiles – the maximum flower tiles that one can have in one play. He thought this signified that our newborn baby was going to be one lucky boy!

As for me, alone in the hospital, I woke up during the night to discover that I was about to be injected with something. When I enquired what the injection was for, I was told it was to prevent milk from coming into my breasts. I was so horrified! I quickly hugged my arms across my breasts and said firmly, "No, merci," then repeated myself more quietly and politely and said, "No, thank you." The nurses tried to coerce me to take the injection, telling me that it was help me get back to normal quicker and retain my girlish figure. The baby, they told me, would get better nourishment from the Enfamil formula, than from breast milk. I was now fully awake and getting angry.

Life in Canada: Ville St. Laurent, Québec 1966

I told them emphatically "Mi sey, No" in my strong Jamaican accent! These darn milk formula manufacturing companies were giving large sums of money to hospitals and towards medical research so that they could get in the way of nature and God's natural plan for babies!

As a result of my refusal to take their injection, I experienced six heavenly days of nursing my baby boy who was brought to my room on schedule and returned to the nursery so that I could have time to rest and recover from childbirth. Such luxury! It was as if I was in a hotel with meals served in bed. Every day, my meal tray was delivered with a red or orange or yellow maple leaf on the tray to match the falling leaves from the trees outside my window. My physiotherapy exercises were strictly monitored and the stitches of my episiotomy were taken care of with soothing heat lamp sessions. I attended baby-bathing demonstrations along with other baby-care lectures. I even bought the *Baby Care* 'bible' written by Dr. Benjamin Spock and felt that I was ready to return home with my baby. What could go wrong?

Baby Brian's first Christmas with Mommy and Daddy

Getting discharged and going home where I was alone without the hospital staff turned out to be a larger problem than I had anticipated. Every time the baby cried, I nursed him. I did not follow a feeding schedule because Dr. Spock endorsed flexible feeding for breast-fed babies. Eddie and the baby slept peacefully, but I was going gung-ho around the clock taking care of the house between frequent feedings. Eventually, I got so tired and worn out that my body was not able to produce enough milk to satisfy a growing baby. So I had to finally agree to Eddie giving the baby one night-bottle feeding of water and glucose so that I could get some rest and replenish my milk supply.

Grandma and Grandpa Wong came up from Jamaica again and were quite helpful preparing meals for our family. They also catered the food for the baby's Christening party. Eddie's best man, Oscar Chin, and his Trinidadian friend, Philip Young Lai, were asked to be the Godfathers. Francine Chen, the Irish-Canadian wife of one of Eddie's Chinese engineering classmates, Ray, was pleased to be the baby's Godmother. The St. Philip's Anglican Church in Ville St. Laurent was not too far away and Rev. Canon Thorpe christened our baby son, Brian Martin Wong. Brian behaved so well during the Baptism service. After the service was over, we returned to our apartment for a nice get-together with our Canadian friends and fellow immigrants who were all making a life far away from our homeland.

As Brian grew into a lovely toddler, I befriended mothers with babies of Brian's age living in our apartment building. His first playmate was Jean-Paul, the toddler of Guy and Suzanne. Because they were French-Canadian, Brian and I learned some French words and phrases. In addition to just learning their romantic language, I also learned something about the sexual exploits of the French Canadians. Guy and Suzanne had a

Life in Canada: Ville St. Laurent, Québec 1966

L-R Suzanne with Jean-Paul, Brian and his baby-sitter Monique

mirror installed on the ceiling above their bed which Suzanne was quite unabashed to show me. Vive la différence!

Through Suzanne, I met other Canadian mothers. As we talked, we realized that they had similar birthing experiences to what I had in the hospital, like almost being injected to prevent the milk from coming into our maternal breasts. After a few "kaffe-klatches," (a coined word for women getting together for coffee), we decided to support a little group that was being formed by like-minded mothers -- the La Leche League. Suzanne became the President and our little group of concerned mothers grew into a large organization and branches started to spread across Canada. I am extremely pleased to have been a part of this now well-established organization that has made such a great impact on hospitals and institutions in terms of endorsing breastfeeding, educating people about the benefits of breast milk as well as assisting mothers with techniques for successful nursing. Our strategy was not to attack the huge milk formula conglomerates but to promote breast-feeding by expounding on its values, both nutritional and emotional. Our next move was to fight the justice system so that breast-feeding in public would no longer be illegal. Today, I give a smile of satisfaction whenever I notice mothers nursing their babies in public, sometimes with and without privacy covers. I'm also pleased to see nursing stations provided in buildings and change stations in public washrooms. This is what I call progress!

Other than Penny, Wilhel and Dorothy, most of the women in our Jamaican Chinese circle, had not yet become mothers, so the four of us would visit each other a lot and celebrate our babies' birthdays together despite the sleet and snow of winter. Some who had gotten or were getting married were Eddie's former roommate, Winston Chin to Faye Yee, Phillip Young Lai to Rose Chin, Eddie's groomsmen, Percy Chen to Myrna Young Kong and Oscar Chin to Myrna's sister, Daphne. Yvonne Toyloy would later marry a Canadian Chinese and Bruce's brother, Malcolm Jue.

Oscar & Daphne's wedding L-R: Myrna (maid of honour), Oscar, Daphne, Percy (best man)

Life in Canada: Ville St. Laurent, Québec 1966

Penny lived downtown and would take her two-year-old son, Andrew on the train to St. Laurent and disembark at Cote Vertu station to visit us. I would pick up Wilhel and we would drive up to Mount Royal Park on sunny days with the toddlers, Brian and Karl. On overcast days, we would go to the bowling alley and somehow the noise of rolling balls and falling pins did not disturb the sleeping boys during nap-time. I already knew Wilhel from my Wolmer's High School days and her son, Karl, was just a year older than Brian. Dorothy is a distant relative of Eddie's and she was married to Calvin Chong, student of Agronomy MacDonald College. Although their

Carol and Brian being visited by Dorothy and baby Oliver Chong

son, Oliver, was younger, he and Brian played well together. In fact, all our children got on well together and we stay-at-home Moms merrily occupied ourselves. As well, we marvelled that we were receiving a princely sum of $6 per month as Child Allowance from the Canadian government!

One day, as I strolled in my local Dominion Supermarket, I met up with another "Wolmerian", Claudette Jacks, who was shopping with her young daughter, Michelle. I found out that Claudette was married to a Trinidadian meteorologist, Mike Nancoo who worked for the World Health Organization and they were living in the same neighbourhood as I. It was such a chance meeting but a happy one given the pleasant memories I had from Wolmer's. Claudette was also a stay-at-home mother with her daughter, Michelle.

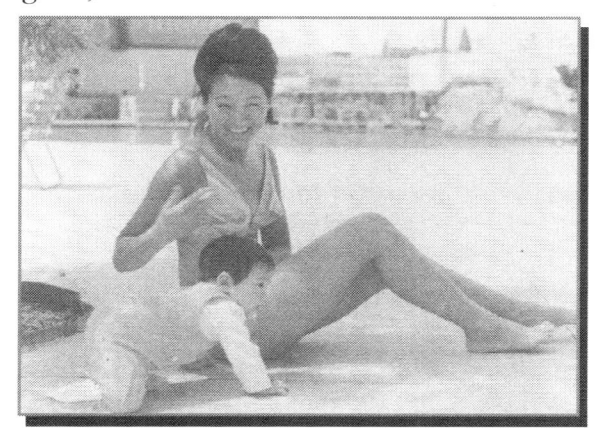

Carol with baby Brian beside outdoor swimming pool

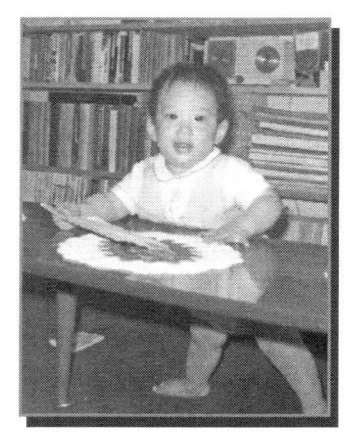

Brian in Royal Court apartment

Life in Canada: Ville St. Laurent, Québec 1966

M.Eng degree *McGill University Convocation 1967* *PHT degree*

I also met another Jamaican girl, Sheila, who lived in our apartment complex. Sheila was married to a French-Canadian, John Mignault, but they did not yet have any children. Sheila was so crazy about baby Brian and his accompanying blue blanket, "tat-tat". He took tat-tat everywhere with him and would caress the satin binding lovingly as he sucked on his pacifier. I think that the smooth slippery feeling of the satin binding reminded him of the satin dressing gown I used to wear while nursing him as an infant.

John worked for British Airways and on his days off the three of us, with Brian in tow, had our own little ritual: We would go "dream home shopping" in the model homes being built in the suburbs of Montréal. Sheila always begged to babysit Brian overnight -- which came in handy when Eddie and I were typing like crazy to finish his thesis for his Master's Degree Program. It was close, but we made the deadline to submit the thesis.

Eddie completed the requirements for his Master of Engineering degree and would be conferred at the Annual Founder's Day Convocation on October 11, 1967. Eddie's graduation ceremony was not at all what I had expected. It was not the large outdoor affair I had seen in American movies. Instead, the ceremony was held indoors at the Montréal Forum without much fanfare; however, since that year's convocation was marking the Centennial of Canadian Confederation, honorary degrees were conferred on the ten Provincial Premiers in addition to the graduating students in all the various faculties. Attending the graduation made it clear to me that although Canadians like much pomp and show, they are more conservative by nature than Jamaicans. I did make a point of taking my photo wearing Eddie's cap and gown, however. After all, I was graduating too – I had earned my PHT degree!

After Brian's first birthday party, Eddie and I planned to travel to Jamaica to introduce Brian to my Williams side of the family in Westmoreland, Jamaica. Once Eddie had graduated and held a job offer from Canadian Bechtel Engineering Company, we decided that it was a good time for Eddie and me to book our flight to

Life in Canada: Ville St. Laurent, Québec 1966

Brian's first birthday party at Pierrefonds

L-R: Ouida, Claudette with daughter Michelle, Carol and Suzanne, supervising gift opening

Jamaica. I had not felt homesick since my arrival in Canada, but I found that I was really looking forward to seeing my family again as a married woman and mother. I was especially eager to see Mama since I remembered all those times when I was growing up and rebelling and she used to say, "Just wait until you become a mother, then you will understand!"

When I wrote her of our planned visit, she quickly wrote back to say how overjoyed she was. In her letter, she included the phrase, "Ah so happy, a don't think ah going to live fi see di day" (I am so happy, I don't think I am going to live to see the day), a Jamaican expression used to express great joy and anticipation. To my horror, only a few weeks before our flight date, Mama's words came true! My sister, Elaine, phoned to tell me that Mama had passed away suddenly. Overseas telephone calls from public call boxes were limited in those days, so we could not speak for a long time. I had barely enough time to assure her that we would be coming for Mama's funeral. I was devastated. Many nights before we left, I sat on our balcony crying until the wee hours of the morning as I reflected on Mama's short life of fifty-two years.

Papa and Mama never really talked to us about Mama's health, and in those days, children were not allowed to ask adults personal questions. In line with Chinese tradition, Papa did not agree to an autopsy of Mama's body for fear of upsetting her spirit so I never learned an official diagnosis for the cause of her death, but, from what my other siblings said about her final years, and what I knew about her medical history, I have deduced the following: many years previously, Mama developed a goiter condition. Her goiter was removed by Dr. Morrison at the old Montego Bay Hospital overlooking the sea. Years later, while I was in high school, she developed thyroid cancer and went to Hong Kong for Chinese medical treatment. When she returned, the cancer was in remission and Mama, living far away from Kingston without oncology services, didn't have follow-up examinations. By the time anyone realized that the cancer had returned, the cancer had spread to her larynx and wind pipe. To try and save her life, Dr. McNeil, a surgeon in Kingston, performed a tracheotomy, removing her larynx and installing a removable pipe in her throat. Mama learned to speak without her voice box, but instead of taking things easy, she was soon back to work in our business and still doing all the tasks that she thought was necessary to please her older husband.

On the day that she died, the Headmaster of the local elementary school, Mr. Dunn, was being buried at the Anglican Church across the road from our place. Many of the locals saw Mama looking on from our gate as the funeral procession led into the church, then she went inside the house. Later in the evening, Mama, as was her practice, removed the pipe in her throat for cleaning, but had difficulty putting it back. Instead of raising an alarm, however, she sat quietly in her room struggling to replace the pipe in her throat. My younger brother, Dick happened to see her and went in to help her with the pipe. While he was there, he noticed that she was having great difficulty breathing and realized that she was in very real danger of asphyxiation. He quickly alerted Papa and Patrick to Mama's condition and then ran next door to the Public Works Department to arrange for transportation to take her to the hospital six miles away. Our car had been taken to Kingston by Donny and Elaine where they were getting passports to travel (Elaine was being sponsored by me to come to Canada and Donny was in the process of beginning Science studies at McMaster University in Hamilton, Ontario).

Patrick sat in the back seat of the car. Mama was laid across the seat and Patrick cradled her head as the Superintendent of Public Works drove to Dr. Carnegie's house. Papa and Dick might have sat in the front seat with the driver. When they arrived, Dr. Carnegie instructed them to leave immediately for the hospital, telling them that he would follow in his own car. When they arrived at the hospital, the staff rushed Mama away, but there was nothing that could be done for her. She passed away peacefully, although Patrick always felt that she had already passed away in his arms en route to the hospital. For years after her death, Dick battled with his resentment towards Papa whom he felt had not treated Mama well during her life. He would recall the numerous times that we had witnessed Papa's harsh outbursts towards Mama when we were children. Elaine always pointed out, however, that although they had long maintained separate bedrooms, Mama used to occasionally sleep with Papa in his bedroom and there were incidents when we could see the affection between them. I think that Elaine struggled with her feelings over Mama's death as well. I think she may have sometimes felt some responsibility for Mama's death, thinking that if she had not taken the car that night, quicker transportation would have been available to take Mama to the hospital. However, it was strange that about the time of Mama's passing while Elaine was staying at Keith's house in Kingston, she and Keith heard rustling noises at the same time in the early night. And strange as it may seem, Elaine's passport disappeared and has never been found up to this day!

It was true that Mama and Papa's marriage had not been easy. As was the practice back in the villages in China, Papa and Mama's marriage was arranged by well-meaning relatives and friends in the late 1930s. These relatives did not, however, take into account some significant differences between the two. Papa was a new immigrant to Jamaica and was just learning to speak English. Mama was Jamaican-born and fluent in English and could speak only a smattering of his Hakka Chinese dialect. He was an only child of his parents and Mama was the youngest of a family of two brothers and five sisters. She was also ten years younger than Papa. I could see why Papa would agree to marry Mama: she was young, intelligent, articulate, outgoing, tall and good-looking. Mama was aware of the tradition of arranging marriages amongst the Chinese and would accept the marriage her older brother arranged for her. Papa was not bad looking either and at least he was taller than she, so she may have decided to take her chances in the marriage with Papa, especially since he was the cousin of her older sister's husband, which meant that she and her sister would be living close to each other in the west end of the island. Despite their very different upbringing, background and ages, and all the ups and downs inherent in married life, Mama and Papa made their marriage work. They raised six children, established a successful business and made a life together in sickness and in health, for better or for worse. They honoured their marriage vows and stayed together for almost thirty years. Only death parted them. Their commitment to each other was definitely an example for me.

Over the years, my dear grandchildren, I have also learned that young children do not fully understand the relationship between married couples. They have little understanding of the negotiations and compromises or the forgiveness and understanding that can exist between a married couple, until they themselves get married. They have no concept of the fact that each person brings his or her own personal history into the marriage. Or that their children would benefit from their histories as well as differences.

As well, we should always choose to think kindly of people, including our own parents, because we do not know what personal demons that person is struggling with in his or her own life. And we should never judge the relationship between two consenting adults in a marriage. Instead, we should simply look at the beautiful end result…..wonderful, secure children and an intact family!

Your loving Ah-Poh

Life in Canada: Ville St. Laurent, Québec 1966

Royal Victoria Hospital, Montreal

*Royal Court Apartments
1105 Jules Poitras, Ville St. Laurent:
(On right, 3rd balcony - home of Eddie,
Carol and baby Brian)*

*Outdoor swimming pool at
Royal Court Apartments*

Life in Jamaica:
Petersfield and Montego Bay
1967

My dear Grandchildren,

My heart was heavy. I was making my way back to Jamaica for my mother's funeral. This was my first trip back since I had left as a single girl. I was returning as a married woman and the mother of a baby son, Brian Martin. I had been planning to make this trip to introduce him to his grandmother. Now that would never happen. We were on our way to bury her. Brian and I were travelling alone, as Eddie planned to join us later.

During the flight, I could not help but once more sadly reflect on Mama's short life. She lived only fifty-two years. Her full name was Gladys Louise Young and she was born in Clonmel District, St. Mary, Jamaica. Her father, Young Bow, was one of the earliest immigrants to settle in this British colony in the Caribbean. No one knows for sure, but he very well might have been an indentured worker on a sugar cane plantation since, following the emancipation of the African slaves, Chinese were brought to the British West Indian colonies as indentured labourers. What we do know is that Young Bow immigrated from Tong Lak Hee Village, Bao On, Guangdong, China, in the late 1800s and did business in St. Mary before settling in Trout Hall, Clarendon.

Young Bow married Naomi Lue. The circumstances of their marriage – how or if it was arranged – are also unknown. They had seven children – two sons and five daughters. The eldest son, Alfred, died as a young man of a brain hemorrhage and the younger, Clarence, took over the family's general store. As was typical in Chinese shopkeeping families, as soon as they were old enough, all the children helped out in the store. Mama's older sisters, Amy, Florence, Nora and Cisilyn, eventually got married and left home, leaving Mama, the youngest child, helping in the store with Clarence and his growing family. Mama worked diligently in the store and got along well with her sister-in-law, Ella, and helped her raise their six children – eldest son, Jackie, and daughters, Cherry, Pat, Carol and Madge. The youngest daughter, Geraldine would be born eight years later.

Earliest photo of Gladys Louise Young

Petersfield and Montego Bay, Jamaica 1967

Amy and Isaac Williams

Mama's eldest sister, Amy, and her brothers were sent to Young Bow's village, Tong Lak Hee, in China to be educated and immersed in the Hakka Chinese culture. They returned to Jamaica as teenagers, fluent in the Dung-Gon (Dong-guan in Mandarin) Hakka dialect. Mama and the rest of sisters, however, attended the local Jamaican schools. They never learned more than a smattering of the Hakka dialect that was spoken by their parents in the home. Amy eventually married a businessman named Isaac Williams (Ngui) and moved to the western parish of Westmoreland. Mama was encouraged to marry Isaac's younger cousin, Papa, and move out to Westmoreland as well. After Mama married Papa, she would occasionally visit her family in Trout Hall and take some of her children with her so that we could get to know Uncle Clarence, Aunt Ella and our first cousins.

I would visit my cousins on my own years later when I started attending Wolmer's High School. The girl cousins also attended high school in Kingston and lived together on Victoria Avenue. Uncle Clarence would check on them when he travelled to the city on business and pleasure. It was customary for Chinese wives to remain at home to take care of the business -- which was open six days a week -- when their husbands left on business, so Aunt Ella usually did not come on these trips, but she would also, on occasion, visit her daughters and her own relatives in Kingston.

Uncle Clarence's son, cousin Jackie, would go on to become a medical doctor, marry a young Jamaican-Chinese lady from the neighbouring district of Frankfield, Clarendon named Dorothy and move to the USA. Uncle Clarence's eldest daughter, Cherry, married Derrick Moo Young and lived in Kingston. Another daughter, Pat, married her distant cousin, Lloyd Young Kong from Guyana, and lived in Kingston also. Lloyd and Pat had met when Lloyd and his brother, Vibert, had come to Jamaica to attend the University of the West Indies, located in Mona, Kingston. Carole, Pat's sister, ended up marrying Vibert and the couple lived briefly in Guyana before returning to Jamaica to work at the West Indies Sugar Company [WISCO] in Frome,

Cherry Moo Young

Pat Young Kong

Madge (Bobbi) Wong

Westmoreland. Madge married a salesman, Harold Wong, and the youngest daughter, Geraldine, went away to university in the USA. She later married Joe Lau and remained in the States.

Mama was a dutiful wife and worked hard wherever Nathan chose to set up his business and always made the best of the primitive conditions she lived under, all the while making improvements that modernized both their stores and their homes. Having had a British education, Mama subscribed to numerous English magazines, which proved helpful in terms of getting up-to-date ideas for merchandise in Papa's stores. It was her idea, for example, to expand the dry goods section of the store with fabric and sewing accessories from England. Mama had learned to sew and taught us to make simple garments and beautified our home with colourful curtains. In later years, I had the chance to add ready-made fashion apparels, millinery items and footwear to the store to keep her customers fashionable. In the rum bar, it was Mama's idea to introduce the malted milk shakes and to offer snow cones. She was so proud of her modern electric mixer and snow-making machine. She also went into the business of bottling and distributing jars of Jamaican pickled vegetables and Scotch Bonnet peppers. Mama was truly ahead of her time!

Mama was a good and organized mother for her six children. She would post a chart on the wall with our schedule for the day for the maids (and us children) to follow. I distinctly remember that eight o'clock was the time to line up for our daily dose of cod liver oil in the morning and that three o' clock was bath-time. Mama always quickly took care of my head lice infestation and my siblings' sores. She religiously detoxified our digestive systems with doses of either castor oil or Epsom salts on specified mornings. After we underwent these procedures, she would reward us later in the afternoon with delicious home-cooked chicken soup flavoured with lots of thyme and scallion and filled with cho-cho, flour dumplings, carrots and macaroni.

Mama was a social, community-minded person who had an outgoing personality. She easily adjusted to living in the remote district of Williamsfield as a new bride. She made friends with the upstanding citizens living in the district and arranged English classes for Papa with the local postmistress, Miss Dawes. When we moved to the seaport of Savanna-la-Mar, Mama became active in the Women's Federation, an organization of the wives of professionals like lawyers, doctors, and teachers, whose efforts were focused on helping the less fortunate women in the community. When we lived in Petersfield, she helped unwed mothers and the orphanage nearby in Water Works. She assisted many of the locals going as farm workers to the USA, and immigrants to England with their job application forms and with obtaining passports and completing travel documents. As a result, Mama was loved by all the residents and customers of the store. She treated the hired help so well that they became an extended part of our family and were devoted to her and, by extension, to us children. Before we were old enough to help in the business, Mama allowed Sister Carmen, Sister P and Novlet, the opportunity to improve their job prospects and better themselves; she also allowed them to live with us and learn business practices like book-keeping. These women all became successful in life and remained lifelong family friends.

Petersfield and Montego Bay, Jamaica 1967

Mama was an obedient wife and went along with Papa's Hakka Chinese traditional ways although she was first-generation Jamaican Chinese. She was careful to demonstrate undying gratitude and filial piety to the patriarch of Papa's family, Uncle Jackson and his family and descendants, in recognition of the fact that it was Uncle Jackson who had sent to China for Papa and his cousins. She participated in the ritual of Sunday get-togethers with the Williams family, even though these occasions must have been somewhat difficult and lonely for her. The wives of the men of Papa's generation were nothing like her. They spoke in Hakka Chinese, a dialect that Mama could hardly understand, and they were envious of her height, beauty, modern clothes and permed coiffure. Mama was also tolerant of the all-night Mahjong sessions in her home while we lived in Savanna-la-Mar and Papa's Mahjong trips to Montego Bay when we moved to Petersfield. I was the one disturbed by the noise of the shuffling Mahjong tiles and the *gah-choks* (rapping on one's head by the knuckles) or ear-twisting by the elders, Jackson, and other players. My siblings did not seem to mind as they made their way between the mahjong tables hoping that some of the players would give them some "sore foot" (money) if they were winning and in a good mood.

Luckily, Papa was not a gambling addict and was fairly disciplined when it came to managing his financial affairs and cultural obligations. Mama did not complain when Papa sent some of their hard-earned profits back to China to support Ah Neung (Chan Lam Keow), the woman to whom Papa had been betrothed in China. Despite the fact that they were never officially married, she was still considered to be his Number One Wife.

Ah-Neung   *Papa*   *Mama*

Mama was a modern woman, who, despite having borne six children, took pride in her full figure. She was quite fashionable and chic. She always wore make up and favoured bright red lipstick. She would have the local dressmakers sew us girls pretty dresses in the latest fashions. The dresses were of such high quality and so well made that, as a teenager, I was more than happy to show off my clothes to the other girls at boarding school. As a matter of fact, the white dress that Mama mailed me for my confirmation at St. Luke's Parish Church was so glamorous with its lace and rhinestones that I had to borrow a more modest dress from another student, Hilary, to wear instead! Mama loved glamour. I know that she loved to read Hollywood movie magazines because on numerous occasions, she told me that I was named Carol after the movie actress, Carole Lombard, and Mearle, after the actress Merle

Oberon (although my two names were incorrectly spelled by the registrar on the birth certificates when I was christened).

Although our family had always employed house maids, Mama insisted that we children learn to make our beds and tie up the mosquito nets that hung over the beds to protect us during the night. She taught us table manners and had the maids prepare healthy westernized food for us and encouraged us to drink fresh milk. Mama would use a cocktail shaker to serve us cold Milo or Ovaltine drinks. We looked forward to the Jamaican-style beef soup with pumpkin, yam, and dumplings that the maids cooked on Saturdays, and, on occasions, on Sundays. She learned how to make Hakka Chinese *baos* with either meat or sweet bean filling as well as how to cook traditional Hakka dishes from the hired Chinese men who worked in our store. After I left home, she tried to teach my sister Elaine these recipes, but, to her regret later in life, Elaine did not pay much attention during these lessons.

Mama using her first gas stove and oven

Mama loved cooking and baking and was always trying out the recipes she saw in her *English Home Journal* and *Mrs. Beaton Cook Book*. She fashioned an oven by lining a wooden box with tin sheeting and added a cast iron pot of hot charcoal in the center of the insulated box. She created her own refrigerator in a similar fashion: by getting the local tinsmith to line a wooden box with tin sheeting inside of which she would place a block of ice purchased from the ice truck coming from the ice factory in Water Works. She would make gelatin desserts from agar-agar to be stored in her make-shift refrigerator along with her frosted cakes. In later years when we got electricity and the business grew in Petersfield, Mama was delighted to have her modern kitchen installed complete with an electric stove and oven, refrigerator, stainless steel sink, formica-covered counters and cupboards, and matching long dining table to accommodate our extended family and many friends. This dining table served many land-crab feasts and many impromptu guests and even salesmen passing through Petersfield.

We children owe Mama a debt of gratitude for having taken care of our formal education. She sent each of us to the best school suited for our individual personalities. She kept abreast of our progress at school and at our boarding places plus made arrangements for our transportation to and from our schools. She made sure we had an appropriate amount of pocket money (although she could not control the extra money slipped to us by Papa). She felt her daughters should have piano lessons despite the added costs of these lessons from the family coffers. I will be

Petersfield and Montego Bay, Jamaica 1967

Mama in Kowloon, Hong Kong   *Mama and Ralph at Grotto, Hong Kong*

eternally grateful that she chose to send me to an Anglican School – Wolmer's High School for Girls – an experience which helped shape my adult life in so many positive ways.

In retrospect, I believe Mama lived a short but fulfilled life, especially when she went to live in Hong Kong, although the trip was really for medical treatment. She was secure enough to stay with the woman who was treated as Papa's Number One Wife and her adopted son, Ricardo, who had escaped the war-torn days by fleeing to Hong Kong. She also met and got along with Papa's other relatives who had escaped from the Chinese Communist Revolution to the safety of the British colony. The Hong Kong Government placed the refugees and all the hillside squatters into a Resettlement Area after a great fire broke out on the hillside. Years later when I had the opportunity of living in Hong Kong, I visited this area. It was a massive concrete complex of small apartments. Each apartment had a simple cooking facility with a small eating table that had to be folded up against the wall so that a bed could be folded down from the opposite wall at night. The common washroom was outside in the corridors, and running alongside one wall was a concrete trough with running water – that was it in terms of sanitary convenience.

Relatives of the refugees, like the Williams [Ngui] family, sent money to help them raise their standard of living and relocate out of the Resettlement Area. Some were able to buy the birth certificate of a deceased person to acquire a Hong Kong ID card in order to obtain papers or passport that would allow them to travel and join relatives overseas. When Mama arrived in Hong Kong in the late 1950s, the early years of desperation were over. The Williams relatives were quite settled and happily working in the Kowloon area. Ricardo's brother-in-law owned a car that was used to take Mama sightseeing and on other outings. Mama made friends at the Roman Catholic Church where she worshipped. A woman named Una became a very close friend.

When Mama wrote home, she did not dwell on her medical treatment. She was obviously happy and excited to be in Hong Kong, a most modern and vibrant city teeming with life and oriental wonders. Although she must have missed us – there

Petersfield and Montego Bay, Jamaica 1967

were so many airmail letters that we received during the time she was away – I cannot help but feel that she also enjoyed some sense of freedom from all the responsibilities that came with having a husband, a business and six children. And I would like to think that my taking care of my younger siblings and helping in the business with Papa allowed Mama some peace of mind on her medical holiday in the Orient.

Mama returned home and after she got settled, I left home to get married and live in Montreal. The following year, she wrote and told me that she attended Keith and Shirley's wedding in Kingston. Similar to my wedding day, only one parent could afford to be away from our thriving business at a time, so Papa, Patrick, Dick and Elaine were left minding the store, rum-bar and grocery shop. Mama wrote often and she liked writing long letters to keep me up-dated on what was happening in Petersfield and all the family gossip. I knew she relished hearing about my new experiences living in Canada so I would reply with long letters too. I must have inherited the love of writing and keeping in touch, from her. Eddie and I were delighted when she mailed us some of Papa's specially dried beef, "Nu-nuck gun". She still did not mention much about her illness but Elaine in one of her occasional cards, did say that she was seeing a specialist, Dr. McNeil and was feeling much better.

Mama and Ricky at Tiger Balm Garden

Mama's marriage was not ideal but she made the best of it and raised her children as best she knew how. My only regrets are that with her early passing, I never had the opportunity for mother-to-mother talks with her and that she did not have the opportunity to immigrate with Papa and us to Canada in the 1970s. Mama was always ahead of her time and I believe that she would have certainly fitted into the Canadian lifestyle and taken full advantage of the community courses offered in cooking, baking, floral arrangement and gardening. She would have been a terrific grandmother too!

As Brian and I watched our plane touch down on the runway of Montego Bay airport, we could see Elaine and my good friend Jeanie, one of my bridesmaids, waving to the plane from the outdoor gallery overlooking the tarmac. We were overjoyed to see each other and they were so excited to finally meet one and a half year old Brian who, I must say, travelled so well on his first plane ride. Elaine was so excited to hold and take care of her first nephew that she insisted on putting him into the car. While doing so, she accidentally banged his head. To this day, she has never forgotten how terribly she felt as she tried to console her crying nephew whom she was meeting for the first time. Needless to say, after the pain and the resulting bump subsided, Brian forgot everything about the incident!

Petersfield and Montego Bay, Jamaica 1967

Arriving in Petersfield District, despite the unhappy circumstances, it was good to be back in my old room and be with my father and younger siblings once more. On the day of the funeral, we all drove in the family car, the same red Chevrolet Impala sedan I used to drive. I had driven this spacious car on many occasions as a single girl, but on this trip, I had to hold Brian on my lap, and my younger sister Elaine was at the wheel. In those days, there were no safety seat belts installed in the car and a child car seat was unheard of. When we arrived in Kingston, we went directly to the Sam Isaac's Funeral Home to see my dear mother. She was laid in her wooden casket looking serene and peaceful. Looking at her, I felt thankful that she passed away peacefully and quickly without having had to suffer through a lengthy bout of sickness and pain.

The funeral service was held at Holy Cross Catholic Church at Half-Way Tree. My in-laws, Kelly and Catherine, drove down from Montego Bay and took care of Brian while I walked beside my father behind Mama's coffin as it was wheeled up to the altar. The church was filled with family, relatives and friends, including Uncle Abraham who could not stop talking during the procession about his shock at Mama's sudden passing.

Mama had a Roman Catholic Church funeral although she had started out her life as an Anglican. In fact, she had brought up all of us children in St. Peter's Anglican Church, which was directly across from our store and home. As children, we spent many hours at church on Sundays. During the week we would help ring the bell and set up the hymn notices. Mama had even arranged for me to be confirmed at St. Luke's Anglican Church while at boarding school. Then, the Roman Catholic priests started coming to the rural areas of Jamaica and converted a lot of the Chinese. Father Knight in Savanna-la-Mar converted Mama. Afterwards, she sent my younger sister to Alpha Academy, a Catholic School in Kingston. I recall one evening, Father Knight coming to our house and told Mama and Papa that they should remarry in the Catholic Church because, since they had not been married in the Catholic Church, they were, in his opinion, "living in sin." Papa was livid and marched him out of the house saying that he had his wedding photo to show that they were married by a parson and that Father Knight sinned more than he did! Papa was never a church-going person but supported our local churches in the district. After this incident, however, he was not at all impressed by the Roman Catholic faith. Nevertheless, Mama continued to quietly worship at the Catholic Church and would have been very happy to know that we arranged to have her funeral service in the Holy Cross Catholic Church.

After Mama's funeral service, the hearse led the procession to the Chinese Cemetery on Waltham Park Road for the burial service. Mama was laid to rest as we gathered around her grave. On our way back to our cars, I noticed the local Jamaicans living in the area were sitting or leaning silently on the surrounding wall of the cemetery and had been looking on with unabashed curiosity – but also with sympathy – at the ceremony.

All of us, including Papa, decided to return home to Petersfield, Westmoreland, immediately although it was about four hours away, driving along the south coast. At

Petersfield and Montego Bay, Jamaica 1967

one point in the middle of the night during the long journey through the unlit countryside, Elaine decided to pull into a closed service station for us to sleep as we were all so drained and tired. As the sun rose the next morning, we woke up to find that where we had parked in the dark was dangerously close to the open and uncovered deep service bay. If we had driven one more inch forward, we would have fallen in. I believe that perhaps Mama's spirit was watching over us and keeping us safe that night.

Eddie eventually flew in from Montréal to join us so Brian and I went to stay with his parents in Montego Bay on the north coast of Jamaica. Brian had an enjoyable time in Petersfield given all the attention he received, and was not too perturbed by all the mosquito bites he received, which, to my dismay, became sores. He had a lovely time in Montego Bay as well. He loved being initiated into the salty seawater of Doctor's Cave Beach and being shown off to our Montegonian friends and relatives.

Mama in front of Aunt Cissy's house, Windward Road, Kingston

One weekend, we borrowed Grandpa Kelly's brand-new Green Opal car to drive along the north coast to Kingston where we stayed with my eldest brother Keith and his wife, Shirley, in Havendale. We decided to go sightseeing in Cinchona in the hills overlooking the city. It was cool and scenic but the drive was so steep that Eddie burned out the clutch of the brand-new car. He would have to sort out this disaster with his father upon our return to Montego Bay. During our visit, we noticed that in whatever room Brian slept, a grey-brown moth was always on the ceiling of the room. We knew it was always the same moth because its right wing had been clipped. We couldn't help but wonder if perhaps the moth was Mama's spirit watching over her first grandchild too!

Eventually, it was time for us to fly back to our new family life in Canada. It was only when I was about to leave Jamaica that I fully realized that I had truly lost my mother, the woman who gave me life, nurtured me with love, care and guidance until womanhood. She had shaped my life by setting me an example of womanhood that was characterized by community-mindedness, family consciousness, an outgoing and friendly spirit, and an overall zest for life. As the plane left Jamaica, I whispered a thank you to her and promised her that I would touch the lives of those around me in a positive way like she had done and that I would also pass on all her good qualities to her grandchildren.

Your loving Ah-Poh

Petersfield and Montego Bay, Jamaica 1967

Mama and Ah-Neung in Kowloon, Hong Kong

Life in Montréal, Toronto and Jamaica
1968 - 1969

My Dear Grandchildren,

When I returned to Montréal, Québec, I could not help remarking on the welcoming reception we received going through Canadian Immigration – and we were not the only ones to experience this welcome. Friends who had arrived on a Visitor's Visa had told me that when they were going through Immigration at the airport, they were asked if they would like to apply for Immigrant Status! Imagine, in the 1960s one could get one's landed immigrant status in Canada just like that!

The friendly attitude towards Jamaicans at this time was mainly because of the relationship between our Canadian Liberal Prime Minister, Pierre Elliott Trudeau, and Jamaica's Prime Minister, Michael Manley, of the People's National Party. Both Trudeau and Manley had attended the London School of Economics in England in the 1940s.

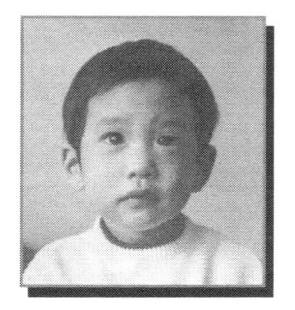

Because it was so easy to do at this time, Eddie and I applied for immigrant status and sponsored my sister, Elaine, to migrate to Canada as well. We thought that having immigrant status in Canada was also important since we had a Canadian-born son who held his own Canadian passport.

I loved motherhood and staying home to take care of Brian who was such a nice toddler. Brian had such a pleasant personality. Eddie would take the bus to

Brian's passport 1967

Brian's passport 1972

Brian learning to swim at Royal Court Apartments indoor pool

L Eddie with Brian

R Carol with Brian

197

Montréal, Toronto and Jamaica 1968-1969

Eddie, Carol & Brian on the trunk of the Corsair car

work at Canadian Bechtel on Décarie Blvd., leaving our second-hand Corsair car for Brian and me to use in the day. On days when we did not feel like going out, Brian and I enjoyed either the indoor or outdoor pool in our apartment complex.`

We were happy to share these facilities with Eddie's youngest uncle, Washington, his wife, Sheila, and their two sons, Craig and Duane. "Washy" decided to bring his family back to live in Montréal after working for a few years in Jamaica as a chemical engineer. And we had the pleasure of having them stay with us until they found their own apartment. We helped them get settled and shared many family visits whenever possible. On occasion, we would splurge by taking the families out for dinner at Mouette's Seafood Restaurant specializing in Maritime lobsters..

Owning a car gave us the freedom to go tent camping with my cousin, Audrey, and her husband Rennie, who was doing his medical residency at the Montréal General Hospital and fellow Civil Engineer, Aston, and Jean, plus Eddie's sister, Ouida. Ouida had been one of my bridesmaids and, after graduating from McGill University, was working and sharing an apartment with Delores and Doreen. We went to Québec campsites and travelled across the U.S. border to New York State camping by Lake Placid and hiking to the Ausable Chasm via Plattsburg. Brian took to camping well and especially liked being outdoors wearing nothing but his diapers! He was well-behaved on these trips and we hoped this early camping experience would influence him to continue camping and enjoying nature later in life.

Since the rent at Royal Court Apartment was constantly being increased, we decided to move even further out of the city to 4550 Cloverdale Avenue, Pierrefonds, Dollard des Ormeaux. We chose to

Carol and Eddie's first canvas camping tent

live near the train station, so that Eddie could take the train to his engineering office. Little did we and other university graduates who moved out to this new apartment building know, but this new development was deemed a low-income area and was surrounded by subsidized housing. Within a week after moving there, Brian's blue stroller was stolen and we discovered that the furnace did not work efficiently. One bitterly cold winter, we had to turn on the electric stove and oven to help keep the apartment warm! At least each outdoor parking space had an electric outlet to provide block heating for the cars! Lucky for us, we did not have house guests during the winter.

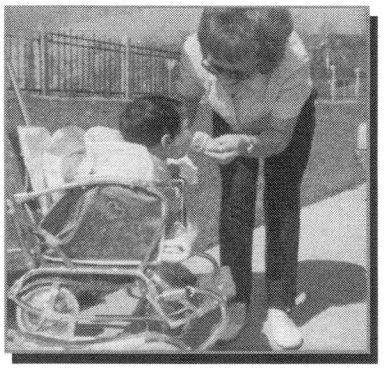

Scottish Aunt Irene treating Brian to an ice cream cone, and below, his Murray clan tartan kilt

Summer guests that year were Eddie's relative, Winston, and his friend, Beverly, who came from Ottawa to visit us just as we were in the middle of packing to leave the province – Québec was no longer La Belle Province! You see, the previous summer, Montréal hosted Expo '67 and it was an especially good time to enjoy the city as millions of visitors arrived for the event. We had a number of house guests from Jamaica that summer, like Harry and Marianne, Benny and Sheila, Eddie's parents, who arrived with their bookkeeper, Mr. Miller, and his wife, Herman and Anna, and others. The city was teeming with excitement and activities at the site on Isle St. Helene. The students had enjoyable summer jobs working there and everyone was happy – except the FLQ political party.

General DeGaulle had paid an official visit from France in 1967 and got the Francophone Québecois all riled up for separation from the rest of Canada. He gave a rousing and inciting speech, ending dramatically with the call: "Vive Le Québec libre!" There were street demonstrations and bombs placed in postal boxes. This unrest culminated in 1970 with the kidnapping of a British diplomat, James Cross, and a Québec minister, Pierre Laporte, by French-speaking activists, but already many foreign-owned companies had started pulling out, including Eddie's company, Canadian Bechtel.

Eddie was offered a transfer to their head office in San Francisco but we were not fond of the idea of living in the USA and decided to move to the neighbouring province of Ontario. We already knew that Toronto was not as cosmopolitan and swinging as Montréal, but when we were passing through the city on our honeymoon, we had noticed that Toronto was spread out with many green parks and seemed very clean and family oriented. We were now thinking that Toronto would be a city that was well-suited for young families like ours.

Montréal, Toronto and Jamaica 1968-1969

Actually, this willingness to migrate and start over has been the history of our Hakka Chinese people. The Hakkas originated in the Central Plains of the Yangtse River and, due to social unrest and hostile invaders, they slowly migrated southwards over the centuries. There were five major Hakka migrations towards south-east Meixian Province and south to Guangdong Province, before the Hakkas were involved in further immigration overseas or across Asia. The Hakka were considered to be the migratory tribe of the Han Chinese and were called "Guest people" -- *Ke-Jia Ren* in Mandarin, *Hak-Yan* in Cantonesese or "Hakka" in English. Whenever there was unrest in their host province, the Hakka people would peacefully move out and start over somewhere else. The Hakka people are well-known for their hard work, endurance and tenacity, as well as their focus on the survival of their families. Wherever they went, they overcame hardship in their new homeland and they never forgot their Hakka traditions, culture and values, which were based on Confucius teachings: respect for elders, help each other, educate and care for the young!

Most folks hate moving but I like moving because I feel I have turned a new page and am embarking on another stage of my life -- even if, as when we moved to Toronto, I have to sleep on a mattress on the floor! Brian also slept on the floor on his crib mattress – which he enjoyed because instead of calling for Eddie or me to lift him out of his crib, Brian could simply walk off his bed and search for dry cereal on his own in the kitchen before coming into our bedroom to awaken us. We had rented an apartment on Leith Hill Road in Willowdale, overlooking the Don Valley Parkway and Sheppard Avenue intersection. From our window, Brian also enjoyed watching the various huge vehicles working at the Fairview Mall construction site. We were happy to learn that there were other Jamaican Chinese living in the area, like Aston and Shirley Shim, as well as other former Montréalers fleeing Québec, like Roger and Barbara, Aston and Jean, Audrey and Rennie, plus Novlet and Russell, who chose to set up his optometry practice in Hespeler, Ontario.

Eddie found another job at the engineering firm of William Trow and Associates; however, soon after finding that job, Eddie's father, Kelly Wong, contacted us to tell us that he had been diagnosed with shingles. He wanted us to come to Montego Bay, Jamaica and manage his supermarket business so that he would be free to seek Chinese medical treatment in Hong Kong where his parents were living in Tsuen Wan. Eddie was not happy in his new job and I was pregnant with my second child so we felt that, since we were not yet fully settled in Toronto, the time was actually right for us to make such a move. Besides, we believed that if your family needs assistance, you do not hesitate to help them. So we packed up and flew to live in the Wong family home at 10 Foster Avenue, Montego Bay, Jamaica. Great-Grandma, (*Ah-Poh Tai*) Catherine, was one of the rare Jamaican Chinese housewives who did her own housework without the help of local maids; nevertheless, she did not seem to mind our intrusion.

Kelly's Supermarket Ltd. was the first supermarket in the western part of the island and Great-Grandfather Kelly was an astute businessman. He was also very progressive. To further his knowledge of English he had taken Dale Carnegie courses, "How to Win Friends and Influence People" and to further his networking and

Kelly's Superservice Ltd L-R: Maas Ken, Alfred, Missa Chin

toastmaster skills, he joined the Masonic Lodge and International Rotary Club. As a result, Great-Grandpa Kelly's business was thriving, especially at this time when the hotel industry in Montego Bay was expanding. Great-Grandpa Kelly supplied the hotels in the area and delivered goods to the rich and sometimes aristocratic vacationers who had started to frequent Jamaica. The world was only just discovering what we already knew (and still know): Jamaica is one of the most beautiful places on earth. To appeal to his rich clientele, which included people like the British Lord Beaverbrook and American socialites, Great-Grandpa Kelly's stock included high class food and drink items, plus top class champagne like Dom Pérignon.

Kelly's Supermarket Ltd. served the local people also and introduced them to self-service. Since the arrival of Chinese shopkeepers, to Jamaica, serving customers had not changed very much: the shopkeeper stayed behind the counter and served the customers the items that were also behind the counter. A shopping centre with aisles of goods from which customers could serve themselves was quite the step towards modernization of the "shop industry" at that time. When we arrived, it was fairly clear that Great-Grandpa Kelly wanted us there to really just supervise the activities at the supermarket. Great-Grandpa Kelly's half-brother, Maas Ken, Missa Willie, Lascelles and Missa Chin, the truck driver could be counted on to do most of the everyday tasks needed to keep the business running. In addition, Great-grandpa Kelly sponsored his nephew William from Hong Kong to help while learning the business. William would later open his own store and eventually settled down in Jamaica. He was happy to meet us, his Jamaican family, and especially his eldest cousin Vernon, when he and his wife, Dorit visited from Austin, Texas, U.S.A

We returned to Montego Bay to find that friends whom we had during our teenage years, like Tony, Jeff, Herman, Dell, Loraine and Rose, were, like us, now married and starting to have babies. When we arrived, our first visitor was Leslie 'Jeff' who

Montréal, Toronto and Jamaica 1968-1969

Carol pregnant in front of supermarket with 2-year-old Brian

brought his young son, Darren, to meet Brian. As Brian showed off his toy helicopter that he had brought with him from Canada, the two boys became instant friends. Our circle of young families would meet at Doctor's Cave Beach, each other's homes for birthday parties, and at the Chinese Club on Creek Street where most of the Chinese community met socially. Eddie's cousin from Kingston, Dudley, came to work at the Barclay's Bank branch at Westgate Shopping Center so he was also a frequent visitor when he was not back in Kingston visiting his family and his girlfriend, Carmen.

The Caribbean Sea and tropical sunshine was good for my pregnancy and I felt great and agile enough to play badminton and go water-skiing well into my advanced stage of pregnancy. Eddie's childhood friends, Edmund and Donald, would arrange water-skiing on Sundays and it was on the evening after one of these wonderful days at the beach, while washing the sea salt out of my hair, that I started having mild contractions.

Before leaving Toronto, my pre-natal care had been provided at Toronto Western Hospital; after arriving in Montego Bay, I continued pre-natal care with Dr. Marco Brown at his clinic on Corner Lane off Charles Square. Early the next morning, Eddie and I checked into Dr. Brown's clinic. Then Eddie went off to the supermarket which was not too far away on the other side of Charles Square. Just like with Brian, I did not find the contractions too severe; but unlike my experience in Montréal, the nurse and Dr. Brown were not offering to administer epidural spinal injections. The birthing process in Jamaica during those days was unhurried. Everyone just let nature take its course; and so, without duress, Gordon Harrison Wong entered our world on August 28th, 1969 in the Chinese Year of the Rooster.

Perhaps because of all the physical activities that I had been engaging in during my pregnancy, Gordon weighed less than Brian at birth – 6 lbs. 10 ozs – which was still more than the average weight for an Oriental baby. Gordon was a good-looking baby – especially when he was dressed in the pink cotton chemises I bought for the baby's layette with the hope that this second baby would be a girl! Regardless of my wish for a little girl, three-year old big brother, Brian, was thrilled to have a baby brother; and like typical Chinese grandparents in those days, the Wongs were delighted to have another male child to carry on the family surname.

Brian laughing with Carol and baby Gordon

My unlimited maternity stay at Dr. Brown's clinic was most comfortable. Mrs. Brown, an English lady, served delicious British home-style meals everyday using her own silverware. While I was there, the baby was taken care of in the nursery which helped me to recover very quickly – so much so that one day, I decided to get out of my dressing gown, put on my now enormous maternity dress and take a taxi to have my hair done at Jeanie's Beauty Salon and return to my hospital bed all without my family knowing. I had to sneak away to do this because the old Chinese tradition was that after childbirth the new mother should not wash her hair or even dare to go outside of the home for one hundred days! Nowadays, that time has been reduced from 100 to 30 days!

Without a crib at Foster Avenue, baby Gordon slept in a folded baby box suitable for traveling which I had bought at Storkland in Kingston. I was now an experienced nursing mother, so Gordon nursed well. He put on weight rapidly and gained chubby cheeks. When he was six weeks old, Great-Grandpa Kelly returned from his medical trip. Like my mother, he seemed to have enjoyed his stay in Hong Kong and was pleased with the medical treatment he had received there. During his absence, we had enjoyed the tropical, laid-back lifestyle and decided that Jamaica would be the best place for us to raise our boys. When we advised Great-Grandpa Kelly of our decision, he expressed some concern. He reminded us that Jamaica had only received her Independence from Britain in August, 1962, and he was apprehensive about the future of Jamaica. He might have been expressing a commonly expressed worry of local Jamaicans at that time; namely, "Black man cyaan rule demselves" ("Negroes are unable to govern themselves"). His concerns might also have reflected his own memory of the turmoil in China that accompanied its change to a Communist state.

While keeping Great-Grandpa Kelly's advice in mind, Eddie and I decided that we would make the move back to Jamaica while the country was still seemingly stable and getting settled as a self-governing entity. Eddie and I planned to go back to Toronto to fetch our belongings out of storage and settle in Kingston where Eddie would be able to find an engineering job that would allow him to maintain continuous work experience in his profession. While we were making these plans, Elaine's sponsorship papers to Canada came through. She needed to go to Canada to be registered, so she decided to accompany us to Toronto. We planned that all of us – Elaine, Eddie, Brian, baby Gordon and I – would fly to Toronto and through their kindness, we would stay with Jean and Aston Wong in their home in Scarborough.

Baby Gordon on plane to Toronto at 6 weeks of age

Although it was only October when we returned to Toronto, a freak snowstorm greeted us – welcoming Elaine to the Great White North. Jean and Aston were most hospitable. Jean was expecting her first baby and didn't mind babysitting Gordon.

Montréal, Toronto and Jamaica 1968-1969

Elaine helped with Brian, which meant that Eddie and I were free to pack a trailer with our household belongings, including a new gold and white upholstered sofa set bought at a nearby furniture store, to be shipped to Jamaica. We also bought a dark green Dodge Dart sedan, and once we were ready, we packed it to the hilt, and headed off on a long, long drive to Florida, USA which would be our departure point for Jamaica.

On our drive down to Florida, we stopped at Corning, New York to visit the Corning Ware and Steuben Glass Factory. In Washington, D.C., we toured the White House, Arlington Cemetery, Lincoln Memorial, Washington Memorial and other historical sites. We stopped by the naval Base in Norfolk, Virginia, before driving carefully and with much apprehension through the southern states before, to our great relief, finally reaching Florida. In Florida, we enjoyed the water show at Cypress Gardens, toured Kennedy Space Centre and other tourist attractions before reaching Miami. Once in Miami, we stayed with family friends, Moi (née Lee) and Roger Hamilton.

Jean and Aston with Sheldon and Derrick

Finally, after shipping our car to Jamaica, we boarded the flight to what we believed would be our luxurious life. We looked forward to having the help of live-in maids and enjoying the warm tropical weather all year round. The words of Harry Belafonte's popular song, " Island in the Sun", and words from the new national anthem captured our feelings well: Jamaica, land of sea and sun; Jamaica, Jamaica, Jamaica, land we love!

Your loving Ah-Poh

Brian, baby Gordon and Carol at the White House, Washington, D.C.

Water Show at Cypress Gardens, Florida

Life in Kingston, Jamaica
1970

My dear Grandchildren,

Settling back in one's tropical homeland is so much easier than settling in a new and foreign country!

As returning residents with a proper bill of lading from Great Lakes Trans Caribbean Line, we did not have any difficulty clearing our container of household effects and personal belongings. It was the same for our 1969 Dodge Dart four-door sedan listed as C$3000 on the Import License documents. We stayed with my eldest brother, Keith and his wife, Shirley until we bought a flat-roof concrete three-bedroom house at 18 Lords Road, in New Kingston which was a newly-developed area mid-town and close to Half-Way Tree. The residential area was considered a middle-upper class neighbourhood away from the commercial area on Knutsford Boulevard.

Upon our return, my first duty was to go and see my father and siblings in Petersfield, Westmoreland. Here, it was no trouble to let the word out that "Miss Carol" was looking to hire a live-in maid to stay with her and family in Kingston – even though we were located almost at the opposite end of the island from Westmoreland. In fact, even before the end of my overnight visit, Lurline showed up and expressed interest in working for me in Kingston. I had known Lurline from my childhood days. She had been a classmate at Petersfield Elementary School. Her grandmother, "Miss Georgie", was a fair-skinned mulatto woman

18 Lords Road, New Kingston

who had dominated the left-section of the store piazza in front of my parents' place of business when I was growing up. One day, Miss Georgie just appeared with her wood and glass case of baked goods and parked herself on this section of the piazza to sell her items. From then on, every day she took up this space, such that it became understood in the community that this was her place of business. Papa and Mama allowed anyone to eke out a living on the store piazza so long as they did not become involved in any fights or block the entrance into our store. Miss Georgie and Lurline's parents were well-known to us in the community. They respected our family

Kingston, Jamaica 1970

and were happy that Lurline would be working for me and would be safe with me in the big city of Kingston.

Eddie found a job with the Consulting Engineering firm of A. J Benghiat and Associates. His boss, Fred Benghiat was an English Engineer who was married to a Jamaican-Chinese lady named Norma. We had a good working relationship with them, especially with Norma who was quite clever and artistic. Norma used to produce colourful picture postcards. On one side was a photograph of a delicious looking Jamaican dish and the recipe for the dish was printed on the back of the card. These postcards were great souvenirs for tourists. Locals also mailed them to Jamaican friends who were living abroad.

The engineering firm's major project at that time was building a Transshipment port in Kingston Harbour. Around this same time, the famous Myrtle Bank Hotel was demolished so that a deep-water pier could be built to accommodate luxury cruise ships bringing tourists to our beautiful "Island in the Sun". The tourist industry in Jamaica was booming. This was a time when the whole world began to recognize Jamaica's natural beauty – the Blue Mountain range, clear blue sea and white sandy beaches. It also helped that Jamaican singing artists were gaining international recognition. They were indeed ambassadors for Jamaica and Jamaican music was being played all over the world, especially among the Jamaican diaspora in Britain and the United States of America.

Our return to Jamaica and living in Kingston meant a period of making new friends. Eddie enjoyed meeting the other engineers in the firm like John, Garth, and Donald. Donald, a Jamaican-born Chinese, was married to Cynthia whom I had met some years before in this way: Cynthia and her sisters, Enid and Marie, were touring the island with their salesman cousin, Leslie (who, coincidentally, was also my cousin on his mother's side of the family). When the sisters arrived in Petersfield, they introduced themselves to my father, as the daughters of Mr. and Mrs. Osmond Chung who were so indebted to him "for saving their lives".

Apparently, my father and the Chungs had been on the same cargo ship migrating to Jamaica from China in the early 1900s. The ship had delivered its banana cargo in England and was returning to Jamaica to pick up another shipment. En route, they stopped in Montréal where they picked up Chinese immigrants to Jamaica who had travelled across Canada from Vancouver to meet the ship. My father did not know the Chungs before this journey, although they had similar backgrounds in that they all were travelling to Jamaica on the invitation of relatives who were already settled on the island and had hopes that they could make a better life for themselves in the Caribbean.

The ship was not a passenger ship and the Chinese immigrants found themselves holed up in the lower deck of the ship. With not enough food and medicine for the journey by sea, the Chungs got ill. Apparently, Mrs. Chung was more feeble than her husband and terribly seasick. My father, who was a strapping, athletic young man, did what any other Hakka Chinese would do for his *Chee-Gah ngin* (own people) who found themselves in difficulty and nursed them back to health by just caring for them.

Kingston, Jamaica 1970

Upon landing safely in Kingston Harbour, they separated going to the opposite ends of the island – the Chungs continued on their journey to Port Antonio, Portland and my father went on to Petersfield, Westmoreland. But the Chungs never forgot what my father had done for them. After many years of eking out a living and raising a family of their own, their three grown daughters were, on this day, standing in front of Papa paying their parents' respects. Papa was thrilled and we children were amazed to learn this story of Papa's benevolent past.

Cynthia and Donald became good friends. Our children grew up together in Jamaica and our friendship continued after both our families migrated to Canada later in life. Here, even in our golden years in Toronto, Ontario, we remain friends. I have never met Marie again but Enid with husband, Lennie migrated to Toronto along with their eldest sister, Pearl and husband, Eric whom I finally met and got to know as well.

John, another of Eddie's co-workers, was English. One day, he invited Eddie to go sailing with him and another English landowner and farmer living in St. Mary, Les Dutton and his English wife, Sue. The Duttons owned a 32-foot sailboat named "Argo" which was moored at the Royal Jamaica Yacht Club (RJYC) off Palisadoes Road. I was eventually invited to go sailing on weekends and we got along well with the Duttons and the rest of the crew which included Sue's bachelor cousin, Richard, and Monica, daughter of a family friend.

Sue was such a lovely person and apparently felt very much at home in St. Mary. She treated her hired help very well without any hint of British colonialism or colour prejudice. Les and Sue had three sons and they would often leave their youngest, Paul, with our maid, Lurline so that he could play with Brian when we went sailing. We would sail around Kingston Harbour and frequently anchor off Lime Cay to cook the lobsters we caught with metal trident poles while snorkeling. There is nothing as tasty as freshly-caught lobster boiled in a pot of sea water!

We competed in a number of harbour races together. These often ended with dinner at the RJYC after docking at the marina. Before we had dinner, however, we would all have drinks to unwind and would rehash the race strategy once we were docked at our berth. Les loved his liquor as much as the British crew loved our Jamaican rum and Red Stripe Beer. These conversations about races could get serious; however, Monica and I were happy just to relax on the foredeck with our ice-cold, refreshing ginger beer. We did not have a real care about our placement in the race!

Sailing on 'Callaloo' L-R: Richard, John, Eddie, Garth, Skipper Les, Carol, Sue

Kingston, Jamaica 1970

Sometimes, we competed in overnight races to Bowden, St. Thomas and back. These races could become dangerous. If the weather was rough, we would have to clip on safety harnesses while on deck. The harnesses were mandatory if one was on deck at night as it was pitch black. With Captain Les at the helm, we would start between East Farewell Buoy and Plumb Point Lighthouse and head for Bowden Harbour finishing between the Northern tip of the United Fruit Company Pier and Watson Spit. The return leg of the race would be from Bowden observing all Channel markers via the East channel and the main Ship's channel in Kingston Harbour finishing between Mark 1 and Club West. The top contenders in these races included Skippers Maurice Facey sailing "Tiara", Owen Plant sailing "Picante", Keith Jones in "Cocoban", Jim Davidson in "Tonteria", John Lethbridge in "Scandale" and Ralph Mahfood in "Desiree".

Sometimes there were weekend races to Port Antonio. The course of these races would start from Mark 1 and the RJYC racing committee boat in a westerly direction towards Port Antonio by way of the ship's Channel, leaving East Farewell Buoy to starboard and Morant Point to port. The finish would be between the northern end of the Finger Pier at the EJAA marina and the White Cage Buoy in the west Harbour, south of Navy Island in Port Antonio. There were even week-long races to Montego Bay or Lucea and even longer races to Miami, Florida, but I did not like to leave Lurline alone with the boys for more than an overnight absence so I did not go on these longer races.

Eddie got seasick frequently but loved every minute of sailing with this lovely group of expatriates and rubbing shoulders with the wealthy upper-class Jamaicans like the Pitters, Thwaites, Nunes, Duffs, Grants, Phillipsons, and Birches. In time, I became very involved with these families as well. I was elected to various committees that did everything from organizing the Regattas, to the Inspection of the Fleet by the RCYC Commodore and Flag Officers, to more social events like, the Children's Swim Meet, Social Evenings, Fashion Shows and Tea Parties.

Harbour race - "Callaloo" with red, white and blue spinnaker

The following year, Les and Sue bought a bigger Cal 40-foot sailboat which was aptly named *Callaloo*. With this better vessel, we began winning more of the keenly contested races. The bigger sailboat also meant that more crew was needed and thus Garth, another of Eddie's co-worker, became a regular member of our crew. Not only were Eddie and I enjoying sailing on *Callaloo*, we were also getting to know the Duttons more and we liked them a lot. We had the opportunity to see their property in St. Mary and I noticed the devotion of their household help and the farm hands. They owned an apartment in Constant Spring for whenever they were in Kingston, especially on weekends for sailing. On one of these weekends, Les suddenly became ill. He was so sick that he was hospitalized at Medical Associates. When he was stabilized, Sue drove back to their apartment only to receive a phone call that Les had taken a turn for the worse and passed away. Eddie and I, and all of their sailing buddies at RJYC were so saddened. We all attended his funeral at St. Peter's Church in Port Royal. Appropriately, his cremated remains were scattered in the Caribbean Sea he loved and enjoyed from the deck of his Cal 40 sailboat by his bereaved wife Sue and his three sons, Peter, Hugh and Paul.

The Lampart family: Garth holding Trudi, Peggy holding Marc

Sue continued sailing *Callaloo* but it was obvious that things were not the same without Skipper Les. Sue began coming into Kingston less and less, especially after her sons all began attending school back home in England. A few years later, I received a wedding announcement card that advised me that on 03 August 1976, Susan Marling Dutton quietly married Colin Charles Adams in Blossom Village, Little Cayman, British West Indies in the presence of Sue's three sons and Colin's three sons, Charles, Neil and Mark. The card indicated that the new Mr. and Mrs. Adams were making Grand Cayman their place of residence.

Even though we no longer sailed together, we found ourselves spending more time with Garth and his wife, Peggy (Marguerite). We got along so very well that when I had a third son, Jason, I asked them to be Jason's Godparents. We met their immediate families and learned that within his family, Garth was called "Peter". He and Peggy did not have any children and later adopted two local children, a daughter, Trudi and a son, Marc. I thought that their decision to provide a secure, loving home for these local children was a very noble thing to do. These children would be very fortunate to have parents like the Lamparts.

We spent many wonderful times together. On one occasion, we decided to climb to the Blue Mountain Peak. The Blue Mountain Peak is the highest point in Jamaica. On a clear day, one can see all the way to Cuba from the peak. This trek was planned with other employees of Benghiat & Associates. We drove as far up the mountain range as Mavis Bank via Papine and Gordon Town. This part of the trip was seventeen miles. Then we drove another six and a half miles to Whitfield Hall where we parked our cars after fording a river at Mahogany Vale. Whitfield Hall hostel is 4,200 feet above sea level and is the last inhabited house on the way to Blue Mountain Peak. Here we started our ascent up the Blue Mountain on foot. It was a warm and sunny day and we enjoyed viewing the coffee plantations and surrounding verdant hills dotted with

Kingston, Jamaica 1970

houses in the distance. A mule was hired for Peggy who seemed undaunted by the height of her saddle from the winding path. Despite the fact that the path got more and more narrow the higher we climbed, her mule was sure-footed. Thirty shillings (British sterling) was well worth the cost of hiring that mule!

The sun began to set as we continued hiking. The sunset was beautiful but by then we were all getting so tired and winded that we were not admiring our surroundings very much. By nightfall, we reached the hut where we would spend the night. It cost one shilling per night per person to stay at this hut. We had already paid for our group at Whitfield Hall hostel. The hut was almost at the peak and we planned that we would rise early the next morning and climb to the top of the peak to view the sunrise. By the time we arrived at the hut, it had gotten really cold. Another set of hikers sharing the hut with us lit a fire but the wood was damp which caused the hut to be filled with smoke. Everyone was coughing but we all remained inside as it was too cold to venture outside. The beds inside the hut were not comfortable either. They were metal spring beds without mattresses but we were too exhausted to care and as soon as we lay down on them, we promptly fell asleep.

The self-appointed leaders of the group awakened us early the next morning. When we finally made it to the peak, we were so elated that we did not mind that we could not see Cuba in the distance. It was so early that the morning mist had not been burned off by the rising sun. Soon, we began our descent. As expected, our descent was much easier than our ascent and Peggy did not need to ride her mule the entire way back to our parked cars. What an achievement for all of us!

Peggy and Garth and Eddie and I also spent a lot of sociable times with my other girlfriend, Venn whom I met when I went to work at Caribbean Estate Management Company as a real estate agent. Venn was a most efficient receptionist and Gal Friday for our American boss, Mr. Cowan. It was obvious why he wooed her away from British American Insurance Company where they had both worked.

Venn was Jamaican and had, coincidentally, attended my alma mater, Wolmer's High School for Girls. Venn was in a lower form at school and did not board at the Wolmer's hostel so we did not get the chance to meet during school days. She married a Jamaican Chinese, Ken Yap and they have two lovely daughters, Simone and Marsha. We three couples spent great times at each other's homes and have remained friends over the years despite all the changes that have happened since, including Garth passing away in

The Yap family: Ken and Venn with daughters Simone (L) and Marsha (R)

Kingston, Jamaica 1970

Jamaica, Venn and Ken migrating to Washington, D.C., and Eddie and I migrating to Canada.

Another important person in our circle of friends in Kingston was my bridesmaid, Jeanie. In 1968, Jeanie had married a Jamaican Chinese young man named Peter and started a family of her own. Peter was the son of Lizette and Austin Chong, who were friends of our family when we were growing up in Savanna-La-Mar. Lizette and my mother were good friends. They gravitated towards each other because they shared many similarities. They were both first-generation Jamaican-born Chinese who were very westernized, outgoing and community-minded. As a result, both families got along well and we children spent many happy times together. We were so close that at one point, Miss Liz, with every good intention, had even tried to arrange a serious relationship for me with one of her cousins from Black River!

Godparents Mr. Forrest and Dulcie at baby Gordon's christening

About the time that Eddie and I returned to Jamaica, Jeanie and Peter moved from Westmoreland to Kingston along with Jeanie's parents, Gordon and Norma Forrest. It was good to have long-time friends living near us again. Mr. and Mrs. Forrest had become good friends of my family when they were living in Petersfield and when my second son, Baby Gordon, was to be christened at St. Lukes' Parish Church, the same church where I had been confirmed as a teenager, I thought it would be nice to ask Mr. Forrest to be Baby Gordon's Godfather. Norma told me years later how pleased he was to be asked and I was thankful he agreed. In absentia, Eddie's old school-chum, Donald, was the other God-father and I asked my cousin, Dulcie to be Baby Gordon's Godmother, to her delight.

Dulcie and family lived at the end of the "widest street in Jamaica", Great George Street in Savanna-La-Mar and she used to work at the Barclays Bank branch. She was given a promotion and was transferred to Kingston so she was happy to babysit the boys during the week after work and drive home to Savanna-La-Mar on the weekends. This was very convenient for me as Lurline needed to have the weekday evenings off and Eddie and I had started to play competitive badminton on weekday evenings also.

We met wonderful friends at Abbey Court Badminton Club like Eddie and Nora, Eustace and Joan, David and Gladys, Daphne, "Spokey" Leslie, Barbara and many others. We played against other top badminton clubs in the Inter-club League matches such as Norbrook Badminton Club, Transom Club, U.W.I, Y.M.C.A, Club

Kingston, Jamaica 1970

The Shortwood Giants Badminton Team
Back L-R: Orlando Lai Fatt, Stanley Shim, Norman Chin Lue, Gregory Yapp, Desmond De Pass
Front L-R: Norman Chin You, Pat Lyn, Carol Wong, Jo Lai Fatt, Mike Chin

India and Rainbow Badminton Club. I enjoyed playing in a different league for Shortwood Giants and was very happy competing with people like Barry and Winston Lue, Orlando Lai Fatt, Desmond De Pass, Yvonne and Gregory Yapp, Stanley Shim, Norman Chin You, Pat Lyn, Diane Tenn, Mike Chin, Frank Young, Norman Chin Lue. We also played socially at Orlando and Jo's house as well as on the home courts at Major and Mrs. Bradley's. Of course, it was not all about competition. There were also celebration and victory dinners at Casa Monte Hotel and lots of fun time just playing badminton in the open air under the starlit skies.

When the Jamaica National Arena was built, Badminton Championships were played indoors. Despite the improper concrete flooring which led to sore joints later in life as well as knee and back injuries, it was a treat to play without prevailing winds. Growing up in a Third World country allowed us lots of freedom but we also had to cope with the shortcomings of backward technology and accept what facilities were available to us.

My dear Grandchildren, like everything in life, there are pluses and minuses and it is up to the individual to balance both and be grateful for small mercies.

Your loving Ah-Poh

Life in Kingston, Jamaica
1971

My dear Grandchildren,

By 1971, our little family was well settled back in Jamaica. The household was running smoothly and we did not regret moving to Kingston.

At this time, Eddie and I received two wedding invitations. Eddie's sister Ouida, who had been one of my bridesmaids, was getting married to Brian Graville in Montréal, Canada in June and my cousin, Ickia Lue was getting married to Alex Chung, nephew of John R. Wong in July at Sts. Peter & Paul Church in Kingston. Eddie and I decided to attend both weddings. We would attend Ouida's wedding first and afterwards, fly across the Atlantic to go on a European holiday. The decision caused me a dilemma because, as much as I wanted to travel, all I could think about was how I was leaving my two young sons for about a month back home in Jamaica. Brian was not yet five years old and Gordon was almost two years old. I could not bear to be apart from them for such a long while.

Eventually, I came up with what I thought would be the best compromise – all four of us would fly to Montréal. We would rent an apartment in the same apartment complex as Eddie's uncle, Washy, and his wife Sheila and their two boys. Their boys were just a bit older than Brian and Gordon. I figured that if we spent about a week in Montréal after the wedding, the boys would be able to become acquainted with and be comfortable with their relatives. At that point, Eddie and I would leave the boys with Washy and Sheila and head off on our European holiday. We would then return to Montréal, pick up the boys and head back home to Jamaica.

I guess the communication between Washy and Sheila and us was not very good because upon our arrival in Montréal, just as we were getting settled into our rented apartment, we learned that Washy, Sheila and their boys were planning to go to Jamaica -- before our scheduled return from Europe. To compound matters, Sheila's two nieces, Lisa and Stacey, had arrived from California to spend time with their cousins before they would all head off to Jamaica. It was going to be a handful for Washy and Sheila -- taking care of six kids under 8 years of age!

All the kids were having a grand time playing together and getting reacquainted so I decided not to totally disrupt our travel plans. Instead, I asked my very good Scottish friends, Irene and Ian, now living in the suburbs of Lachine, to take care of Brian and Gordon when Washy, Sheila and the other children left for Jamaica. Irene and Ian were happy to do so, but in hindsight, I think that we should have all moved over to Irene and Ian's home immediately after making this decision so that the boys could

Kingston, Jamaica 1971

have become acquainted with our Scottish friends before we left for Europe. It must have been traumatic for the boys to be taken away by their new guardians after weeks of being taken care of by relatives and playing with Craig, Duane, Lisa and Stacey! Oh well, hindsight is always 20/20! I guess we never thought of this alternate plan because we were committed to the short term rental on the apartment and it did not occur to us to just give up the apartment. Added to that, we had the distraction of my youngest brother, Donald (Donny) and my sister, Elaine who had made plans to meet us in Montréal so that we could show them around La Belle Province. Elaine was coming up from Jamaica for the first time to acquaint herself with Montréal because she was planning to migrate to Canada shortly.

At that time, Donny was attending McMaster University in Hamilton, Ontario and was in the Science program with the hope of getting into medical school to become a doctor. When he arrived in Montréal, the boys were happy to see him again. Gordon, our toddler, found it difficult to call him "Uncle Donny" and kept calling him "Dan-Dan" to the amusement of all the other children. We had lots of fun being together, especially in the evenings when we gathered at Washy's now crowded apartment for dinner with all six children gleefully playing together. Dinner time was busy, noisy and chaotic; the chattering children were fed first, then the table cleared for the next seating of adults. And there was the clean-up afterwards.

The Chins, the Williams, the Wongs and all the children attended Ouida and Brian's wedding ceremony at St. Philip's Church in Montréal West and the reception after at The Martinique Hotel, 1005 Guy Street, downtown Montréal. Eddie and I had previously met Brian Graville who was an English metallurgist from Kent. We all went to dinner at Mouettes Seafood Restaurant where tea and coffee were 20¢, clam chowder 85¢ and a lobster dinner was $8.50 and they instantly liked Brian when he proceeded to use his hands to eat his steamed lobster with relish. Ouida and Brian would reside in Baie D'Urfé, Québec before moving across provinces to Ontario within a few years.

The children were totally happy. Washy and Sheila figured they would be able to cope with our children in addition to their own children and their nieces, and it was agreed that Irene and Ian would come and relieve them of Brian and

Brian and Ouida Graville's wedding, Montréal, Québec

Kingston, Jamaica 1971

Gordon before they left for Jamaica. Elaine had taken her flight home and Donny had returned to university, so it was time for Eddie and me to begin our European holiday. We flew first to London, England where we stayed in the home of Harvey and Joyce Lou-Hing who were the parents of Merryl and Linda. Merryl and Linda were sisters who had recently married Eddie's childhood friends, Donald and James. Donald and James went to London to study Accounting after finishing high school at Cornwall College. It was in London that they met and married the two sisters. Merryl and Linda's family had migrated to England from Guyana via Trinidad many years before.

Washy, Sheila and son Duane Chin

Donald married the older sister, Merryl and James, the younger, Linda. Completing their studies, they returned home to Montego Bay with their wives and we were delighted to meet them. We became lifelong friends. Our children all grew up together. They attended the same Montego Montessori school and we continued our friendships when we all migrated to Toronto many years later.

Harvey and Joyce were very hospitable considering they were meeting us for the very first time. They were a very outgoing and friendly couple who liked to open their house to young people so we met other family members and friends of their two sons, Terry and Robin. James' brother, Edmund was also visiting from Jamaica so Joyce and Harvey were happy to take all of us around. They took us to the dog races and night clubbing. For sightseeing, Eddie and I bought a 7-day "Go-as-you-please" ticket for £2 and two shillings each, that is, two English guineas per person. This ticket pass allowed us unlimited use on London's famous red double-decker buses and the efficient Underground Railway for a week. We were fortunate to be there for the birthday celebrations of Queen Elizabeth II and the Trooping of the Colours. The ceremony was so impressive. We lined the sidewalks close to Buckingham Palace Gates to watch the Changing of the Guards as well. It was fascinating to see the historical places we had been reading about in our school history books like London Bridge, Westminster Abbey, Tower of London, Tate Gallery, British Museum, Trafalgar Square, Soho

Queen Elizabeth II on her birthday

Kingston, Jamaica 1971

L-R: Carol, Joyce Lou Hing, Edmund Hew, Terry Lou Hing

and other such places. Plus, we also got to eat fish and chips wrapped in past editions of newspaper! We did not give any thought to whether this traditional way of serving fish and chips was unsanitary! We experienced typical English weather as well -- needless to say, we had to purchase umbrellas and raincoats for walking around the streets of London.

One evening, we went to see *Pyjama Tops* at the White Hall Theatre of Adult Entertainment. This was a controversial sex comedy at the time because nude swimmers performed in a "see through" glass swimming pool on stage. We also saw the controversial American Tribal Love-Rock Musical, *Hair* at Shaftesbury Theatre and attended the Royal Tournament 1971. It was then in its 31st year at Earls Court and it cost us 80 pence per person to attend. We did not spend all our time in London. We rented a car and visited Warwick Castle – one of the great fortifications constructed during the 14th century by Beauchamp, Earl of Warwick, plus the quaint English towns and rolling verdant countryside. We could only drive by Balmoral Castle since it was being occupied by the Royal Family when we went to see it. We also drove to Oxford, the City of Spires and thought of Eddie's brother, Vernon who had studied at Oxford University as a Rhodes' Scholar. We loved visiting Stratford-upon-Avon. I could not help thinking about my English Literature teachers when we visited properties like the house where Shakespeare was born, Anne Hathaway's cottage and Mary Arden's house. The admission fee at that time was only four shillings.

To visit Scotland, we took an overnight train to Edinburgh and, on the strict orders of our friends Ian and Irene, stayed at a traditional Bed and Breakfast so that we could experience a full Scottish breakfast, including porridge! When I first met Irene in Montréal, she used to tell me about the hearty and healthy Scottish breakfasts she ate growing up. She insisted that a breakfast was not a breakfast

Eddie at Warwick Castle, England

unless one had porridge that "sticks to your ribs". Irene also arranged for us to stay with her parents in Lomond Gardens, Fife so we rented a car to drive up to Stirling Castle and other monuments associated with Mary Queen of Scots. We also visited the Abbey and Palace of Holyroodhouse founded in 1128 by David I for successive Scottish monarchs and Linlithgow Palace built by James I in 1425. Other historical places surrounding the Firth of Forth were Dundrennan Abbey and Inchmahome Priory where the Cistercian monks sheltered Queen Mary during the Battle of Pinkie. We drove further around The Trossachs, past Auchtermuchty, which was the home of Ian's parents. After visiting Irene's parents in Fife, we ended up in the beautiful Lake District

Carol flanked by Irene's parents and brother Ian

Irene's father was a coal miner with a quiet disposition and had a real heavy Scottish accent so we did not speak with him as much as with Irene's mother who was outgoing and high-spirited like Irene. She worked in a pub and made sure to take us there to show us off to her customers – "a real, live Chink from Canada"! We found the Scottish people to be more friendly, chatty and happier than the English folks. We were made to feel totally at home with Irene's family even though we had never laid eyes on them before!

Next, we flew to France and stayed on the left Bank of Paris. We thought that the Parisians were the absolute opposite of the Scots. They were not very helpful and quite snobbish, looking down on our Québecois French when we used it to try and find accommodations. "Chambre pour deux" got us the smallest room on the highest floor without any washroom facilities …and there was no building elevator either. They were not polite to foreigners on the street either and things were quite expensive. Regardless, it was exciting to see the Tour Eiffel, Arc de Triomphe, the Louvre, sidewalk cafes and everything that Paris is famous for. We even took a day trip to Versailles which, with its splendid display of French opulence in the Palace and beautifully manicured courtyards, was well worth the trip.

From there we flew on to Holland where we were happy to stay in the home of Eddie's Aunt Lucille and her tall, pleasant Dutch husband, Erik, a chemical engineer.

Eddie at Versailles, France

Kingston, Jamaica 1971

They lived outside Amsterdam in the wooded area of Putten. We would join the merry throng of cyclists riding to the Putten train station, leave our borrowed bicycles at the station and hop on the train to Amsterdam. The trip cost two kronas. We would return later in the evening to pick up our bicycles and ride back to their house. Occasionally, Erik and Lucille would drive into Amsterdam after work and meet us for dinner in the city.

We will not forget Erik's love of fine dining – or what we found to be his strange ritual when making a toast. After making his toast, Erik would gaze deeply in the eyes of the person being toasted, shake his head quickly from side to side, before putting his lips to the glass and taking a sip. All this would be done without ever breaking his gaze. For many years afterwards, Eddie and I adopted Erik's funny ritual as our own private toast. Over the next few decades, we were to meet Erik and Lucille again in Canada and even later, long after Lucille had passed away, we would once again visit the back woods of Putten, to enjoy fine dining and drink many toasts to our now elderly Dutch gentleman friend, Erik.

The refuge of Anne Frank and family during the Nazi occupation

Our sightseeing around Amsterdam included the Canal Tour. I had only recently read the *Diary of Anne Frank*. The story was still so vivid in my mind that I found myself becoming very emotional as I passed the house where she and her family had been hidden. Eddie and I could not resist visiting the largest permanent diamond exhibition in the world at A. Van Moppes and Son where we could only gaze in awe at the diamonds displayed. Another highlight of the trip was walking around Amsterdam's infamous Red Light District. The novelty of seeing the ladies on display in the show windows was a real eye-opener for us! We thought the Dutch way of dealing with prostitution was so innovative and practical in comparison to the prudish attitudes the rest of the world seemed to have. We were particularly impressed to learn that the "ladies of the night" received regular health checks so that their customers could be confident of their state of health. Plus, by being so open about the world's oldest profession, Holland created the biggest boom for tourism in Amsterdam – although I don't know if it was a big boom for the prostitutes. It seemed like the Red Light District was filled more with curious onlookers like Eddie and me than actual customers. In any case, whether or not they were interested in soliciting business from a prostitute, curious tourists still brought in revenue to the city!

Dan Stratt, Amsterdam, Holland

One day, we visited downtown Amsterdam only to witness Dam Stratt Square was still being hosed down by police officers to get rid of the young, pot-smoking hippies who camped there at night on the steps under the imposing National monument. Who would have guessed that in the next millennium, Amsterdam, in the typical liberal-minded Dutch fashion, would legally allow the smoking of marijuana in its famous coffee shops. Nowadays, people can smoke marijuana freely in a safe and controlled environment – a very Dutch way of doing things! Tourists can visit these "Amsterdam Famous Coffee Shops" or take a two-hour walking tour to cover the History of cannabis, medical marijuana, and industrial uses of Hemp.

Before leaving Holland, we took a trip to Rotterdam which boasted the newly-built Euromast Space Tower overlooking the busiest harbour in the world at the time. From there, we planned to take the train to Copenhagen, Denmark. When we arrived at the station, however, we were astonished to run into Arthur and Ann Lowe from Norbrook Badminton Club! Fancy meeting another couple from Jamaica in a distant European city! We could not believe that they were arriving in Holland just as we were leaving.

In Copenhagen (Kobenhavn), Eddie and I stayed at an extremely clean Bed & Breakfast house belonging to a nice and demure Danish lady. She explained to us how the public transport system worked and we marveled that the public buses used the honour system of payment. Passengers paid their fares when they disembarked at the rear doors where the boxes for payment were installed. The bus driver was just content with making his way through traffic and opening the front door for passengers to enter. He seemed to totally ignore those passengers disembarking. What an honest set of people in those days!

Kingston, Jamaica 1971

Copenhagen's "Little mermaid"

We were delighted to see the symbol of Copenhagen, the famous statue of the Little Mermaid sitting on a rock in the sea by the harbour. We especially enjoyed Tivoli Gardens. Everywhere was lit up and there were nightly performances and exhibitions – the whole place had a festival atmosphere.

We walked around the Stroeger area of cobblestone streets lined with restaurants and gift shops before reaching the Town Hall Square which was surrounded by more restaurants alongside the canal and warehouses and marinas. The whole area had a very different ambiance to the canals in Amsterdam. We thought that the Danish people were more polite and orderly than the Dutch. I also really liked their furniture. Danish furniture design was pleasingly simple and they used very unique fabrics for their furnishings. Because of travel weight restrictions, I could only purchase yards of open weave drape material to bring home with me. It's been 40 years since that trip, but you will still find that fabric hanging in my home today!

It had been a wonderful European holiday, but I was anxious to see my little sons, Brian and Gordon, and take them back home to Jamaica. Our Scottish friends, Ian and Irene who were now taking care of them in Montréal brought them to meet us when we arrived back at Dorval Airport. I was happy to see them again but I was horrified to see Gordon dressed in one of Irene's daughter's pink outfits. Apparently, Gordon had gotten much bigger during our absence and had outgrown his clothes so Irene thought it would be cute to dress him in Tracey's clothes. Brian was a bit taller and was quietly smiling when he saw us. Clearly, he recognized his mother and father, but Gordon was wondering who we were. That nearly broke my heart and I could only hug my pretty little boy dressed in pink oh so tightly.

After spending a few days with our dear friends and reacquainting ourselves with the boys, we all flew back home to Jamaica, and I vowed never to ever leave them for such a long time again!

Your loving Ah-Poh

Life in Kingston, Jamaica
1971

My dear Grandchildren,

Our house in Kingston backed onto the property of the Friends Preparatory School (run by the religious group of American Quakers) which opened up onto Worthington Avenue. We thought that it would be most convenient for Brian to attend that school since it was almost in our backyard. All we would have to do was to create an opening in our back fence for Brian to attend his first school.

Not long after we made that decision, however, I learned of Mona Preparatory School where one of my past teachers at Wolmer's High School for Girls, Mrs. Vidal Smith, was the headmistress. We decided to send Brian to Mona instead. I did not mind dropping off Eddie at work so that I could have the car to take Brian to Mona Preparatory School and then pick him up at the end of the school day and later, drive back to pick Eddie up from work as well if it meant that Brian would be studying under the leadership of a woman I respected and admired!

Having a live-in maid made this transportation arrangement even more convenient. By this time, my first maid, Lurline, had become involved in a personal relationship in Petersfield and wanted to move back to that area. She suggested that her younger sister, "Cutie" could replace her. Since I knew Lurline's family background so well, I had no problem hiring Cutie and having her move into the maid's quarters adjoining our house. She doted on Gordon! She did not allow him to learn to help himself -- even when eating. Cutie would spoonfeed him after picking out all the bones from his meat and removing the shell off his hard-boiled eggs, long after he was old enough to do such tasks for himself. As a result, Gordon became spoiled and lazy at the dining table, traits that I believe he carried with him into his adult life. But Cutie was not all to blame; I spoiled him too. When it was time for him to begin school at Friends Preparatory School, Gordon would cry because he did not want me to leave and, since I was allowed to bring in my sewing or letter-writing materials, I would sit at the back of the classroom just to make him happy. After many weeks of this behaviour, however, I decided that it was time to get firm with him and left him to cry after I walked with him through the back fence and took him to his classroom at school. Needless to add, the following morning I was dismissed as no longer needed!

Eddie and I decided that it was time to make another attempt to have a baby daughter. There was a three-year age difference between Brian and Gordon and I felt that the age difference was too wide as they were not able to have a very close relationship at this time during their childhood because Gordon was too young to be a playmate to Brian. So, I planned that my next child would be only two years younger than Gordon. There were about two years' difference among all of my

Kingston, Jamaica 1971

siblings and we had grown up quite close. There was always someone close enough in age to you to be a partner in crime, which made for good sibling memories once we reached adulthood. I soon got pregnant for the third time. Once more, Eddie suffered instead of me through the morning sickness that expectant mothers always experience during their first trimester of pregnancy!

I felt hale and hearty throughout my pregnancy – healthy enough to start planting a vegetable garden in the backyard. I had not been very interested in domestic matters when I was growing up, and was especially uninterested in gardening. That was a task always handled by Mama and the yardboys. Nevertheless, I planted a garden and soon discovered that I had a natural green thumb. I was really good at growing bok-choy. I quickly learned, for example, that cabbage cannot be left to mature so long for the outer leaves to fold in because the already folded head of tender cabbage will soon open up and become tough and inedible. Anyway, I was so good with growing Chinese bok-choy that I had to sell the surplus to John R. Wong Supermarket in our neighbourhood. Mrs. Wong was happy to offer this oriental vegetable to her Chinese customers and I was pleased that my new hobby was profitable.

Around this time, Attas & Defour, consulting engineers in Port of Spain, Trinidad, accepted Eddie's application to attend a Seminar on Highway Engineering held in September 1971 at the University of the West Indies (UWI) Cave Hill Campus in St. Augustine, Trinidad. The seminar was just for a few days and, since my cousin, Dulcie was willing to babysit her godson, Gordon, and Cutie was there to take care of Brian, I decided to take this opportunity for one last trip before I would be home-bound with our next infant. Eddie and I flew British West Indian Airways (BWIA) to Port of Spain and stayed in Centeno with our friends, Delores and Wilson Look Kin whom we had met during our 1960s university days in Montréal.

Carol pregnant with Jason visiting Centeno, Trinidad

Delores is Jamaican Chinese and the sister of our young friend, Norman Chin You who was attending Loyola College. Delores had been working with Seagrams in Jamaica when she was transferred to their office in Montréal. Initially, she had lived with her brother, Norman, but she later became the roommate of her cousin, Doreen Chin and Eddie's sister, Ouida. Delores had met Wilson, a Trinidadian Chinese, when he was studying Agronomy at MacDonald College, a part of McGill University located in St. Anne de Bellevue. They fell in love, tied the knot and moved to Trinidad after Wilson's graduation.

Apparently there is a lot of flooding in Centeno because most of the houses are built on concrete stilts. The space below the houses is used as a covered car port. The town next to

Centeno heading in the direction of Port of Spain was Tuna Puna. I found this to be an amusing name and it was hilarious when the locals would hail the mini-buses shouting "Tuna Puna" or simply "Puna"! When Delores and Wilson were at work and Eddie attended his seminar, I would visit my cousin, Winifred (Winnie) who lived in Maraval. Winnie is the granddaughter of my father's Uncle Jackson. She had left Jamaica for England to study hairdressing. While she was in England, she met Tony, a Trinidadian Chinese who was studying in London as well. The two had married and, after briefly residing in Jamaica, moved to Trinidad to raise their son, Dean. On our visits, Winnie taught me how to make macramé hand bags which was the rave in Trinidad at this time.

Trinidad was another British West Indian possession. It is located south of Jamaica, close to Venezuela. Their natural resource is oil which brought much wealth to the country. They also boast the first Chinese Governor General in the Caribbean, Sir Solomon Ho Choy. The dynamic scholar and politician, Dr. Eric Williams was their Prime Minister at the time I visited the island. Many East Indian and Chinese indentured labourers had settled in Trinidad during the late 1800s so Wilson and Tony would have been second or third generation Trinidadian-Chinese. I did not think that Trinidad was as beautiful as Jamaica and their main beach, Maracas, was so disappointing to visit. The sand was coarse and a paler shade of brown and the sea was rough with frightening waves and a strong undertow from the Atlantic Ocean. The neighbouring island of Tobago, however, is where one could find white sands and beach resorts comparable to my beautiful island of Jamaica.

At the end of our visit, en route to Jamaica, we visited the nearby Dutch Island of Curaçao and stayed in Willemstad. Curaçao is one of the Netherland Antilles along with the islands of Aruba and Bonaire. Willemstad was a quaint village. There was a

Pontoon bridge and colourful buildings along canal, Curacao, Netherlands Antilles

Kingston, Jamaica 1971

swinging pontoon bridge over the waterway and rows of colourful stores, each painted in their own colour and design, lined the banks. Willemstad reminded me very much of the downtown canals in Amsterdam. Their beaches are not very white and the island gets heavy trade winds. Their national symbol is the Divi-Divi tree which is bent and wind-blown as expected but I still purchased a gold charm of the tree to be added to my travel bracelet of charms.

Gord and Brian on swing of gym set

Returning home to my two little sons was, as always, a joy. I am so grateful to Dulcie and Cutie's care and devotion to them while I was away. I also felt comfortable leaving the boys with Cutie and Dulcie because I knew that our home was surrounded by good neighbours who would help if there ever was an emergency. Our neighbourhood was deemed middle-upper class and our neighbours were quite friendly. On Lords Road, our next door neighbour was a Jamaican-Chinese engineer with an American wife. They also had three sons and a cute daughter, Melanie. The youngest, Jamie was Brian's age. He used to come over and play on our gym set in front of our lawn and under a tree separating our properties. Jamie's other brothers were teenagers, much older than himself. The oldest had his flowing hair "heavily waxed" to form "Rasta dreadlocks". Occasionally, I would see him on the flat roof of their house having a casual "spliff" of marijuana with other Rastafarians while a transistor radio would be blaring away. Their parents owned a construction company and were not usually at home during the daytime.

The Rastafarian Movement is a cult consisting mostly of descendants from the Negro slaves captured from the coast of Africa. They consider Emperor Haile Selassie of Ethiopia to be their God and call for repatriation to Africa. Most Rastafarians are vegetarians eating "Ital" (salt free) food and finding solace in smoking marijuana. Marijuana, known as "ganja" in Jamaica, is a banned substance on the island. Many young people, although not necessarily of African heritage, like my neighbour's son, were attracted to the lifestyle of the Rastafarians, including the smoking of marijuana. Marijuana was originally grown in Jamaica for its medicinal uses but when its hallucinogenic qualities were discovered, smoking for that purpose became popular. The plant grows easily and can be cultivated prolifically in the warm Jamaican climate and as such, it became an important product in a developing drug trade between the Jamaican masses and other countries in South and Central America as well as with the United States of America.

Kingston, Jamaica 1971

Our neighbours across the street owned the Gore Manufacturing Company which produced concrete building blocks. We discovered that they were an understanding set of people one afternoon when Brian had accidentally and unwittingly released the emergency brake of our car which was parked on our sloping driveway. The car slowly reversed out onto the road and almost hit down their fence. Our neighbours a few houses down were, like Eddie, originally from Montego Bay. Micheline was French-Canadian and her husband, Michael's family owned a construction company called Sharpe Construction in Montego Bay. Eddie's family and Michael's family knew each other well. They would become our lifelong friends as well, especially after we shared experiences such as moving back to Montego Bay at the same time and migrating to Canada at the same time too. For this latter move, we even shared a trailer for household effects. Michael and Micheline have two sons, Andrew and Christopher and a daughter, Melanie who were our children's ages. Around the corner from them lived Matthew, Janet and Harvey Lyn who opened a business, "Gifts Oriental" in the Premier Plaza next to Tropical Plaza on Half-Way Tree Road.

A few houses up on Lords Road, were four Chinese families known to us. Nuke and Violet's house was easy to find because their motorized fishing boat was always parked prominently on their front lawn. Violet is Eddie's cousin and they were a religious couple. Next to them was the Chung family who owned the well-known Chinese products store, Nam Keung on Barry Street in Chinatown. Their unmarried daughter, Ena lived with them and her friend, Liz, lived next door with her parents, Mr. & Mrs. Lyn. We all felt very comfortable and happy in our neighbourhood.

It was soon time for the new baby to come. We moved Brian and Gordon into one room with new bunk beds so that the third bedroom could be converted into a nursery. Once more, I had included pink chemises in the layette as I was again hoping for a baby girl. I had completed all the baby preparations and all I had left to do was just wait. One day, I felt some mild contractions. As this was my third baby, I did not panic or rush to go to the hospital. Instead, I took the time to shower, wash my hair and have something to eat before phoning Ena to see if she would be able to come down and help Cutie to babysit the boys. We had already made arrangements with Ena to come down to help when it was time for the new baby to arrive, so she was ready to walk down to our house in no time. Eddie then drove me to Medical Associates on Half-Way Tree Road. Once we got there, however, the relaxed pace changed as the nurses began to frantically try and locate my Obstetrics/Gynocologist Dr. Burrows. Apparently, I was dilating very quickly! Perhaps my friends were right – I had been playing too much badminton too far into my pregnancy.

I was wheeled into the delivery room -- as was the custom at that time, Eddie was not with me – and the nurses gave me a brown paper bag to breathe into hoping to delay the pushing urge because Dr. Burrows had not yet arrived. As soon as Dr. Burrows arrived and was scrub-ready, the baby literally slid out. All Dr. Burrows had to do was to announce that it was another boy baby and show me my third son, Jason Stuart Wong. It was 28 November 1971, in the Chinese Year of the Pig.

Kingston, Jamaica 1971

The Jamaican nurses were most efficient and the baby was taken to the nursery while I was wheeled back to my room to recuperate. I only stayed in the hospital for a few days however, before we returned home to two boys waiting eagerly to play with their new baby brother. I had asked Eddie to place the birth announcement in the *Daily Gleaner* with the opening phrase, "Another prince, Jason Stuart Wong, born to Edward and Carol Wong". The next day, however, to my horror, I read our birth announcement: "Another son, Prince Jason Stuart Wong born to Edward and Carol Wong"! I received quite a few phone calls from close friends wanting to know how could I name my baby "Prince" but everything was cleared up at the baby's christening at St Luke's Parish Church.

On Jason's Christening Day, our friends, Garth and Peggy Lampart officiated as Jason's Godparents and a reception dinner was held at our home on Lords Road. I recall that when I was busy preparing the dinner, Baby Jason's diaper needed changing and he began crying because of the discomfort of the dirty diaper. Eddie was still scornful about changing a dirty diaper so, instead of changing the baby, Eddie began swinging Jason in his carrying seat to hush him until I was free to change him. Eddie did not, however, check that the safety belt of the carrying seat was buckled. As Jason cried louder, Eddie began to swing the seat more vigorously hoping to quiet him. After a few of these vigorous swings, my little baby fell forward out of the seat and flat on his little face crushing his nose. Needless to say, I was so angry with Eddie! Poor Baby Jason had a sunken nose bridge with a huge black and blue mark across his chubby face!

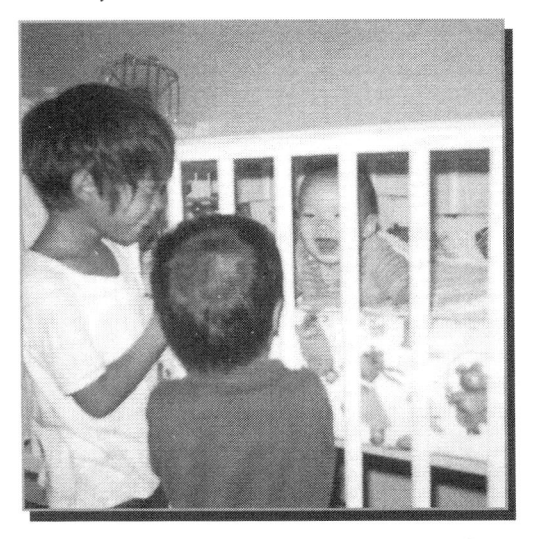

Brian and Gordon visiting Jason through crib slats

Having a newborn baby did not disrupt our regular practice of driving our maids home to visit their family on the weekends. We would take that opportunity to visit with the Williams side of the family in Petersfield, and then visit with the Wong side of the family in Montego Bay on the way back. However, there was one change that needed to be made to this practice: with a new baby and a fixed car-bed in the back seat, there was no more space to take our black Labrador dog, Malcolm, on these trips.

On Friday mornings, I would drive Eddie to his office and return home to pack up the kids, maid and dog by late afternoon. The car would be jam packed. I would then drop Malcolm off at the home of Ewart and Hope, who had originally given Malcolm to us as a puppy. They were happy to have Malcolm stay and visit with his siblings. I would then proceed to pick up Eddie from work and then we would start our journey. Eddie would drive to Old Harbour and through Mandeville continuing on the south coast of Jamaica to Petersfield, Westmoreland where we would overnight. On Saturday afternoon, we would head inland driving north to Montego Bay to overnight again

Kingston, Jamaica 1971

and the following day, drive on the north coast back to Kingston via Fern Gully and Bog Walk.

When we arrived in Petersfield on Friday evenings, there would be many cousins and friends gathered at my father's home. The store would be closed. With the advent of televisions in homes, the movie theatre business had been discontinued. The theatre housed another badminton court. Now there was both an inside and the original open air badminton court for all to use and enjoy. The number of badminton players had gradually increased over the years. Not everyone at these gatherings played badminton, however. Some people played dominoes and others just socialized. Brian and Gordon got accustomed to the noisy gathering and enjoyed playing with the cats and dogs, as well as sleeping under the protective mosquito nets.

On Saturdays, I would spend some time in the store. The regular customers were always happy to see me. I would also pay a visit to the post office next door. The postmistress, Miss Icy, was by then, almost reaching retirement, but many of the original staff, who had been so kind to me as a child remained at the post office. They were pleased that I had not forgotten them although I was now grown-up. After the delicious, traditional hearty fresh beef soup with the family at lunch time and Cutie's arrival from visiting with her family, we would pack up the car again to head for Montego Bay.

Saturday evenings, we would find the Chinese community of Montego Bay at the Chinese Club on Creek Street where they also played badminton and dominoes. The next day, we would meet up with family and friends again at Doctor's Cave Beach and spend happy times splashing in the blue Caribbean sea and playing in the sand. Then, as we did in Petersfield, we would help ourselves to items from the family business. In my father's store, Nathan Williams & Sons Ltd., we would find hardware and household items we needed and at Kelly's Superservice, we would pack up mostly grocery food items. We would then head back to our home on Lords Road, Kingston laden with goods and good memories.

When I reminisce about both sides of our families, their welcoming hospitality, their generosity, and the wonderful times shared together and all the pleasant times that are etched in my memories, I have to conclude that family is simply the greatest and most important people in our lives! They also form sturdy and strong roots for our family tree!!

Your loving Ah-Poh

Kingston, Jamaica 1971

God-parents Garth and Peggy holding baby Jason at his christening, with smiling father looking on

Baby Jason creeping on a table by the pool

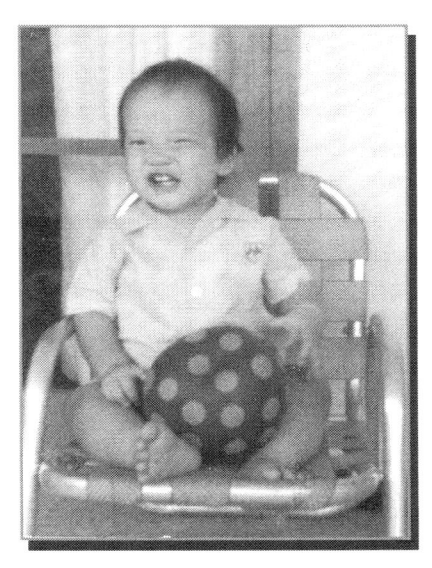

Jason on the front veranda at Lord's Road

Life in Kingston, Jamaica
1972

My dear Grandchildren,

Returning to one's own family home is the best and most comforting feeling as our dog Malcolm would attest to – he was always so happy to be home after we fetched him from our friends after a weekend of much appreciated dog-sitting.

Our maid, Cutie, had been fraternizing with the maid next door who regaled her with glorious tales about life in the city. So, it was inevitable that, upon hearing these stories, Cutie would want to leave our family and seek a more exciting job in the big city. I really do not blame her for wanting to leave us – she was a young, simple country girl who wanted more out of life than just taking care of other people's children and home. I could quite understand the desire for a more exciting life as well. I myself had been enjoying the city life by going out to night clubs like Club Havana, Club Inferno Discotheque, Sombrero Club. Club Havana was owned by the Chin family who were in-laws of one of my cousins, Dorothy. This was a hot spot during this era because Mr. Chin would frequently engage Cuban troupes to perform at his club. The shows were terrific – the music and dances were most entertaining, plus the performers, especially the girls, were so attractive and buxom in their colourful frilly Spanish costumes. There were also fancy restaurants and facilities to be enjoyed in the surrounding hotels in New Kingston like Sheraton Hotel, Pegasus Hotel, and the Terra Nova Hotel. I loved the fashion shows by Carole Issa or by Daphne Logan that were presented during their High Tea Parties.

Adventure and excitement came in all different forms in those days. One day while sunbathing poolside at Courtleigh Manor Pool, I suddenly missed toddler, Gordon who had been playing beside my lounge chair. Looking around, I saw Gordon struggling in the water and without hesitation, I jumped into the pool to rescue him from drowning. Brian and Gordon had been swimming in the pool wearing water-wings for flotation. They had taken off their water-wings to eat lunch and had not put them on again. Gordon had forgotten that he was not wearing his water-wings and had decided to go back into the pool. Gordon was not the only person who had forgotten something that day. As I comforted a spluttering Gordon, I noticed that the top of my bikini was floating and bobbing merrily on top of the water in the pool. Apparently, I had loosened the top of my swimsuit to avoid a sun-tanned mark on my back and had forgotten this in my panic to save Gordon! After this episode, I began teaching the boys to swim using drinking straws to "bubble up". This was a fun swimming technique for kids to understand the dynamics of inhaling and exhaling while in the water and creating bubbles to get accustomed to having water in their face without fear or panic.

Kingston, Jamaica 1972

It was an exciting time for the national arts in Jamaica as well. The stage theatre scene was very lively with local stage plays performed at the Barn Theatre on Oxford Road and Jamaican Cultural pantomimes at Ward Theatre. The Little Theatre Movement and the National Theatre Trust were being formed during this period. The National Dance Theatre performances were most energetic and vibrantly choreographed by dancers like Rex Nettleford and Eddy Thomas. The Jamaica Heritage Singers were formed some time later. The John Peartree Art Gallery on Haughton Avenue featured celebrated Jamaican artists like Barrington Watson, Ainsley Peter Chung, Karl Parboosingh, Buddhai and Alexander Cooper to name a few. When I was leaving Jamaica and wanted paintings reminiscent of Jamaica, I purchased paintings by Alexander Cooper from his exhibitions at Hill's Galleries and Devon House. Mr. Cooper at the age of 20, had won a government scholarship to the Jamaica School of Arts and Craft. After winning various art competitions, his paintings found their way into private and public collections in Europe and North America having exhibited in New York, Washington, Philadelphia and New York. When I was living in Montréal during Expo '67, I was pleased that he was commissioned to produce the brochure for the Jamaica Pavilion and the many, many people who attended, including myself and friends, framed this brochure as a work of art.

The Daily Gleaner and *Star* newspapers promoted the all-island beauty competitions recognizing that there were gorgeous Jamaican girls of all shades and skin colour. There were crowns for everyone from Miss Ebony to Miss Mahogany to Miss Sandalwood in the Miss Kingston & St. Andrew Beauty Contest! The Chinese Jamaican community held their own beauty contests as well. Winners included Annette Chang, Miss Chinese Jamaica 1954, Barbara Tenn, Miss Chinese Jamaica 1955 and later, Melanie Chang, Miss Chinese Athletic Club 1963. I believe my cousin Cynthia Williams was the only Williams brave enough to have entered a beauty contest.

Of course, there was also a Miss Jamaica Beauty Contest annually. The winners went on to compete in international competitions like Miss World and Miss Universe. These beautiful women, like my schoolmate Carol Crawford (Miss World, 1963), Patsy Yuen (second runner up in Miss World, 1973), or Evelyn Andrade (who, when she competed in the Miss Universe competition in 1954 became the first coloured woman to compete in a major beauty contest), sure put Jamaica on the map! Somehow, Jamaicans do make a mark in foreign countries! I believe that in the case of our beauty contestants this was because when these women were surrounded by so many other beautiful people from all around the world, their tropical personalities shone through and made them stand out from the crowd.

Shopping in Kingston was getting more modern at this time as enticing and attractive foreign goods became more available. At Tropical Plaza, for example, business was brisk at Lee's Fifth Avenue. This was a store owned by Lee Issa, a member of a long-standing Syrian business family in Jamaica. The All American Department Store owned by the Wong Pow family and Magic Kitchen owned by Wolfgang Hohn, a newcomer from Germany, were also popular. In addition to bringing state-of-the-art kitchen appliances and gadgets into Jamaica, Wolfgang ran a craft business teaching the local Jamaicans to make wooden and straw furniture and items out of locally produced materials. The expatriate Todd family also helped developed the local Jamaican arts with their pottery business in Highgate, St. Mary. Another thriving business, located in a different plaza, also comes to mind. This was a baby store called Storkland which was owned by the Wong family (Arthur, Stanford et al, no relation to us). I patronized the store on every trip I made to the area. The CARIFTA (Caribbean Free Trade Agreement) trade agreement was in effect at this time. It made a positive impact on the local garment industry where we saw an increase in local manufacturing especially at Davon Corporation owned and operated by David Chin and Donald Chin. The economy was good and everything was going so well in Jamaica.

My older brother, Keith and his wife, Shirley decided to open a clothing boutique. I suggested the name "Gazebo" for the boutique and volunteered to help them get their business established. About the same time in Liguanea, Shirley's sister, Marie, was opening her own hair salon. I suggested the name "Cygnet" after a baby swan, but the Jamaican painter who made the sign spelled it "Signet". Despite the misspelling, the sign – and name – was readily accepted.

Brian, Carol and Shirley at Gazebo Boutique

Gazebo was located in the newly opened shopping plaza, Twin Gates, which was owned by the Chang family. They also owned the Lenn Happ Supermarket at one end across from the Twin Gates Pharmacy which belonged to their relative, Ricky, and was run by the family. Other stores that come to mind were Mann's owned by an English gentleman, Derek Game, and Susan Fashions operated by Susan Alexander, daughter of Moi and Carlton Alexander. Carlton was the CEO and Managing Director of Grace Kennedy Ltd. and a most popular person among the Chinese community. Although he was not Chinese, he obviously favoured the Chinese in his business and social life. I remember Moi (née Yap) as a very quiet and nice lady and Carlton as an outgoing and dynamic person with a smiling face. At the other end of the plaza was Music Mart managed by Donny Young.

Donny's older brother, Roy is married to Violet (Vi) Lym whose family lived in Darliston, a district near to Petersfield. The Lym family was close to our family especially since one of Vi's sisters, Pat, married Papa's nephew, John. We spent many happy times at their home in Darliston and got to know the extended families of Vi and Roy, Ann and Easton, Angela and Bobby, Jean and Phillip. We also became very

Kingston, Jamaica 1972

L-R: Valerie Lym, Donny, Crosby Lym, baby Howard and mother Pat Chin, married to cosin John

friendly with the unmarried siblings, Crosby and Valerie, who were closer to my age. We used to go to many beach picnics and various parties together. Crosby bought a Thames truck and we loved to travel in the open back. I was thrilled when he taught me how to drive such a big vehicle, especially negotiating the wide turns. Mr. and Mrs. Lym used to tell me that they were eternally grateful for my father's kindness. During the war time, when rice was in short supply, my father's relatives, with disdain, would tell him not to give rice to the half-Chinese families: "Mek dem nyam breadfruit" (make them eat breadfruit) – a fruit that is used as a starch by local Jamaicans. My father believed in showing kindness to everyone and so, despite the advice of his relatives, he would send rice to the half-Chinese families he knew because food shortage was becoming critical at that time. The Lyms were not the only family to relate such a story to me. Many times throughout my life, people would come up to tell me about some act of kindness that Papa had done for them. Such stories made me feel so proud to be his daughter!

When Cutie left my employment, I did not miss her as much as I missed her cooking! I had to get back in the kitchen like I had to do in Canada. I was never a good cook and never did like cooking, but I managed regardless. One year when the Jamaican Open Badminton was scheduled at the National Arena, my brother, Patrick and a distant cousin Barry, came to stay with us in order to compete in this all-island championship. They did not do very well and I do believe that my self-taught survival cooking experience in Montréal might have contributed to their loss at the Men's Doubles title! Another year, my sister, Elaine was competing in the Mixed Doubles Championship with Eddie and having made it to the finals, they lost – but this time, not because of my cooking! Eddie had decided to take Brian to the arena, perhaps to give me a break since I was managing three kids on my own without a maid. They had to wait until late in the night for the final match to be played. It got so late that Brian became over-tired and started crying so much so that Eddie and Elaine had to forfeit their match. Elaine was never so disappointed in her life and probably never slept a wink that night. She might have blamed Brian for the loss, but it was actually Eddie's fault for not being able to cope with the embarrassment of a crying child and playing through the final game. In fact, we lived close enough for Brian to have been taken home to me, but it was Eddie's decision and he decided that they would all return home. Needless to say, Elaine was sure they would have won their final match and captured the crown. Hopefully, she will forgive Brian as he forgave her for banging his head against the car when he was a toddler!

Without a maid, I had to also give up my part-time sales job at Caribbean Estate Management (CEM) which was really something that I did to occupy my time more than anything else since I was not a good salesperson for Stony Hill Development. Neither did I do well for Key Homes in the Camrose Development! I just did not have the patience to deal with the unrealistic demands of the "hoity-toity" Jamaicans returning from England who were the target market of these developments. However, I did rent an apartment at Worthington Court Apartments to a returning resident. Unfortunately, this resident did not really meet the expectations of the dignified landlord! I think that the CEM secretary, Venn, probably had a lot of explaining to do to Mr. Schroeder when Mr. Schroeder realized the low class status of his tenant! Oh well!

One day, a local boy in a clean and freshly ironed khaki school uniform came to the gate looking for a gardening job and I was impressed by how tidy and respectful he was. I already had a regular gardener, Seebert, so I asked this young man, named Norman, if he would consider coming and living with us as a house-boy instead. Norman lived nearby with his grandmother and he was more than happy to go and get his belongings and move into our maid's quarters. Norman was around 15-years old, a polite and decent boy who had been well brought-up by his grandmother. At night, his father would come home intoxicated and, in his drunken state, would, with no cause, beat the sleeping Norman. I believe that the father's drunken violence might be the reason why Norman's mother had left the home. Without Norman's mother there as a target anymore, the father was turning his violence on his son. As was so typical of Jamaican grandmothers, Norman's grandmother had willingly taken in the child that her worthless son had basically neglected. In Jamaica, many fathers would abandon the mothers of their children, which led to mothers having multiple fathers for their children. It meant these women often had to struggle to support their children, and grandmothers often had to help raise these children. Norman lived in a wooden house in a tenement yard surrounded by other houses, but when I went to his home one day to meet his grandmother, I was impressed by how tidy the dirt yard was and immaculately swept.

Norman loved to play with Brian and Gordon and he would act just as childish as the much younger boys. I felt that due to unsavory circumstances at home, Norman had been forced to grow up quickly – sometimes, his young face would reflect the harsh realities of his life. I always felt so sympathetic towards him and liked seeing him behaving silly like my young sons. On Saturdays, Norman would take Brian to the movie theatre. They both enjoyed the western films. On returning home, they would reenact the scenes hiding behind the sofa and shooting at each other with their fingers while Gordon would look at them quizzically. Norman had been really well-trained by his grandmother. He kept the house more clean and tidy than the female maids we had! Every weekend he would wash and iron his khaki school uniform in readiness for school. As he moved up to the higher forms in school, it was obvious Norman needed more time for studies – and for his social life! He wanted to be out with his teenage school friends and started staying out late at night and needed a nap after school. I am not sure if he was a good student but his ambition was to be a photographer and I wish I could have helped him realize his goal. Later, when we were planning to move back to Montego Bay, I offered him a room to live with us

Kingston, Jamaica 1972

there and an apprenticeship with my cousin, Daisy and her husband, Isaac of Tenn's Photo Studio, but Norman did not want to uproot his life or to leave his grandmother alone in Kingston. I lost touch with Norman, but I have often thought about this kind and decent boy, trying to grow up without parental support and guidance and wondered how life turned out for him.

On one of our weekend family visits to Petersfield, Lurline, my first maid, brought a woman named Gurscella, to see me. Lurline knew that Cutie was no longer working for our family. Gurscella was Lurline's neighbor and friend and she needed a job. Apparently, Gurscella was fed up with having children for various irresponsible fathers – seven in all -- and had decided to leave home to earn money to care for her many children. The children were living with her in a small wooden house built next to her mother's and Gurscella felt confident that her older daughters and her mother would be able to keep an eye on the younger children while she worked in the city. Gurscella was dressed neatly and was more mature than either Lurline or Cutie. I thought she had a pleasant, smiling face – it reminded me of the woman on the Aunt Jemima pancake mix box – and she obviously loved children since she had so many of her own. We came to an agreement and Gurscella – who was stout, but moved quickly – hastened to get her belongings so that she could return to Kingston with us.

Gurscella – whom we called Gurzel for short-- was happy taking care of Brian, Gordon and Baby Jason in the absence of her own children. She scolded the boys as if they were her own and encouraged them to eat up their meals by warning them that if they didn't, "Timmoti coming tonight and Timmoti coming to get yu" (Timmoti is a Jamaican folk-tale about a village ogre). She was especially protective of Jason since he was the baby. Gurzel would be so devastated when any of the boys were hurt, that she would be in tears until I got home. She was always especially cross with them if they disobeyed her warning about playing in the pick-up truck in the driveway since Gordon had already fallen out in the past. Gurzel also had a sense of humour and whenever she was asked what we were having for dinner, she would always give the same reply with a grin: "Saltfish tail and jancro liver" (the tail of a salted cod-fish and the liver of a vulture). In other words, dinner would be a surprise.

Papa with Vincent Lee at DisneyWorld, Florida

There were quite a few weddings in 1971. I recall Marie Plinton married Vincent Yap Young at Stella Maris Chapel. Eddie's cousin, Pam Wong, married Maurice "Harry" Lyn and Nelson Yu Choy Lee married Chang Pui Fung at Holy Cross Church followed by a reception at International Restaurant.

Kingston, Jamaica 1972

Nelson is the son of Vincent Lee, the man who gave Papa the idea of opening a movie theatre. Vincent, Papa and another friend, David "Ah-Young" Chin were gambling buddies who later went on a trip to Disney World courtesy of their winnings. They would pick up Papa en route to Montego Bay to play Mahjong whenever they were going from their district in Little London, Westmoreland.

Another wedding celebrated in 1972 was the marriage between my younger brother, Richard "Dick" Williams to Margaret Taylor who was a contract teacher from Belfast, Northern Ireland who had been assigned to Mannings High School, Savanna-La-Mar. Margaret was a good tennis player who met our cousin Bim Williams first, because his family had a tennis court in their backyard. Later on, he took her to play badminton at Dick's home in Petersfield. There Margaret and Dick met several times to play badminton, during which time their love for each other blossomed and bloomed. This wedding was particularly special because it was the first family celebration to bring all the family together since the arrival of our stepmother, Chan Lam Keow. In accordance with Hakka cultural tradition, we called her "Ah-Neung", a Hakka title for an older and respected aunt. Ah-Neung had been betrothed to my father at birth and he had every intention of returning to marry her after he had migrated to Jamaica and earned some money. While he was in Jamaica, however, China closed its doors to immigration and emigration during the upheaval of

Richard (Dick) and Margaret Williams' wedding
Back row L-R: Ricky, Claire Morgan (matron of honour), Eddie, Carol, Keith, Shirley, Patrick
Front row L-R: Brian, Ah-Neung, Dick, Margaret, Papa, Gordon

Communism. Years later, Ah-Neung escaped mainland China and made it to Hong Kong where she was supported by Papa. After my mother passed away, Papa was encouraged by his relatives to send for her to join him in Jamaica, which he did.

During Ah-Neung's separation from Papa, she adopted a son and a daughter. The daughter had married and left home long before Papa sent for Ah-Neung, but her son, Ricardo (whom we called Ricky), was able to secure a birth certificate and a British Passport while living in Hong Kong so he could travel and Papa sponsored him to Jamaica. When Ricky arrived in Petersfield, we embraced him as our eldest brother and Papa's Chinese son. Ricky and Papa bonded quickly because of their shared fluency in speaking their Hakka dialect and Ricky was also very industrious. He would wake up very early to kill a chicken from our coop and prepare it for cooking later in the day. Then, he would have his breakfast and was ready to open the store – all before everyone else was up! While in Hong Kong, he had learned how to sew, so he was able to use material from the store to sew his own clothes. Ricky was anxious to learn English, the Jamaican way of doing business, and how to cope with the local Jamaicans. I remember that one evening while helping us collect tickets at the lower door of our Venus Theatre, one man decided that he would like to enter without a ticket. When Ricky tried to prevent him from entering, the man hit him in the face with a bicycle chain. The chain caused an ugly gash and a nose bleed. We were all so upset by the incident – and even more worried when Keith, my elder brother, angrily chased after the assailant. Keith returned safely, however, and the other local patrons calmed him down, so eventually, the show did go on. But the incident served as a lesson for Ricky and us that we had to practise a certain amount of restraint and tolerance when dealing with the local people – even when we caught them trying to cheat us in one way or another.

We had fun teaching Ricky to dance after the store was closed and very soon he was going out with us and adopting our Western ways. He was so hard-working and ambitious that it was not long before Papa arranged for him to have his own store in Locust Tree, another district not too far from Petersfield. Another uncle, Uncle Sin Goh, would continue to mentor and keep an eye on him in this new business. Ricky also worked very hard at his own business and, as I've said before, eventually saved enough to go back to Hong Kong and marry a young lady named Diana. When they returned, he and Diana moved to Old Harbour where they ran a successful business and started a family before migrating to Toronto. Their children are Melvin, Juliet and Marcos.

Brian at Mona Preparatory School with Sean and schoolmate

In 1971, with Gurzel firmly in charge of the household, I resumed being active on the Parent Teacher Association of Mona Preparatory

School, which Brian attended. Brian was a good student and made friends with Sean, the son of Beryl and my cousin, Dr. Wilson Williams. One of the things that I used to organize to raise funds for the school library was a supper and fashion show on the lawns of Jamaica House I was not only involved in organizing fashion shows, I sometimes modelled as well. I was also asked to be a fashion model for fundraising tea parties organized by the Immaculate Conception High School Alumnae Association. Other times, I was modelling fashions for businesslady, June Lee Fatt, whom I had met through the badminton circles. When I met her, June had recently competed in the Rothman International Badminton Tournament and won the Ladies Singles title in the "B" division. I guess the height and stature that I had inherited from my parents was unusual for a Chinese person as there were no other Chinese girls modelling on stage in those days; or perhaps, I was just more bold and more experienced with modelling than other Chinese girls since I had grown up with a liberal first generation Jamaican Chinese mother who did not mind me parading on stage for our Anglican Church tea parties in Savanna la Mar during my teens.

At this time, Eddie and I were also freely enjoying the sporting life of Kingston and would play tennis at Liguanea Club which, in its colonial days, had excluded local residents from membership. In 1971, however, with dwindling membership and a lack of funds to keep the club running, locals were welcomed. More and more exclusive clubs had to follow suit and we found ourselves able to attend events like New Year's Eve Dances held at the Constant Spring Golf Club.

Eddie and I also started playing competitive badminton Inter-Club Leagues and championship matches at the Jamaica National Arena. This allowed us to enjoy a wider network of badminton enthusiasts. As result, I got involved with the Jamaica Badminton Association (JBA) and was elected on the Council along with President Richard Roberts, Frank Parslow, Allan Feres, Norman Haddad, Eddie Chin, Reg Cardoza, Bob Weston, Lucien Tai Ten Quee, and others. I was appointed on the Finance, Schools, Entertainment and Publicity Committees. During my time at the JBA, we eventually were organizing six tournaments throughout the year and working hard to have badminton included as one of the sports competed for in the Central American and Caribbean Olympic Games.

The Carreras Open and the All Jamaica Badminton Tournaments attracted entries from the top level female players like Pauline Laman, Barbara Tai, Margaret Parslow, Norma Haddad, Christine Bennett, Helena DaCosta. The male entries included Keith Palmer, Richard Roberts, Tony and Mike Garcia, Peter Wong Ken, Richard Wong, Paul Nash, Tony Wong.

The veterans noted were Alan Feres, Justin Wilson, Frank Parslow and Keith Evans while the teenage juniors were Geoff (19), Jennifer (18) and Beverly (16) Haddad. *The Daily Gleaner* reported one record breaking event – when Jennifer and Beverly Haddad became the youngest players to win an All Jamaica Ladies Doubles title by defeating Margaret Parslow and Christine Bennett. Another dramatic tournament upset was when the unseeded Eddie Wong – your Ah-Goong -- trounced top-ranked player, Mike Garcia. In later years, more and more competitive Jamaican Chinese players emerged including Nora and Eddie Chin, David and Gladys Chin, Joan and Eustace

Kingston, Jamaica 1972

Tony Wong presenting trophy to Paul Nash while Van de Groot looks on

Lyn, Daphne Chin Loy, Barry Lue and Yvonne Yapp, George Hugh, Leslie Chong, Bobby and Junior Moo Young, the Lyeow brothers, the Ivan Chin family – Gary, Clifton, Kevin, Andre, Lillith and little Brett, who was shorter than the bottom of the badminton net on the court.

The Rothmans International Open Badminton Tournament attracted top male international stars like Jamie Paulson, Yves Paré and Ken Delf from Canada, Roy Diaz Gonzalez, Victor Jaramillo and Esteban Reyes from Mexico in the first year. In the following year, female players joined from USA (Pam Stockton), Holland (Joke Van Beusekom), Sweden (Lene Koppen) and Nancy McKinley and Barbara O'Brien from Canada. In later years, male and female European players from Britain (Ray Stevens, Derek Talbot, Mike Tredgett and Margaret Beck), Germany (Wolfgang Bochow), Denmark (Erkland Kopps, Elo Hansen and Fleming Delfs), Sweden (Sturre Johnsson and Thomas Khilstrom) started to include Jamaica in their circuit. I am sure that the fact that they got to have a wonderful tropical holiday, in addition to competing, was part of the attraction for them!

From Malaysia, Dominic Soong Chok Soong and Saw Swee Leong came along with Herman and Ade Chandra from Indonesia. Pedro Aegua was a lone competitor from Peru. A contingent from Guyana (Ian Leach and Keith Hendy) and Surinam (Reggie Ching Jong, Ray, Noel and Ruel Sjauw Mook and Ro Caster) arrived in the following years.

After a few years, younger players arrived from Mexico (Ricardo Jaramillo and Jorge Palazuelos) as well as Beena Narwani, Tony Chen and Neville Babooram from Trinidad, West Indies. Our Jamaican youngsters got in the action too. They were teenagers Anna Kay Van De Groot, Georgina Hew, Christine Chung, Andre Chin, Vernon Green, Ricky Vaz, Victor Ziadie, Barrington Lue and Brian Haddad.

In no time, we got quite friendly with all the foreign players and started arranging sightseeing tours and parties. The sport of badminton was not heavily sponsored anywhere in the world at that time, so the players were happy to be billeted in local homes, taken on trips by us driving them around and attending parties in our homes. They loved dancing to the Jamaican music of Bob Marley & the Wailers, Jimmy Cliff,

Kingston, Jamaica 1972

Desmond Dekker, Toots and the Maytals, Dobby Dobson, the Skatalites, Prince Buster and others. The girls liked learning the Ska dance steps and their favourite song was "My Boy Lollipop" by Millie Small.

One year, some European badminton competitors were staying with me at my in-laws' home since I had arranged for them to be flown over to Montego Bay to give demonstration matches at the Chinese Club. They loved the white sands and warm sea at Doctor's Cave and the hospitality of the Montego Badminton Group. Late one night while sleeping, I heard some splashing in our pool outside my bedroom window and when I cautiously peeked out, there they were, these European guys and girls, skinny-dipping! I went back to sleep and was thankful that the bedroom of my less liberal-minded in-laws was at the far end of the house away from the swimming pool area because I do not think they would think kindly of this outlandish behaviour!

Before I joined the JBA, the past president, Major Balfe Balfour, had been attempting for years to form a Caribbean Badminton Association which would include Trinidad, Guyana and Surinam, but without much success. Eventually, in 1970, after meeting with all the four National associations in Trinidad, a Regional Badminton Confederation was formed and Jamaica won the Inaugural Quadrangular series losing only one of 42 matches played. Last year in 1971, the JBA hosted the Caribbean Badminton Championships (Caribaco) at the Jamaica National Arena which was opened by Governor General, Sir Clifford Campbell in the presence of Ambassadors and High Commissioners from Surinam, Trinidad and Guyana.

Other than JBA organized tournaments, Abbey Court Badminton Club organized, for the first time, an Open Tournament sponsored by Davon Corporation and Van-Del

Guyanese badminton team on Discovery Bay tour after Caribaco tournament

Kingston, Jamaica 1972

Limited. Entries came from all over the island – Montego Bay, Savanna-la-Mar, Mandeville and Ocho Rios. President Lucien Tai Ten Quee and Captain Eddie Chin were pleased to receive 220 entries – an all-time high number of entries in the history of the sport in Jamaica. Eddie Wong was the Vice-Captain and other committee members were Melvin Cooke, David Chin, Daphne Chin Loy, David Lyew and Eustace Lyn.

The major upset in the Open Division was that all-island Champion, Keith Palmer, got ousted in the semi-finals by Tony Garcia who went on to meet No.2 seed and eventual winner, Richard Wong. In the Closed Division, the Montego Badminton Group players (Eugene Chin, Philip Chin, Victor Lyn Shue, Leslie Chin, Jean Chin, Angela Tenn, Vera Chin, Linda Hew) and cheering squad from Montego Bay earned much popularity during the tournament and won for themselves four of the five final matches. Angela emerged a triple champion winning the ladies singles against No.1 seed, Liz Kelly; the mixed with Victor Lyn Shue; and ladies doubles with Vera Chin against Andrea Nash and Pat Lyn. Victor earned a double champion winning the Men's Singles and the mixed with Angela against the Mandeville pair of Neville Atkinson and Barbara Thomas, but missed out in his efforts at the triple when he and Leslie Chin could not hold the better pair of Barrington Lue and Derrick Chin.

My involvement with the JBA did not impede my participation in these games and I was pleased to have been able to compete in the Ladies Singles event and capture the title from Judith Lyeow. I also had much success in the Ladies Doubles with various partners like Joyce Marr, Yvonne Yapp and Linda Hew. I also had various partners in the Mixed Doubles event, people like Derek, Barry and Derrick. Naturally, I competed with Eddie in the Married Couples event – which caused a lot of stress on our marriage, especially when we were trounced by better opponents like Frank and Margaret Parslow, Joan and Eustace Lyn, David and Gladys Chin, Eddie and Nora Chin or Allan and Ellen Pitts!

In truth, I was not on the same level as Eddie when it came to badminton. Before we were married, while I was playing for fun on my backyard badminton court in Petersfield, Eddie was playing on the McGill University badminton team in Montréal, so he had a lot more coaching and training than I had. In fact, in addition to playing in a higher division of the Inter-Club League and having tournament partners like Eddie Chin and Eustace "Tassy" Lyn, Eddie was a strong enough player to have been invited for special training with a view to being possibly selected for the Jamaica National team.

My dear Grandchildren, as a result of our love for badminton and tennis, our lives and our children's lives would be greatly influenced by these racquet sports for many, many years to come.

Your loving Ah-Poh

Life in Jamaica:
Not-to-Worry, Montego Bay,
1973 – 1974

My dear Grandchildren,

Life was good in Jamaica. Most Jamaicans were enjoying a stress-free lifestyle and all classes of Jamaican society were getting along together harmoniously.

Jamaica received her independence from Britain on 06 August 1962 while the Jamaica Labour Party (JLP) was in power. By 1973–1974, Jamaica was under the leadership of the eloquent and charismatic Prime Minister, Michael Manley. He was the younger son of a previous Prime Minister, the British-educated Queen's Counsel, Sir Norman Washington Manley, who formed the Peoples National Party (PNP) which was now the ruling political party.

The opposing political party, the JLP, was formed by Norman Manley's Trade Unionist cousin, Sir Alexander Bustamante in 1938. Now, the JLP was led by Leader of the Opposition, Edward Seaga. The Jamaican currency had previously been British Sterling – pounds, shillings and pence – but after independence a conversion was made to Jamaican dollars and cents. One British pound was equivalent to $2 JA, ten shillings to $1 JA and one penny to one JA cent.

Business and the economic trade was booming so much that your paternal great-grandfather Kelly Wong, who had been encouraging us to join him in his well-established business, Kelly's Superservice Ltd., bought a larger and fully furnished house. The house was large enough to accommodate our family of five and was meant as a further enticement for us to move to Montego Bay. Eddie was getting good engineering experience having attended another engineering course, Ocean Engineering, at the University of California, Berkeley in Los Angeles, USA, but he was only receiving a salary of $430 JA a week with an annual bonus of $50. What was even worse for him, however, was the fact that he was working for someone else. By offering us a share in the business, his father was making an offer Eddie could not refuse: to become self-employed and still be able to keep up his civil engineering experience on a part-time basis at the north coast office of Warnock Hersey Caribbean Limited at a salary of $6,000 JA per annum working two days per week.

When he made his offer, great-grandfather Kelly was also counting on my past business experience in my family business to help make his business work. This arrangement was satisfactory to me as we could now quit making the weekend visits to the western end of the island. I would be closer to my side of the family as well, and our maid, Gurzel, would be able to use public transport to go home for visits on

"Not-To-Worry", Montego Bay, Jamaica 1973-74

Entrace to Wongs' residence "Not To Worry", Brandon Hill, Montego Bay

Driveway leading to lower level and parking area

Back patio overlooking swimming pool

her own. So, we packed up and rented our house to the Clarke family. Mrs. Clarke was the daughter of a Mr. Wong who was a salesman I knew years ago when I used to run the family business in Petersfield. The Clarkes would later purchase 18 Lords Road when we decided to migrate to Canada later on.

Eddie's parents, great-grandfather Kelly and great-grandmother Catherine, had lived for years in a modest wooden house at 10 Foster Avenue. Now they were making a drastic change by moving to an upscale architecturally designed concrete house with wooden shingled roofing on the side of Brandon Hill overlooking the wooded area of Mount Salem, the Cornwall Regional Hospital, Bogue Heights and out towards the Caribbean Sea. The fully-furnished house and property was purchased from an American expatriate lady who was returning back to her homeland. She had given the property an appropriate name, "Not to Worry". There was a white house-sign bearing the name posted prominently at the entry gate from the street. The entrance was protected by a cattle trap of metal pipes across the driveway. The paved driveway curved downhill to a leveled car park. Midway down the hill, the house was securely appointed.

After you entered the house through the double dark mahogany wooden front doors, you would be welcomed into the living room leading out onto a wide open patio overlooking the rest of the sloping property. On either side of the living room were the bedroom areas. Great-grandfather Kelly and great-grandmother Catherine shared the master bedroom suite next to the kitchen. Our family would have the two bedrooms and a bathroom on the opposite side of the house. Eddie's and my bedroom overlooked the round swimming pool at one end of the terrazzo-tiled patio. The boys' bedroom overlooked one of the doghouses belonging to Dixie, a fierce Rhodesian Ridgeback, guarding this side of the property. The other doghouse near the car park on the opposite side of the house belonged to a German Shepherd Alsatian named Tanaka. Our family black Labrador Malcolm would be kept inside the house for our added safety.

The stairs from the kitchen led to the lower level where there was the car-park and self-contained and sparsely furnished servant's quarters. The servant's quarters were a two-bedroom space, so we converted one bedroom into an office and kept the other bedroom for our maid, Gurzel. The lower level living-room, dining-room and kitchen were furnished with our own furniture brought from Kingston. On the lowest level of the sloping building were the laundry facilities, kids' play area plus the storage area and pump room for the swimming pool. The swimming pool was half-fenced around. The exposed side overlooked the bottom of the sloping property which was bordered on three sides by tall pine trees for privacy. Our neighbour below us was a retired JLP politician who would eventually become a Governor General of Jamaica, Sir Howard Cooke. To the north side lived Mrs. Wilson, a professional pianist who made her living performing at the hotels and offering private piano lessons. On the south side was an American expatriate family who sometimes had children visiting.

The gardens at the top of the premises had sloping lawns, majestic palm trees, flowering bougainvillea and hibiscus plants, coleus hedges and other flowering trees.

"Not-To-Worry", Montego Bay, Jamaica 1973-74

An Otaheiti apple tree and dwarf coconut trees bore profusely, as did the other ground provisions planted. We were able to retain the services of the past gardener, Egbert who was a quiet and gentle man of Maroon heritage. Maroons were the descendants of runaway African slaves who hid in theCockpit Country and successfully defended themselves against the British. They were so successful in the guerilla warfare they practised that eventually the British signed a treaty with them. The Maroons settled peacefully in Maroon Town after slavery was abolished in 1833 and a subsequent mandatory apprenticeship for the slaves ended in 1838. Egbert came to work by bus from Maroon Town every weekday and kept the professionally landscaped property in fine form, just as it had been many years before. When the previous owner eventually died in the United States, Egbert swore he would see the ghost of "Missis" sitting in the living room. He was also a good companion for Gurzel who became housebound because of the remoteness of Not-to-Worry and he kept her abreast of life outside Montego Bay. Egbert passed away years after we migrated to Canada and when the property was sold, the new owner could not afford to keep him in employment. We heard he had died of lung complications and wondered if he was in any way affected by the powdered chlorine he had used to maintain the swimming pool all the years that he had been working at Not-to-Worry. I will always remember his good manners and respectful attitude to us and the children.

Before Eddie's classmate, Donald, got wind of us returning to Montego Bay, he had written to me about helping the Chinese Club to form a Montego Badminton Group (MBG) and assisting with getting top badminton players to come to Montego Bay after the tournaments were completed in Kingston. In one of his letters, Donald promised to have "a roast suckling pig on hand to greet you upon your arrival" in Montego Bay. We did find a very warm welcome for us in Montego Bay and immediately started attending MBG meetings at James and Linda Hew's home. Later on, we took turns hosting the meeting at each other's homes. Once formed, the MBG elected chairman was Donald; captains were Victor and Leslie; treasurer was Linton, assisted by David Chin; secretary was Merryl; committee members were Horace, Mandison, Jean Chin, Angela, Rosie, Jean Lue and David Lai representing the juniors.

We started with a Badminton Exhibition by international players following the Rothman International Badminton Tournament 1973 with a "Braata Barbecue". The exhibition was very successful as many Montegonians could not have afforded the time and effort to go and see badminton played at such a high calibre when these players were in Kingston. The international players enjoyed this break from competitive play and were happy to spend some recreational time on the north coast in the tourist capital of Montego Bay before moving on to compete elsewhere in the States. At a later date, we would also host Pat Davis, leading English coach and author of many badminton coaching books who held coaching clinics during the evenings after sightseeing during the daytime. He would refer to me in his later correspondence as "his chauffeuse". As a MBG member, I would go with the Montego Bay contingent to compete in matches held at the National Arena playing Singles, Ladies Doubles with Linda Hew, and Mixed Doubles with Richard Chin and Clifton Hew. Eddie was busy learning the supermarket business and working as a part

-time residential engineer inspecting work done on a coastal highway so he was not able to be away in Kingston for these JBA organized tournaments.

At the Rothman International Badminton Tournament in Kingston, we stayed in Linda's brother-in-law's home. George "Geggie" Hew is James's older brother who married Pamela and had two children: Georgina and Jonathan. The upset of the Ladies Singles in the Closed Division was that Georgina, a 13-year old student of Priory School, knocked out the Number One seed, Yvonne Yapp and also 13-year old, Andre Chin captured the Men's Singles title from top seed, Barrington Lue. Before Georgina won the Ladies Singles trophy, she beat her Aunt Linda and defeated Number Two seeded player, Carol Wong in the hard-fought three-setter final match. Luckily for us, Georgina did not enter the Ladies Doubles so Linda and I were able to capture the crown from top seeds, Yvonne Yapp and Joyce Marr. Without a doubt, Georgina inherited the racquet sport gene in the Hew family as her uncle, Ernest was an All-Jamaica Badminton Champion before he went to study at the University of the West Indies Medical School. His siblings George, Esme, Edmund and James were also excellent badminton and tennis players.

The 1974 badminton exhibition in Montego Bay at the Chinese Club premises on Creek Street was again arranged in association with the JBA following the Rothman's International Tournament. The foreign players were flown down on a chartered flight for the "Badminton Extravaganza". The contingent included Asian players from Indonesia and Malaysia so we planned to host a "Tiger Barbecue" which included Wuhan soup, Chen Sing Chicken, Kung Fu spare ribs, Chow Choy and Wang Yu fried rice. The cost was $4 per person, or 50 cents for people who only wanted to watch the exhibition. It must be said that the Mexican, Trinidadian, Guyanese and Asian players were easier to accommodate than the delinquent, free-spirited European players. They were not party animals or heavy drinkers and were quite modest in their behaviour off court.

We also arranged friendly matches with the Savanna-la-Mar badminton players in Petersfield and the badminton players from the Alcan Sports Club, Mandeville. The away matches were always enjoyable and sociable, especially in Petersfield where the hosts would organize land-crab feasts followed by whichever fruit was in season or plentiful like June plums and mangoes. Domino games were also arranged and everyone had a wonderful time and made great memories of shared camaraderie, regardless the results of the matches played.

The Montego Badminton Group (MBG) was now affiliated with the JBA and was included in their newsletters. The JBA newsletter included a long piece that noted that the MBG was a very active club that had recently concluded their club league of three teams namely "The Radicals" captained by Carol Wong, "The Strugglers" captained by Jean Chin and "The Overdogs" captained by Linda Hew. The winning team was "The Radicals". The Kelly Superservice Knock-out Tournament was also held and won by The Radicals again. The numerous entries in the Annual MBG tournament vied for silver Challenge Cups sponsored by Jamaica Car Rentals, Cornwall Betting, BOAC, Overton Plaza, and the China Doll restaurant in the "A" Division and the "B" Division.

"Not-To-Worry", Montego Bay, Jamaica 1973-74

Carol at MBG trophy presentation at "Not To Worry"

The prize-giving party took place at the home of Eddie and Carol Wong in Brandon Hill and prizes were handed out by the Vice-President of JBA, Mr. Lucien Tai Ten Quee. The trophy cup winners were: "A" Division Men's Singles – Victor Lyn Shue; Ladies' Singles – Carol Wong; "B" Division Men's Singles – Tommy Lee; Ladies' Singles – Karen Chin; Men's Doubles – Tony Tai and Linton Chin with runners-up Johnny Gurzong and Chris Brown; Ladies' Doubles – Jean and Sharon Chin with runners-up Daisy Tai and Karen Chin; Mixed Doubles – Linton Chin and Linda Hew with runners-up Bertie Sharpe and Karen Chin.

At the MBG annual general meeting, the following were elected to serve :-

President	Mr. Leslie Chin
Captain	Mr. Tony Tai
Vice-Captain	Mrs. Carol Wong
Hon. Secretary	Mrs. Daisy Tai
Hon. Treasurer	Mr. Walton Chin
Committee members	Eugene Chin, Mandison Chin, Horace Lue, Edmund Hew.

While the MBG flourished, the Chinese Club building was falling into disrepair so attempts were made to locate the land title from solicitor, David Hew in Kingston and the members of the Chinese community were called together at a Chinese New Year Dinner with an aim to revive the club. Many years before, Mr. James Chin had left the property for the Chinese community and a two-storey building was built for the Chinese as a meeting place especially for Chinese New Year celebrations. Over time, the elders neglected the building and their children grew up and went away to study or work elsewhere. The main level was sturdily built with a concrete foundation and the upper level had a wooden flooring, railings and shutters with zinc roofing. Upstairs was the main hall with a stage and downstairs was a patio with a kitchen, men's and ladies washrooms, storage and a caretakers room. The clubhouse was surrounded by breadfruit trees and the patio overlooked the badminton courts and an abandoned tennis court. At the rear of the building was the home of Mr. Masue Chin and the ice factory was next door. The creek ran along Creek Street towards the sea so to enter the property one would have to go across a concrete bridge spanning the narrow creek which was sometimes filled with a collection of miscellaneous debris following a heavy rainfall.

Plans were made to build two indoor badminton courts adjoining the aging Chinese Clubhouse and a groundbreaking ceremony was held. Eddie was too busy to take care of the planning so newcomer, Terry Larsen started drawing up the architectural plans. Terry was an architect originally from the American mid-western State of Nebraska who had come to Jamaica with his petite blond wife, Bonnie to work on the Cornwall Regional Hospital where he met Eddie. They became our good friends and were invited to join all the functions at MBG and other community events. When Terry's contract was up and he had to return to the States, Bonnie stayed at our home until he was settled in Boston, Massachusetts. Later in life, they settled in Bryan, Texas where Terry became a lecturer at the Texas A & M University and we have remained long-distance friends to this day.

Terry Larsen, architect, receiving badminton prize from Wally Chin, at MBG trophy presentation

Eddie and Carol at ground-breaking ceremony of Chinese Club expansion

Our single friends started to settle down and we attended the wedding of Horace Lue and my cousin, Jean Chin at St. James Parish Church with reception at the exclusive Round Hill Hotel. The venue was the same for Edmund Hew and Paulette Lee Sang. Philip Chin tied the knot with Sandra Noyes at the Anglican Parish Church too but their reception was held at the Richmond Hill Hotel, owned by Stanley and Stephanie Chin which had a lovely view overlooking the city. Norman Chin You got married to Audrey Chin at Holy Cross Church, Half-Way Tree and the reception was held at Mee-Mee Chinese Restaurant, Northside Plaza in Kingston.

My only sister, Elaine was getting married to her cousin, Chester Chin at St. Basil's Roman Catholic Church on Bay Street in Toronto and the reception was to be held in Chinatown on Dundas Street. Papa, my brother Patrick, and I flew up for this long-awaited wedding. Elaine and Chester knew each other as teenagers because our families are related and lived about three miles from each other in Westmoreland. We

"Not-To-Worry", Montego Bay, Jamaica 1973-74

lived in Petersfield, while the Chin family lived in Whithorn District. Elaine and Chester shared a love of photography and they set up a photo studio named "Cheslaine" upstairs in our home on the back verandah so you could say their love developed in the dark room as they processed the rolls of film! Chester was a great guy and everybody loved him, including my mother to whom he was so obliging and respectful.

Before returning to Jamaica, Eddie and I had sponsored Elaine to come to Canada as a permanent resident and after working at Eaton's Department Store and settling down in an apartment on Keele Street, she in turn, sponsored Chester to Canada. He began working at Weston Bakeries and now they were planning to get married and start a family. Without a doubt, I already knew that Chester would be a devoted husband to Elaine, a wonderful father, a caring son-in-law, a kind brother-in-law and an extremely conscientious worker in terms of providing for his family and others.

Chester and Elaine as teenagers

I arrived ahead of time to help Elaine prepare for her wedding and to help outfit the wedding party. Her bridesmaid was her past roommate, Lorna and her matron-of-honour was Terry, a friend whom she had met at Eaton's in the cosmetic department. There was a party held at the party room in their apartment complex so we met some of Elaine's friends and other invitees to the wedding like Mike and Phyllis Cooke; Phyllis was her boss at the Eaton's branch at Shoppers World. Elaine and Chester owned an old red sedan car which they named "Lulubelle". She cost the 'exorbitant' sum of $200. I was to drive her to the wedding and reception so that they would have a car to drive to an unknown hotel for their wedding night. At the end of the reception, Patrick and I would be driven back to their apartment by a tipsy Mike who scared Patrick with his erratic driving, but we arrived safely to welcome the newly-wedded couple the following day.

Papa returned home to Petersfield after the wedding, but Patrick and I accompanied Elaine and Chester on their one-week honeymoon to Montréal, Québec. We stayed

Groom Chester and bride Elaine

Papa and Elaine

Elaine, Patrick and Carol at Mount Royal, Montréal

Elaine and Chester with "Lulubelle" car

Patrick, Carol and Chester in front of Beaver Hall

with our friends, Washington and Sheila Chin in Pointe Claire and I rented a car so we could all go sightseeing every day. Since I had lived in Montréal before, I knew all the sightseeing spots. The car rental for the week was $45 plus 0.07 cents per mile and the sales tax was 8%. Elaine and I were quite curious about the gay bars which were just beginning to open up in Québec. We went to check them out and were in awe and admiration of the beauty and exquisite make-up worn by the gay guys. Although it should have been Elaine and Chester's honeymoon, all four of us had a wonderful time together. At the end of the week, Elaine and Chester flew back to Toronto, and Patrick and I returned to Jamaica.

My three sons, Brian, Gordon and Jason did not even miss me while I was away since their father was home with them, their grandparents were nearby and they were used to Gurzel running things in the home. The boys were now quite settled in Montego Bay and enjoyed attending the private Montego Montessori School. I had read about the Montessori method of schooling and the aims of the Italian founder, Marie Montessori so I was so very pleased that an English expatriate, Miss Rosemary Branwhite decided to open the first Montessori school in Jamaica in Montego Bay not very far from where we lived in Brandon Hill, actually at the bottom of the hill and next to Overton Shopping Plaza. She was assisted by another expatriate, Mrs. Gorham, whose children also attended the school, and Miss Claire Hugh from Guyana.

"Not-To-Worry", Montego Bay, Jamaica 1973-74

Devoted maid Gurzel and "her boys"

All the students were from middle and upper-class families so there was a lot of financial support for the school from the wealthier families. Miss Branwhite was very open-minded, unsurprisingly so since the Montessori teaching method values open-concept. She accepted all the ideas and help from the Parent Teachers Association. Our Christmas concert also revealed this willingness to be open to different ideas and experiences.

At the concert, Swedish parent, Marianne Hastings had her daughters, Anna and Marie, share their Swedish Christmas tradition of Santa Lucia. Her son, Paul and my three sons sang solo Christmas carols. Tears came rolling down from my eyes as I watched and listened to Brian singing "The First Noel" in a clear cherub-like voice, Gordon giving his rendition of

Montego Montessori Christmas concert
Front row of angels behind Mary and baby Jesus L-R: Gordon, Jason, Jeremy, Paul, Desmond

"Baby Jesus, We will Rock You" with a lisp and a raspy voice, and three-year old Jason singing "Away in a Manger" in a loud voice with a Jamaican accent so beautiful that it would melt your heart.

When we asked Miss Branwhite if it would be okay to take the children out of school for our family holiday to Florida, she highly endorsed our travel plans saying that the education received from travelling to foreign places could not be replicated in the classroom. As a result, we did not delay our flight plans to Orlando, Florida and stayed at Sheraton Catalina Hotel outside of the Disney World Theme Park. At that time, Jamaica had only one television station which broadcast only in black and white so it was extremely difficult to pull the children out of the hotel room when they discovered that the room had a colour television with so many stations to choose from! However, we made it to the famous Disney World and opted for the two-day pass costing $11.50 per adult and children $9.50. We were awestruck by the crowds, pavilions, rides and all the entertainment geared for children in the "Small, Small World" ride. Cinderella's Castle was magical as were the Disney cartoon characters walking around the grounds. Jason was terrified of them but Gordon and Brian enjoyed every moment. I could not believe the patience the boys demonstrated when we had to wait in line for hours to have caricature sketches of each of them. These were done by artists as we exited the movie theatres after seing *Snow White and the Seven Dwarfs*. Anyway, it was worth the effort as today, I can show you the framed sketches of your fathers at your age! I guess having children early in life allows one to have a higher level of patience and tolerance for such adventures.

Brian and Gordon in a hug from Wally Walrus

The first day at Disney World, we spent the entire day – right up until the fireworks lit up the night skies – within the Magic Kingdom. On the second day we visited Fantasy Land, Adventure Land, Frontier Land and Tomorrow Land and ended the day at the Pioneer Music Hall in the Fort Wilderness campground resort with a dinner and a show. All the boys ended up sleeping at the table during the show and it was good that we had rented a car for our late nights. Poor Brian, as the eldest, had to be awakened to walk drowsily to the car while the other boys were carried by Eddie and me. Another reason why it pays to have children when one is younger and stronger!

"Not-To-Worry", Montego Bay, Jamaica 1973-74

On our non-Disney days in Orlando, we took it easier and visited the Lion Country Safari where the admission was $5 per adult and $2.75 for children and the John F. Kennedy Space Center and space shuttle launch site. In Cape Canaveral, we also visited the Museum of Sunken Treasure. We drove out to the Ringling, Barnum & Bailey Circus World where we saw our first Imax film which was the most revolutionary motion picture process ever developed at that time. It felt as if we were indeed watching -- actually participating in – a live circus. Outside, there were tame circus elephants to ride, a college of clowns, a museum of exotic wonders, and a weird and wonderful theatre of supernatural illusions. I guess we really were in the world's largest, grandest and best amusement park as the hand-out flyers read! Visiting Sea World also blew our minds with its realistic Hawaiian village, dolphin feeding pool in a tropical lagoon, a seal and penguin stadium, a fountain fantasy, and a whale and dolphin stadium. There was another world of the sea with sharks, sea turtles and exotic fish in a huge 150 thousand gallon salt-water aquarium adjoining a Japanese village with a Pacific tide pool.

We even drove farther away from Orlando to visit Busch Gardens in Tampa and rode the Trans-Veldt Railway for a close-up view of wild animals in their natural surroundings. The boys could feed and pet the parrots after the trained bird circus and watch the elephant, chimpanzee and sea lion shows.

Brian and Gordon with birds at Busch Gardens

"Not-To-Worry", Montego Bay, Jamaica 1973-74

Eddie and "My Three Sons" in Mickey Mouse t-shirts

We continued driving along the Gulf Coast to St. Petersburg to visit the MGM Bounty, Florida's first marine-historical exhibit of the world famous sailing ship. We retraced the history of Captain Blythe, who took more than one year to sail from Britain to Tahiti in 1787, and First Mate, Fletcher Christian who led the most famous mutiny in the maritime history. I felt a special thankfulness to Captain Blythe for taking hundreds of breadfruit tree plants to be planted in Jamaica. The breadfruit was brought to the island originally to feed the African slaves on the sugar-cane plantations but today it is one of the unique food specialties of Jamaican cuisine.

We ended up in Miami and stayed at the Holiday Inn before flying back home -- with lots for the boys to tell the other children at the Montego Montessori School.

Travelling abroad is indeed one of the best ways to broaden one's mind and is best shared with loved ones. This family trip was the first of many, many more to come in our lives!

Your loving Ah-Poh

"Not-To-Worry", Montego Bay, Jamaica 1973-74

Vernon's visit from Austin, Texas L-R: Dorit, Vernon, Eddie, Grandpa Kelly with Brian, Carol with Gordon, Grandma Catherine, Ouida

MBG Dinner L-R: Linda, Elma, Carol, Eddie, Donald

MBG Dinner L-R: Errol, Jean, Jeff, Polly, Rosie, Wally, Merryl, Linton

Life in Jamaica:
Not-to-Worry, Montego Bay,
1974 - 1975

My dear Grandchildren,

Our family felt very secure living in the tourist area of Jamaica. We were also very aware of the many foreigners coming to enjoy our Island in the Sun and of the benevolent acts of many of these foreigners.

One of our overseas visitors was Mr. Johnny Cash, international superstar of American country music. His family planted cotton in Arkansas and after enlisting in the U.S Air force, he married his wife, June Carter of the famous Carter family of folk music legend. Johnny was part Cherokee Indian and he wrote bitter protest songs about the neglected American Indians and put on benefit concerts at Indian reservations to raise money to support their causes. His compassion for the down-trodden affected him in other ways. He played at many of the U.S Penitentiaries and large prisons like San Quentin and Folsom which inspired him to write "Folsom Prison Blues and "I Walk the Line". At this time, many foreigners were investing in Jamaica, like his friend and hotelier, John Rollins who built the Rose Hall Intercontinental Hotel outside Montego Bay. Johnny Cash fell in love with Jamaica and Jamaicans so he purchased the Cinnamon Hill Great House from his friend, John and became a frequent visitor to Jamaica.

Johnny Cash

Mr. Cash would bring his entire group down to Rose Hall and give benefit performances to raise money for the SOS Children's Village for unwanted children in Barrett Town. This was a cause which was very dear to the hearts of both Johnny and June Cash who contributed thousands of dollars for the construction and furnishing of the SOS house and environs. They also performed benefit concerts to build the Jamaica House Garden Theatre in Kingston, along with a basic school accommodating 150 children with added donations from Mr. and Mrs. John Rollins.

The International Service Clubs did their charitable part also. Great-grandfather Kelly and Clinton Chin were active in the Rotary International Club. Linda and James Hew and cousin, Rosa and Dockie Chin were representatives of the Montego Bay Kiwanis Club. Uncle Donald Chin encouraged Eddie to become a member of the Lions Club of Montego Bay. It was then only natural for me to become a part of the Lioness Club to raise funds to aid the Salt Spring Basic School and other charity work needed in the area for local children. My Chinese friends like Merryl, Elma and Delsie were

"Not-To-Worry", Montego Bay, Jamaica 1974-75

Delsie Chin and other Lionesses

also involved as Lionesses so we had to share our time between our charity work and organizing Christmas parties for the children of the Chinese Club as well. But it was fun for me. I enjoyed feeling more integrated in the Jamaican society and meeting more people in the hotel industry, the East Indians in the In-bond business, and the expatriate professionals. I loved being part of a broader community where everyone was doing their best to give back to the community that we all shared; and being part of a movement in which everyone of all races was having a good time working together, respecting each other, accepting our differences and enjoying each other's company!

At the same time, work continued on reviving the Chinese Social & Athletic Club (CSAC) in Montego Bay and following the Chinese New Year's dinner invitation to the wider Chinese community, an Annual General Meeting was held on May 14, 1975 and the executives and committee members were elected. Draft constitutions were adopted, membership fees were fixed at $20 per adult, $10 per child and $50 per family. Engineering designs and architectural drawings were in the process of being completed by Eddie Wong and Terry Larsen. Pledges that had been made at the Chinese New Year's dinner had almost all been collected by Carl Chang, a newcomer who had recently opened The Western Sports store in Overton Plaza. Sports programs were planned to include domino tournaments (Edmund Hew), football leagues (P.C. Chin), basketball matches (Eddie Wong), volleyball competition (Eugene Chin), tennis (Linton Chin) and table tennis league (Carl Chang). Cooking classes would be offered by Vivian Yap and Chinese classes to be arranged by Carol Wong. Harding Wong Shui was appointed Club Photographer and Carol Wong was put in charge of the CSAC scrapbook.

Re-entering the Wong family business was much easier this time around because Great-grandfather Kelly, through his contacts via Rotary International and perhaps his Masonic Lodge, seemed to have cornered the market supplying the hotels and most of the local businesses. In fact, the business had become more wholesale than retail. As a result, we had a counter of ladies employed to take the orders from smaller shop-keepers from remote districts and Kelly's half-brother, Ken, nicknamed Korean, was totally in charge of supplying the goods and supervising the men hired to assist him. We had a truck driver, Missa Chin, to transport goods to and from the cold storage and make deliveries to the customers and do any other work that included transportation. There was also a chauffeur, Missa Willie to drive me and the children when needed. Eddie soon learned the work needed to run the office, deal with the salesmen and keep track of the business accounts. I was the trusted cashier and was not at all phased by having to make large cash transactions or to make the bank lodgments. One of our staff, either Alfred, nicknamed "Gun-tukka", or Lascelles Fuller would inconspicuously drop the bank deposit bag off at the Charles Square branch of the Bank of Nova Scotia without fear of being robbed.

This was not, however, very stimulating work for me and with Gurzel taking care of the house and kids, I decided to work part-time for Eastern Airlines at the newly named Donald Sangster International Airport, formerly the Montego Bay Airport. We bought a Mitsubishi Minivan which was suitable for me to drive to work and pick up the children. The van was totally white in colour so I had a broad pink stripe painted around the perimeter of the van which gave it a more feminine – and personal – look.

White mini-bus with pink stripe, Gordon sitting on step

I was selected to attend a training class on basic ticketing and tariffs in Miami for two weeks. I was to depart after work, but I almost missed my flight because I was waiting for Eddie to bring the children to the office at the airport to say good-bye. He did not show up and I waited so long that the plane door was actually closed before I went to board the plane. Because I was friendly with the ground crew, they rolled the steps back to the plane and re-opened the door to let me board -- which was really against regulations. During the flight, I wrote Eddie a very cross, scolding letter and mailed it as soon as I arrived in Miami.

My other Eastern Airlines co-trainees were Olive and Jennifer who were happy to be away from their families but I was not comfortable going out after training as if we were still single girls. In the daytime, I hung out with other Eastern Airlines employees from other countries in South America and the Caribbean. I ended up most evenings attending the Gusman Philharmonic Hall and the Coconut Grove Playhouse all by myself. I enjoyed the work of the then budding choreographer, Bob Fosse, who was making his debut in *Pippin*, a musical comedy. I loved these bigger productions of live theatre and was quite thankful that my years at Wolmer's High School had given me the exposure to and an appreciation for stage productions and the fine arts as well which I wanted to pass on to my own children and grandchildren later in life.

When I returned home to Jamaica, my three sons were excited to see me not only because of the gifts I brought back from the States for them, but because they were waiting to tell me all about the musical production they were rehearsing for. The production was called *Antics* and was about an ant colony. Brian was the main lead, playing the part of the ant named Voran, while Gordon and Jason were in supporting

"Not-To-Worry", Montego Bay, Jamaica 1974-75

L-R Alice, Jason and Jeremy as baby ants

Boys' antics in "Antics" costumes

roles. They all had singing parts and after a few more rehearsals, the show was performed at the Fairfield Theatre to a packed audience of parents, friends and students from other schools. After a great performance, we treated our talented sons to icecream at Burger House near the City Centre Shopping plaza with other parents, Marianne Hastings and Yvonne Jones and their children/members of the cast, Paul, Anna, Maria and Ronald. Later on, we were so pleased that the performance was taped by a Mr. Marzouca and we received a recording of *Antics* on a cassette tape which I have to share with you all someday.

Fairfield Theatre was situated on the grounds of the Fairfield Golf and Country Club which had excluded Chinese and local Jamaicans in colonial days. Because of their exclusivity, the membership fees were prohibitive and very soon, they were in financial hardship and started opening up to locals. Before that, we could only read in the local newspaper, *The Daily Gleaner*, that the likes of British tennis player, Fred Perry, Americans Arthur Ashe, Althea Gibson and Gussie Moran in her frilly tennis underwear, pretty Maria Bueno from Argentina, handsome Australian Ken Rosewall were in town and playing tennis at Fairfield. It was the same snobbery that had been evident at the Montego Bay Racquet Club and certain hotels in the area. One Chinese lady, Mrs. Chin, was forbidden to enter a hotel named Sunset Lodge near Chatham beach. Many years later, she ended up owning the same hotel which was renamed "Jack Tar". My dear Grandchildren, what goes around, comes around and no one can predict the future!

Tennis became less elitist when the Jamaica Lawn Tennis Association fielded a Davis Cup team to play internationally and in the Caribbean. Like badminton, the cigarette company, Rothmans of Pall Mall Ltd., began to sponsor tennis tournaments too, such as the Rothmans Tennis Spectacular at the National Arena in Kingston. They organized a promotion on the main King Street downtown during which traffic was blocked off and some of the international tennis stars gave a demonstration game on a tennis court marked out on the asphalted street. Some of the tennis stars were Illie Nastase (Rumania), Martin Reissen, Billy Martin, Clark Graebner, Eugene Scott, Bob Lutz (USA); Buster Mottram, Roger Taylor, and flying Englishman, Gerald Battrick from Britain; Swede Ove Bengtsson, Italian Andriano Panatta, Charles Pasarell from Puerto Rico and our Caribbean boys: John Antonas and Leo Rolle from Bahamas; and Lance Lumsden, Dennis Davis and Richard Russell from Jamaica.

The first Jamaica Tennis Week was held at the Montego Bay Racquet Club and co-sponsored by Air Jamaica and the Jamaica Tourist Board. This was given worldwide publicity and events were Grand Masters Mixed Doubles, Senior Doubles, Junior Veteran Doubles, and Senior Pro Celebrity exhibition matches which were hosted by tournament director, Bill Talbert, U.S Davis Cup captain. This was going to be a fun tournament and entries received included Harry Hopman, Australian Davis Cup captain; Oleg Cassini, famous tennis wear designer; Neil Simon, playwright; Hank Greenberg, Hall of Fame baseball and tennis celebrity; Jinx Falkenberg, television and radio star; Doc Liberman; George Hoehne, industrial designer; Hon. Robert Payton, U.S Ambassador; R. Hunnewell, banker; Fred Manha Kovaleski, U.S Senior Doubles winner; Chuck Mc Kinley, Wimbledon champion; Sarah Palfrey, world and U.S champion; Don Budge, world champion; Dick Savitt, Wimbledon champion; Senator Jacob Javits of the U.S Foreign Relations Committee; Pauline Bets, U.S Ladies Singles champion; and more. There was much excitement as the illustrious players started to arrive and somehow I became involved, especially when Harry Hopman volunteered to hold tennis clinics for over 40 children selected mainly from tennis clubs and the "ball boys" from hotel courts. I recall George Hew phoning me from Kingston to enter this tournament and later on, told me how disappointed he was to be paired with Harry Hopman who was getting on in age and was not as competitive anymore. In the end, George was happy to have met this small, delightful Australian gentleman.

In the badminton world, the People's Republic of China was emerging as a significant force and I was advised by the JBA that a goodwill team of twelve officials and players from China were coming to give exhibition games at the National Arena in Kingston. I was asked whether the MBA would like for the team to give demonstration matches in Montego Bay as well. I

Australian tennis coach, Harry Hopman, demonstrates to Sharon during free clinic

"Not-To-Worry", Montego Bay, Jamaica 1974-75

Visiting Chinese team with Mayor Sinclair (back row) and MBG Captain, Leslie Chin

immediately stated: "Of course we would!" We arranged for the team to stay at Palm Beach Hotel courtesy of Leslie Hew and took them sightseeing on the north coast. Needless to say, they were most courteous, appreciative, polite and gracious. We were quite pleased that the team travelled with their fluent interpreter and efficient secretary -- and noticed, that, of course, there were also officials with the team to keep an eye on them.

Having lived abroad, our family also enjoyed sightseeing on the coast and on weekends we would often stay at different tourist areas. When we stayed at Negril Beach Villas, we would invite other families like Merryl and Donald's, James and Linda's, Edmund and Paulette's and Mandison's to join us for a day visit. We would visit the lighthouse, spend most of the day on the seven mile long beach and go sailing on our 16ft. Bonito sailboat. These get-togethers would create childhood friendships among our sons and Desmond, Tricia, Ginny, Jeremy, Justine, Simone, Glen, Tracey and Katherine. Another favourite place to stay was at the Coconut Cove Villas and Caribbean Villas in Discovery Bay. The Michael and Micheline Sharpe family would go with us to visit the Crocodile Farm and watch Ross Kananga wrestle the crocodiles. Their children Andrew, Christopher and Melanie, were good company for Brian, Gordon and Jason while they investigated places like the Green Grotto Caves, Columbus Park and Runaway Bay.

Our annual summer family holiday that year was spent visiting my sister, Elaine and husband, Chester, in Toronto, Ontario, Canada. We stayed at their apartment in the Tuxedo Court Apartment complex on Markham Road and the boys were so rambunctious, we had the neighbours living beneath us complaining a lot and hitting the floor with their mop-sticks. Brian, Gordon, and Jason, who had grown so wild and unfettered in Jamaica did not realize the restrictions of living in a high rise apartment. Elaine and Chester had just bought their new white Toyota Camry car as their red "Lulubelle" sedan had just expired. They had also decided to take over a business establishment called the "Windjammer Seafoods" which was like a Fish and Chips take-out shop on Wellington Street, Markham. They were in the corner unit of a shopping plaza and got along well with the other unit owners as well as the previous Italian owners of the Windjammer. We were able to get around by ourselves and I enjoyed a lot of live dinner theatres at Teller's Cage, Mississippi Belle, Old Angelo's, Second City and O'Keefe Center where I went to see Tony Randall and Jack Klugman as "The Odd Couple". I just love going to live stage shows whenever we travel abroad!

It was a treat to dine at Toronto's unique theatre restaurant, Ed's Warehouse. Several years prior, one of North America's most flamboyant and successful merchandiser, Mr. Ed Mirvish purchased the Royal Alexandra Theatre, which was considered to be one of the finest theatres in the world. The lack of dining facilities in the immediate area, prompted him to purchase an adjoining warehouse building in which he created an elegant dining room. In keeping with his theatrical motif, Mr. Mirvish had used much of his famous collection of antiques to create a truly fabulous restaurant with Old World splendor and charm. The décor featured the world's largest collection of Tiffany-type lamps. At that time, it was said that every night over three hundred people enjoyed a superb dinner of roast beef or steak and we were happy to be one of them.

Eddie sailing with Gordon and Brian

Our Toronto visit was timely because my youngest brother, Donny had just arrived from travelling for months after receiving his Bachelor of Science degree from McMaster, University in the Fall of 1974. No one in the family was able to attend his convocation ceremonies but we were proud that one of our six siblings made it through university and would be entering medical school as was Papa's and every Chinese parent's dream. We, his siblings, were just happy to see the results of our family slaving away in our "Chiney Shop" to be able to afford Donny's university expenses. I was also mighty relieved because while Donny was at McMaster, I had written him warning against the dangers of doing drugs or smoking pot, so prevalent in North American universities during the hippie era. As a worried big sister, I kept in my scrapbook the air letter in which he admonished me for even thinking he would do anything illegal and reassured me that he was "clean".

During his post-graduation tour, Donny had been sending me picture postcards from backpacking and hitchhiking all over Europe and Asia with his friend, Dave. In

October, they took the train from Amsterdam, Holland to Denmark and planned going through France, Spain, then Monaco. I got another postcard the following month that they had taken a train from Brussels, Belgium and Luxemburg. Because of bad winter weather, they headed south hitchhiking to Milan, Florence and Rome, Italy where they saw enough paintings, sculptures and cathedrals to last a lifetime. In the new year of 1975, he was in Athens, Greece which was his favourite country so far because the Greeks were so friendly and honest. Plus, Donny admired their enjoyment of life expressed through their dancing, eating seafood and drinking wine. Donny was not shy to join in the Zorba style dancing where rows of men dance in a line with arms around each other's shoulders.

Donny and Dave spent a week on the peaceful island of Mykonos before going on to Turkey and Iran where Donny developed an interest in the Islamic faith. He was taken with Muslim mosques, Persian carpets, Arabic scripts and the incredible bazaars filled with exotic women, veils, robes, turquoise stones, handicrafts and spices. He found the people beautiful and hospitable, the food, especially rice dishes, tasty and cheap, and the various musical instruments and music totally fantastic. He spoke with Muslims coming back from their pilgrimage to Mecca and even met up with other young Canadians.

They then moved on to Kathmandu, Nepal and found the place to be like some type of medieval fairyland. In some places, it felt like one had gone back one hundred years in time! He had a chance to go trekking in the beautiful Himalayas but would not dare attempt to see Mount Everest which was extremely far away and way too strenuous. The people in this area were a mixture of Tibetans and Indians so Buddhism and Hinduism co-existed. Donny wrote that ever since he had arrived in the East, he had been happier than he had ever been in his life and wished that I could have shared this experience with him. He found everything, everyone and everywhere overwhelming and attained spiritual enlightenment. From New Delhi, India, he flew back to Amsterdam via Cairo, Egypt and felt a shock when he re-encountered European civilization after being so long in the Far East. His last postcard said he was having the time of his life but he had not received any correspond-ence from us and he could hardly wait to see us again as there was so much to tell of his travels.

While we were in Toronto, Donny showed up at Elaine's apartment door. We were all shocked when we saw him because he arrived wearing a turban, a white tee-shirt, a green and

Donny with his Indian sitar

white checkered sarong and Indian leather sandals. He was tall and thin with a scanty beard but had a look of peace and contentment on his face. He did indeed have lots to tell us – including tales of the parasites he had contracted and recovered from during his journeys! Brian, Gordon and Jason were mesmerized by his stories and practised chanting with him. Brian even got to try on his turban.

L-R: Donny, Gordon and Brian meditating

I was very pleased that Donny had, like our other siblings, kept in touch with me while he was travelling. I recall getting picture postcards from Dick when he went to Mexico with his male friends and later with his wife, Margaret when they visited Niagara Falls, Toronto and Saskatchewan where Margaret's uncle lived. Elaine was sure to send me postcards from her very first flight out of Jamaica to Miami, Florida and, as an only sister, never forget to send me birthday cards. I guess my father was right: the eldest daughter becomes the mother in the mother's absence. I suppose I bore that role and responsibility long after we were all grown-up.

To Papa's relief, Donny returned to University of McMaster but he did not enter Medical School. After having become involved in mystic Eastern religions on his trip, Donny felt that practising medicine was not what he would like to do with his life. Without telling Papa, he started working at the University library instead, with the intention of saving enough money to return to India to help Mother Teresa with her work caring for the poor and dying. Donny headed back to the slums of Calcutta as soon as he had the air-fare. That was all he needed because Mother Teresa's convent would provide board and lodging. It took awhile for Papa to come to the realization that Donny was not going to give him the honour of having a "Doctor Son", but eventually Papa was able to come to a compromise with Donny: Papa asked me to write to Donny to say that even if he did not want to become a doctor, he should return to Canada immediately and find a job instead of "kicking stone and watching the leaves fall off the trees". I guess writing this letter was a duty that fell on me as the elder daughter. Plus Papa was not able to write English well. In fact, I recall only

"Not-To-Worry", Montego Bay, Jamaica 1974-75

receiving one letter from Papa in my life – which I promptly pasted into my scrap book. His air letter was written from Hong Kong where he had travelled to after attending my wedding in 1965. It informed me of his safe arrival and that he would be sending me via sea mail two Chinese cheong-sams, which are traditional Chinese dresses, and a Chinese silk duvet for my matrimonial bed. I was amazed that he would write to me – and in English as well. As a result, I treasured his letter and have kept it safely up to this day of writing to you, my little Grandchildren.

To close, I will tell you that Donny obeyed his father and found a job with the Canadian University Services Overseas (CUSO) working in Kandy, Sri Lanka. He and his fellow Canadians taught the Sri Lankans to plant soya beans and make soy-based food like tofu and tofutto ice-cream. He enjoyed going up in the peaceful tea plantations in the mountain and met a 90-year old Buddhist teacher so he began his studies in Buddhism. He would return with his colleagues on home visits but in no time he would disappear to the South-east Asia again. Many years after, Papa passed away and Donny was finally ordained in Sri Lanka as a Buddhist monk and became the Venerable Bhante Kovida.

Your loving Ah-Poh

Chins, Hews and Wongs stay at Negril Beach Villas L-R: Paulette, Linda with Jeremy, Claire, Eddie and kids - Tricia, Desmond, Jason, Glenn

The Wongs' 16-ft. Bonito sailboat

Life in Jamaica:
Not-to-Worry, Montego Bay,
1975 - 1976

My dear Grandchildren,

When we returned to Jamaica after our holidays in Canada, trouble was already brewing in paradise . . . . especially in the city of Kingston.

When Jamaica received Independence from Britain in 1962, the ruling political party was the Jamaica Labour Party (JLP) led by Prime Minister Alexander Bustamente. The JLP continued in power until, in 1972, Michael Manley and the People's National Party (PNP) swept into office. It was rumoured that members of the PNP brought guns into Jamaica to arm Manley's supporters and intimidate JLP supporters in the poor illiterate ghetto areas. Nevertheless, Manley led a great campaign and he was very charismatic. Many middle-class Jamaicans like our family, agreed with his party's argument that there was too wide a gap between the wealthy and the poor Jamaicans. Manley's political slogan was "Better must come" and he self-styled himself as the Biblical character, "Joshua" who would "lead his (poor) people out of bondage". Many of us educated middle-class folks, voted for "Joshua" and helped to create the biggest landslide election victory in the history of Jamaican politics.

Soon after the PNP came to power, the now Prime Minister Manley started preaching against capitalism and began endorsing democratic socialism, particularly in the urban area. This was a philosophy that only reminded the Chinese in Jamaica of the tumultuous events in China that had occurred with the rise of a Communist state there. Such anxious feelings amongst the Chinese Jamaicans were amplified when Manley opened up relations with Communist Russia and Cuba, who started sending doctors to the island to assist our medical system. Rumour had it that these people also brought with them their Marxist ideology and Russian arms which many believed were used to train the disillusioned youth in the hills. In the meantime, violence continued in the ghetto areas between the PNP and JLP supporters. After his victory, Manley tried to recall the guns from the ghetto by creating an amnesty requesting guns to be handed into churches. Needless to say, not many guns were handed in to the reverend pastors or priests. It was rumoured that many guns were buried in remote areas instead. A Gun Court was even established to combat the rising gun violence, but to no avail.

To bring about his vision of democratic socialism, Manley's government targeted the businessmen. Instead of recognizing that the business classes served the community in important ways and that they had worked hard and sacrificed to be able to provide their families with beautiful homes, the success of the business classes was pointed to as evidence of crimes of dishonesty against, and exploitation of, the masses. Instead of suggesting that the business classes be admired and imitated, it was hinted that they should be hated for their seeming success and superior lifestyle. Manley himself uttered words that were understood to be a solemn promise to tax the rich middle and upper-class business people out of their homes in Cherry Gardens, Beverly Hills, and other fine high-bracket residential areas throughout the island. Mr. William Strong, in his column "You can Quote me" in *The Daily Gleaner* October 1974, suggested that such sentiments had not just emerged with Manley, when he noted that other seasoned PNP politicians in the Jamaican political landscape had been equally guilty of setting up the businessman as target for public contempt, ridicule and even hate.

Marxist Socialists in the PNP portrayed businesspeople as the enemies of egalitarianism. Yet the Jamaican businessman - resilient, realistic and single-minded, as perhaps no other businessmen in the Caribbean - had a long history of serving a thankless community, feeding, clothing, housing, financing, transporting and generally providing all manner of public service to their communities, as well as providing thousands upon thousands of jobs to other Jamaicans. As a result of this inflammatory rhetoric, verbal attacks against Jamaican businessmen began to be followed by actions of a more ominous nature. There was an increased rate of robberies against businesses, often Chinese. Some of these attacks proved fatal, such as when my dear girlfriend Carmel lost her life from gunshot wounds as she returned home one evening with her brother and children asleep in the car.

In 1975, Jamaican journalist Ron Marshall reported in his article for the Fall issue of *The Pagoda* that, at the instigation of PNP youth organizers, hundreds of unemployed Jamaicans had invaded private properties in Portland and Westmoreland and announced that these properties were now "captured lands". This was a new mentality amongst the have-nots – that they had the right to "capture" other people's properties. One of the organizers hailed this action as the first revolutionary strike in a confrontation between the socialist movement and the capitalist class. It was surmised that some of these radical youth leaders were West Indian students who had also been involved with the setting of a fire in protest in the Computer Room siege at Sir George Williams University in Montréal during the late 1960s, actions that had dismayed the University faculty, the Québec government and shamed other overseas Caribbean students and visitors like myself.

In the meantime, Manley did nothing to alleviate the growing concerns of the business class. Instead, he increased the levy on the aluminum bauxite companies, an action which made foreign investors very nervous. The added revenue from these levies was supposed to fund programs to help the poor, but they were squandered when Manley launched a disastrous Impact Program. Manley proudly claimed that he had put money in the pockets of the poor by offering free schooling and clean-up campaigns (where people were paid for cleaning up the roadsides). These "Crash Work" programs did not, however provide the long-term impact on alleviating poverty. It would have been better if Manley and the PNP had devised a program which, while providing employment for the masses, would benefit the country in terms of real and continuing production. It seems that no one reminded Manley of the proverb: "Give a man a fish and you feed him for a day; teach a man to fish and you feed him for a lifetime."

After only three years in power, Michael Manley and the PNP had produced an economy teetering on the brink of bankruptcy. Edward Seaga, leader of the JLP, warned of financial chaos in a speech that was published by *The Daily Gleaner* in December 1975, and it became known that the police had seized the tapes and transcript of Seaga's speech. Added to that disaster, the normal trickle of immigrants who left the island to seek the greener pastures of North America had turned into a vast swell. In 1974 alone over 21, 000 Jamaicans voted with their feet against the PNP policies and left the island. The queues at the American and Canadian Embassies were long and all the Chinese elders were advising their families to start looking about their immigration papers as well.

I reasoned that since Eddie had his Master's degree in Civil Engineering from McGill University, we had a Québec marriage license, our first son Brian was born in Montréal and held a Canadian passport, plus we had already lived in Canada, we would not have much problem reinstating our Canadian immigrant status if and when we were ready to leave. We were in no rush to go back to Canada and face the harsh winter conditions again so quickly after our return! Additionally, life outside Kingston was not really affected too much by Manley's "Politics of Change" and the tourism and sugar-cane industries in the western parishes were still doing well.

All the same, I started collecting U.S dollars from the customers at Kelly's Superservice and purchasing US dollars from the airport staff while I was at work at Eastern Airlines in readiness for my departure sometime in the future. I invited my sister, Elaine to bring her Canadian friends to visit Montego Bay at my expense with the understanding that they would reimburse me at some later date. There was a general feeling of insecurity in the country and many people started to mail money out of the country. In response, the post offices were directed to scan the letters to prevent money leaving the country. Money wrapped in carbon paper, however, proved to be a good way to thwart this scanning, so the post office started to stick pins through the letters to detect the residue of the carbon paper. Many other clever devices and plans were concocted to outwit these searches so that people could send their money where they wanted to. After all, everyone has a right to do whatever he or she wants with his/her hard-earned savings!

Life was still good in the western parishes of Jamaica and in our "Not-to-worry" family home. Gurzel's family was also well-taken care of. Gurzel was even allowed to load up with slightly damaged goods from Kelly's Superservice for her home visits on weekends. Her eldest daughter was attending Teacher's College and when she visited us, she sat at our dining table while her proud mother served her. Gurzel's other children were attending school and she was able to provide school uniforms and school fees for them all. As she had wanted to be, Gurzel was now totally independent of the various worthless fathers of her children. Our children and the

"Not-To-Worry", Montego Bay, Jamaica 1975-76

Kids' poolside party for Ian Chin

children of our friends were happy at their respective schools and were always delighted to come to our house for birthday swim parties. At one party, we were not told that Brian's school friend, Xavier could not swim and in the excitement of everyone else jumping in the pool, he also did. Luckily Great-Grandfather Kelly was home and saw him struggling in the water and jumped in to save a sputtering Xavier from drowning because I had left the pool area for a short while.

The children, Brian, Gordon and Jason, loved driving in my white mini-bus with its pink stripe. There were three rows of seats and sometimes I would remove the middle row so that I could replace it with a custom-fitted sponge padding that fit the floor space. This was excellent for long trips because the boys could play, sleep or lay around in this space whether we were driving or parked. In those days there were no safety seatbelt laws in place and the children found it fun to roll around on the floor of the van as we navigated the winding Jamaican roads! These types of roadways did not allow for much speed and there were not many vehicles on the roads so with the Good Lord watching over us, we did not have any accidents or mishaps. When I was not working at Eastern Airlines or Kelly's Superservice, I would make day trips to Petersfield to visit my father and siblings. Papa looked forward to these visits. He used to like my bringing him fresh water coconuts to mix with his Scotch and loved giving the kids things from the store.

In light of what was happening in Kingston, Papa insisted that each of the boys ought to have a suitcase and he outfitted them each with their very own little brown suitcase, which turned out to be ideal for carrying their toys and personal belongings. The boys were especially delighted that the suitcases had flip locks with keys to secure their special things that they did not want to share. Many, many years after the boys grew up, I used these suitcases to keep their little toys and card collections of T.V. stars, such as Farrah Fawcett, Lee Majors as Steve Austin, the Six Million Dollar Man or Wonder Woman, comics, puzzles and their other childhood memorabilia.

Because I was driving a minivan, when I picked up my children from school, I would also collect those living on Brandon Hill, like Eddie and Melanie, Desmond and Tricia and Jeremy. Dropping off Eddie and Melanie at their parents, Sheila and Benny Chin's home, was always a good stop -- especially when their fruit trees were bearing. At Desmond and Tricia's home, there were bunny rabbits in a hutch for the children to play with. Sometimes Desmond and Tricia would stay at our home until their parents would pick them up and this was very okay with the head of our household, Gurzel, who became popular among our circle of friends and their children.

Gurzel would also go to the Chinese Club with us and at one Children's Christmas

"Not-To-Worry", Montego Bay, Jamaica 1975-76

Kids performing L-R: Eddie, Gordon, Desi, Tricia, Brian
(Hidden) mothers Carol and Merryl

Party, she even performed a musical number with our family. The Wong family was like the Von Trapp Family featured in the movie *The Sound of Music*. Our whole family would sing together at various events at the Chinese Club. Our famous song was our rendition of "Abdul Abulbul Amir" which was selected by Eddie. On one of my trips to Kingston via a local Jamaica Airways ten-seater propeller plane, I bought a guitar for Eddie's birthday, but he just set it aside. After many months, I met a Jamaican pharmacist who had recently arrived from England and when I mentioned the neglected guitar, he offered to teach me to play the guitar. After hours of me practising the guitar around the house, and the teacher sometimes coming by to give me a lesson, behold, Eddie started showing an interest in the guitar! After that, I could not get access to the guitar anymore.

I did not mind, however, because I was really more fond of playing the piano and regretted not continuing my piano classes during my high school days. I also surmised afterwards that being able to play the piano gave one a good base for reading music for all musical instruments; similar to how playing soccer provides the footwork base needed for all sports. Hence, I decided to ensure that my boys would learn to play the piano and play soccer. Thus, when, on

The Wong-Von Trapp family performing

another trip to Kingston, I heard that the music teacher at Immaculate Conception High School was selling her piano, I bought it and had it delivered to Montego Bay. This brown wooden upright German Konig piano has now been in our family for over forty years. After the piano arrived at our home in Brandon Hill, Brian and I started taking piano lessons from Miss Clarisse Crawford, who was an accomplished pianist in the Montego Bay hotel scene.

I had been taking Brian, Gordon, Jason and our friends' children to French classes at the Alliance Francaise de la Jamaique. Madame Lucienne Weltscheff, the French wife of the owner of Ramparts Inn, formed the Montego Bay Branch and I was appointed head of the Entertainment Committee. Even though we had no plans to move at this time, Eddie and I felt that somehow, one day we would be returning to Canada where French is the second official language (English being the first), and we wanted to prepare our sons for such a move by having them learn the French language. The Entertainment Committee, in collaboration with the Cultural Services of the French Embassy, brought world-famous classical guitarist, Jean-Pierre Jumez to perform at the Fairfield Theatre. Monsieur Jumez's repertoire covered the entire history of guitar music but had a special concentration on contemporary music from all over the world. Our big stage production was Voltaire's acclaimed play *Candide* which was performed by the Jean Gosselin Theatre group from France. We also hosted a reception for the talented cast poolside at Ramparts Inn where we also met Monsieur Gosselin and diplomats from the French Embassy. At the end of the reception, and after many cocktails, it was inevitable that the foreigners would take advantage of the typical warm Jamaican evening and change into skimpy swimwear so that they could dive into the pool under starlit skies while the coconut trees gently waved in the cool breeze. The guys could not take their eyes from the beautifully cut green bikini worn by one of the actresses!

The Entertainment Committee also held screenings of French films like *Les 400 Coups*, *Les Grandes Manoeuvres*, *La Guerre est Finie*, *Max et les Ferrailleurs*, and *Martin Soldat*. We also showed French films at the children parties like *Aladdin et la lampe Merveilleuse* and hosted Festivals of French Theatre for all schools throughout the island where French was taught. Our selection came from schools in Savanna-la-Mar, Lucea and Montego Bay. As the children learned French, Madame Weltscheff added an accelerated course for adults and also a beginner's course using modern picture books and audio-visual methods. Needless to say, Eddie and I registered for these classes along with my friend, Carmel Chin. Jamaica should be so

Alliance Francaise children's class
L-R: Gordon, Desmond, Brian, Colbert,
Claudine Weltscheff (in front)

thankful that this individual French hotelier, Madame Weltscheff formed a branch of the Alliance Francaise de la Jamaique and brought her culture to Jamaicans. I myself appreciated this education and the exposure it gave my family to another culture. It also made me wonder, many times, what makes someone, like Madame Weltscheff, have such a desire to preserve, perpetuate and promote her culture even when living so far away from home.

Carmel was the wife of one of Eddie's classmates, Junior of the Henry Chin family on Barnett Street. I met her when one of her sons, Paul, started attending Montego Montessori School. Like me, she was fun-loving and we used to go on day trips to many places when our children, including her other sons, Shane and Kurt, were in school. We were not bashful about spending the day at Hotel Hedonism in Negril and ventured up as close to the nudist area as was allowed! At other times, we would spend days splurging at Stella's Beauty Spa at Half Moon Hotel. We would have full-body Swedish massages, herbal facials along with lunch and relax by the poolside. Her parents, Mr. and Mrs. Robbie Young were already living in Toronto and we used to talk about moving to Canada as we were also getting quite concerned about the political unrest in Kingston and the future of our children in the island. Little did I know that within a few years, the political unrest would progress outside of the city and reach Montego Bay. A robbery at her home in Irwin would take her violently away from my life. I shared so many wonderful times with my kindred spirit, Carmel, that it is no wonder that I would keep in touch with her parents when living in Toronto in later years as a way of staying connected with her spirit.

Our children were progressing well in all aspects of the Montego Montessori School, including swimming competitions at Chatham Hotel swimming pool as arranged by the Rotary International Service Club. Also, I was approached by Mrs. Gorham to form a Cub Scout Troop and I appointed myself to be the leader "Akela". To organize the Troop, I had to fly to Kingston to attend a weekend course given by the Scout Association of Jamaica. I had been a Girl Guide during my high school days at Wolmer's High School for Girls so I already had some of the basic training, but I was not familiar with this younger branch of Cub Scouts and Brownies. Brian and Gordon were enrolled in the troop, as well as their friends, Paul Hastings and Ronald Jones. One of our greatest thrills was to march in the parade with other scouting troops through Charles Square as many

Montego Montessori Cub Scout Troop members

Montegonians waved from the sidewalks. Such marches were enhanced by the music provided by the Boys Club Band which was formed and supported by another benevolent expatriate, "Papa Pablovich" who provided all the instruments, uniforms and lessons for the budding local musicians. I do not think that the government ever truly realized how much foreign immigrants loved Jamaica and gave back to its people. Likewise, many businesspeople, like the Chinese, helped the local citizens who lived around their "Chiney Shops" by giving credit, sponsorship, donations and simply helping out the community despite their racial differences.

I should also note that the Montego Bay Chinese Sports & Athletic Club was open to local Jamaicans since its inception. Even Black Americans working in Jamaica were free to attend the Club. I remember one such man attempting to block a volleyball shot. We were all horrified when the ball hit his splayed fingers so hard that one finger was pushed back to expose the digit bone! We could hardly bear to look! At dominoes, Victor Belmonte would emerge winner at the tournaments. At badminton, Johnny Gurzong and Chris Brown would play in the Men's Doubles club championships. Our Junior badminton players included people like Bertie Sharpe, Tony Begg, Sandra Mullings, Michael Campbell, Trevor Barrett, and Ian Miles. The Jamaica Badminton Association applauded our junior badminton development which developed the skills of our local Jamaican as well as Chinese members' children, Justin Lue, Karen Chin, Sharon Chin, JoAn, Richard & Elaine Chin, Arthur Chin, Desi Chin, Andrea Chin, Peter and Tommy Lee, Philip and Bobby Chin, Rodney and Lindy Lee, Joey Chin, David Lai and many other teenagers.

Later on the Caribbean Regional Badminton (CARIBACO) was formed and some of our junior badminton players were invited to try out for the Junior National Team and Peter Lee was selected. Afterwards, we were happy to entertain the Junior team from Guyana after the championship in Kingston. The leader, Lorie Lewis and his players were taken around to see the tourist sites, like Dunn's River Falls, and we enjoyed their company while they played badminton with us in the evenings. Carol Lee, Jay Manson-Hing and Tracey Lee were also Junior Team members who come to mind, and who, I would have the pleasure of meeting again in

Montego Badminton Group L-R: Jean, Merryl, Joey, Sharon, David, Glen

Toronto many years later after they had grown up and migrated to Canada.

For junior tournaments in Kingston, I escorted a huge contingent to the Under 19 Division and later on, a horde of us entered the Abbey Court Tournament where we swept most of the trophies. I recall that some of the adults stayed at Cynthia and Johnny Chuck's residence but what I remember most of all was that we had great camaraderie and were proud to have made a great impression in the Jamaica National Arena.

Victorious MBG badminton competitors at Abbey Court Tournament
L-R (back): Justin, Victor, Clifton, Tony, Leslie (Jeff)
L-R (front): Carol, Sheree, Angela, Sharon, Lindy, Richard

Love blossomed amongst our badminton stars. Victor Lyn Shue and Angela Tenn decided to tie the knot and Eddie Williams and Sharon Wong got engaged. Sharon Chin turned sweet sixteen while Lindy Lee and Richard Chin turned 18-years of age. Our married members started to have children whom they brought out to the Chinese Club. Some of the little ones were Eddie's god-daughter, Simone Hew, Nadia Chin, Serena and Aurora Lue, Darren and Diane Chin, Jonathan Chin, Vanessa Chang, Tiffany Chung and numerous others. These children were already starting to play around on the badminton courts and chasing the badminton shuttlecocks in the wind. Brian entered a fun tournament with Karen Chin and was thrilled to receive his very first badminton trophy.

Brian would go on to take tennis lessons at the Montego Bay Racquet Club with pro Basil. The Jamaican father-son team of Irving and Richard Russell had been hired at this club which years before was not open to local folks. As a result, some of the Chinese community like Esme Lee, Edmund Hew,

Tennis group at Montego Bay Racquet Club
L-R: Chris, Buff, Esme, expat, Alice, expat
(Kneeling) Mr. Nagai

"Not-To-Worry", Montego Bay, Jamaica 1975-76

Jean Chin, Buff and Alice Kong, Ah-Goong and I and other locals started playing there on Sunday mornings and during weekday evenings.

Brian and I also signed up as Tae Kwon Do students when my badminton friend and champion, Barbara Lai brought Master Sam Soo Han (6th degree black belt) and his students from Kingston to Montego Bay. They gave a splendid demonstration at the Overton Plaza which resulted in starting a local branch with a group of keen students. Lessons for this Korean art of self-defense were held at the Blessed Sacrament Church Hall and Brian looked handsome in his white dubuk uniform.

Tae kwon do class: Carol (fifth left), Brian (centre front)

That year, Brian, Gordon and Jason voted that our annual family holiday should take us back to Disney World in Florida, USA. This time they thoroughly enjoyed the visit. They had already had a "trial run" sometime before, and, since Jason was older, he was more appreciative of this wonderland for kids. He was no longer scared of Mickey and Minnie Mouse, Donald Duck and Goofy as they paraded around the grounds. Like a mother hen, I liked to keep a tab on my children in a crowd, but in order not to draw too much attention from others as I did this, when I wanted to know where they were, I would quietly make the sound of an owl. When they heard the "woo-woo" sound, they would either let me know where they were or come back to me.

On this trip, the crowd was overwhelming at the Monorail station and our family got separated as the trains arrived for different destinations. When I gave the motherly "woo-woo" sound, Brian and Gordon gathered around me but Jason was not in sight. I hurriedly went around the area making more "woo-woo" sounds in desperation until a distraught Jason finally appeared. We were so relieved! If he had boarded the wrong train, it would have been a disaster and it would have been almost impossible to find him over all the acres of the theme park! Jason had also been so worried when he could not find us.

From that time forth, Mommy's "woo-woo call" became the official Wong family call – even long after our sons grew up, got married and left the home! And very soon, you, my dear Grandchildren, will begin to hear it and learn to love it!

Your loving Ah-Poh

Life in Jamaica:
Not-to-Worry, Montego Bay, 1976

My dear Grandchildren,

We continue to give back to our community in Jamaica, even as violence spread among the masses.

Our Lions and Lioness Clubs continue to raise funds for the less fortunate in our Parish of St. James and our Montego Bay branch of Lions International Clubs was getting recognized worldwide in their overseas publications for its work. We were invited to their International Convention in Honolulu, Hawaii and a group of us planned to proudly carry our Montego Bay banner at the Convention among the other groups from all over the world.

Eddie and I planned for a more extended trip than simply attending the Convention and although I was comfortable with Gurzel running the house while we were away, for added peace of mind, I asked the Chinese teacher at the Montego Bay Montessori School, Clare Hugh, to stay at our house to assist Gurzel with taking care of Brian, Gordon and Jason in our absence. Aunt Valerie Chung would be on call as well. My cousin, Valerie was now working full-time at the Royal Bank branch in Montego Bay and boarding with our young "Uncle Joe", his wife, Lucia and their children, Ian and Theresa. Valerie's mother, Aunt Doris, is related to Papa and the family lived in Savanna-la-Mar where the family business was.

We asked our efficient travel agent friend Merryl to include a Pan American Tour of the Far East to follow the Lions International Convention. En route to the Convention, Eddie and I flew non-stop to Los Angeles and headed for Hollywood, Beverly Hills. We immediately took a tour of Universal Studios, walked along Sunset Strip and checked out the Walk of Fame in front of Graumann's Chinese Theatre. We saw the famous Hollywood Bowl and visited the notorious Hugh Hefner's Playboy Club of Playboy Bunnies with their cotton tails.

After Los Angeles, we flew to Las Vegas where there was a huge celebration and salute to "America's Bicentennial 1776 –1976" at Dunes Hotel and Country Club. I thoroughly enjoyed the Liberace Show at Las Vegas Hilton. I was so impressed by his flamboyance and the ease with which he played his shiny, glittering pianos. Liberace was a really entertaining showman showing off his jewellery, fur coats and cars on stage. As usual, throughout our trip, I mailed the boys a picture postcard from every city we visited, including one of Liberace. When we got home, I found out that the

"Not-To-Worry", Montego Bay, Jamaica 1976

Eddie at the Hollywood Bowl

postcard that impressed them the most was the postcard I sent of Liberace because to them, he looked so funny and outrageous.

From Las Vegas, Eddie and I flew on to San Francisco in one of Howard Hughes' Airwest Super DC-9 jet and stayed at the Hotel Californian. We took a Ding How tour of China Town and rode the cable car to Nob Hill, Golden Gate Bridge, the Japanese Centre and the shopping district of Union Street. We had to quickly purchase warm clothing because it was so windy and cold especially when we visited the famous Fisherman's Wharf. At this time, San Francisco had the largest Chinese population outside of mainland China since the Chinese started arriving from Tai Shan, Guangdong Province during the 1800s to join the gold rush and seek their fortune on "Gam San" (Gold Mountain).

It was a treat to fly United Airlines and land on the tropical and sunny island of Oahu, Hawaii and stay at the Outrigger Hotel in Waikiki. There were an estimated 45,000

The Montego Bay Lions and Lionesses at Hawaii Convention

members attending this 59th Annual Convention and the delegates represented more than 1,140,000 Lion members from 149 nations and geographic locations around the world. This four-day convention commenced with a street parade that began at Ala Moana Park and then stretched down the main thoroughfare of Kalakaua Avenue. It was so exciting and almost overwhelming to be a part of this 4-5 hour parade which was so large that colourful floats and marching bands covered approximately one and a half miles along the beachfront. There were keynote speakers for each day and, at the final session, nationally known economist and business administrator, Joao Fernando Sobral of Sao Paulo, Brazil was installed as the 60th President of Lion's International, the world's largest service club organization.

Despite how busy we were, we found time to take the Circle Island tour of Oahu to see many oriental temples, bonsai gardens, residential districts of Nuuanu Plai and the lookout at Kamehameha. We drove along the picturesque coastline highway of the Pacific and watched the restless surf splashing white against the black volcano rock. On the windward side, we continued through Kaneohe, Heeia, Kahana Bayu and Puna Luu; stopped at a famous Mormon Temple, then continued through rolling fields of sugar cane and endless pineapple fields nestled in the valley. On the leeward side of the island, we went up to the base of Diamond Head volcanic crater, and followed the foothills of the Koolau mountain range to view the beautiful Hanauma Bay. We entered Sea Life Park, then the world's largest exhibit of marine life, and continued along the coast through Wimanalo and the old Hawaiian town of Kailau and Kaneohe, passing massive banana groves to return to Waikiki Beach.

We also took the Pearl Harbour cruise to visit America's largest Pacific Naval Base and the sunken USS Arizona, USS Utah and Ford Island. The best and most enjoyable stop was the Polynesian Cultural Center which was a massive complex. The Center is a non-profit educational and cultural centre run by the Church of Jesus Christ of Latter Day Saints (Morman). The Centre aims to educate visitors about the arts and crafts of various Polynesian cultures. This trip was well worth a whole-day visit to participate in the many activities representative of the cultures of Samoa, Aotearoa (New Zealand), Fiji, Hawaii, Marquesas, Tahiti and Tongo. It truly was a day well spent!

After a most enjoyable Lions Convention, we bid farewell to our newly-made Lion and Lioness friends and prepared for our trip to the Far East. I recall that when one of the Lions members from Guyana heard that Eddie and I were going on to a trip to the

Carol at Polynesian Cultural Centre

Orient, he was quite concerned and warned us not to go to China. He proceeded to tell us of a Guyanese friend's father who felt he would like to take a tour back to his homeland in China after years of working and making a life in Guyana. This man had lived in Guyana since the pre-Communist days. When his tour group got to their first city in China, they all had to submit their passports at their hotel before they spent the night. The following morning, Chinese officials returned the passports, all except the one belonging to the man from Guyana. The tour group organizers were told that the man from Guyana had taken ill during the night and that he was hospitalized. The group was advised to continue on to the next city on their itinerary and that this person would join them as soon as he had recovered. When the group arrived at the next destination, however, they were informed that the Guyanese passenger that they had left behind had passed away, and that they did not need to interrupt their tour or contact the man's relatives in Guyana as the officials in China would handle these issues. However, when the man's relatives arrived in China to collect his body, the body had disappeared and no one could give them a satisfactory account of what had transpired. The family members remembered that in his youth, before he left China, the man had been involved in some anti-government activities and they wondered if his past was somehow connected to his sudden death and disappearance. I do not know if that story was true or not, but I did reassure our Lions friend that China was not on our itinerary.

As our Jamaican fellow-members headed home, Eddie and I began our Pan-Am Orient Adventure. We first flew to Tokyo, Japan and stayed in the fabulous New Otani Hotel where we were welcomed warmly and received kimonos to wear and keep. We have kept those kimonos safely to this very day. The gardens were so immaculately kept and the soothing waterfalls lent a peaceful atmosphere. On the busy streets of the Ginza, we found the Japanese people to be so well-dressed, civilized and polite even when they did not understand our English. We ate at small family restaurants and thought it was so practical to have plastic replicas of meals in the windows to display their menu items.

Our group tour included a Night Club tour where the Geisha ladies performed and served us in a tea ceremony. They were wearing their traditional and beautifully embroidered silk kimonos with Obi sashes at the back which was such an exquisite sight. Next stop was the Kokosai Theatre where all of us were amazed by the Japanese variety show and enjoyed every cultural item on our program.

The following morning, we were literally pushed onto the "Bullet train" that travelled at 150 miles per hour to the ancient city of Kyoto. We visited the Kinkaku-ji Temple otherwise known as the Temple of the Golden Pavillion belonging to the Rinzai sect of Zen Buddhism. In 1397, Lord Yoshimitsu,

Japanese performance at Kokosai Theatre

the third shogun of Ashikaga, bought the site and enjoyed it initially as his villa but later changed the name to Kitayamaden Palace after adding a new gilded pavilion with a deep pond around it. Here he retired from the Shogunate and devoted his life to the development of Japanese culture through trade with China. After Yoshimitsu's death, the palace was converted back to a Zen temple. It provided a beautiful, quiet and peaceful setting for this inscription:

SCRIPTURE WITHOUT WORDS

How fresh it is like morning dew
An open flower
How clear it is, the note of singing birds
The clouds are calm, the waters blue
Who has written,
"Scripture without words"

Mountain is sharply etched
Woods are colourful
Valleys deep and rapid streams with spray
Moonlight is clear
In softly breathing wind
Man reads in the quietness
"Scripture without words".

Our tour also included Nijo Castle built by the first Tokugawa shogun, Lord Leyasu (1542 –1616) and the Old Imperial Palace built by Emperor Kammu in 794 and rebuilt in 1854. Eddie and I were absolutely fascinated during the tour of Kyoto Handicraft Centre to see the ancient technique of Inaba cloisonné as well as the rare process of finger nail weaving of exquisite fabrics. Our bus trip to Nara to see one of the oldest shrines in Japan, known for its 3,000 stone lanterns in the compound, was just as

Eddie at Old Imperial Palace, Kyoto, Japan

"Not-To-Worry", Montego Bay, Jamaica 1976

Eddie and deer at Nara, Japan

interesting. While there, I made sure to write a prayer for our safe return home and the well-being of our sons in Gurzel's care and placed the prayer in one of the stone lanterns. The holiest object of the Todaiji Temple was the Great Buddha measuring 53 feet tall and weighing 450 tons. It remains the largest of its kind in the world. After visiting so many magnificent temples and shrines, it was refreshing to walk around Deer Park where more than 1,000 tame deer roam freely about mingling with tourists and begging for tidbits. The popular belief is that the deer are sacred messengers of the goddess enshrined in the adjoining Kasuga Shrine. It was just nice to pet them and I wished that Brian, Gordon and Jason were here to play with them all.

We next flew to Singapore and were greeted with "Selang Datang" which means "Welcome" by the Singapore Airline hostesses. The Singapore Airline hostesses could very well be the friendliest and nicest airline hostesses in the world. It was very hot and rainy but we were feeling most comfortable, especially as we were surrounded by the friendly Chinese population who all seemed noticeably disciplined. The place was very clean and everything, even the Night Market, seem orderly and sterile. It is amazing to know that Singapore is about the same size of Jamaica, and yet, had become so productive and progressive since becoming an Independent Republic in 1965. Hakka Chinese Prime Minister Lee Quan Yew was then in power and ruled with an iron fist. He had not forgotten about the harsh and unfair treatment of the Chinese by the Malays when he decreed his policies against them in his country. It was said that he had curtailed their migration into Singapore and it was feared that any male Malay marrying a Singaporean for immigration purposes would be castrated to prevent procreation. To us, the cause of Singapore's prosperity compared to Jamaica's lack of financial growth seemed obvious: Singaporeans are more hardworking and far more educated than Jamaicans and more civic-minded and determined to build their country unselfishly for the betterment of everyone.

We were visiting Singapore during the time period of the American Hippie. Singapore had endorsed a law that all males entering the country had to have their hair cut short, to above their shoulders. There were barbers stationed at the airport to ensure that people complied with the rule – if they did not, they would leave on the next available flight out of Singapore. The same strictness was felt in the hefty fine imposed for any piece of garbage, even a candy wrapper, dropped on the floor. Chewing gum was forbidden, which I thought was a good law that curbed a nasty habit brought in by foreigners. The traffic downtown was not a problem since there was a law forbidding cars from entering the city without a permit. This encouraged the use of public transport as people left their cars outside the city limits safely and appropriately.

Our sightseeing included a city and west coast tour with lunch served while we enjoyed an Asian cultural show. We also visited the famous Tiger Balm Garden, a

"Not-To-Worry", Montego Bay, Jamaica 1976

House of Jade, Jurong Bird Park and a tour of Johore Bahru. It was neat to hire a tri-shaw which was a two-wheeled rickshaw pulled by a lean Chinese man pedalling a bicycle. We also enjoyed seeing images of the national symbol of Singapore, a Merlion, which is a mythical character with a lion's head and the body and tail of a mermaid, all along the waterfront.

Flying on Pan Am's 707 Jet, we left Singapore and arrived at the Don Muang Airport in Bangkok, Thailand and checked into the Indra Regent Hotel. We did not mind going on another tour of temples to see the newly discovered Golden Buddha at Wat Traimit. The Wat Po was the most extensive temple in Bangkok which housed the colossal Reclining Buddha and the ornate white

Carol beside the Merlion, national symbol of Singapore

Italian Marble temple of Wat Benchamabopit. The boat and barge cruise was fun. We cruised along the winding canals by long-tailed boat and landed at a Thai farmer's house to watch monkeys climbing coconut trees and plucking coconuts. We also witnessed a fight between a mongoose and a cobra snake and saw repulsive snake pits of hissing snakes of all lengths. The floating market tour was most colourful with fruits of strange varieties like prickly rambutans and purple mangosteens while numerous boats jostled for business. Going through the Royal Palace Grounds, it was hard to believe we were in such an exotic place with its own dazzling Emerald Buddha Temple. My favourite place was

Eddie and Carol with Golden Buddha in Thailand

"Not-To-Worry", Montego Bay, Jamaica 1976

the Thai Village Cultural Show presented at Rose Garden in Nakom Pathom where we saw huge elephants at work, Thai boxing matches, cock-fighting, Hill tribe and other folk dancing. We also witnessed a Thai wedding ceremony and a Buddhist monkhood ordination ritual. It was also quite an experience to dine in Baan Thai restaurant which was a genuine teak Thai-style house with private dining rooms in which we sat cross-legged and listened to old-style Thai music played on ancient traditional instruments. The Thai classical dancers were exquisite in their beautiful glittering costumes and graceful in their body movements, especially when using their hands and fingers which were accessorized with extended and pointed fingernails. I also found it very difficult to resist buying Thai silk material after touring the silk farming industry!

Furama hotel, Hong Kong Island

We next boarded Pan Am's 727 jet flight to Hong Kong and stayed at the fabulous Furama Hotel in Central District on Connaught Road across the harbour from Kowloon where my mother had stayed with relatives some years ago. Our stay coincided with the Miss Universe Beauty Contest which was hosted at our hotel. As a result, the lobby was always filled with camera crew, spotlights being strategically set up and a constant buzz of excitement.

We fulfilled our Wong family obligation by taking a ferry across the harbour to Tsuen Wan to visit your Great-great-grandfather (Ah-Goong Tai Tai), Henry Wong and Great-great-grandmother (Ah-Poh Tai Tai) who lived there. In the early 1800s, Henry had left his wife to make a living in Jamaica. He was not industrious and tried different ways to make a living but was never successful enough to send for his wife to join him in Jamaica. Instead, he had children with a local woman and continued to eke out a living. Eventually, he returned to his wife and village in China, while in the meantime, his Chinese son, Kelly, migrated to Jamaica where he became a successful businessman. With Kelly's concern for his parents, Henry and his wife were able to move to Hong Kong where they lived comfortably in an apartment in Tsuen Wan.

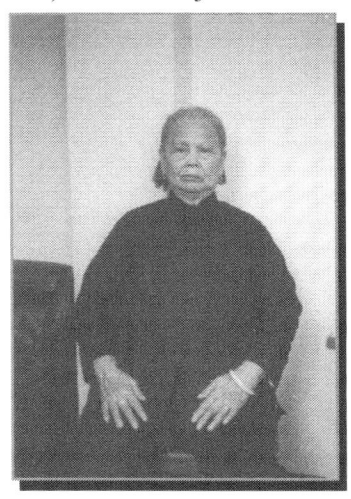

Hong Kong was, at that time, still a British Crown

Ah-Poh Tai

Ah-Goong Tai

Colony consisting of 236 islands and islets, many of them waterless and uninhabited. The colony also included a portion of the Chinese mainland east of the Pearl River estuary adjoining the province of Guangdong. This area is known as Kowloon and the New Territories. The largest and most important island in the colony is Hong Kong Island which, together with adjacent islets, has an area of 29.2 square miles. It is 92 miles southeast of Guangzhou (Canton), and 40 miles east of Portuguese Macau. On the mainland facing Hong Kong Island, is the ceded territory of Kowloon which, with Stonecutters Island, has an area of 4.3 square miles. The New Territories were leased from China on June 9, 1898 for 99 years. Between Hong Kong Island and Kowloon lies Victoria Harbour, one of the world's most natural harbours. It was known in Cantonese as "Heung Gong" meaning "Fragrant Harbour", which, over time, became Hong Kong.

In 1937, following the Japanese invasion of mainland China, thousands of mainland Chinese fled to Hong Kong and many more, including members of our Wei family, arrived in the early 1950s during Mao Tse Tung's Communist regime. The British government in Hong Kong began building multi-storey blocks of flats in 1954 for the resettlement of squatters in the Kowloon area. This was preceded by a great fire among the squatters who had set up unsightly shacks along the hillside. They were also issued Hong Kong Identification cards in the interim.

Squatters' shacks of refugees from China   *Government resettlement apartments, Kowloon*

Despite Hong Kong Island's steep and rugged terrain, post-war building development was spectacular. Great blocks of flats, many of them erected by the government for low-salaried workers, cling to almost perpendicular hillsides. Many narrow side streets are so steep they must be stepped like the famous Ladder Street in Western District past Central District which was the commercial area. Banks, merchant houses and warehouses helped to make Hong Kong wealthy and prosperous as a trading port. To cope with Hong Kong's rapid industrial and population growth, three new towns were being developed in the New Territories when we visited; namely, Tsuen Wan, Tuen Mun (Castle Peak) and Sha Tin.

This heavily populated city stop of Hong Kong was the most harried stop on our itinerary at that point. The people were aggressive, noisy and constantly on the move. The crowds were overwhelming and everywhere was super busy. Nevertheless, I

"Not-To-Worry", Montego Bay, Jamaica 1976

Ancient Chinese junk with red sails in Hong Kong harbour

found Hong Kong very fascinating, exciting and full of life. We attended a dinner and show at Miramar Theatre and found it to be most cultural. We also drove out to have dinner and a show on Tai Pak, one of the floating restaurants in Aberdeen, which was quite a novel way of dining; another day, we went up to Victoria Peak on a funicular tram. That was unusual and a different method of getting to the highest point. Victoria Peak overlooks the busy harbour full of all types of watercraft. It was a sight to behold -- especially if we caught sight of red sails of an ancient Chinese junk. We could view planes landing at the Kai Tak Airport nestled in the dense Tsimshatsiu area; the gnarling fingers of high rise apartments reaching to the skies; and the busy Central District of commerce where old wooden tram cars wound their way among the heavy traffic dotted with red Hong Kong taxi cabs. The view was interesting and spectacular!

Our next destination was Taipei, Taiwan which was like a smaller and more orderly version of Hong Kong. The city was busy and at one of the restaurants, we had our first experience of Mongolian barbecue where slivers of raw meat and vegetables were cooked on an iron dome heated from flames underneath. I was quite curious to visit the Imperial Palace and Museum to see the trove of Chinese art, craft and treasures which, it was claimed, were taken out of China when Mao and his Communist army took over and General Chiang Kai Shek and his Kuomintang army fled to Taiwan. It was quite an enlightenment to discover an indigenous tribe living remotely up into a hill area on our one-day trip to the Wulai Aboriginal Village. We had to be transported there by push-car which was manually pushed by aboriginal tribesmen. Their cultural folk dance performance was very delightful and they all looked relaxed, happy and friendly.

Wulai aboriginal girls with our tour guide, Taiwan

We flew next to Vancouver, Canada – and arriving there was like taking a breath of fresh air. After our time in the Far East, Vancouver seemed spread out and the population seemed sparse. The majestic Rocky Mountain range was visible from all parts of the city and the sky ride we took from Grouse Mountain gave us a good view of the city.

Bull riding competition at Calgary Stampede, Alberta, Canada

The Canadians were most polite, quiet and seemed to walk much, much more slowly than the Cantonese people. Taking the ferry to visit Victoria, British Columbia seemed so dull when compared to the crowded ferries plying across Victoria Harbour in Hong Kong. While in Vancouver, Eddie and I had a nice visit with my cousin, Audrey, her husband, Rennison and their children, Sulan, Anita and Neil whom we had not seen since they left Toronto, Ontario to settle on the west coast.

Our next flight took us to Calgary, Alberta and was a bit more exhilarating because we arrived during the annual Stampede. It was lovely to see so many people dressed up in western cowboy wear and cowboy hats while the native Indians were wearing leather-fringed jackets or Indian dress. They kept their hair long and the women braided their hair in plaited pig-tails. It was strange to visit an Indian village and see them still living in teepees and wigwams like in the western movies. The chuck wagon races, bare-back bronco riding and other stampede action was all new and exhilarating to me. It was good to see the Canadian Mounties to remind me that we were truly in Canada. Eddie and I stayed at the Empress Hotel and after the stampede, we took a bus trip further into the Rocky Mountain range to the most beautiful and picturesque town of Banff where I felt I like I had been transported into a picture postcard. As well, it was unbelievable to be on the vast Columbian Ice Fields and later bathe in the Sulphur Hot Springs on top of Banff Sulphur Mountain. What an experience!

Eddie was getting homesick and not traveling well so we flew into Toronto to unwind and spend a few days with my sister, Elaine and husband, Chester. However, before returning home to Jamaica, we still had one more stop to make: a visit to our dear friends, Bonnie and Terry in Boston, Massachusetts. Terry had been sent from this architectural office to work on the Cornwall Regional Hospital in Montego Bay and had returned to Boston after that work was completed. Although Eddie was still not feeling well, we had a nice visit going around Boston's Freedom Trail, learning about

Paul Revere and the American Revolution; Benjamin Franklin and the Governors during the 16th Century; the Boston Tea Party and the Boston Massacre; Faneuil Hall and Quincy Market where the American Revolution began. It was so quaint to dine at Ye Olde Union Oyster House built in 1826 and Longfellow's Wayside Inn in Sudbury, located 20 miles out of town and built in the 1870's.

Finally, we flew back to Jamaica. At the airport, one of my suitcases disappeared in the time it took us to get from the terminal to our car where our chauffeur, Missa Willie, had come to meet us. Things had changed during our absence, as short as it had been. I could sense a change of attitude in the Jamaican people. The political situation in the city of Kingston had escalated and the discontent was moving into the countryside. There was much violence in the shanty areas like Trench Town and Tivoli Gardens because the PNP supporters were being favoured to get work and handouts while supporters of the opposition JLP were being overlooked. Even the police were no longer non-partisan. A police crackdown on crime had resulted in criminals leaving the Kingston area and seeking refuge in the other parishes farther away from St. Andrew, including Montego Bay where I was now living, and areas like Roaring River close to my hometown in Petersfield, Westmoreland. Bob Marley captured the sentiment of this troubled times by writing songs and sang about the suffering, gun violence and redemption in the ghetto areas. He lamented these conditions when he sang, "No woman, nuh cry" and appealed for an end to violence when he sang, "One Love, let's get together and feel alright".

The leader of the Opposition Party, Edward Seaga, called for the end of the "Crash work" programmes that were wasting and squandering public resources and leading the country into total financial chaos. The economy was surrendering to massive inflation and the foreign exchange reserves were evaporating to nothing. It was becoming clear that the PNP government was collapsing into a state of panic, searching hysterically for enemies and plots to blame for their own failures. Manley picked on the productive business-class and preached that they were wealthy because they had exploited the masses and the masses were becoming more and more resentful in their frustration because of their poverty and lack of education. As a result of the Marxist youth arm of the PNP further "capturing" land around the island, the uneducated masses felt that they too could "capture" rooms in anyone's houses or one of the cars parked in a garage, or any other property they felt like possessing. The masses were made to feel hard done by the middle-classes and to believe that they had the right to capture anything their hearts desired without working for it! As these events unfolded, many middle and upper-class people packed up and left the country.

Similar to some countries in Southeast Asia, the low-key, humble Chinese people became targets on whom the masses could vent their frustrations. The Chinese were often scapegoats to blame for the financial woes of the masses. In Jamaica, most Chinese immigrants, like my father, had arrived from China in the early 1900s with only the clothes on their backs, and had worked hard under primitive conditions, scrimped and saved diligently to educate and provide a better life for their next generation. Now, all that hard work and sacrifice was held against them. When a

Financial Intelligence Unit (FIU) was created to search for hidden accumulations of US currency, Chinese Jamaicans, among others, were targeted for business, home and garden searches and other forms of harassment. This made the middle class, professional and more affluent Jamaicans extremely nervous. Furthermore, they felt that the government confiscating their hard-earned money, even if it was in US dollars, was tantamount to robbery. The masses were also demonstrating resentment against Chinese children who attended school alongside them – even though these children were, like Eddie and me, fully integrated into Jamaican society and had parents who had contributed so much to help build up the nation. It was said that these public attacks on the Chinese by politicians served as a diversion to distract people from the government's own party members who were squirreling money out of the country themselves to tax-haven countries like Switzerland in Europe and nearby Cayman Island.

Prime Minister Michael Manley, our "Joshua", made matters even worse when he gave a rousing speech on television in which he stated that if anyone did not like his democratic socialist policies, he or she could leave – he said there were, after all, five flights to Miami leaving daily from Jamaica. After that statement, many more members of the middle-classes prepared to migrate. Some considered moving to the surrounding islands or places in Central America like Costa Rica. Those who were wary of the Canadian winters joined the long queue at the American Embassy with thoughts that the weather in Florida would be more tropical and closer to their existing business places in Jamaica. Families were split up as mothers and children left to establish residency in new homes in new countries while the fathers remained in Jamaica to keep their businesses running until the mothers and children were settled. This practice would indeed cause a stress on many marriages. A cloud of suspicion began to develop amongst friends and even amongst family members. Many people made plans to leave under a veil of secrecy for fear of being reported and subjected to searches by Manley's Financial Investigation Unit. This meant that many times, children would arrive at school to find that their classmates had disappeared the night before – left with their families on one of the five flights out of Jamaica as Manley had suggested, without even saying good-bye to their friends or leaving behind any way of maintaining contact with them.

My dear Grandchildren, Ah-Goong Eddie and I felt that the time had come for us to heed our parents' warning and join the mass exodus out of Jamaica by applying for our landed immigrant status in Canada. Like our migrating Wei family Hakka Chinese ancestors, we were forced to move on in search of a better life for you, our next generation.

Your loving Ah-Poh

"Not-To-Worry", Montego Bay, Jamaica 1976

Eddie and Carol at the Hakka walled village, New Territories, Hong Kong

Hakka mothers carrying their babies on their backs, New Territories, Hong Kong, overlooking the border with China at Lo Wu

Show featuring the culture of various Hawaiian Island, at the Polynesian Cultural Centre, Oahu, Hawaii

Life in Jamaica: "Got-to-Worry", Montego Bay, 1976 – 1977

My dear Grandchildren,

I changed the name of our house from "Not-to-Worry" to "Got-to-Worry" on the prominent white signboard at the entry to our property. It was a simple act -- removing the first black metal letter "N" and replacing it with a letter "G" – but it signified a lot to everyone passing the gate of our house. It signified that all middle and upper-class Jamaicans like myself were indeed worried, getting paranoid and fearful of the situation creeping over our homeland.

Never in the history of Jamaica had a Prime Minister been propelled into the leadership with so vast a popular vote and such a vast reservoir of good will; never in the history of our homeland had such a great expectation of our new political leader aroused such great expectations in the hearts of his electorate; but sadly, it is equally true that never in the history of Jamaica had so popular a leader dissipated this vast reservoir of goodwill in so short a time. By 1976, our country was consumed with bitterness, frustration, fear, suspicion and division among its citizens.

In the business world, despite the increased levies on the Bauxite companies, foreign reserves were drying up because of government squandering of these funds and the failed Impact "Crash Work" Program. As a result, there were food shortages and food prices rose as demand outweighed availability. Many entrepreneurial locals started a peddling trade. It was mostly the women who would go abroad to purchase small but much-needed items, like onions, and return to sell them at inflated, exorbitant prices. Business places had to scramble to find items for their customers. I even heard that my cousins were taking my father's goods off the delivery truck at will and without Papa's permission. These economic difficulties were further compounded when the Minister of Tourism declared that Jamaica did not need tourism and our illiterate hotel workers began to be told that serving foreigners was akin to the re-enslavement of the black people. Jamaica's tourism industry, built around Jamaica's God-given natural beauty, was also damaged by bad service and the numerous reports of violence in the foreign press.

The political world was split in my homeland and there was trouble in paradise. On the one hand, within the ruling PNP were the young leftist radicals who were demanding swift changes in the traditional structure of Jamaican society and not caring whether they rendered the society apart in the process; and, on the other hand, there were the older, but saner minds, who were against hasty changes that would create fear and uncertainty. At this point, the more articulate radicals, with their political science educations, were unable to be controlled by Prime Minister Manley. It is a pity that he and his older, and supposedly wiser, colleagues had not yet fully appreciated the fact that only an atmosphere of calm and confidence would encourage skilled and productive professionals, including medical doctors, to remain in the country. This class of Jamaicans was leaving in increasing numbers in response to Manley's disastrous policies, a situation that was not helped when Manley announced that Jamaica walked hand-in-hand with Cuba and invited hordes of Cuban technicians into the island and sent hundreds of students to Cuba to be indoctrinated. Such policies created an unhealthy exodus of nation-builders from Jamaica.

When Manley realized that he had caused a mass exodus, he tried to stem this flow by making it illegal for anyone to leave Jamaica with more than $50 JA in their possession. It was such a ridiculously low amount of money -- $50 JA was not enough to even pay the taxi fare from any airport – that clearly, Manley's real intent was to keep people, and their money, in the island. Little did he realize that by instituting this provision, he made people more paranoid and desperate to get themselves and their money off the island – and desperate people started being more creative and thinking of more clever ways to spirit their hard-earned money out of the country. Many anecdotes could be written about the numerous ways money was sneaked out of the country -- some sad, some funny, some disastrous -- but thankfully, most were successful. Sometimes, however, people in Jamaica would send money to their family and friends abroad in a variety of ways, but these friends or family members would later claim that they had never received any such money. Whether they were being truthful or not, no one could tell. Money couriers, people entrusted to get money out of the island and transport it to someone else, sometimes claimed that they had been robbed before they could deliver the money, or that they had delivered the money when the recipient claimed to have never received it. Of course, such claims could not be verified without fear of reprisals since thefts like this could not be reported and investigated. It was more than money that was lost, however, when these incidents occurred. The repercussions were that there was a huge loss of trust and friendship and the creation of estranged relationships among family members.

One funny story circulating amongst the Chinese Jamaican community about trying to smuggle money out of the country during this period was that of a Chinese man being strip-searched at the airport. Feigning ignorance of the reason for the search, he asked, "A wha' you looking for?" and when he was told "Missa Chin, we a look fi money", he gloatingly replied, "Yu a look fi mi money? Money gaan last week and mi go today". I do not know if, after that encounter, he was able to walk out onto the tarmac with a smug look on his face or whether he was delayed longer than necessary out of revenge so that he would miss his flight – a common practice of disgruntled and outwitted FIU officers.

There were other stories of Chinese families being able to leave successfully with their money by travelling on the same flight with loyal Jamaican servants who sat separately from their bosses carrying the stash of cash that they would both take to the bank and deposit upon landing in the new country. We also heard of money being boldly smuggled out of Jamaica in cigarette packets, socks, underwear and even baby diapers.

Most people were like me, however. Upon deciding to leave, we opted to stay within the law and take money out of the country in the value of household and personal effects. We thought that it would be better to take your wealth with you in the form of these items than simply leave it behind; and besides, you would also have the items to sell in case your family fell on hard times. Although I am not a materialistic person and never admired high-end items, I was happy to spend a lot of time in the months prior to leaving Jamaica flying frequently to Kingston to purchase new and solid mahogany furniture from Jamaica Heritage, Jamaican straw goods and kitchenware from Magic Kitchen, silverware and stationery from Times Store, bed and bath linen from Hanna's, and children's toys from Storkland. In Montego Bay, I purchased rattan furniture from Rattancraft, jewellery from Henriques and Swiss Store, fine Irish linen table cloths and napkins, Irish, French and Swedish crystal sets, wooden oriental chests, English bone chinaware, Lladro and Lalique figurines, imported cosmetics and perfume from Duty Free stores, plus paintings and other artwork from Stacy's Galleries. There were also imported ladies fashions from Temptation Boutique and men's wear, including silk ties, from Northern Hub. From Kelly's Superservice, I obtained non-perishables items and tinned items, such as corned beef, condensed milk, Milo, Ovaltine, Horlicks, Fry's Coco powder, and soap and laundry detergent. The carpenters made a wooden crate for my used piano and also for each concrete garden pot purchased from Maffessanti supplies. I was stocking up in preparation for packing a 40 ft. trailer of personal effects for shipping to Canada. I knew that I was taking a chance when I packed the powdered laundry detergent because I had heard of my friend whose trailer was stopped in transit and searched for hidden US currency. When the FIU officers were searching, they viciously slashed the upholstered furniture and when no money was found, they spitefully opened the large boxes of laundry detergent and maliciously scattered it all over every item in the trailer.

It was a difficult time. Officers in police cars were roaming around the street in search of trailers in the process of being packed and neighbours who held grudges against each other, were reporting each other to the police as well. Those who were unable to leave the country began describing their friends as rats deserting the sinking ship and draining the country, as if their friends were not simply taking their own well-earned proceeds from their hard labour with them when they left. As a result of such tensions, our trailer was not parked near our home but was parked secretly out in the deserted re-claimed area of Freeport. Each night, after the supermarket was closed, we used our delivery trucks to transport our items to Freeport and packed the trailer under the cover of darkness and away from snooping eyes. The loyal staff of the supermarket could be trusted as well as our friends, Michael and Micheline Sharpe and George and Terry Leung, who would share our trailer bound for Montréal.

Eddie and I had decided to return to Montréal because we had such a wonderful time starting out in our marriage in that cosmopolitan city, our first son was born there, and we had only lovely memories of our time in La Belle Province. It made sense that we would migrate back to that city so familiar to us when we left Jamaica. As expected, since we had been former permanent residents in Montréal, Eddie had an engineering degree from McGill University, we had a Québec marriage license and a Canadian-born son, we easily satisfied the criteria necessary to obtain landed immigrant status for our family of five – mother, father and three sons all under the age of 12. We did not waste any time once we had received our landed status and immediately flew to Montréal, even though it was winter, to register the entire family, after which time we planned to return to Jamaica to pack up the rest of our belongings.

When we arrived in Montréal, we were met at the Dorval Airport by Uncle Washy and we stayed with his family in Pointe Claire. During our stay, we cleared customs and received our trailer of household effects and personal belongings which had been sent ahead of time from Jamaica. We stored our belongings in Morgan's Storage Company with a plan to return the following summer. Brian, Gordon and Jason were so happy to play with their cousins, Craig and Duane. They were also delighted and fascinated by the snow and the cold weather –

L-R: Gordon, Jason, Brian, with Eddie tobogganing

so much so that their dripping noses did not bother them at all! They were having fun and especially enjoyed Christmas shopping in the indoor malls where they were fascinated by the huge variety of toys and games that they had never seen or heard of before.

Afterwards, we went to stay with Eddie's sister, Ouida, her husband Brian Graville and their toddler, Diane who looked like a china doll. Spending Christmas holiday with family in Baie d'Urfé was nice and the suburbs were much quieter and more of a white winter wonderland than the city. We were happy to also share the Christmas holidays with old friends from university days who had remained in Montréal after we had left for Toronto and Jamaica in 1968. We exchanged news about the current situation in our respective countries. They informed us about the uneasy political climate in Montréal at that time. They

L-R front: Gordon, Diane, Brian, Ouida
L-R back: Carol, Jason, Eddie

told us that French Canadians still wanted independence from the British and that discontented, radical Québecois and hot-headed Front de Libération du Québec (FLQ) political party members were constantly demonstrating. And we told them the news about the political atmosphere in Jamaica – how it was just as tense with the economic despair and the growing divide between the haves and the have-nots, even among the Blacks themselves in Jamaica. With most of the visible minorities migrating, the Black masses had started turning their resentment against the lighter complexioned Blacks who were more educated and well off.

Brian, Gordon and Jason with Santa Claus at Fairview Shopping Centre in Montréal

I felt relieved that, with the exception of Brian who had Canadian citizenship by birth, our entire family now had registered with landed immigrant status in Canada and our household belongings were safely stored in Montréal. We flew back to Montego Bay after Christmas 1976 and started planning for our departure to Canada. We thought that perhaps our time in Canada would be short, only a few years – just enough time to educate our children – after which time, we would retire somewhere on the Jamaican shores bathed by the warm, blue Caribbean Sea. To those Chinese Jamaicans who were also contemplating migrating elsewhere but were apprehensive about resettling in a new country, I encouraged them by pointing out that our Hakka ancestors had migrated over the centuries whenever necessary and even our parents had been brave enough to take a ship, which was no Royal Caribbean Cruise Line, to venture abroad and eke out a living in a tropical island that they had only just heard about. They had no idea about the geographical differences and the inhabitants of the island when they left – they did not even know the language of the new country. At least we were fluent in English, had grown up in the western hemisphere and, having studied geography, had more knowledge about the country we had chosen to migrate to.

There was continued unrest in Jamaica. Tension was felt all around. There were more and more reports of crime and violence, especially against the Chinese who were perceived by the general public as hoarding US currency. My cousin's house was searched and the garden dug up by the FIU who was given this authority to conduct such searches by the government. More Chinese leaving the island found themselves harassed at the airport. Montego Bay, as well as other parts of the island, seemed more and more deserted by the productive middle-class. This absence was noticeable at the Chinese Sports and Athletic Club. The membership had dwindled and a new committee needed to replace those members who had left the land of their birth. The President was now Horace Lue, Vice-president Eugene, Secretary Jean, Treasurer Esme, Games Captain, Steve and other committee members were William, David, Clifton, Carl, Charles, Donald and others. Despite the changes happening in Jamaica, life went on and the club continued, albeit with the East Indian merchants increasing the membership of the club. Some of the East Indian In-bond merchants had been migrating out of Jamaica as well. In fact, when packing my trailer, I bought items of family room furniture from our friends, the Daswani's. We never actually discussed our inevitable migration during this purchase; we all just nodded our heads knowingly throughout the transaction.

Ladies tennis group L-R standing: Inge, Marjorie, Liz, Jean Kneeling: Sister Marita, Carol

Our tennis group was dwindling as well. Dr. Delisser's lovely wife, Liz and Dr. Ludlow Burke's family left, but holding down the fort were Esme, Edmund, Jean, Buff and Alice, and a few expatriates still with valid working visas. In the meantime, Jamaican medical doctors were heading to Canadian provinces like Saskatchewan, which did not require them to sit the medical examinations again, while the younger Chinese doctors, who had graduated more recently, were willing to head for progressive Canadian cities like Toronto, where they were confident that they would successfully sit the Ontario qualification exams and open lucrative practices.

Eddie and I kept busy with our charity work at Lions International Service Club. Our inductor, Donald, was now the President with Arnold Chin, Winston Chin and Ernest Wong included among the officers for 1976–1977. The Lions Club of Kingston officially launched the Sight Foundation with a full-time ophthalmologist, Dr. Man, providing services at the Eye Department of Kingston Public Hospital and the University Hospital. A mobile clinic was set up for patients in the rural areas around the entire island. By 1976, it had served over four hundred patients. This was an excellent and meaningful service for Jamaicans living in the countryside and the Lions Club Sight Conservation Committee was to be commended for having organized the service. I recall that among the Lions Club of Kingston 1976 administration was Lester Lee as Secretary and Dr. Michael Woo Ming as volunteer medic. Despite the fact that so many Chinese Jamaicans were giving back to the greater Jamaican society, they were, on some levels, afraid of the very society that they were helping. Many, on their return home from doing these good deeds, were wary of stopping at traffic lights for fear of being robbed and were prepared to break the law by going through a red light if need be. Kingstonians were being victimized and robbed while driving and had taken to locking themselves in their cars and being on the constant look-out for life-threatening and seemingly suspicious movements around them. What a life!

Montego Montessori School carried on despite the dropping enrollment caused by families packing up and leaving Jamaica. Soon, the children learned not to ask any questions if one of their classmates suddenly was not at school anymore. Still, we made the best of the situation at hand and our Montessori Cub Scout Troop and other students took a lovely train trip to Appleton Estates and visited the Ipswich Caves as well. The students were excited about the all-island Spelling Bee competitions, especially Gordon, who was already

Lions President Donald Chin greeting visitors to The Reg Perrin Clinic near Montego Bay

showing signs of being a good speller. We parents became worried, however, that the working visa of the English headmistress, Miss Branwhite would not be renewed. Since Jamaica's Independence, foreign teachers were slowly being ousted from the country, much like how the British Army had been ousted. These were big mistakes since law and order was slowly eroding without the presence of the Army and there were not many qualified teachers left on the island, even at the only Teacher's College and Mico Training College. Our Montego Bay branch of the Alliance Francaise de la Jamaique was winding down, Ramparts Inn was up for sale, and Madame Weltscheff was selling off her lovely copperware collection as she prepared to leave.

In addition, my own father was investigated by the FIU, which was a division of the Ministry of National Security. While Dick and Margaret were on holiday in Europe in 1976, the FIU came on the suspicion that the family was hoarding foreign currency. They ordered the business closed while they searched and ransacked the entire premises. Papa was calm and allowed them free access to the store, grocery shop and living areas upstairs and downstairs, while he sat in his office playing his usual game of Solitaire. Without any success at finding money, the officers did not leave empty-handed: they confiscated Dick's licensed rifle, his coin collection and Margaret's treasured personal papers and irreplaceable family photos, to their dismay and disgust on their return from holidays. We also learned later that all through the fruitless search by the FIU officers, Papa was sitting on his hard-earned and accumulated foreign currency. Bravo, Papa, your grandchildren would say you are just too cool! And your children believe that we inherited our ingenuity from you!!

"Got-To-Worry", Montego Bay, Jamaica 1976-77

This incident coming so close to home was the impetus we needed to get going on taking one of the "five flights a day to Miami", which Prime Minister Michael Manley was offering Jamaicans. A State of Emergency was instituted in 1976. This drastic measure followed the election returning the PNP to power for a second term, which caused another wave of violence and an even greater mass exodus overseas.

It was getting too difficult to remain. We felt compelled to leave Jamaica because our children's education was in jeopardy and it was exhausting to have to live under a constant veil of secrecy and suspicion. I was also so aware that the world that I had grown up in, when friendly relations with local Jamaicans was the norm and I felt part of a broader community of Jamaicans, was disappearing. Now, instead of feeling at home, I felt that the local Jamaicans, under Michael Manley's rule, were chasing me, my family, relatives and friends out of the land of our birth.

Your loving Ah-Poh

The boys bidding farewell to Montego Montessori School, Montego Bay

Life in Jamaica:
"Got-to-Worry", Montego Bay, 1977

My dear Grandchildren,

I had left bitter winters in Montréal, Québec, Canada and the rigid, uptight life-style of Canadians and had returned to Jamaica hoping to enjoy the relaxed lifestyle in the island for as long as I could. But the Marxist indoctrination sweeping the island was warping the mind-set and behaviour of my fellow Jamaicans and I felt it was definitely time to leave my beautiful homeland.

In these very troubled times, Eddie and I had to plan carefully how we would leave Jamaica. It was as if we found ourselves in some kind of espionage thriller just because we wanted to migrate to the safe refuge of Canada. I refused to do as other families had done; namely, leave Eddie doing business in Jamaica while the children and I set up lives in Canada. For me, the Wong family would stick together. Sink or swim, at least we would do it together.

To avoid suspicion that we were leaving, we agreed that Eddie would leave Jamaica first with Brian, almost 11-years old. They would fly to Toronto where Eddie would find a job, and I would follow later with eight-year old Gordon and six-year old Jason. We decided to settle in Toronto instead of Montréal because we had learned that the separatist movement had been victorious in Montréal. The FLQ political party in Québec had won the recent elections and Premier, René Levesque was in power. He had decreed that all signs and labels must be written in French first, with English following. French would be the first language of the province and all immigrant children would be compelled to attend French schools. I always felt that learning another or even more languages would be beneficial but it would be difficult for my boys, especially the eldest, Brian, to start learning all his academic subjects in French. Another draw to moving to Toronto was that my siblings and other Jamaican Chinese friends had been settling in Ontario without any language adjustment and their children were happily learning in the Canadian school system. I considered that migrating to Montréal at this time would be like jumping from frying pan into the fire! Hence, we decided to migrate to Toronto and at a later date send for our belongings that we had previously stored in Montréal.

Since migrating families were subject to harassment at the airport, we bought non-refundable two-way plane tickets for Eddie and Brian so that it would look as if they were only visiting Toronto. Obviously, we would lose the cost of the return portion of the tickets, but we felt that this loss was worth it. To complete the ruse, Eddie and Brian would travel lightly without much luggage and we would not say good-bye to anyone. While they were gone, I would dispose of our house on Lords Road in New Kingston and sell my signature white minivan. Fortunately, your Great-grandfather Kelly would continue to stay at the house in Brandon Hill and business would carry on as usual at Kelly's Superservice. This would also help reduce suspicions that we were planning to migrate. In a similar fashion, my father would continue to carry on the business in Petersfield after my brothers Patrick, Dick and his wife, Margaret migrated to Toronto. At a later date, Papa would sell the business in Petersfield and join us in Toronto but Grandpa Kelly would keep the business for his half-brother, Ken to operate with his own immediate family.

Paranoia was setting in all over the island. Manley and his cohorts were unable to stem the tide of Jamaicans migrating or curb the flow of money leaving the country and rumours were flying that his next desperate move would be to start closing the airports. This rumour hastened the flight plans of those who were ready to go but were just, as we used to joke, "waiting to turn off the lights". On the date that it was rumoured that the airports would be closed, however, I knew that I would not be quite ready to "turn off the lights" as I had not yet disposed of our first house and vehicles. My eldest brother, Keith and his wife were not quite ready to leave either, so we decided to fly over to the nearby island of Cayman for the weekend just in case the rumour was true. We figured that if worst came to worst, and Manley really did close the airports, our assets would be captured in Jamaica, but at least we would not be imprisoned on the island. There were many other Jamaicans on the Cayman Airlines flight that day, all of us obviously hedging our bets with regard to the possibility of the airports closing, but everyone was pretending that they had not heard the rumours. We all pretended that we were just going away for a brief holiday (or, for some of us, that we wanted to quietly and inconspicuously deposit our hard-earned cash in this tax haven).

We spent a nice weekend in Cayman Island and listened keenly to the radio for news of Manley shutting down the airports in Kingston and Montego Bay. In the meantime, we went sightseeing and visited a turtle farm much to the delight of Gordon and Jason. The Caymanians were warm and friendly, and had no realization of the plight we Jamaicans were in since they had a steady and level-headed government running their little island. They were still welcoming folks to invest in and boost their economy. Since there was no sign of the airports in Jamaica being closed, we returned at the end of the weekend to finalize our matters at hand, determined not to hang around longer than necessary in our most beautiful island which was being ruined by misguided Marxist politicians.

The tenants at our house on Lords Road were willing to purchase the house and needless to say, as they were aware of the fact that we, like so many Jamaicans, were probably trying to flee the country, they drove a hard bargain, offering to buy the house at a lower price than market value. Many local Jamaicans recognized that they had a good chance of purchasing homes in more upscale neighbourhoods around Kingston since many of the fleeing owners were trying to sell them so that they could leave the island. In my case, I did not feel that I had much choice in the matter, so I signed the deal and hired the law firm of Myers, Fletcher & Gordon to close the sale and handle any final matters in my absence. After the sale was finalized, one of their lawyers brought the payment for the house in US currency to Miami, Florida and contacted me in Toronto to collect the money. It was a "hush-hush" deal and I knew that I was vulnerable – there was a very real chance that the money from the sale would never arrive in Miami, but I felt I had no choice but to trust the lawyers. At least they were reputable legal men, I thought.

I was tying up the final loose ends. I practically gave away my dear minivan to my relative, Joe rather than simply leaving it in the driveway where it might be "captured" by some local fanatic of democratic socialism. I decided to give our Dodge Dart car to Missa Willie, our chauffeur and faithful employee. My friends, Edmund and his wife, Paulette would find employment for our loving maid, Gurzel at their bakery in Hopewell, Hanover. Our genteel Maroon gardener, Egbert would continue working for Grandfather Kelly and remain in employment while we were gone.

As was the case when Eddie and Brian left, I bought return air fares for Gordon, Jason and myself to go to Toronto. We planned that Missa Willie would just drive us out to the airport without any fanfare or protracted goodbyes with our friends and family. As I was an employee of Eastern Airlines, I made sure to take advantage of our employee discount by making a number of stops on the way to Toronto. Gordon, Jason and I would fly to Austin, Texas, then New Orleans, followed by a stop in Atlanta, Georgia before arriving in Toronto. As well, the night before, I took my excess baggage allowance luggage and last-minute packing in carton boxes to be checked in and loaded onto the plane without scrutiny.

Gordon and Jason about to board the Air Jamaica flight leaving Jamaica from Sangster International Airport, Montego Bay

"Got-To-Worry", Montego Bay, Jamaica 1977

The next day, after bidding farewell to Missa Willie, my playful children and I checked in at the Eastern Airlines counter. As I had pre-loaded our larger boxes and luggage, we appeared to be travelling with little luggage, just like cheerful holiday-makers going on a short vacation. It was all so casual. In the departure lounge, the boys sorted through their miniature Eastern Airlines travel bag and played with their marbles, matchbox cars and other knick-knacks. When we had gone through security, the boys had innocently opened up their little shoe-box size brown suitcases to display other toys and keepsake items for the Customs officers. I took a photograph of Gordon and Jason in front of our Air Jamaica aircraft to record this day. As we sauntered along the tarmac and climbed the stairs into the plane in brilliant sunshine, I looked back and had one last silent look at Sangster International Airport and the picturesque view beyond.

Gordon and Jason were now seasoned travelers so they buckled up and craned their necks to look out through the tiny window as the plane taxied to the runway. As our plane took off from the ground and into the skies, I leaned back, closed my eyes and thought of the Peoples National Party's election slogan, "Better must come". Better must come, I agreed, although for us, better would not be in Jamaica.

We were met in Austin, Texas by Eddie's older brother, Vernon who was amazed at the number of carton boxes we had brought along with our luggage. Luckily, he had come alone with a car big enough to accommodate us and our belongings. He was a professor of Theoretical Physics at the University of Texas and probably did research for the US space program which he was not privy to speak about. Dorit, his wife, was at the house which was in a quiet, secluded part of town. It was a beautiful, quiet spot, but the boys were scared of the huge trees and surrounding forest-like atmosphere having just seen the movie *Grizzly* which was about Grizzly Bears roaming the forest. Gordon and Jason shattered the quietness with their Jamaican exuberance which Dorit felt might disturb the nest of birds above the porch so I had to keep shushing them to be quiet.

Gordon and Jason visiting LBJ ranch with Uncle Vernon

"Got-To-Worry", Montego Bay, Jamaica 1977

River boats on canal alongside River Walk, San Antonio, Texas

The next day, Vernon took us sightseeing around Austin and proudly showed us his sailing club where his laser sailboat was kept. He was equally proud to show us around the original home and ranch of President Lyndon B. Johnson who, by that time, was living in the White House following the assassination of President John F. Kennedy on November 22, 1963. One day, we took the Greyhound bus to visit San Antonio where many people mistook Gordon for a Mexican boy. We enjoyed the wide, flat, river-boat cruise along San Antonio's River Walk – Paseo del Rio – as the strolling Mariachi bands played. The concrete channels creating the River Walk commercial area were built as part of the overall flood prevention program completed in 1929. Flood control gates at the south and north ends of this horse-shoe-shaped bend in the channel protected the area from high water levels. Seven-year old Gordon wrote a message to his elder brother, Brian on a picture postcard of the nice red river boat we were on and I mailed it to Brian's mailing address in Toronto.

The San Antonio River was named for Saint Anthony de Padua in 1611 when the Spaniards arrived and built missions as Spanish outposts with an aim of bringing their religion and civilization to the indigenous native Indians. One of the outposts was an impressive two-storey stone structure that was meant to house the Spanish Cavalry company from Alamo de Parras in Mexico, hence, the name "Alamo" which means cottonwood in Spanish. After Mexico won her independence from Spain, Texas, in turn, sought hers from Mexico in 1835. Mexican General Martin Perfecto de Cos was sent to San Antonio by Dictator General Santa Anna to liquidate the rebellious Texans who had converted the mission compound into a fortress. Mexican General Cos was defeated and an infuriated General Santa Anna arrived to exact his revenge on the Texans.

This famous historical event was known as the Battle of the Alamo. At the museum on the actual site of this battle, we learned about the thirteen fateful days in 1836

"Got-To-Worry", Montego Bay, Jamaica 1977

Jason and Gordon in front of the Alamo, Texas

when Texan Colonel William Travis answered Mexican General Antonio Lopez de Santa Anna's surrender ultimatum with a cannon shot. The defenders of the Alamo at first withstood the onslaught of the Mexican army. When their ammunition and supplies were all but exhausted, they committed themselves to die as patriots who valued freedom and fought against Santa Anna's intolerable injustices and decrees rather than surrender. Among the brave heroes who died inside the Alamo were James Bowie who was an Indian fighter and famous for his use of the Bowie Knife, James Bonham and Davy Crockett, a frontiersman who had brought his Tennessee boys to fight as reinforcements in the Alamo.

After the fall of the Alamo, the angered Texans and American volunteers led by General Sam Houston launched a furious attack on the Mexican army at San Jacinto shouting "Remember the Alamo!" They routed the Mexican army in minutes and captured General Santa Anna. Texas was free and a new Republic of Texas was born. An independent nation for nearly ten years, Texas was officially annexed to the United States in 1845.

Our friends, Bonnie and Terry Larsen, now living in Bryan, Texas, drove the long way to Austin to get us and our belongings to stay a few days with them. Bryan was not a large city and the main point of interest in that city was the Texas A & M University where Terry was a lecturer in Architecture. We would be flying out of Houston International Airport so they drove us the long distance to the airport in their two-door sedan. The car was jammed packed with our immigrant boxes. In fact, the car was so full that we had to keep the trunk open during the journey! As planned, we arrived a day earlier than our flight so that all of us could spend the day touring the AstroDome. After that, the Larsens left and the boys and I spent the rest of the time at AstroWorld, one of the Six Flags theme parks. This was an eye-opening experience – our first visit to an amusement park of this magnitude. The rides were filled with screaming people and I was thankful that Gordon and Jason were too short to be allowed on most of them!

The following day, we arrived at the Holiday Inn in the Latin Quarter of New Orleans. This was such a quaint stop on our journey. It was fun going around the area in a horse drawn buggy. We also walked around the Latin Quarter and marveled at the ornate wrought iron balconies of the Spanish influenced architecture. We also walked to the city park where buskers entertained pockets of tourists. Of everything we saw in New Orleans, however, I think what impressed Gordon and Jason the most was the colour television in our hotel room!

Bonnie Larsen with Jason and Gordon in front of her and Terry's dream car, Bryan, Texas

The flight between New Orleans and Atlanta, Georgia was not long and soon we had landed in a super busy airport terminal building. We took a tour of downtown Atlanta. One of the stops on the tour was the Peachtree Gallery, which at this time was the most recently built high-rise building in the city. The rest of the downtown area looked a bit dilapidated but the city looked more appealing when we drove out of town past stately Georgian mansions to the Stone Mountain Park. This was a Park that was used

Gordon and Jason at Stone Mountain, Atlanta, Georgia

all-year round for outdoor activities like sailing, fishing, golfing, camping, hiking and horseback riding. The highlight of Stone Mountain was that it boasted the world's largest work of sculptural art, which was carved on the world's largest granite mountain in 1970. The carving is of the figures of President of the Confederacy, Jefferson Davis, and of Generals Robert E. Lee and Stonewall Jackson, all heroes of the American Civil War. It is said that the carving is much more than a monument to the Old South, however; it is also a reminder to all men that out of change and social crisis can come even firmer strength and unity. It is a memorial to a critical period of American history which, though tragic, gave birth to the united nation they have become.

It was particularly appropriate that we visited this memorial so close to our arrival in our new home in Canada. On the flight to Canada, while Gordon and Jason slept, I closed my eyes and silently said a prayer of thanks to my Heavenly Father for all His great mercies and protection. Then I reflected on my life thus far. In the first Chinese Zodiac cycle that started my life, I lived a happy and carefree childhood in a land of lovely people who had a formative influence on my life. In the second Chinese Zodiac cycle, my life had been shaped by an excellent British education combined with an invaluable "salt-fish shop common sense" education in my father's business. My third cycle thrust me to into blissful married life and blessed motherhood.

Now I was about to start my fourth cycle of the Chinese Zodiac with a new chapter in my life in a peaceful foreign country. There had been considerable stress in our lives the last few years we had lived in Jamaica, but now I was looking forward to a new period of great opportunities and good fortune for me and my family in the land of the Maple Leaf.

At this point in our family history from Jamaica to Canada and back, I close with much love and hope in my heart for you, my dearest grandchildren.

Your loving paternal grandmother,
"Ah-Poh" Carol Williams-Wong

More Favourite Photos

Patrick after bodybuilding workout

Dick at gate to Petersfield family home

Picnicking up in Newcastle with Peggy Lampart and Eddie (right) and other families (below)

305

More Favourite Photos

More Favourite Photos

Wedding Day

18 September 1965

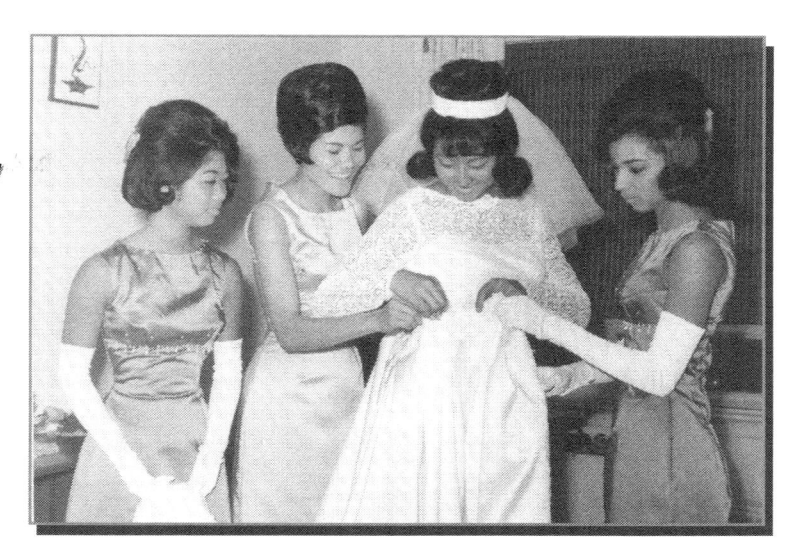

307

More Favourite Photos

Top: Confetti shower on church steps

Middle: Keung's speech, Wilhel in foreground, Penny behind her

Bottom: Listening to speeches - Bim & Lorna, Yvonne Toyloy, Rennie & Audrey in foreground; Norman, Daphne, Neville, Ko-ko, Jim, Myrna in background

Wedding Guests

More Favourite Photos

Left: Eddie & Carol's first dance

Below: Norman & Althea

Foreground L-R: Russell & Novlet, Althea & Oscar
Back left: Arthur & Wilhel

More Favourite Photos

Brian

More Favourite Photos

Gordon

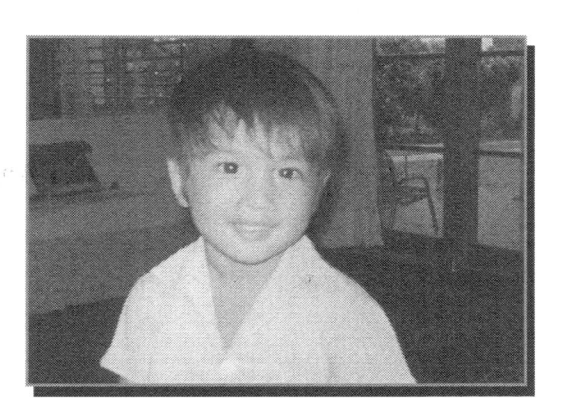

More Favourite Photos

Jason

More Favourite Photos

The boys and their friends

Top left: Tricia, Jeremy, Jason   *Top right: Brian, Ronald*

Bottom: the Sharpe family L-R Gordon, Jason, Melanie, Christopher, Andrew, Brian, mother Micheline

More Favourite Photos

Top: Birthday donkey ride - in cart L-R driver, Serena, Brian, Jamie; on ground L-R Simone, Marsha, Paul
Bottom left: Jason, Brian, Eddie, Gordon *Bottom right: Andrew, Brian*

More Favourite Photos

Top: Gordon's birthday party

Middle: Jason's birthday donkey ride

Bottom: Gordon cutting birthday cake with Diane

More Favourite Photos

Miscellaneous

Top: Donny at McMaster University

Bottom L-R: Faye, Washy

Top L-R: William, Gordon, Jason, boys

Bottom L-R: Brian, Duane, Craig

More Favourite Photos

Left L-R: Ricky, Linette, Stephanie, Ray Chen

Below left: Eddie & Carol
Below right: Arthur & Wilhel with baby son Karl

L-R: John Mignault holding Brian, Sheila, Carol, Ouida, Washy with Duane, Sheila with Craig

More Favourite Photos

Left: Philip & Rose Young Lai's wedding, maid of honour Elorene

*Below left L-R: Winston, Novlet, Jean, Ina
Below right Audrey & Carol with ice sculpture*

*Bottom Front L-R: Brian, Glen, Gordon, Oliver, Jason
Back L-R: Eddie, Carol, Philip Chen & friend, Dorothy, Calvin*

More Favourite Photos

Right L-R: Yvonne Thompson, Tony Tai, Linton Chin

Below left: Carol, Tony Williams
Below right: Carol, Uncle Joe Chin

Bottom L-R: Carol with other Scouting leaders in training

More Favourite Photos

The E.G. Wong Family

More Favourite Photos

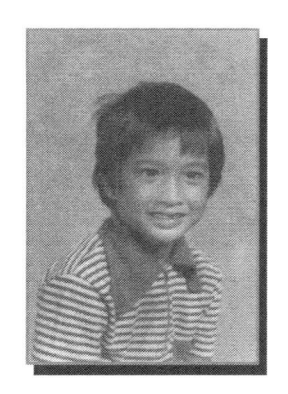

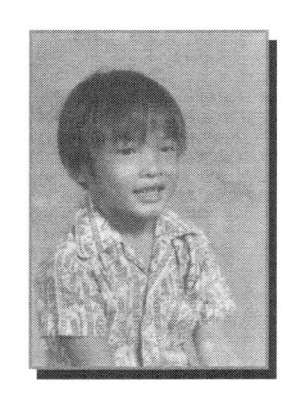

Appendices

1. Map of Hakka Chinese Migration — 324
2. Jamaican Hakka Family Relations Chart — 325
3. Map of China (including Hong Kong) — 326
4. Map of Niu-Foo Village, Bao On, Guangdong — 327
5. 20th Century Timeline — 328
6. The Wei Jin Xiu Furong (Chun Yin) Family Chart — 329
7. Foreword from *Our Family Tree* — 332
8. Descendants of Wei Gen Choi — 334
9. The Nathan Williams Family Chart — 336
10. The Gladys Young Williams Family Chart — 337
11. The Wong Family Chart — 338
12. The Williams Families in Jamaica — 339
13. Map of Jamaica — 346
14. Coat of Arms of Jamaica / National Anthem of Jamaica — 347
15. Map of Canada — 348
16. Coat of Arms of Canada / National Anthem of Canada — 349

Appendix 1: Map of Hakka Chinese Migration

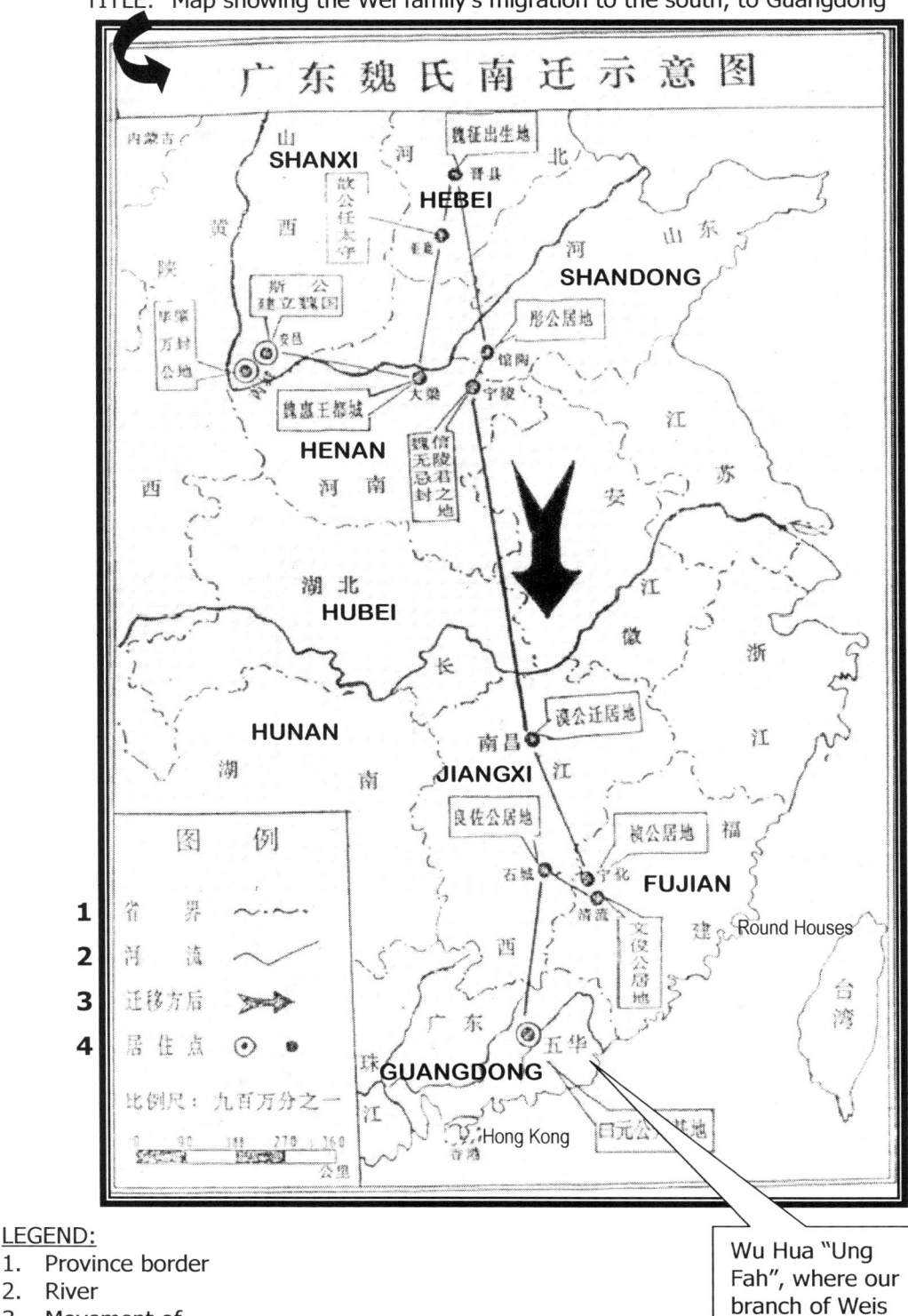

TITLE: "Map showing the Wei family's migration to the south, to Guangdong"

Wu Hua "Ung Fah", where our branch of Weis arrived with Maolin Gong.

LEGEND:
1. Province border
2. River
3. Movement of migration
4. Settlement/Residence

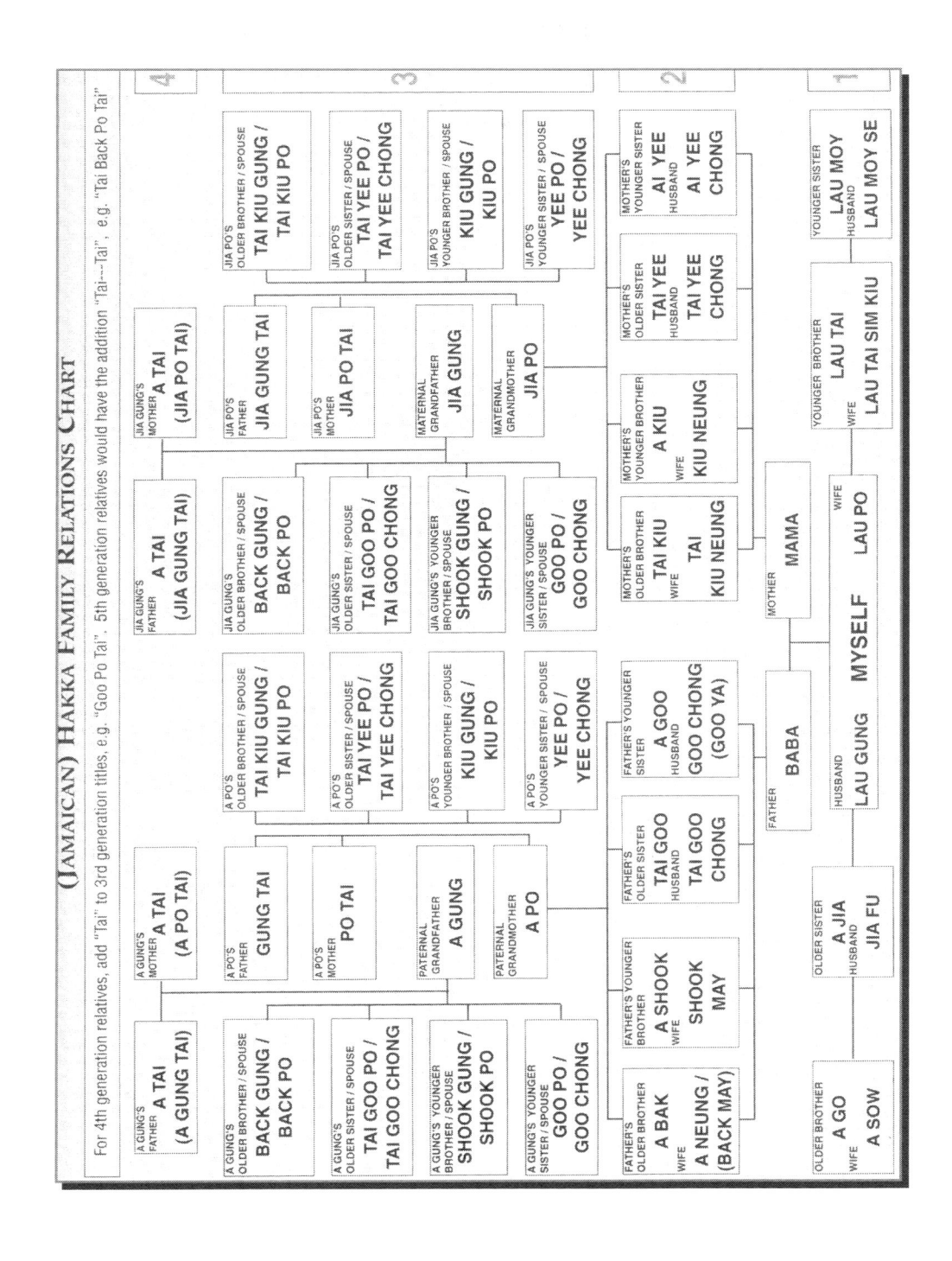

Appendix 2: Jamaican Hakka Family Relations Chart

(JAMAICAN) HAKKA FAMILY RELATIONS CHART

For 4th generation relatives, add "Tai" to 3rd generation titles, e.g. "Goo Po Tai". 5th generation relatives would have the addition "Tai---Tai", e.g. "Tai Back Po Tai"

Generation 4

- **A GUNG'S FATHER**: A TAI (A GUNG TAI)
- **A GUNG'S MOTHER**: A TAI (A PO TAI)
- **A PO'S FATHER**: GUNG TAI
- **A PO'S MOTHER**: PO TAI

- **A GUNG'S OLDER BROTHER / SPOUSE**: BACK GUNG / BACK PO
- **A GUNG'S OLDER SISTER / SPOUSE**: TAI GOO PO / TAI GOO CHONG
- **A GUNG'S YOUNGER BROTHER / SPOUSE**: SHOOK GUNG / SHOOK PO
- **A GUNG'S YOUNGER SISTER / SPOUSE**: GOO PO / GOO CHONG

- **A PO'S OLDER BROTHER / SPOUSE**: TAI KIU GUNG / TAI KIU PO
- **A PO'S OLDER SISTER / SPOUSE**: TAI YEE PO / TAI YEE CHONG
- **A PO'S YOUNGER BROTHER / SPOUSE**: KIU GUNG / KIU PO
- **A PO'S YOUNGER SISTER / SPOUSE**: YEE PO / YEE CHONG

Generation 3

- **JIA GUNG'S FATHER**: A TAI (JIA GUNG TAI)
- **JIA GUNG'S MOTHER**: A TAI (JIA PO TAI)
- **JIA PO'S FATHER**: JIA GUNG TAI
- **JIA PO'S MOTHER**: JIA PO TAI

- **PATERNAL GRANDFATHER**: A GUNG
- **PATERNAL GRANDMOTHER**: A PO
- **MATERNAL GRANDFATHER**: JIA GUNG
- **MATERNAL GRANDMOTHER**: JIA PO

- **FATHER'S OLDER BROTHER / WIFE**: A BAK / A NEUNG (BACK MAY)
- **FATHER'S YOUNGER BROTHER / WIFE**: A SHOOK / SHOOK MAY
- **FATHER'S OLDER SISTER / HUSBAND**: TAI GOO / TAI GOO CHONG
- **FATHER'S YOUNGER SISTER / HUSBAND**: A GOO / GOO CHONG (GOO YA)

- **JIA GUNG'S OLDER BROTHER / SPOUSE**: BACK GUNG / BACK PO
- **JIA GUNG'S OLDER SISTER / SPOUSE**: TAI GOO PO / TAI GOO CHONG
- **JIA GUNG'S YOUNGER BROTHER / SPOUSE**: SHOOK GUNG / SHOOK PO
- **JIA GUNG'S YOUNGER SISTER / SPOUSE**: GOO PO / GOO CHONG

- **JIA PO'S OLDER BROTHER / SPOUSE**: TAI KIU GUNG / TAI KIU PO
- **JIA PO'S OLDER SISTER / SPOUSE**: TAI YEE PO / TAI YEE CHONG
- **JIA PO'S YOUNGER BROTHER / SPOUSE**: KIU GUNG / KIU PO
- **JIA PO'S YOUNGER SISTER / SPOUSE**: YEE PO / YEE CHONG

Generation 2

- **FATHER**: BABA
- **MOTHER**: MAMA

- **MOTHER'S OLDER BROTHER / WIFE**: TAI KIU / TAI KIU NEUNG
- **MOTHER'S YOUNGER BROTHER / WIFE**: A KIU / KIU NEUNG
- **MOTHER'S OLDER SISTER / HUSBAND**: TAI YEE / TAI YEE CHONG
- **MOTHER'S YOUNGER SISTER / HUSBAND**: AI YEE / AI YEE CHONG

Generation 1

- **MYSELF**
- **HUSBAND**: LAU GUNG
- **WIFE**: LAU PO

- **OLDER BROTHER / WIFE**: A GO / A SOW
- **OLDER SISTER / HUSBAND**: A JIA / JIA FU
- **YOUNGER BROTHER / WIFE**: LAU TAI / LAU TAI SIM KIU
- **YOUNGER SISTER / HUSBAND**: LAU MOY / LAU MOY SE

325

Appendix 3: Map of China (including Hong Kong)

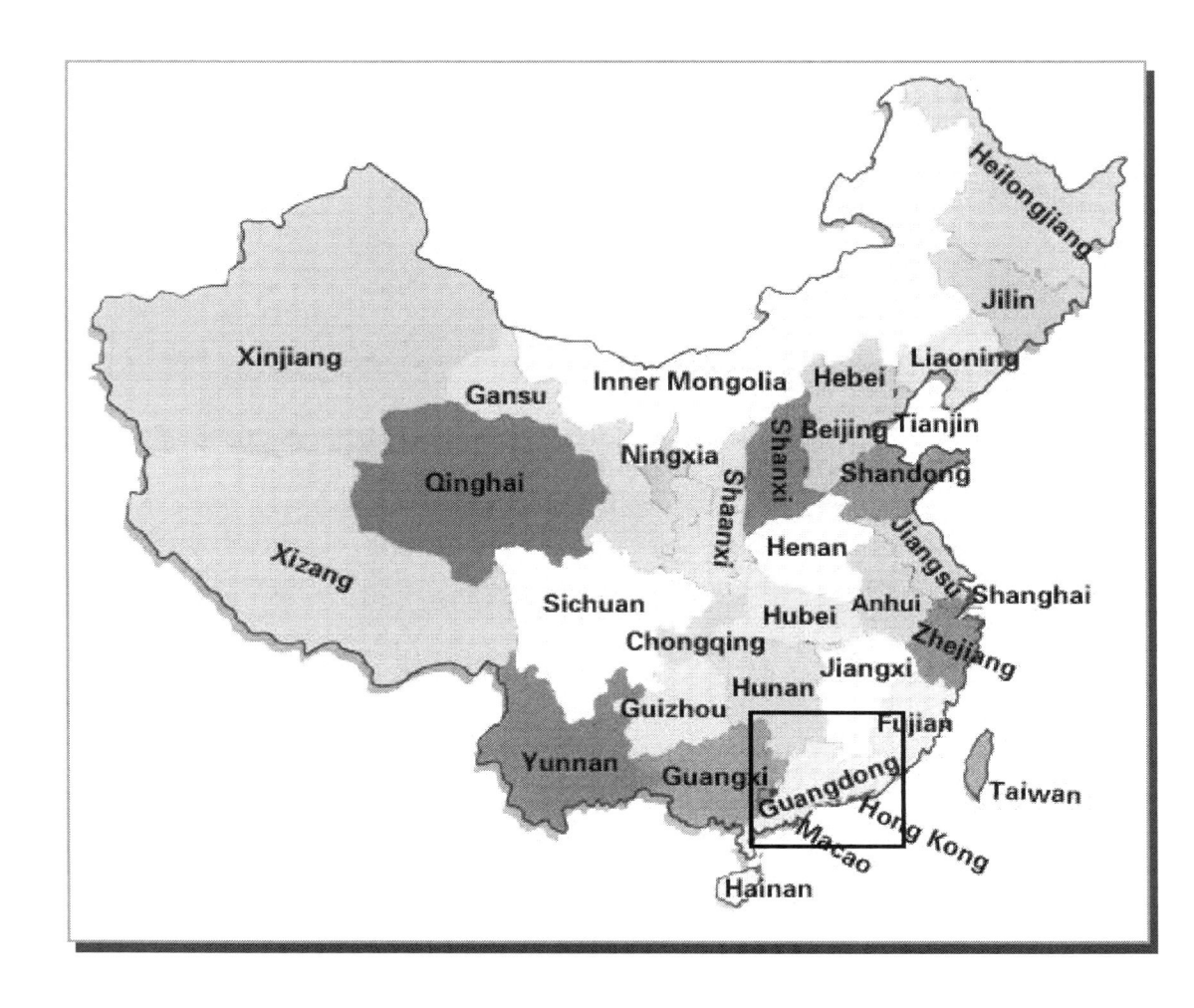

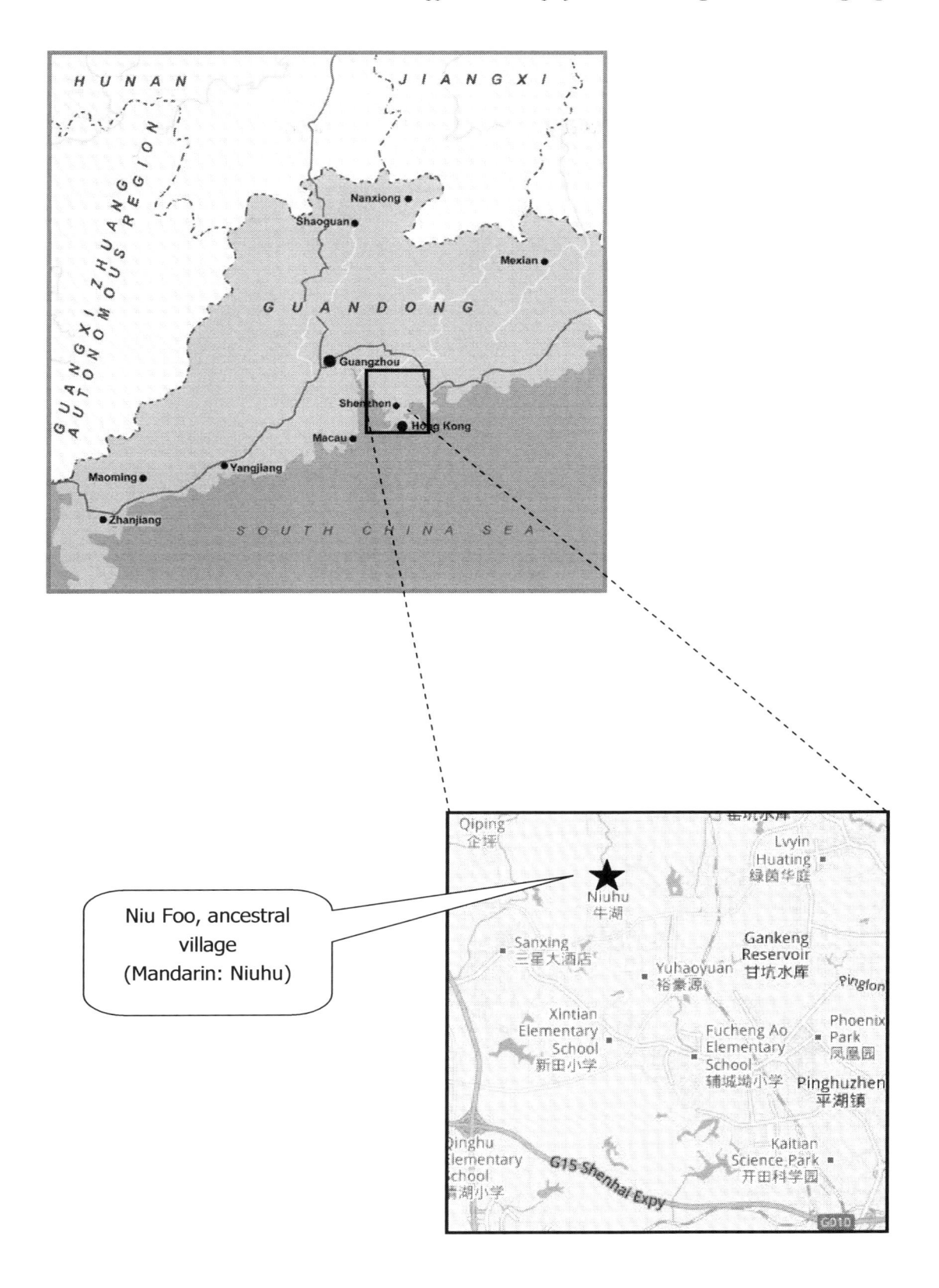

Appendix 4: Map of Niu-Foo Village, Bao On, Guangdong

Niu Foo, ancestral village (Mandarin: Niuhu)

Appendix 5: 20th Century Timeline

CHINA ----- 20th CENTURY EVENTS ----- WORLD | WEI FAMILIES

Year	China/World Events	Wei Families
	Boxer Rebellion 1898-1901	
1910	Republic of China founded 1912	**First to migrate to Jamaica from Niu Foo:** Wei Huineng (Fwee Len) / John Williams circa 1905
	World War I, 1914-18	
	Russian Revolution 1917	First migrations to Guyana
1920	Civil Wars 1920-37	First migrations to Trinidad
1930	Great Depression 1930s	**Second wave of migrations 1920s and 30s:** after 1906 most went to Guyana first, then on to Jamaica or Trinidad.
1940	Sino-Japanese War 1937-45	
	World War II, 1939-45	Many migrants sent their children back to China to learn the culture and return later to help in the family business. Most returned safely but some got trapped there after Mao Zedong took over and formed the People's Republic of China in 1949.
1950	Civil War: Nationalists vs. Communists. Communists took over 1949	
	Korean War 1950-53	
1960	Cuban Revolution 1959	
	Jamaica and Trinidad Independence 1962. Eric Williams PM Trinidad 1962-81	
1970	Guyana Independence 1966. Forbes Burnham PM Guyana 1966-80	**Migrations from the Caribbean to Canada, U.S.A. and U.K. 1970s and 80s:** most left Jamaica to escape the violence and disastrous economic situation after PM Manley took over.
	Michael Manley PM Jamaica 1972-81	
1980	Cultural Revolution 1966-76	
	Deng Xiaoping PM 1978-92	
1990	Berlin Wall fell 1989	As families prospered and China opened up to the West, many elders make the pilgrimage back to the ancestral village of Niu Foo, Bao On, Guangdong.
	1st Gulf War 1990-91	
2000	Tiananmen Square protests 1989	
	Hong Kong returns to China 1997	

A Typical Journey

They started from Niu Foo on foot or bicycle to catch the train coming from Canton to Hong Kong. There they took a boat across the Pacific to Vancouver, then by rail across Canada to Montreal. There they boarded a banana boat bound for the Caribbean. The whole trip usually took 3-4 months.

Appendix 6: The Wei Jin Xiu Furong (Chun Yin) Family Chart

Wei Family Tree: Jinxiu Furong (Chun Yin)

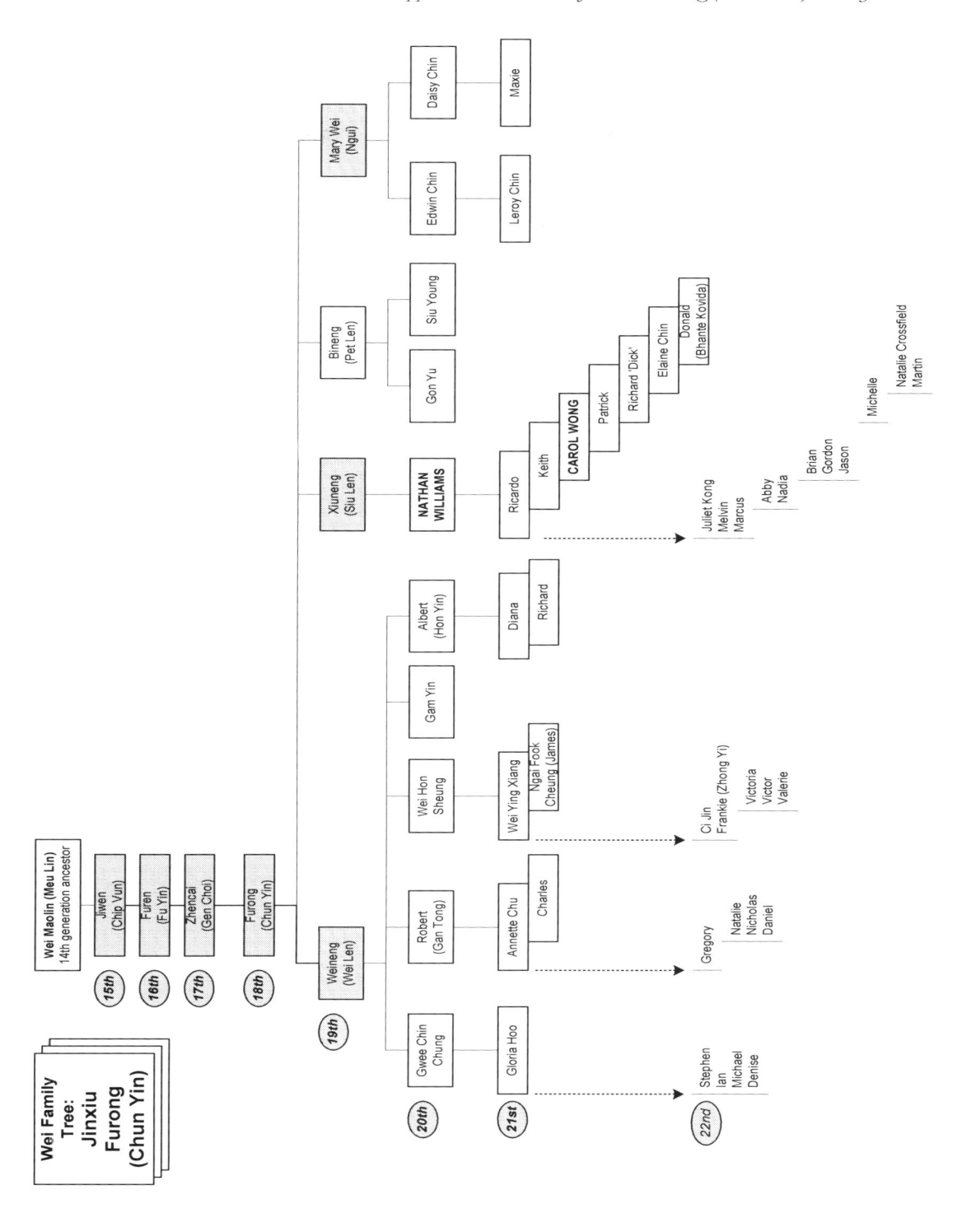

- Wei Maolin (Meu Lin) — 14th generation ancestor
  - **15th**: Jiwen (Chip Vun)
  - **16th**: Furen (Fu Yin)
  - **17th**: Zhencai (Gen Choi)
  - **18th**: Furong (Chun Yin)
    - **19th**: Weineng (Wei Len)
      - **20th**: Gwee Chin Chung
        - **21st**: Gloria Hoo
          - **22nd**: Stephen, Ian, Michael, Denise
      - Robert (Gan Tong)
        - Annette Chu
          - Gregory → Natalie, Nicholas, Daniel
          - Charles
      - Wei Hon Sheung
        - Wei Ying Xiang
          - Ngai Fook Cheung (James)
            - Ci Jin
            - Frankie (Zhong Yi) → Victoria, Victor, Valerie
      - Gam Yin
      - Albert (Hon Yin)
        - Diana
        - Richard
    - Xiuneng (Siu Len)
      - **NATHAN WILLIAMS**
        - Ricardo
        - Keith
          - Juliet Kong, Melvin, Marcus
        - **CAROL WONG**
          - Patrick
            - Abby, Nadia
          - Richard 'Dick'
            - Brian, Gordon, Jason
          - Elaine Chin
            - Michelle
          - Donald (Bhante Kovida)
            - Natalie Crossfield, Martin
      - Bineng (Pet Len)
        - Gon Yu
        - Siu Young
    - Mary Wei (Ngui)
      - Edwin Chin
        - Leroy Chin
      - Daisy Chin
        - Maxie

Excerpted from *"Wei Family History in the Americas and Caribbean"* 2011

Author's Note:

The following pages contain five appendices excerpted from *"Our Family Tree"* 1992:

Appendix 7: Foreword from "Our Family Tree"

Appendix 8: Descendants of Wei Zhencai (Gen Choi)

Appendix 9: The Nathan Williams Family Chart

Appendix 10: The Gladys Young Williams Family Chart

Appendix 11: The Wong Family Chart

Appendix 7: Foreword from "Our Family Tree"

Dedicated to the
memory of

WEI, BACK TSEUNG
NATHAN WILLIAMS

NOV. 1904 - JUNE 1990

Appendix 7: Foreword from "Our Family Tree"

Dear Family & Relatives,

While my father, NATHAN WILLIAMS(WEI, BACK TSEUNG) was alive, he instilled in me a strong sense of "family" and placed the "elder daughter" responsibilities squarely on my shoulders especially after my mother, GLADYS LOUISE YOUNG, passed away on July 16, 1968 in Jamaica, West Indies. He constantly told me about the history of the Williams family in China, reminisced about the hardships faced while settling in Jamaica during the 1930's and shared the adjustments of the inevitable migration to Canada.

My husband, EDWARD, sons, BRIAN, GORDON and JASON and I had the good fortune of living in Hong Kong for three glorious years from 1978-1981. This gave us the wonderful opportunity of visiting the ancestral villages of our respective families in the Kwangtung Province of China. The Williams village of NU FOO is only a few miles from the Wong village of SOO SEK HAH and across the Shum Chun border from Hong Kong. We met some of our relatives, ate specially prepared meals and experienced life in rural China.

During my father's stay with us in this period, he also introduced us to the many Williams relatives who had previously escaped from China during the Cultural Revolution and had sought refuge in Kowloon, Tsuen Wan, Tai Po and the New Territories. My mother was already known to them because she had previously lived in Hong Kong for a short while when she went to get Chinese medical attention in the 60's.

In 1980, when my younger sister, ELAINE CHIN, visited us in Hong Kong, we made another trip to NU FOO where we had the euphoric feeling of sitting on our father's chair in his house and standing in the ancestral hall he always spoke about. We met some more relatives, visited the grave-sites including my grandmother's tomb where her bones are still kept in the huge urn and toured the surrounding verdant region of GUN LAM HEE where decades ago "Papa" had walked to play many basket-ball games and soccer matches with his cousins and friends.

The following year, we all returned back to living in Canada with a good feeling and sense of identity as we had indeed "found our roots".

When my father passed away at my home in Unionville, Ontario on June 10, 1990, I felt one generation of our family's history had faded and should be documented before another is lost. Since "Papa" had frequently expressed the regret that his name would not be perpetuated because he did not have any male grand children bearing the surname "Williams", I decided to take it upon myself to pursue the creation of our family tree with the hope of achieving his wish, that is, to perpetuate his memory and family line onto future generations to come. (At the same time, it was only natural to also research my mother's genealogy for the benefit of my immediate family).

While pursuing the Williams genealogy, I discovered from cousin CYNTHIA WILLIAMS living in Washington, U.S.A., that my uncle ROBERT WEI (who used to live in Trinidad, W.I.) had also the similar insight of researching our family's history from China to the West Indies. His documentation is written in Chinese so it was only fitting that I should continue our family's history from Jamaica to Canada and written in English. We spent hours comparing our findings and I learned more about our heritage in the mean-time.

Appendix 7: Foreword from "Our Family Tree"

One of my 1993 resolutions was to have this task completed by June and in order to expedite this production of our family tree, I decided just to concentrate on my father's branch because I learned that the Williams family tree is very very huge with many, many branches and too numerous "Twigs". I would also conclude only up to my generation with the hope that our descendants will continue to up-date.

Apologies for any mistakes or omissions.......
I do not claim every information to be totally correct so please do not hesitate to make your own corrections & additions; if possible, place Chinese characters and proper names where appropriate. Better yet, why not take out your very own branch of the family tree to reproduce and use this documentation as an instigation to starting your very own family tree.

Doing my family tree and researching our family history has been rewarding mostly because it gave me a chance to reflect upon my parents' life and appreciate their destiny. In his own way, throughout his life and with testimony from his peers, "Papa" was a fair and hard working businessman, a kind and helpful friend, a concerned and caring parent, a loving and generous grandfather ....and always quick-witted with a unique sense of humour that leaves behind many heart-warming memories and anecdotes.

Needless to add, this finished product is dedicated with much love and devotion to the memory of my father, NATHAN WILLIAMS (WEI,BACK TSEUNG) on the third anniversary of his passing from this world.

MAY HIS NAME BE PERPETUATED FOR GENERATIONS TO COME !

Elder daughter,

(Mrs.) CAROL WONG (NEE WILLIAMS)

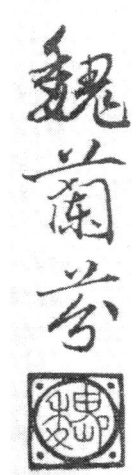

(Dec. 1992)   L - R: GORDON, EDWARD, CAROL, BRIAN AND JASON

Appendix 8: Descendants of Wei Zhencai (Gen Choi)

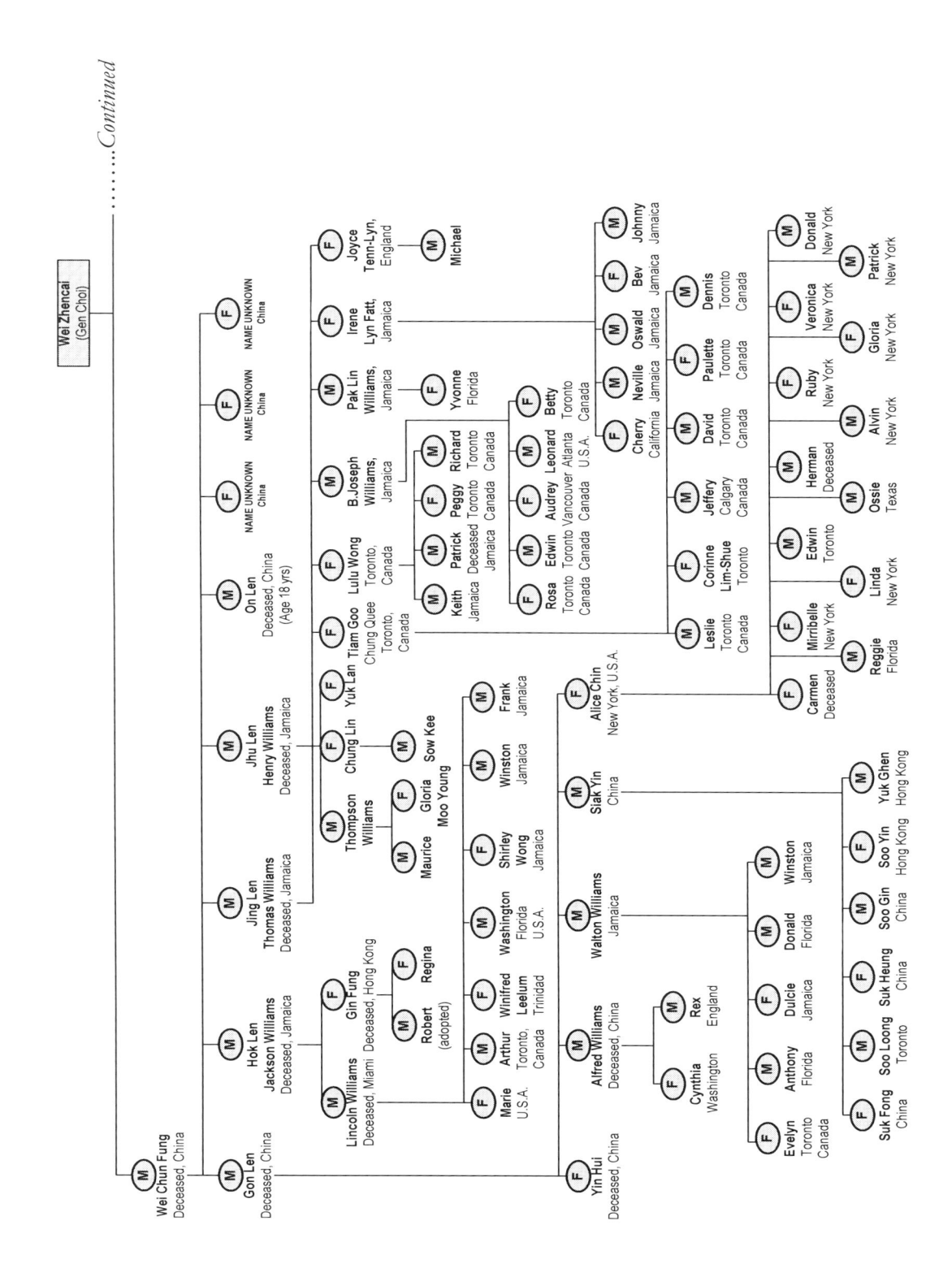

..........*Continued*

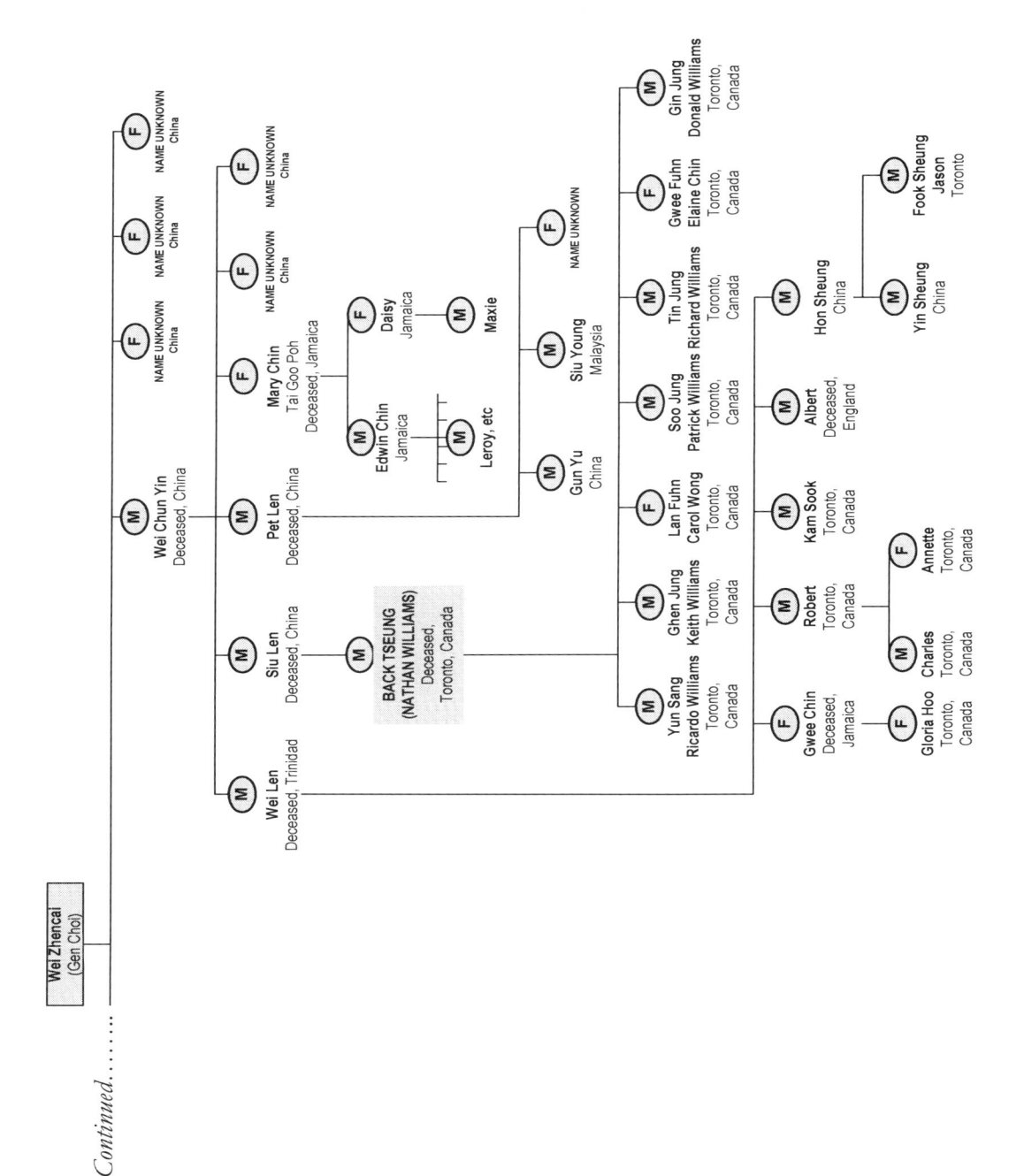

Appendix 8: Descendants of Wei Zhencai (Gen Choi)

Wei Zhencai (Gen Choi)

Continued........

- **Wei Len** — Deceased, Trinidad
- **Siu Len** — Deceased, China
  - **BACK TSEUNG (NATHAN WILLIAMS)** — Deceased, Toronto, Canada
    - **Yun Sang / Ricardo Williams** — Toronto, Canada
    - **Ghen Jung / Keith Williams** — Toronto, Canada
    - **Lan Fuhn / Carol Wong** — Toronto, Canada
    - **Soo Jung / Patrick Williams** — Toronto, Canada
    - **Tin Jung / Richard Williams** — Toronto, Canada
    - **Gwee Fuhn / Elaine Chin** — Toronto, Canada
    - **Gin Jung / Donald Williams** — Toronto, Canada
    - **Gwee Chin** — Deceased, Jamaica
      - **Gloria Hoo** — Toronto, Canada
    - **Robert** — Toronto, Canada
      - **Charles** — Toronto, Canada
      - **Annette** — Toronto, Canada
    - **Kam Sook** — Toronto, Canada
    - **Albert** — Deceased, England
    - **Hon Sheung** — China
      - **Yin Sheung** — China
        - **Fook Sheung / Jason** — Toronto
- **Wei Chun Yin** — Deceased, China
  - **Pet Len** — Deceased, China
    - **Mary Chin / Tai Goo Poh** — Deceased, Jamaica
      - **Edwin Chin** — Jamaica
        - **Leroy, etc.**
      - **Daisy** — Jamaica
        - **Maxie**
    - NAME UNKNOWN — China
    - NAME UNKNOWN — China
    - **Gun Yu** — China
    - **Siu Young** — Malaysia
      - NAME UNKNOWN
  - NAME UNKNOWN — China
  - NAME UNKNOWN — China
  - NAME UNKNOWN — China

Appendix 9: The Nathan Williams Family Chart

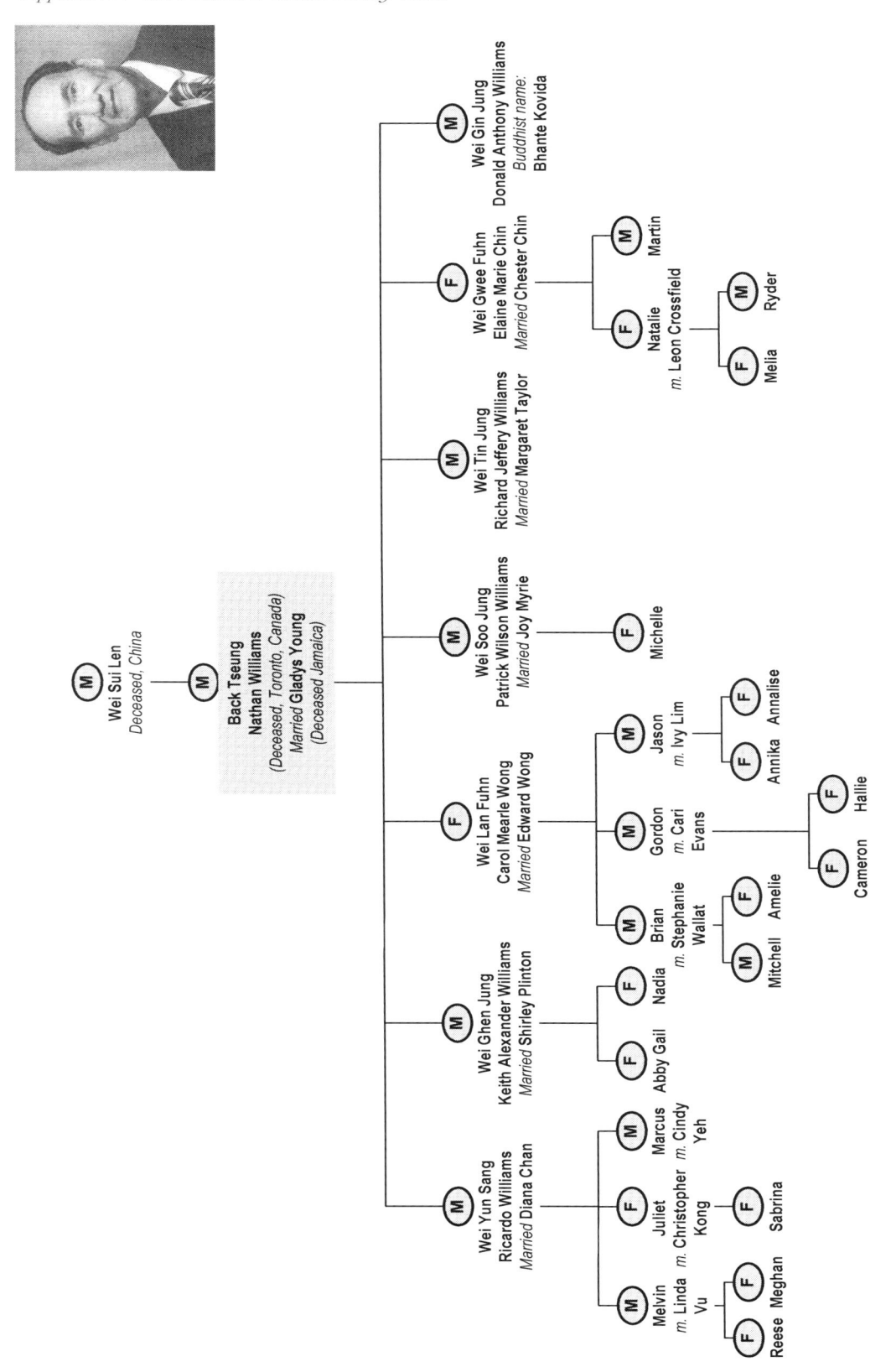

- Wei Sui Len — *Deceased, China*
  - Back Tseung / **Nathan Williams** *(Deceased, Toronto, Canada)* / Married **Gladys Young** *(Deceased Jamaica)*
    - Wei Yun Sang / Ricardo Williams / Married Diana Chan
      - Melvin / *m. Linda Vu*
        - Reese
        - Meghan
      - Juliet / *m. Christopher Kong*
        - Sabrina
      - Marcus / *m. Cindy Yeh*
    - Wei Ghen Jung / Keith Alexander Williams / Married Shirley Plinton
      - Abby Gail
      - Nadia
    - Wei Lan Fuhn / Carol Mearle Wong / Married Edward Wong
      - Brian / *m. Stephanie Wallat*
        - Mitchell
        - Amelie
      - Gordon / *m. Cari Evans*
        - Cameron
        - Hallie
      - Jason / *m. Ivy Lim*
        - Annika
        - Annalise
    - Wei Soo Jung / Patrick Wilson Williams / Married Joy Myrie
      - Michelle
    - Wei Tin Jung / Richard Jeffery Williams / Married Margaret Taylor
    - Wei Gwee Fuhn / Elaine Marie Chin / Married Chester Chin
      - Natalie / *m. Leon Crossfield*
        - Melia
        - Ryder
      - Martin
    - Wei Gin Jung / Donald Anthony Williams / *Buddhist name: Bhante Kovida*

Appendix 10: The Gladys Young Williams Family Chart

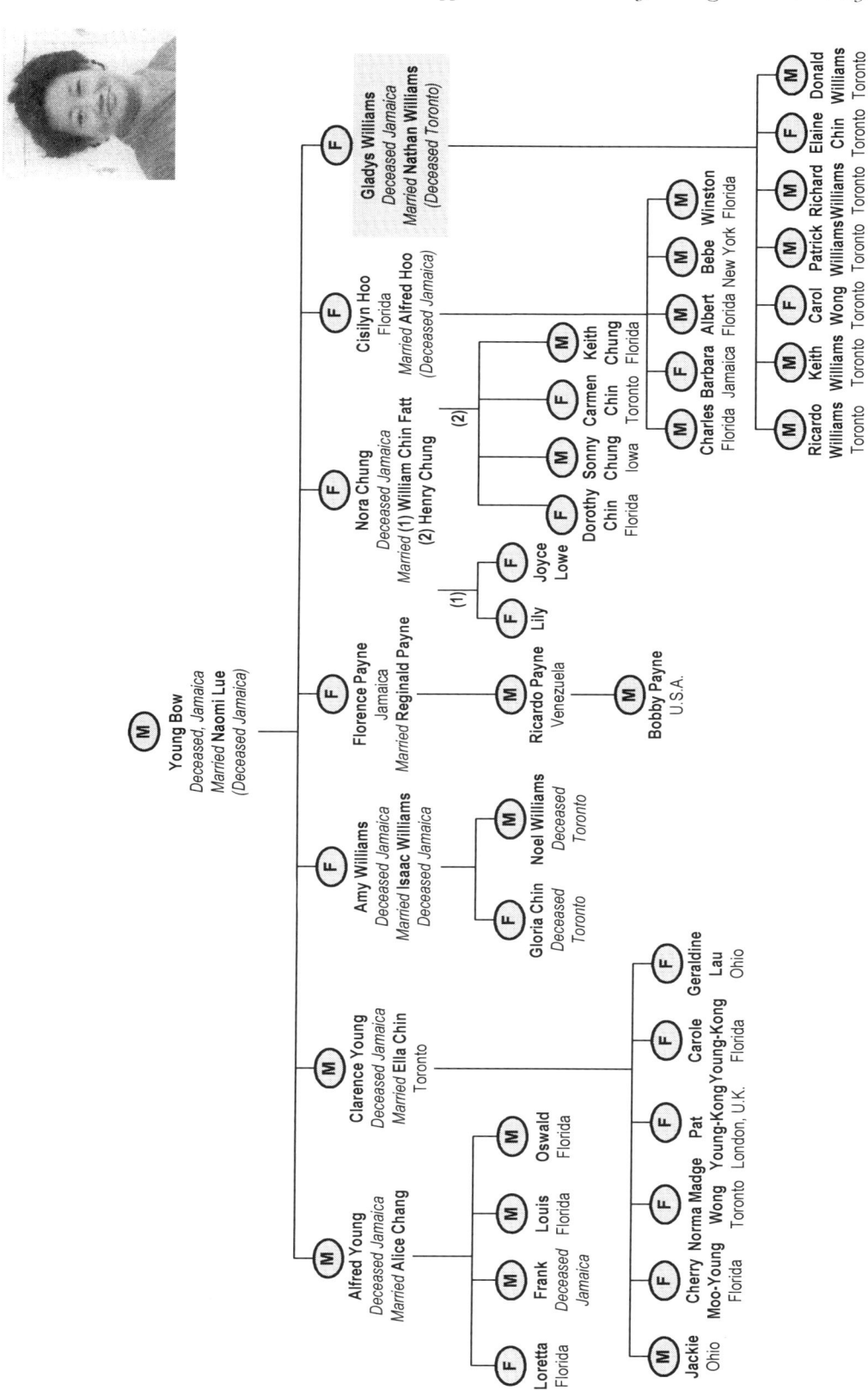

Young Bow
Deceased, Jamaica
Married Naomi Lue
(Deceased Jamaica)

Children of Young Bow:

- **Alfred Young** — *Deceased Jamaica, Married Alice Chang*
- **Clarence Young** — *Deceased Jamaica, Married Ella Chin* — Toronto
- **Amy Williams** — *Deceased Jamaica, Married Isaac Williams, Deceased Jamaica*
- **Florence Payne** — Jamaica, *Married Reginald Payne*
- **Nora Chung** — *Deceased Jamaica, Married (1) William Chin Fatt (2) Henry Chung*
- **Cisilyn Hoo** — Florida, *Married Alfred Hoo (Deceased Jamaica)*
- **Gladys Williams** — *Deceased Jamaica, Married Nathan Williams (Deceased Toronto)*

Children of Alfred Young:
- Loretta — Florida
- Frank — *Deceased Jamaica*
- Louis — Florida
- Oswald — Florida

Children (next generation of Alfred Young line):
- Jackie — Ohio
- Cherry Moo-Young — Florida
- Norma Young — Toronto
- Madge Wong — London, U.K.
- Pat Young-Kong — Florida
- Carole Young-Kong — Florida
- Geraldine Lau — Ohio

Children of Amy Williams:
- Gloria Chin — *Deceased Toronto*
- Noel Williams — *Deceased Toronto*

Children of Florence Payne:
- Ricardo Payne — Venezuela
- Bobby Payne — U.S.A.

Children of Nora Chung:
(1) Lily; Joyce Lowe
(2) Dorothy Chin — Florida; Sonny Chung — Iowa; Carmen Chin — Toronto; Keith Chung — Florida

Children of Gladys Williams:
- Ricardo Williams — Toronto
- Keith Williams — Toronto
- Charles Williams — Florida
- Barbara Chung — Jamaica
- Albert Wong — Florida
- Carol Wong — Toronto
- Patrick Williams — Toronto
- Richard Williams — Toronto
- Bebe Chin — New York
- Elaine Chin — Toronto
- Donald Williams — Toronto

337

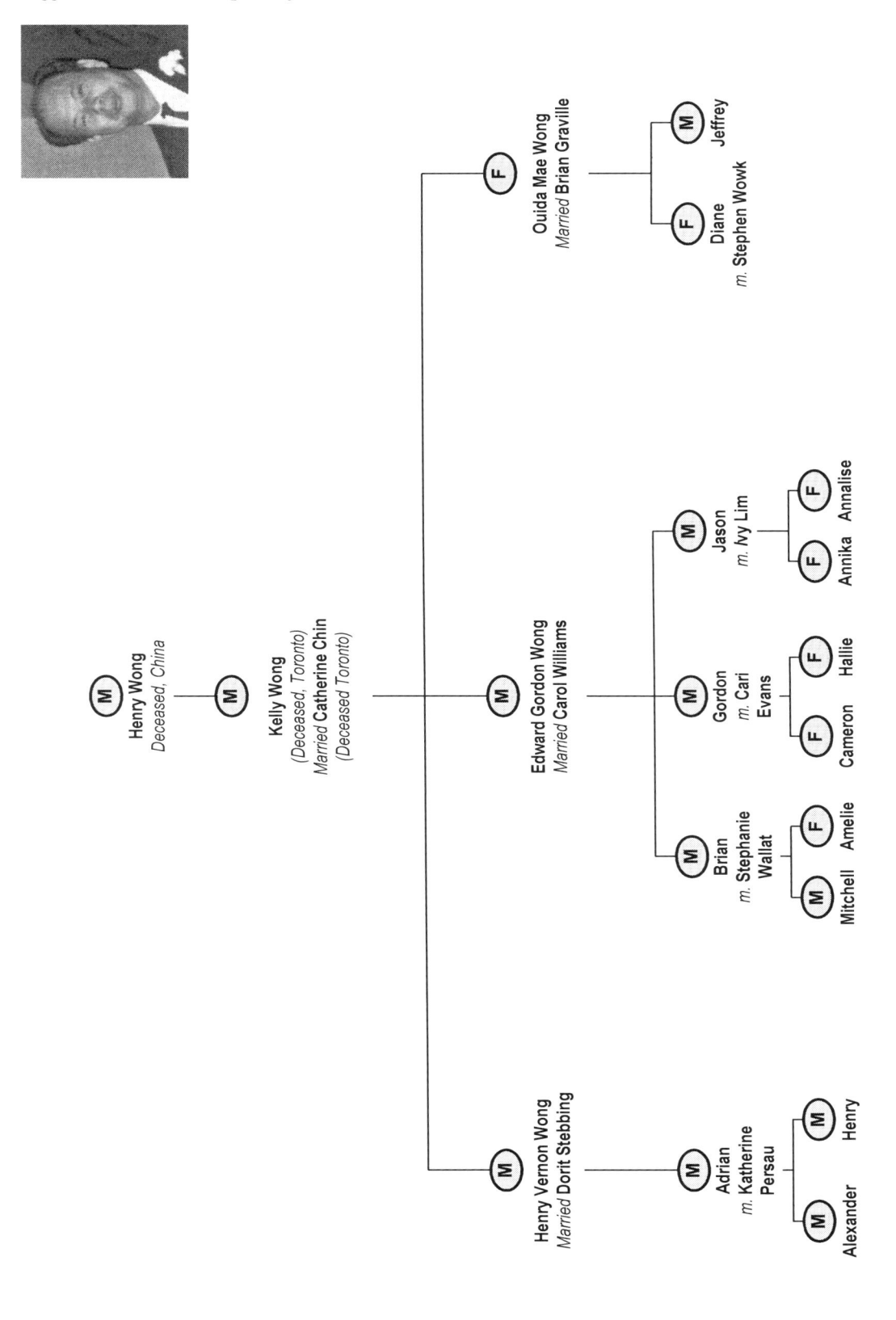

Appendix 11: The Wong Family Chart

- **Henry Wong** — *Deceased, China*
  - **Kelly Wong** *(Deceased, Toronto)* — *Married* **Catherine Chin** *(Deceased Toronto)*
    - **Henry Vernon Wong** — *Married* **Dorit Stebbing**
      - **Adrian** — *m.* **Katherine Persau**
        - Alexander
        - Henry
    - **Edward Gordon Wong** — *Married* **Carol Williams**
      - **Brian** — *m.* **Stephanie Wallat**
        - Mitchell
        - Amelie
      - **Gordon** — *m.* **Cari Evans**
        - Cameron
        - Hallie
      - **Jason** — *m.* **Ivy Lim**
        - Annika
        - Annalise
    - **Ouida Mae Wong** — *Married* **Brian Graville**
      - Diane — *m.* Stephen Wowk
      - Jeffrey

Article adapted from "Our Family Tree" dedicated to my father, Ngui Bak Seung (Nathan Williams)

The Wei families are Hakka people whose origins can be traced back to the year 661 BC during the Tang Dynasty. Our ancestors lived in the northern regions of China in Henan (Hakka=HO LAM) Province. Due to social unrest and because of hostile invaders during that era, the Hakka people moved in different directions but our ancestors travelled southwards and eventually settled in Guangzhou Province. The Hakka people (Mandarin translation: Ke Jia Wen) have since been known as a migratory tribe, being "guest people" (Cantonese HAK=guest, YAN=people) of several regions in China.

During the 19th century, the 17th generation ancestor WEI ZHENCAI (GEN CHOI), worked very hard for merchants in Canton, saved diligently and became quite wealthy. He built the ancestral village with nine adjoining houses, similar to North-American town-houses, surrounding the ancestral hall ('TIANG') where weddings and other festive occasions were celebrated with relatives and neighbouring villagers.

The village was named 'NIU FOO' after the lake that was situated nearby (NIU=cow, FOO=lake in the Hakka dialect). The lake was beautiful, the fruit trees were abundant and a large well supplied fresh water for the entire village where other families, including the Chin, Tenn, Lee and Lo families, lived together peacefully. The Wei families lived in the old section called "Lao Wee" and the Chins lived in the new section, "Sin Wee". Everyone followed the teachings of Confucius: respecting elders, helping each other, educating and taking care of the young.

Wei Gen Choi had two sons and eight grandsons. The only record of his daughters or granddaughters is granddaughter Mary Wei, because she came to Jamaica (At that time, girls were not considered important to be documented as they would inevitably get married and move away to another village of the spouse's family). Over the years, Gen Choi became a respected landlord after buying surrounding rice fields for the family's cultivation and for renting out to other people. He was an astute businessman as he also bought shops in nearby towns and the rent collected from all his tenants bought viable trading commodities such as rice and 'wet sugar' (a mixture of cane sugar and molasses).

When Wei Gen Choi died, his sons and grandsons mis-managed his business. The lands were sold, shops closed and the remains of the business were divided up among the family. The womenfolk toiled in the fields as well as in the homes while some of the men-folk lazed around and even took to smoking opium. Around this time, China was defeated in the "Opium Wars" with Britain and Hong Kong was now ruled by the British. In 1845, the Americas opened up and started recruiting labourers to work on building the Panama Canal and constructing the railway across Canada; also the gold rush was beginning in California. Many Hakka people went to Hong Kong to sign up as contract labourers. Those who went to Panama became exhausted by overwork and suffered from the prevalent tropical diseases; this resulted in a high death rate. The survivors demanded to leave Panama and the authorities shipped 475 Chinese workers to Jamaica because of its close proximity and the need for workers in the sugar factories and cane-fields.

By 1870, American companies started large-scale planting of coconuts and bananas in Jamaica and the second batch of Chinese labourers arrived. After their contracts expired, some started small grocery shops of their own. The years that followed 1885 saw Jamaica entering a period of rapid development and there were no laws restricting the entry of Chinese immigrants. Hence it was a simple matter for Chinese to come on their own or invited by relatives and friends, but not as contract labourers. They had the freedom to choose the work they wanted: some became farmers and labourers, but the majority started small businesses of their own. By 1888 the total number of Chinese settlers in Jamaica was about 800.

In 1905, the government formulated a set of immigration laws which marked the beginning of restrictions to the entry of Chinese immigrants. Despite this, the first Williams to arrive was NGUI FWEE LEN. Unable to speak English, he readily agreed to the romanization of his combined names sounding like "Williams" and it is said he was given the name "John" by the local postmistress who was teaching him English.

From then on, almost all members of this line of Wei/Ngui families who came to Jamaica adopted the English surname "Williams". Some of these included the 19th generation family members Ngui Hok Len (Jackson Williams); Ngui Jhu Len (Henry Williams); Ngui Jing Len (Thomas Williams); Ngui Yow Len (James Williams); Ngui Den Choy (Charlie Williams); and Mary (née Wei) Chin. One exception is Ngui Yun Fah (Willie Wee Tom).

In 1926, when Sir Edward Stubbs became governor of Jamaica, the laws restricting Chinese immigration were slackened, so the 1930 census showed the Chinese community numbering 6,000. Among those in the 20th generation who followed their uncles and cousins to Jamaica during the 1930s were: Chun Ming (Abraham Williams); Chung Sang (Isaac Williams); Jung Yu (C.J. Williams); Jung Pin (Arthur Williams); Gui Sen (Willie Ngai); brothers Wei Jung and See Fatt (Ernest and Martin Williams); Sin Chun (Samuel H.

Appendix 12: The Williams Families in Jamaica

Williams); brothers Jun Lin, Jung Foong and Jun Fen (James Williams); Gwee Chin; brothers Biang Lam and Chun Ngen (Alfred and Walton Williams) and their sister Alice Chin; Hon Ming (Lincoln Williams); Chung Sin (Thompson Williams); Bow Kee (B.J. Williams); and my father Bak Seung (Nathan Williams).

The usual route from Niu Foo Village to Jamaica was to travel by bicycle or on foot to the nearby railway station to catch the train to Hong Kong coming from Canton, then steamship to Vancouver via Shanghai and Japan. It took 18 days to cross the Pacific Ocean to Canada. In Vancouver, the Chinese were put in quarantine until they could board the train which took 5 days crossing Canada to Montreal. On arrival, they were kept underground in the train station and forbidden to come above ground until it was time to board a banana ship coming from England and bound for Jamaica. (This was the era of the Chinese Immigration Act, which stopped Chinese immigration to Canada altogether until it was repealed in 1947. The Canadian Government also publicly apologized for the ingratitude shown to the Chinese labourers who risked life and limb to blast through the Canadian Rockies to build a railway linking all ten Provinces of Canada. As well, the Canadian Pacific Railway officials are present at the Annual Wreath-laying at the monument commemorating the Chinese Railroad Workers of Canada in Toronto, Ontario).

Aboard the ship, the Chinese were kept under the lower deck in a huge open dormitory which was hot and smelly. The journey was arduous and long; the food was awful, many passengers were sea-sick and suffered terribly during this ordeal. Many nursed each other as best they could with inadequate medical supplies. Arriving in Kingston Harbour, the passengers were met by relatives and dispersed to various parts of the island. Most of the Williams cousins, like my father, still had to travel another 130 miles of rough, unpaved road by motor car to reach "home" in the Parish of Westmoreland. "Home" was a strange land with a different kind of people speaking an unknown language. They stayed with and worked long hours in their uncles' shops learning the business and communicating with the customers until they could open their own business in neighbouring districts within the parishes of Westmoreland (e.g. Williamsfield, Petersfield, Savanna la Mar, Grange Hill, Frome, Blackness, Little London, Darliston, Bethel Town), Hanover (e.g. Green Island, Lucea) and St. James (e.g. Montego Bay, Cambridge, Catadupa). They faced many hardships trying to eke out a living under primitive conditions, dealing with ignorant and sometimes violent customers for a narrow margin of profit.

The Williams Families were close-knit and helped each other, meeting on Sunday evenings for the men-folk to discuss business, the women to exchange newly-learnt ideas and the children to play together – like ancient "support group meetings" – as adjusting to a new country was difficult and each district apart from each other was isolated. It was also a chance for rest and relaxation, speaking their own Hakka Chinese dialect, eating familiar food and playing mahjong…. a happy and enjoyable day of families getting together which was a treat because their shops were open 6 days a week and most of the time up to 18 hours a day.

In 1949, the Chinese Communist Party over-ran the entire country of China and the Nationalist government moved to Formosa (now Taiwan). Most of the family members still living in Niu Foo Village escaped to Hong Kong and were given refugee status by the British government there. During this exodus, some children whose families had sent them back to China "to learn Chinese culture", did not make it across the border into Hong Kong and remained in China during the entire reign of Mao Zedong. Meanwhile in Jamaica, as business prospered and expanded, money was sent back to help relatives resettle in Hong Kong or to buy birth certificates to apply for passports for some to make their way to Jamaica. A few even managed to sneak out of Communist China by swimming across to Hong Kong or being smuggled out illegally via "snake boats".

Our Williams Families adapted very well and became fluent in the Jamaican "patois" dialect. They integrated into their communities and earned the trust of the local people. They however saw the need for their children to be educated in the British school system. Some families sent their children to the Chinese Public School in Kingston for primary education, but most went through local primary and elementary schools, then attended private Anglican or Roman Catholic high schools and later university for further education. Some were fortunate enough to be sent abroad to universities in the U.S.A., Canada and Britain and after graduation, a few settled abroad to further their careers.

Other branches of the Williams Family, including the Ngai family, and relatives of in-laws with other Hakka families continued to arrive, settling in Westmoreland as well as other parts of the island like Mandeville, May Pen, Lionel Town, Old Harbour, Bath, Kingston etc. For festive occasions, they came together to cook in makeshift open-air kitchens, to eat Hakka Chinese food and celebrate mostly weddings, christening of first-born sons and Chinese New Year. To the delight of children and amazement of the local people, traditional rounds of fire-crackers were hung high and set off to drive away the evil spirits making way for good luck, fortune and prosperity.

The Chinese community in Jamaica kept abreast of each other through the Chinese Benevolent Society, Chee Gung Tong, Chinese newspapers and the

"Pagoda" magazine. They supported the Chinese Construction Association, Chinese Dramatic Club, Chinese Public School, Chinese Cemetery and Chinese Athletic Club, all located in Kingston. They belonged to various business associations over the years. They tried to maintain the Hakka culture, getting together to celebrate occasions like Chinese New Year, "Gah San" (cleaning of the graves & ancestral worship) and "Double 10" or Mid-autumn Harvest Festival.

As the second generation of Chinese who were born in Jamaica grew up in the 1950s and 60s, many sports clubs began to form in all parts of the island and the youngsters travelled to challenge each other in cricket, soccer, basketball and later badminton. This was also a good opportunity for young Chinese people to travel to other parts of the island, meet and socialize at dancing parties, beach parties and picnics. Many romances blossomed and some into marriage, during this era.

The now expanded and English-speaking Williams Families were firmly established in Jamaica by the 1950s, indicated by Uncle Lincoln Williams' appointment as Justice of the Peace in 1955 and Abraham Williams becoming an active Masonic Lodge member.

The successful businesses became diversified from "salt-fish shops" to grocery shops to supermarkets, rum bars to restaurants, from haberdashery & dry goods to department stores and fashionable boutiques, from one-man operations to factories and manufacturing plants. With the help of the now grown and educated children, they bravely ventured into sugar cane plantations (Lincoln Williams & Henry Williams), movie theatres "Venus Theatre" & "Federal Theatre"(Nathan Williams & James Williams), plastic bag and concrete block-making (Jackson Williams family), fruit, chicken and livestock farming (B. Joseph Williams), beauty salons (Winnifred Williams), confectionery (Alfred Williams), millinery (Eleanor Williams) and clothing manufacturing (Shirley & Olive Williams), construction (Wilbros./James Williams family), tourism (Israel Williams), trucking (C. J Williams family) etc., etc.

Although there had been isolated incidents of anti-Chinese rioting in the capital Kingston, the Chinese had become fully integrated into society, contributing in all walks of life and gaining a reputation for being hard-working and peace-loving. While the second generation were adopting Jamaican culture and feeling settled, China opened its doors to the outside world and permits were available for overseas Chinese to return to their homeland, China. The older Hakka people craved the nostalgic village life and familiar countryside, so many returned to visit and reconnect with relatives who were left behind the "Bamboo Curtain"; some stayed with the intention of being buried there.

Appendix 12: The Williams Families in Jamaica

In 1972, the People's National Party (PNP) under Michael Manley's leadership came to power in Jamaica. The ensuing years of "democratic socialism" led many Jamaicans by 1980, including the Williams Families, to seek immigrant status abroad, mostly to the U.S.A. and Canada. Some travelled back and forth trying to keep their businesses viable, but most settled with their families. This exodus was similar to the Williams pioneers seeking a better life overseas in the Western Hemisphere and not without hardship, fear and suffering…..but this time, escaping to a secure environment offering sophisticated life-styles and more opportunities for the younger generations.

Many had never travelled abroad before nor lived in a North American environment, but found work even if it meant "stepping down" in position and finding new careers. These included self-employment (e.g. retail stores, food services) and professions like medicine, engineering, banking, real estate, sales etc. The elders kept busy helping out with household chores, child-rearing, playing mahjong and visiting each other. The children adapted quickly to the Canadian school system and many pursued university degrees in fields such as computer technology, engineering, optometry, medicine, hotel management, etc. We kept in touch with each other by attending family get-togethers and fund-raising functions for various Jamaican charities. Some joined the Caribbean Chinese Association (CCA) and Tsung Tsin Association of Ontario (TTA) which organize social, cultural and sporting events.

Although most of the Williams elders settled with their children and families in Canada, the U.K. and U.S.A., they never lost touch with their ancestral village, Niu Foo, nor forgot Confucian teachings on which the Hakka values are based and they have passed on the "work hard, don't waste, save money" ethics. Money was constantly sent back to help the family members still living there, to repair and refurbish the ancestral hall ('Tiang') which was damaged during the Cultural Revolution, to purchase a mini-van for the villagers and recently to build a new Wei Temple of worship.

Now that several members of our generation have "retired", we too are making the pilgrimage to Niu Foo Village in Guangdong, China to visit where our ancestors were born, lived and died. Nor have we forgotten our place of birth, Jamaica, the land our parents and grandparents adopted and helped build while appreciating our new country where our descendants are being born.

Carol Wong
August 2011

Appendix 12: The Williams Families in Jamaica

Papa and his children 1987

Standing L-R: Patrick, Keith, Carol, Elaine, Dick, Donny

Appendix 13: Map of Jamaica

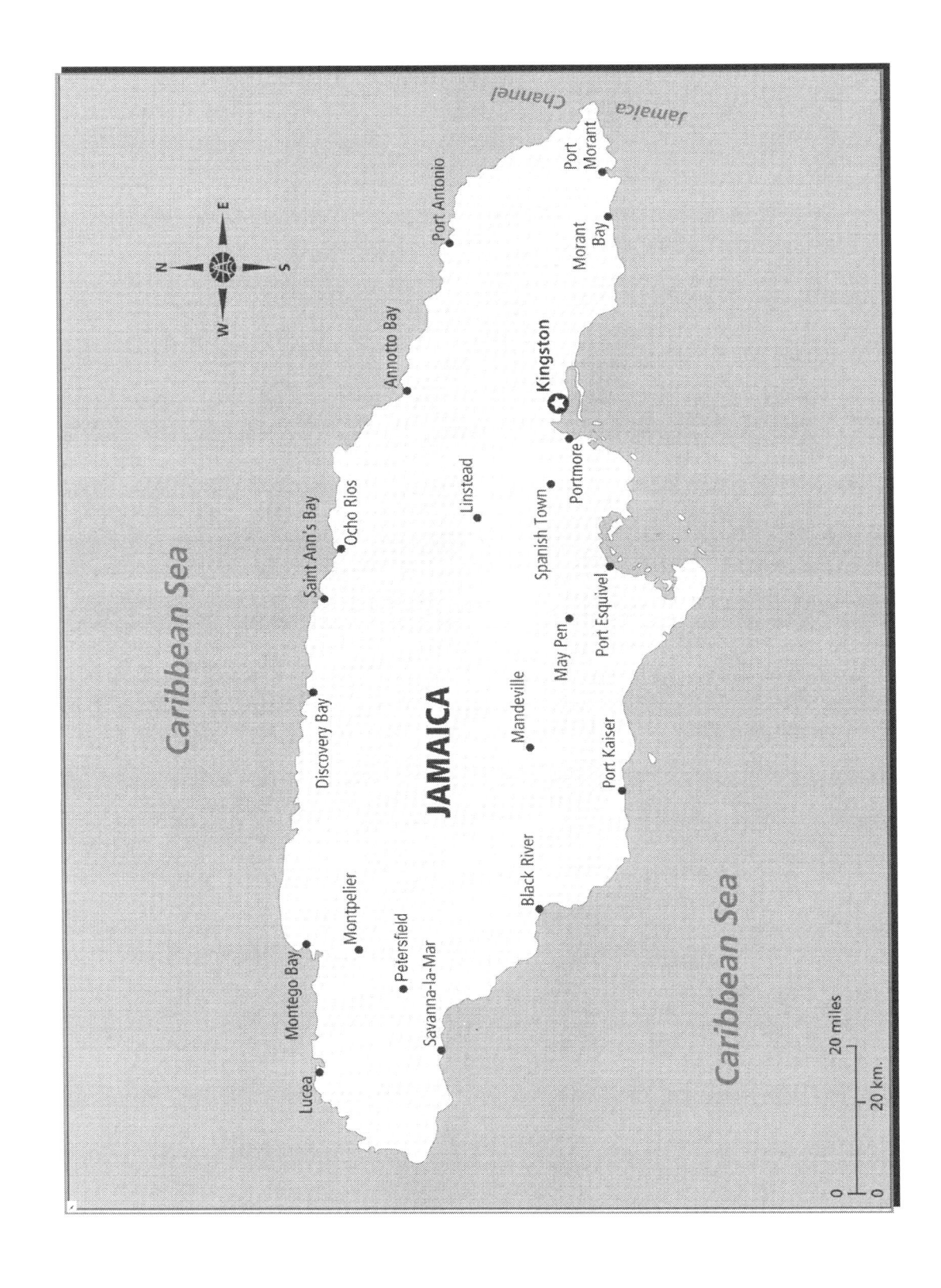

Appendix 14: Coat of Arms and National Anthem of Jamaica

Jamaica National Anthem

Eternal Father, Bless our Land,
Guide us with Thy mighty hand,
Keep us free from evil powers,
Be our light through countless hours,
To our leaders, great defender,
Grant true wisdom from above,
Justice, truth be ours forever,
Jamaica, land we love,
Jamaica, Jamaica, Jamaica, land we love

Teach us true respect for all,
Stir response to duty's call,
Strengthen us the weak to cherish,
Give us vision lest we perish,
Knowledge send us, Heavenly Father,
Grant true wisdom from above,
Justice, truth be ours forever,
Jamaica, land we love,
Jamaica, Jamaica, Jamaica, land we love.

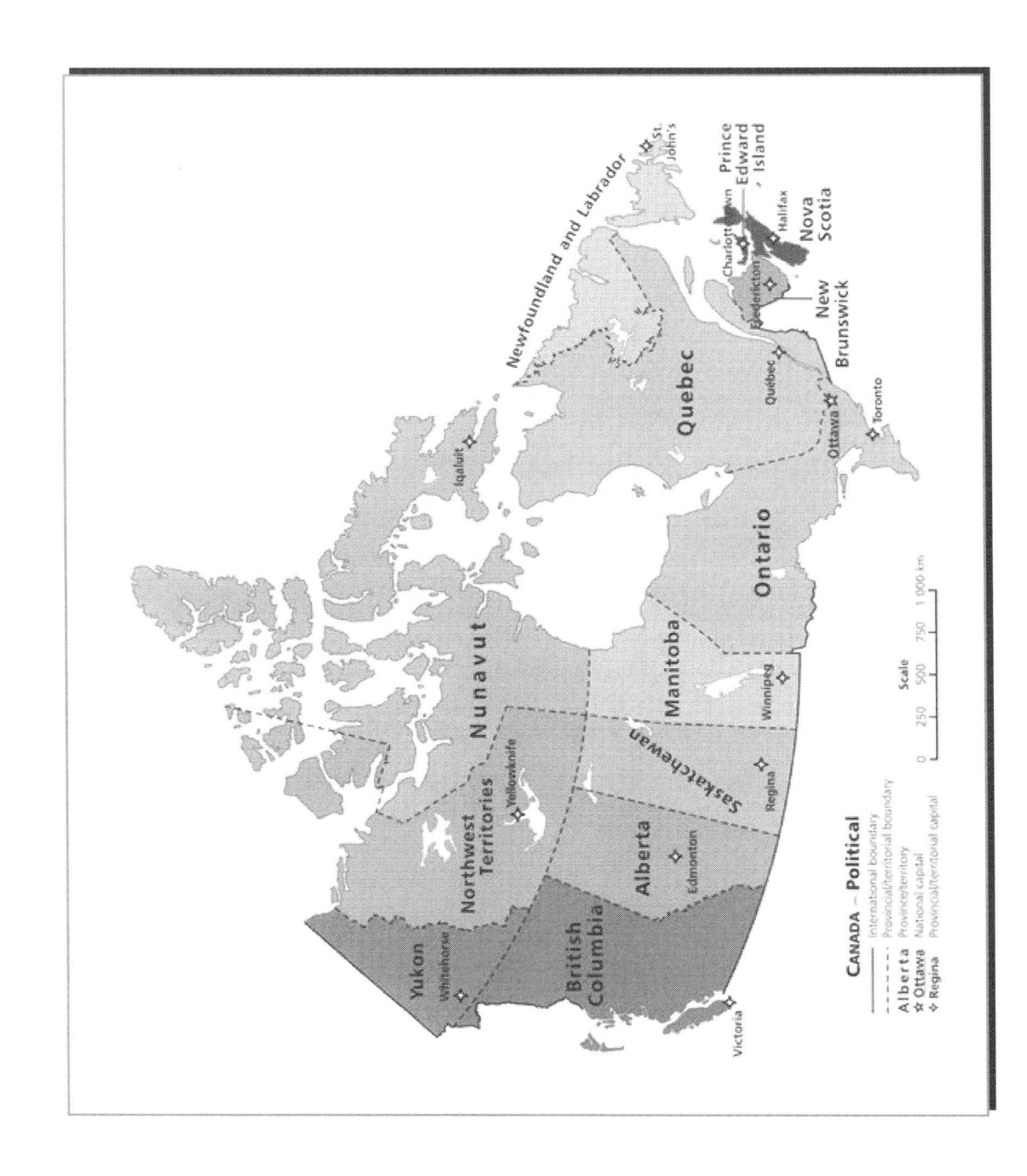

Appendix 15: Map of Canada

Appendix 16: Coat of Arms and National Anthem of Canada

O Canada!

O Canada! Our home and native land!
True patriot love in all thy sons command.
With glowing hearts we see thee rise,
The True North strong and free!
From far and wide, O Canada, we stand on guard for thee.

God keep our land glorious and free!
O Canada, we stand on guard for thee.
O Canada, we stand on guard for thee.

O Canada! Where pines and maples grow,
Great prairies spread and lordly rivers flow,
How dear to us thy broad domain,
From East to Western sea!
Thou land of hope for all who toil!
Thou True North strong and free!

God keep our land glorious and free!
O Canada, we stand on guard for thee.
O Canada, we stand on guard for thee.

About the Author

Carol Mearle Williams-Wong (Ngui, Lan Fuhn) was born in Petersfield, Westmoreland, Jamaica, educated at Wolmer's High School in Kingston, married in Montreal, Quebec, and returned to live in Montego Bay, Jamaica a mother of three sons.

Resettling in Unionville, Ontario, Canada, Carol was active in her community to earn one of the City of Markham Mayor's Senior Hall of Fame awards. As an outstanding President of Unionville Tennis Club, she was bestowed a Lifetime Membership.

Presently, Carol is the Past President of Tsung Tsin (Hakka) Association of Ontario, Canada, where she was feared, admired and respected as the Hakka Chinese Dragon Lady.

She and her husband, Edward continue to reside in Unionville while her children and grand-children are living in Richmond Hill, Ontario; Vancouver, British Columbia and Seattle, Washington, USA.

Made in the USA
Charleston, SC
20 May 2015